THIS IS OUR HOME

THE UNIVERSITY OF
NORTH CAROLINA PRESS

CHAPEL HILL

This Is Our Home

SLAVERY AND STRUGGLE
ON SOUTHERN PLANTATIONS

WHITNEY NELL STEWART

*This book was published with the assistance of the
Authors Fund of the University of North Carolina Press.*

Designed by April Leidig
Set in Caslon by Copperline Book Services, Inc.

Cover art courtesy of the South Caroliniana Library,
University of South Carolina, Columbia.

Library of Congress Cataloging-in-Publication Data
Names: Stewart, Whitney Nell, author.
Title: This is our home : slavery and struggle on Southern
    plantations / Whitney Nell Stewart.
Description: Chapel Hill : The University of North
    Carolina Press, 2023. | Includes bibliographical
    references and index.
Identifiers: LCCN 2023029873 | ISBN 9781469675671
    (cloth ; alk. paper) | ISBN 9781469675688 (paperback ;
    alk. paper) | ISBN 9781469675695 (ebook)
Subjects: LCSH: Home—Southern States. | Enslaved
    persons—Southern States—Social life and customs. |
    Plantation life—Southern States—History. | BISAC:
    SOCIAL SCIENCE / Ethnic Studies / American / African
    American & Black Studies | SOCIAL SCIENCE / Slavery
Classification: LCC HQ541 .S84 2023 | DDC 306.3/620975—
    dc23/eng/20230706
LC record available at https://lccn.loc.gov/2023029873

The ache for home lives in all of us.—Maya Angelou,
All God's Children Need Traveling Shoes, 1986

CONTENTS

ix List of Illustrations

xi Acknowledgments

xvii Note on Language

1 *Introduction*
Home in Slavery

15 *Chapter One*
Demarcating Home and Labor:
Montpelier Plantation, Virginia

43 *Chapter Two*
Concealing for Privacy and Protection:
Stagville Plantation, North Carolina

71 *Chapter Three*
Rooting One's People:
Chatham Plantation, Alabama

99 *Chapter Four*
Projecting Domestic Authority:
Patton Place, Texas

125 *Chapter Five*
Building Stability and Legacy:
Redcliffe Plantation, South Carolina

153 *Conclusion*
Home in Freedom

163 *Appendix*
     Why, What, and How:
     A Note on Material Culture Theory,
     Sources, and Method

169 Notes

239 Bibliography

265 Index

ILLUSTRATIONS

MAP

US South showing the five plantations at the center of this study 10

FIGURES

1.1 Madison mansion and performative core, Montpelier Plantation, VA 17

1.2 Field Quarter, Montpelier 21

1.3 Stable Quarter, Montpelier 24

1.4 South Yard, Montpelier 28

1.5 AutoCAD map, South Yard, Montpelier 30

1.6 African American women sweeping yard 31

1.7 South Yard from Madison mansion, Montpelier 37

1.8 *View of Montpelier* by Anna Maria Thornton 39

1.9 Madison mansion, Montpelier 41

2.1 Walking stick, found in Bennehan house, Stagville Plantation, NC 50

2.2 Henry Gudgell cane 52

2.3 Emancipation Proclamation cane 52

2.4 Bennehan house, Stagville 53

2.5 Dorsal face, cowrie shell, found in slave cabin, Stagville 58

2.6 Ventral face, cowrie shell, found in slave cabin, Stagville 58

2.7 Cut dorsal face, cowrie shell, found in slave cabin, Monticello Plantation, VA 59

2.8 Forked stick with broken tine, found in slave house at Horton Grove, Stagville 64

2.9   Forked stick, slave house, Horton Grove, Stagville 64

2.10 Brick nogging, slave house, Horton Grove, Stagville 65

2.11 Slave house, Horton Grove, Stagville 65

3.1   Whitfield mansion, Gaineswood Plantation, AL 73

3.2   *Plantation Burial* by John Antrobus 85

3.3   View inside wall, Jackson Family Cemetery, Forks of Cypress Plantation, AL 92

3.4   View outside wall, Jackson Family Cemetery, Forks of Cypress 92

3.5   Slave cemetery, Forks of Cypress 92

3.6   Monument to Nathan Bryan Whitfield, Demopolis, AL 93

4.1   Patton mansion, Patton Place, TX 103

4.2   Ceramic sherds, Patton Place 111

4.3   Ladies' fashions, 1853 115

4.4   Receipt, Rachel's purchases, Columbia, TX 120

4.5   Ladies' fashions, 1860 120

5.1   Hammond mansion, Redcliffe Plantation, SC 137

5.2   Slave cabin, Redcliffe Yard 138

5.3   Detail of slave cabin, Redcliffe Yard 140

5.4   Diagram of Redcliffe Yard 141

5.5   African American family, Redcliffe 147

5.6   Instagram post and photograph, Breanna Henley at Redcliffe, 2021 151

c.1   Gilmore cabin, Montpelier 154

c.2   Ceramic pitcher and washbowl, Orange County, VA 158

c.3   Slave cabin, Magnolia Grove Plantation, AL 159

ACKNOWLEDGMENTS

I HAVE ALWAYS CALLED this place—the American South—home. For a long time, I took that for granted. But not every Southerner has been able to do the same, and the reasons for that are deeply rooted in our region's history. Listening to a wide range of experts—academic and public historians, archaeologists and architectural scholars, descendant groups and family historians—has allowed me to begin discovering why this is. I am deeply grateful for every book and article, class and conference session, email and phone call, tour and field school dig I've had to learn from these brilliant folks.

The history faculty at Rice University provided me the scholarly base from which I could explore the past. Jim Sidbury, Caleb McDaniel, and John B. Boles were especially influential in my development as a Southern historian and helped me formulate the kinds of questions I was most interested in. I began to examine those questions through different lenses—material and visual culture—while working as a fellow at the Museum of Fine Arts, Houston's Bayou Bend Collection and the Decorative Arts of the Gulf South formerly known as the Classical Institute of the South. I had the pleasure of learning on the job with Remi Dyll, Jennifer Hammond, Lydia Blackmore, Caryne Eskridge, and Maria Shevzov, among others. I continued this exploration of diverse source types in my dissertation research, during which I was fortunate to receive several fellowships at both archives and museums, including the National Museum of African American History and Culture; the National Museum of American History; the Huntington Library; the American Antiquarian Society (AAS); Duke University; the Virginia Historical Society; and the Winterthur Museum, Garden, and Library. I finished my dissertation at a place built on interdisciplinarity: the McNeil Center for Early American Studies at the University of Pennsylvania. My erudite, intellectually diverse group of colleagues and the Center's enormously supportive environment helped me complete that monumental task.

But I was not yet done figuring out what questions about Southern history and methods for exploring it truly mattered to me. So, after the defense, I took what I had learned from the dissertation—a cultural history of home in the nineteenth-century Black freedom struggle—and made a plan to explore home on plantations from the ground level and in specific communities; and the research that took place over the next four years led to this book. It takes immense privilege to be able to pivot like this, and I could not have done it without funding from the Edith O'Donnell Institute of Art History at the University of Texas at Dallas (UTD); the History and Philosophy program at UTD; the Bass School of Arts, Humanities, and Technology at UTD; and a Cecilia Steinfeldt Fellowship for Research in the Arts and Material Culture through the Texas State Historical Association. I was also fortunate to spend a semester at the AAS as a long-term National Endowment for the Humanities (NEH) fellow, and I am grateful for the expertise and guidance of Nan Wolverton, the AAS staff, and all the AAS fellows.

This kind of place-based research required a car, lots of road-trip junk food, and a willingness to cold-call overworked public and community historians. Thankfully, dozens of smart, kind, engaged professionals welcomed me and all my questions with open arms. In these curators, archaeologists, education managers, state history directors, local and family historians, and descendants I found some of the greatest sources of knowledge about our Southern past. I had the pleasure of getting to know, learning from, and receiving feedback from these folks across the South, including: Terry Brock, Matt Reeves, Christian Cotz, and Elizabeth Chew at James Madison's Montpelier; Sara Bon-Harper, Nancy Stetz, and Jason Woodle at James Monroe's Highland; Vera Cecelski and Julie Herczeg at Stagville State Historic Site; Vanessa Hines and Charles Johnson with the Stagville Memorial Project and North Carolina Central University; Eleanor Cunningham of the Alabama Historical Commission; Paige Smith at Gaineswood Plantation; Lee Freeman with the Florence-Lauderdale Library; Curtis Flowers of Lauderdale County; Chris Elliott, Shannon Smith, Angela Pfeiffer, Kennedy Wallace, Hal Simon-Hassell, and Mark Osborne of the Texas Historical Commission; southeast Texas community historian Sam Collins III; Cary Cordova at the University of Texas at Austin; and Elizabeth Laney, Chelsea Stutz, and Stacey Young at the Redcliffe Plantation State Historic Site. Archives and libraries were still a fundamental part of the research, and I could not have done it without the help of staff at the Wilson Library at the University of North Carolina; Auburn University Special Collections and Archives; and the South Caroliniana Library at the University of South Carolina.

I was fortunate to receive some much-needed feedback on portions of the manuscript through presentations at the McNeil Center Friday Semi-

nar; the Society for the Historians for the Early American Republic meeting; the Southern Forum on Agricultural, Rural, and Environmental History; the Materializing Race Un-conference; the Friday Focus at Bayou
Bend Collection and Gardens; the Slavery and Spatial History, Omohundro Institute Coffeehouse Table Seminar; the Edith O'Donnell Institute of
Art History Workshop; and at two meetings of the Dallas Area Society of
Historians. I also received useful comments during a NEH long-term fellows writing workshop at AAS; special thanks to my fellow fellow, Craig
Friend. Additionally, Annelise Heniz, Alexandra Finley, and John Lund-
berg carefully read chapter 4 and provided indispensable help with telling
Rachel's story. I relied on a cohort of superb material culture scholars—
Zara Anishanslin, Katy Lasdow, Katie Lennard, and Whitney Martinko—to
help me think through how to best articulate the method and theory of our
shared field in the appendix. I published a version of chapter 2 in *Winterthur
Portfolio*, for which Amy Earls, the special issue editors Jennifer Van Horn
and Catharine Roeber, and the anonymous reader all provided crucial direction for clarifying and substantiating my material culture analyses.

I am still astounded by the number of willing colleagues, including senior
scholars, who read the entirety of my book manuscript, gave critical yet con-
structive feedback, and helped me produce a more nuanced book. Amy G.
Richter served as a reader for my book proposal, full manuscript, and revised
manuscript, and at every step of the way, she guided me toward deeper, more
sustained analysis. Two additional anonymous readers also provided feedback at various steps of the manuscript process. To all three of UNC Press's
readers, I express my sincere gratitude. Molly Morgan, archaeologist at Rice
University, generously gave her time and disciplinary perspective to improve
the text. Thavolia Glymph, whose scholarship has been so influential to my
own, served as the invited reader for my manuscript workshop. Her combination of incisive yet reassuring commentary pushed me to stay focused on what
matters, to probe what we can and cannot know from our source material, and
to be confident in my work. Sixteen additional top-notch scholars at my manuscript workshop were essential in helping me create a roadmap for revisions:
Zara Anishanslin, Ashley Barnes, Gregg Cantrell, Annie Gray Fischer, Erin
Greer, Maria Montalvo, Chris Morris, Rich Newman, Natalie Ring, Eric
Schlereth, Nomi Stone, Andrew Wegmann, Dan Wickberg, Ben Wright,
Miller Wright, and my editor Mark Simpson-Vos.

Mark did not just show up to my manuscript workshop; he was absolutely pivotal in making it a success, expertly making sense of so many smart

comments and questions. If I did not know it before, that experience made clear his skill as an editor. Every step of this long process has been easier, less worrisome, and more fulfilling because of his guidance. Beyond his editorial talents, he is a truly kind, patient, and generous person. I so appreciate him and the entire team at UNC Press.

So many people have contributed to this book, directly or indirectly. UTD graduate student Stephen West helped immensely by scanning microfilm at the Southern Methodist University (SMU) Library. The Southern Outrages, a writing group of former Rice students, has been a bright spot over the last few years. I am thankful for these clever, funny, compassionate friends, including Lauren Brand, Andrew Johnson, Wright Kennedy, Keith McCall, David Ponton, Eddie Valentin, Ben Wright, Miller Wright, and of course our fearless La Doña, Maria Montalvo. For more than a decade, Rich Newman and Tamara Thornton have been mentors, giving sage advice and cheering me on. Emily Conroy-Krutz has for years been an inspiration and breath of fresh air in this too-often toxic profession. Lizzie Ingleson has helped me through crises professional and personal, and was always ready with a hug and perceptive insight.

Other folks made sure I was never solely focused on work. Gena and Jordan, Kate and Duncan, Kim, Ash, Kat, Brandon and Julia, Colin and Abby, Mike, Adam, and the D&D Maps and Legends crew (Ben, Annie, Will, Ashley, Jon, and especially our DM and extraordinary hosts, Davis and Linda) made sure I had plenty of fun adventures over the last several years.

Being in academia can be tough, but through it I have met some of the best friends who listened to hours of book talk, sent supportive GIFs and emojis, and distracted me in the best ways. Andrew and Maia Wegmann are unicorns, majestic beings that sprinkle magic over every late-night concert or poetry reading. Nora Slonimsky and Jeremy Levine love frivolity (whether well-mannered or not), and their enjoyment of the best things in life make my life so much better. Annie Gray Fischer and Will Myers are extraordinarily well-read, deeply empathetic people, who also happen to be some of the most fun, silly, and hilarious humans. They make Dallas a better place to call home. Lindsay Chervinsky is my rock, a fierce friend and constant cheerleader. She and her husband, Jake, continue to awe me with their work ethics, their achievements, and their ability to make a seriously delicious cheese plate.

My family has been right next to me every step of the way, and to them I am deeply indebted. I married into a group of exceptionally loving, creative, good people. Kathi, Gil, and Lydia; Eric, Rita, and the kids; Kiki and the broader Wright/Thomas clan make every trip to Wisconsin worth the drive. My aunts, uncles, cousins, and extended Alabama family have always affectionately put up with demonstrations of my latest passion, from cartwheels to history lectures. My two sets of Southern grandparents—Laverne and Royce Stewart, Doris and Carl Knight—instilled in me a love of hard work, for which I am eternally grateful. My sister, Heather Jacquin, is an ebullient and affectionate presence, and my niece, Joy, embodies her name. My parents, Marsha and David Stewart, have been unfailingly supportive presences in my life, whether at the dance studio, swimming pool, or hunched over my computer working during holidays. Frankie the dog cuddled with me during long writing nights, and his affection makes me feel like the most important person in the world. Thankfully, Teddy the cat's haughty glares and occasional contemptuous swipes keep me grounded. My husband, Ben, is my sounding board, my in-house editor, my biggest supporter, my travel companion, my favorite person. He is an exceptional historian and person who fills our home with historiographical debates, lectures on the Wilmot Proviso, loud music, louder laughter, and much love, all of which have made the grueling process of writing a book a bit easier.

With the help of these folks and more, I hope to continue having the pleasure and privilege of thinking, learning, reading, visiting, writing, and talking about our shared Southern home.

NOTE ON LANGUAGE

ACADEMIC AND PUBLIC HISTORIANS continue to debate the terms we should use to describe people ensnared in the institution of slavery. Many have recently adopted the practice of replacing *slave* with *enslaved person* and *slave owner* with *enslaver*. The aim here is to emphasize the humanity of individuals unwillingly bound in the system and to center the active, intentional role of those who willingly bound them, reinforcing that those in bondage were not merely property, and that their enslavement was consistently, violently maintained by individuals as well as governments.

As historians try to accurately and responsibly narrate history, the terms we use are informed not only by the terminology of the past but also by the present day. As Vanessa Holden has argued, historians' choices of terminology should be informed by contemporary communities that have been shaped by the history under discussion—for example, by the descendants of enslaved Americans.[1] Other historians, such as Leslie Harris, assert that choices about terminology can differ depending on the writing context. In long-form historical writing, for instance, the contexts of humanity and violence might be obvious enough that the rhetorical choices of *enslaved person* and *enslaver*—which can sometimes impose burdens on clear prose—may not be necessary.[2]

Inspired by these scholars and by broader conversations over language, readers will find that I employ different terms at different moments. I have used *enslaved individual* or *person* or *laborer* more often and in the context of writing about the lives, work, and world of actual people, while more rarely using *slave* as a modifier (e.g., slave cabin) and in the context of writing about enslavers' views of their property. I have chosen to use *enslaver* more frequently to emphasize the active work of enslaving, but I also include *slave owner* for rhetorical variety. I hope that when readers encounter these terms, they will remember the dehumanizing, violent character of a system that allowed one human to own and control another.

I follow the work of *Indigenous* and *Black* scholars in capitalizing those terms but choose to keep *white* lowercase to emphasize the power differential among these communities in the past and present.[3] I am indebted to the editors of the *Journal of the Early Republic*'s Critical Engagements Forum "What's in a Name?" who brought together an outstanding group of scholars to lay out these and other debates over terminology. Such debates will and should continue, but the forum serves as a useful resource for thinking about how to best articulate our complicated histories.

Lastly, I have chosen (unless otherwise noted) to keep the language of the much-debated Federal Writers' Project–Works Progress Administration *Slave Narratives* in its original form. White interviewers of this 1930s New Deal project recorded the memories of formerly enslaved Americans in what has been termed "black vernacular" or "Negro dialect." (The same was not true for Black interviewers, who rarely used dialect in their transcriptions.) The "Negro dialect" was developed by folklore editor John Lomax to represent a racialized dialect but also to homogenize the diverse speech patterns of various regional dialects, therefore increasing readability while still signaling "authenticity" (or better put, what white people *expected* or *assumed* about Black Southerners) to what was believed to be a mostly white readership. As historian Catherine Stewart argues, the "FWP decisions . . . reveal more about how the black vernacular was used to represent black identity than about the actual speech patterns of ex-slave informants." Even so, Stewart views the narratives as "written versions of oral performances," wherein formerly enslaved interviewees were able to draw on "tropes and rhetorical strategies . . . to enact some measure of authorial control and create counternarratives of black history and identity."[4] So while the exact language of the interviews, as recorded by white writers, likely does not reflect the authentic voices of the formerly enslaved, they still demonstrate centuries-old oral and literary traditions of Black Americans.

THIS IS OUR HOME

Introduction

HOME IN SLAVERY

The coastal breeze filled the room with warm, autumnal air as several Black South Carolinians gathered to write a letter to the president of the United States. These formerly enslaved men had traveled from their homes on plantations around Edisto Island to protest the federal government's plan to give those plantations back to their previous owners. Those owners were white men who had been traitors to the Union; and while they may have legally owned the land, it was not truly theirs. These Black men insisted that they deserved the right to purchase the property, for it was their people's sweat and blood that had made it profitable. Yet there was more to this place and to their claim to it than labor. As one man took up the pen and paper, the rest agreed they would tell the president that although they had "toiled nearly all our lives as slaves and were treated like dumb driven cattle" on these plantations, "This is our home."[1]

THIS IS OUR HOME EXPLORES HOW those forced to live and labor on sites of enslavement nonetheless sought to make meaning of spaces designed for exploitation. On plantations across the region, enslaved people relied on what was around them—the buildings and landscape, the household's objects and its occupants—as they tried to fulfill their aspirations of home.[2] They continually strove and sometimes succeeded in making their involuntary residences feel more like their own, from sweeping yards or building cabins, to hiding objects in walls or burying kin in the ground. These and other homemaking practices produced physical evidence of enslaved people's personal and communal desires, of what they wanted but could not count on from their domiciles: a place of their own, separate from where they labored as slaves; a place with a semblance of privacy and security; a place to root themselves and their people; a place in which to project and protect a degree of power; a stable place for their families to build a legacy for future generations. Across the plantation South, enslaved people struggled to transform sites of forced occupation, of confinement, and of slavery into something more: a home. This book tells the stories of their struggle.

Historians over the past century have offered various explanations for how individuals coped with the captivity and cruelty of chattel slavery, including acceptance, accommodation, resistance, and agency.[3] None of these explanations is wrong, but none is independently sufficient to explain the full range of emotions, beliefs, and actions that constituted life under enslavement.[4] These tactics were not irreconcilable. Together, they convey the multitude of ways that humans, caught in a system of racialized slavery, constantly engaged in what historian Vincent Brown calls a "politics of survival," an "existential struggle" that could be "productive" of something more.[5] Enslaved people sought to do more than simply physically endure. They aspired to make meaning of their survival, and making a home was one way of doing so. This struggle was more than existential, however, taking material and spatial form on estates where enslavers held great sway. But white Southerners never held complete control over Black homemaking. Built by enslaved people and imbued with their own dreams, Southern plantations were Black homes as well as white.[6]

Yet our histories—in books, in movies, and at historic sites—have for more than 150 years tended to overlook or downplay this endeavor, largely as a result of three powerful narratives of plantation life. The first narrative, a product of the pernicious paternalism at the core of Lost Cause mythology, implied that Black people loved and longed for their "happy homes" in slavery and, by extension, longed to be re-enslaved even after emancipation.[7] This profoundly racist misconception denies the very real violence, suffering, and constraints that enslavers imposed upon men, women, and children. In the second narrative, the Big House and its white family became the central, and often the only, story of home on plantations. If Black Southerners were mentioned at all, it was in the context of their work as "servants" for their "employers."[8] This historical distortion, like the Lost Cause myth from which it sprang, similarly elides the true brutality of enslavement. But it also willfully forgets or erases slavery and Black Southerners from the past and, by extension, marginalizes them in the present. The third narrative emerged from a righteous effort to undercut the Lost Cause delusions and instead to highlight the very thing that

these other narratives sought to obfuscate. For good reason, it followed abolitionists in recognizing plantations as sites of cruelty and exploitation.[9] But that
is not the whole story. Black homemaking existed alongside, and was shaped
by, oppression. Implying that only white people had homes on plantations
continues the work of enslavers who, in their campaign to deny Black people
their humanity, vigorously denied unfree individuals the possibility of making
and having homes.[10] Even as many scholars, cultural institutions, and public
figures have laudably committed to exploring more fully the history of slavery in our nation's past, these three narratives have lingered, misrepresenting
what plantations were and, more importantly, what they can tell us about the
majority of people who lived on them.[11]

This Is Our Home exposes the fallacies of these deeply embedded narratives,
revealing the varied ways that enslaved people attempted to make their homes
on Southern plantations despite enslavers' concerted efforts to prevent them
from doing so. The book digs deep, sometimes literally, into five plantations,
in the process examining how residents tried to wrest control over and make
meaning of slavery's spaces. Their homemaking can be found in artifacts recovered from archaeological digs; in extant and digitally re-created built environments; in the objects discovered lodged between cabin walls or those kept in
museums; in legal records that preserved details of domestic practices and possessions; in plantation papers that describe how enslavers surveilled, intruded,
and devastated Black families and homes. White Southerners confined and
challenged Black homemaking, further illuminating the contestation central
to enslavement.[12] Each chapter therefore examines both the Black and white
residents from a single plantation, each located in a different Southern state,
moving—as so many individuals entrapped in the institution of slavery did
during the nineteenth century—from the Upper South of Virginia and North
Carolina to the Deep South of Alabama and west to the frontier of Texas.
The final chapter takes us into and beyond the Civil War and emancipation by
exploring an estate in the cradle of the Confederacy, South Carolina. At each
site, its particular material culture and domestic practices testify to enslaved
people's lives and aspirations as well as to their enslavers' attacks on both.

Beyond the Ideal of Home

At its core, *This Is Our Home* is about something universal yet deeply personal,
timeless yet historically contingent: home.[13] More than simply a shelter or
where we reside, this study defines home as a place we make and give meaning

to, a place that at least partly feels like our own.[14] We associate it with a set of feelings, desires, and beliefs that are both particular to our individual experiences and shaped by communal and social ideals. Through homemaking practices that use the land, the buildings, the objects, and the relationships of our domestic sphere, we try, though rarely succeed, to fulfill our aspirations of home.[15]

But the places called home at the center of this book will look quite different from what historians and the public typically imagine for nineteenth-century Americans. A mansion or even a yeoman's farmhouse is clearly a home, but a slave cabin, a swept yard, and a burial ground? Our conception of what counts as part of one's home, and who is qualified to make a home, is still restricted by the unattainable nineteenth-century ideal of the domestic sphere, one that is inevitably white and well-off.[16] Building on scholars' recent work reconceptualizing domesticity, which moves us past ideology, this study considers tangible realities as much as ideals.[17] Centering the material transformations of homemaking gives us far more room to explore the reality and deeper significance of home for far more people in the past.

Middle-class and elite Americans in the nineteenth century debated extensively about "home" in churches and legislatures, schoolrooms and living rooms, novels and newspapers.[18] In the process, they developed a set of beliefs about what made a "good" home and, consequently, who could or could not make one. Homes should raise good children, inculcate morality, prepare individuals for citizenship, encourage familial love, protect inhabitants from hostile forces, demonstrate material refinement, and provide a comfortable and safe haven from an increasingly chaotic world.[19] Homes were to function as the woman's sphere, in which feminine duty, piety, character, care, and charm thrived.[20] The physical house and its domestic wares were to reflect and encourage these values.[21]

Amid intensifying anxieties over migration, urbanization, gender norms, and unstable boundaries of class, ethnicity, and race, this ideal home and its material form became a powerful tool of exclusion.[22] Many individuals in the past (like many in our present) spent their lives in homes of cruelty, abuse, and neglect.[23] And while all Americans faced the reality that their dreams of home would never be totally fulfilled, certain people had far fewer opportunities to try. This is not to assume that every American wanted the exact same thing, for not everyone held to the ideals of a white, middle-class, Victorian home. Rather, it is the recognition that whatever individuals desired, the possibilities for realizing those desires were vastly different depending on who you were. As historian Thavolia Glymph argues, race and class determined who could claim their home as a sanctuary, and in the US South, slavery had made the distinction "all the more profound and pronounced."[24] While some homes were deemed virtuous and respectable, others were seen as perpetually lacking, unable to adequately instill the values that many Americans held dear. Those homes were overwhelmingly built by and dwelled in by "others": nonwhite, immigrant, impoverished individuals.

Many historians have thus presumed that those deemed "unable" to live up to the ideal may not have wanted or even sought a home; this included enslaved Southerners. Slavery required constant physical and psychological violence, and home is so often associated with ideals of happiness, family stability, comfort, and independence that the cruelty and constraints of slavery seem to belie any possibility of enslaved people making, or even wanting to make, a home within such harsh conditions.[25] Many formerly enslaved writers seemed to agree—especially when writing antislavery tracts designed to outrage Americans who venerated domestic ideals. The authors of slave narratives sometimes remembered their dwellings with loathing, describing them as "a kind of domestic jail" and "prison-house" that enslavers compelled them to occupy.[26] It is understandable, then, that historians have been wary of calling plantations or specific living quarters "home" for enslaved people.[27] This is particularly true for scholars whose explorations rightly highlight the deeply violent nature of enslavement, including those for whom forced labor was the primary characteristic of slavery and of plantations.[28] "Work necessarily engaged most slaves, most of the time," historians Ira Berlin and Philip D. Morgan asserted in 1993. Labor, they wrote, "was so inseparable from life that, for most slaves, the two appeared to be one and the same."[29] Life was labor; labor, life. From this perspective, there was little time, space, or energy left for enslaved people to make homes. This view is especially obvious for scholars who characterize plantations as an "American gulag" or "slave labor camp."[30]

Home seems impossible amid such brutality, but that does not mean people in exceptionally difficult circumstances did not try to find meaning in, and a modicum of control over, spaces of coerced labor, captivity, assault, and enslavement. Writing of his life in slavery, Thomas Jones expressed his belief that enslaved people shared a natural, acute longing for home: "No one can have . . . such intensity of desire for *home* and home affections, as the poor slave."[31] For many enslaved Americans, like most of their free countrymen, an ideal home would be one where family resided and community gathered without fear of confinement, intrusion, physical attack, or detachment. It would be, as theorist bell hooks describes, a "private space where we do not directly encounter white racist aggression."[32] This was impossible in a world where surveillance and separation from loved ones was inescapable, but it did not completely dampen enslaved people's dreams. Frederick Douglass may have claimed that, according to the law, "the slave has no wife, no children . . . no home," but we know that enslaved people nonetheless continued to seek, find, make, reconstitute, redefine, and place great import in family, and the same was true for home.[33] They sought a home even if, as Thomas Jones put it, "it was only the wretched home of the unprotected slave."[34]

While recognizing the brutal, repressive conditions of enslavement, *This Is Our Home* does not assume that life under slavery prevented any hope or realization of home. It follows the call of Black feminist scholars who encourage a more balanced understanding of enslaved life: not only laboring but living, not only subjection but autonomous action, not only suffering but pleasure.[35] Home and labor were never antithetical, and our historical narratives ought not reify the nineteenth-century myths that claimed them to be. Enslaved people's homemaking was still labor, but unlike the labor that enslavers demanded, it was performed for oneself and one's people.[36] Enslaved women and men devoted precious, limited time, energy, and resources to the activities, people, and things that meant something to them.[37] *This Is Our Home* therefore insists that plantations were never *only* spaces of forced labor for enslaved people and that despite slavery's attempts to dehumanize them, Black Southerners were never reducible to their labor.[38] Undoubtedly, plantations were workplaces, and brutal ones at that. They were sites of production and exploitation. But this book asks readers to consider that plantations might also have been something more: What if enslaved people thought of a plantation not only as a compulsory workplace but also as a home? And if they did, how did they manage these seemingly incongruent ideas? How could a plantation be a site of surveillance and violence, a site of the slave trade that treated people as objects to be bartered and sold, while also remaining a meaningful, even hopeful, home?[39]

This requires that we open our conception of home and homemaking to a much wider array of materials, spaces, and practices. Home was never just a house, let alone a multiroom, single-family dwelling.[40] There was certainly no single, universal residence for all enslaved people; their domiciles ranged from cabins of logs, planks, stone, or wattle and daub; single or double-pen, some with lofts or second stories; arranged along a central street adjacent to the mansion or around a yard, far from the enslaving family.[41] Some men, women, and children did not have cabins or even rooms to call their own; instead, they simply slept wherever they could.[42] But the domestic sphere was never confined only to free-standing dwellings or the activities that took place inside them.[43] Enslaved residents sought to make their homes in the many structures and spaces that constituted a plantation or even contiguous plantations.[44] Cabin, garden, yard, quarter, field, forest, burial ground, river: all this together was part of what archaeologist Whitney Battle-Baptiste calls the "captive domestic sphere."[45]

The Material Culture of Homemaking on Southern Plantations

Thousands of manuals, novels, poems, drawings, sermons, and speeches regaled nineteenth-century Americans with stories and advice about what made the ideal "good" home. Reality is harder to find. This is particularly true for understanding the experiences of enslaved Americans, whose homemaking, home feelings, and domestic life were seldom intentionally recorded. Illiteracy and lack of time or materials prevented most enslaved people from recording their own thoughts and actions. Those who did document life on plantations—enslavers, overseers, guests, and other white folks—usually noted enslaved homemaking only when it intersected with their own pursuits. Fortunately, by using material culture sources and methodology, we have the opportunity to illuminate parts of the past that have been hidden, ignored, or misinterpreted.[46] As historian Stephanie M. H. Camp insists, scholars investigating the physical aspects of life "in the quarters" have the opportunity to acquire a new understanding of slavery, for there we can see the "passions with which enslaved people invested their homes, and the larger significance of those passions."[47] Whether products of passion or simply pragmatic responses to enslavers' oppression, enslaved people's material culture is a declaration of their humanity and, thus, of their multifaceted, complicated lives, lives that cannot be fully understood just through what someone else wrote down about them. A material culture of slavery therefore brings the methodology and source base of material culture together with slavery scholars' commitment to questioning all sources for what they are and are not saying.

Scholars of slavery have long bemoaned the imbalance and inadequacy of written sources, and they have developed essential, innovative methods of interpreting these flawed texts.[48] The gaps, silences, and violence of the archive—produced and reproduced through the creation and preservation of historical sources—limit how we narrate history; the archive provides us with only part of the story told from a very narrow point of view.[49] In the case of slavery, the view has been overwhelmingly that of enslavers—their thoughts, beliefs, and actions, even when they are nominally discussing enslaved people.[50] The work of scholars like Tiya Miles, Saidiya Hartman, Marisa Fuentes, and more have shown better ways of reading sources. The phrases these scholars use to describe this undertaking—a "diagonal reading of documents," writing history "with and against the archives," reading *along the bias grain*"— all come back to the same point: we must go beyond what is explicitly written.[51] We are not throwing away the sources. We are questioning them, spending time with them, using imagination and speculation in our efforts to find what is not being said or who is not being represented.

This method, which emphasizes the incomplete nature of the archive, also inadvertently suggests that we should expand our ideas about what exactly constitutes "the archive."[52] Objects—things produced, consumed, altered, and discarded by humans—are legitimate sources for historical exploration. A piece of furniture, a tool, a ceramic dish, or a dress: each is an object, as is a barn, a cabin, a yard, or a manicured landscape. If it has been made or altered by human hands, it can be analyzed and interpreted as a piece of material culture. Artifacts are evidence of individual, communal, and social beliefs, aspirations, and practices; they are also constitutive of them. In other words, objects are both expressive and creative. Material culture is always about more than the physical thing itself. It is about people's ideas and actions, about the relationship between objects and the people who made them, maintained them, lived in them.

As both a source base and methodology, material culture prompts us to expand our notion of the archive; we must learn to analyze and interpret different forms of evidence and place them in conversation with one another to produce a fuller picture of the past (see appendix). A material culture of slavery requires engagement with scholarship outside the typical purview of historians. This means including the work of archaeologists, art historians, and architectural historians who have illuminated the power and the role of material culture and the built environment in the lives and landscapes of enslaving and enslaved Americans.[53] Borrowing techniques from these diverse disciplinary backgrounds, a multistep process allows us to carefully draw out the multilayered meaning of objects that rarely explicitly tell us what they mean. Sometimes, however, material evidence does not survive, while at other times, the words and actions of individuals, as much as their things, reveal new insights. Yet material culture methodology is still useful in these non-material investigations, providing a process through which we can intentionally interrogate what might be absent or obfuscated in the textual archive. Central to material culture methodology is the use of speculation and contextualization to substantiate one's interpretation of a nontextual source. Readers will thus confront rhetorical signs of speculation: "possibly," "perhaps," "conceivably," "likely"; all are expressions meant to connote hypotheses that can be supported with additional evidence to suggest a plausible interpretation. Reading objects requires imagination, which historians may be suspicious of in this otherwise supposedly "objective" discipline.[54] Of course, all historians hypothesize, make guesses, and choose certain interpretations over others. But material culture encourages a fuller embrace of speculation, though only when done carefully and with ample supporting evidence. This means gathering all relevant sources from the material as well as from the written and visual archives to offer reasoned and responsible possibilities. Through this process, we can contextualize the material world and the physical actions that created it to reveal something about the people who were a part of it.

The ability to gather a diverse evidentiary base drove the selection of the plantation sites at the center of this study: Montpelier in Virginia, Stagville in North Carolina, Chatham in Alabama, Patton Place in Texas, and Redcliffe in South Carolina (see map).[55] While each site is unique—expressing geographic, temporal, agricultural, and size variation—all contain representative elements of plantation living during the nineteenth century. Evidence from these sites includes letters, plantation papers, and probate records of enslavers; published memoirs and Works Progress Administration (WPA) interviews with individuals formerly enslaved on the site; historical images like sketches, paintings, and photographs; accounts from guests and travelers; maps of historical landscapes; extant and reconstructed buildings; records of archaeological digs and architectural studies; and artifacts preserved or recovered from various areas of each plantation. Surviving objects, buildings, and landscapes, while rare, are particularly important for this study, as the material culture found within and around plantations show a range of homemaking activities not typically present in the textual record. Through these assemblages of various sources, Montpelier, Stagville, Chatham, Patton Place, and Redcliffe reveal some of the many ways and reasons that enslaved people struggled to make their homes.

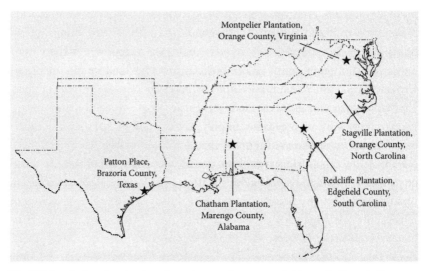

The US South showing the five plantations at the center of this study. Stars indicate location and text boxes provide name and county. (County names are antebellum, not modern.)

At Home on Five Southern Plantations

In five chapters, *This Is Our Home* explores five plantations across the US South, with each chapter delving into one site.[56] Each chapter, along with the introduction and conclusion, begins with a vignette inspired by primary sources. The scope and focus changes from chapter to chapter: some concentrate more on spatial arrangement, landscape, or built environment; while others emphasize particular objects, domestic practices, or individual residents.

We begin in the Upper South with chapter 1's exploration of Montpelier Plantation, where enslaved residents used architecture, domestic practices, and the Virginia landscape to materially manifest a separation between their homes and the spaces where they were forced to labor for others. In the early nineteenth century, Montpelier's owner James Madison engaged in similar practices of differentiation, establishing visual cues and material barriers such as fences and tree groves throughout the plantation. These markers divided areas that James and his wife, Dolley, considered part of their home from those areas associated with enslaved labor. Yet even in the areas that enslavers coded as Black, and therefore as worksites, enslaved residents like Ralph Philip Taylor and his mother defined their homes, including through the African diasporic landscaping tradition of keeping swept yards.

South of Montpelier, people enslaved at Stagville Plantation in North Carolina, like Ephram Hart, attempted to create private, protected homes among the dangers that surrounded them. Chapter 2 takes an in-depth look at artifacts that enslaved individuals deposited within dwellings during the first half of the nineteenth century, including a walking stick, a cowrie shell, and two forked sticks. Amid uncertainty and unease fostered by the enslaving Bennehan-Cameron family, Black Stagville residents concealed meaningful objects in the hope that such actions and the artifacts themselves would safeguard them and their families.

The next two chapters move us along the path of the Second Middle Passage, from the Upper South to the Deep South and beyond. Chapter 3 follows Cresy, Chloe, Phebe, and others on a journey from North Carolina to Alabama that their enslaver, Nathan Bryan Whitfield, forced upon them in the 1830s. Through the creation of burial grounds on Chatham Plantation in Alabama, and through their mortuary practices and possessions, these enslaved migrants endeavored to establish a sense of rootedness in a place to which they had no ancestral connection.

Chapter 4 takes us farther west to slavery's frontier in Texas, where for much of the 1840s and 1850s, an enslaved woman named Rachel lived as the lady of Patton Place. There she displayed a command over the plantation through her own command of the behaviors and belongings that provided white Southern women power in the home. Rachel consistently battled disgruntled local white citizens, including the enslaving Patton family, who believed her domestic power was dangerous, and who would ultimately tear her from her position on the plantation and force her to make home elsewhere. All the while, though, Rachel continued to rely on the domestic practices and possessions of ladyhood to exercise some control over her life.

We then turn back east as the Civil War and Reconstruction forever altered home on Southern plantations. Chapter 5 shows how James Henry Hammond, one of South Carolina's most fervent proslavery advocates, destabilized the families and homes of his enslaved laborers while at the same time building his dream home as an enduring monument to his mastery, to white supremacy, and to slavery. But just six years after Redcliffe's completion, slavery was dead, and the aspirations of Black Southerners to establish homes where their families could grow and thrive together became more possible. While some quickly left the plantation, other families stayed put, making the place they had long resided as enslaved people into their homes as free people.

The conclusion demonstrates the continued importance of home and homemaking to Black Americans long after emancipation. The immediacy and fervor with which formerly enslaved people fought for their homes shows that they had long been thinking and working to realize these aspirations. Although slavery was no more, the limitations enslavers had placed upon Black homes remained, evolving into increasingly effective methods of surveillance, intrusion, and displacement. The struggle to maintain control over one's home persisted amid the terror of Jim Crow, through the hope of the Civil Rights Movement, and into the uncertain present.

ENSLAVERS VIEWED EVERY INCH of their plantations as their own, but their control was never complete nor fully recognized by Black residents; even a plantation mansion contained enslaved homemaking.[57] In plantation spaces, we can find individuals engaging in a range of activities that sought to transform them, sometimes permanently and sometimes temporarily, into something else. Located in the context of the captive domestic sphere, we can understand Black homemaking on plantations as a form of what scholars call Black placemaking, one of the many ways people of African descent transformed spaces of trauma into "sites of endurance, belonging, and resistance."[58] Black homemaking—whether the everyday practice of sweeping a yard or the sacred ritual of burying a loved one or the construction of a new cabin—attempted to turn the plantation's spaces of violence, bondage, familial separation, and coerced labor into a place where enslaved people could do more than simply survive.[59]

Homemaking was not unique to nineteenth-century Black Southerners. People across time and space have used their domestic possessions and practices to create meaning where they lived. Investigating homemaking on Southern plantations reveals one context among many in US history when certain groups were deemed undeserving of calling this nation home; one context among many when privileged groups used their homemaking to deny the same to marginalized groups; one context among many when those marginalized groups themselves utilized tactics of homemaking to challenge those in power; and though they did not always win, they regarded home as a core component of their living, their coping, their survival.[60] The land that those South Carolina freedmen declared was their home in the 1860s would be returned to their former enslavers, yet this did not stop their pursuit of a place to call their own.

The struggle between enslaved people and their enslavers to make their homes on the same land, with (and often in spite of) one another, was a constant and significant part of the on-the-ground struggle over slavery and freedom. And so we begin with a plantation that, by the end of the eighteenth century, had been home to generations of both Black and white families. There resided an heir to a large estate, one of the nation's "Founding Fathers," who was determined to make his home exactly what he desired. There also resided nearly one hundred enslaved people, unwillingly bound to labor for James and Dolley Madison yet determined to make their homes within the spaces of slavery at Montpelier Plantation.

Chapter One

DEMARCATING HOME AND LABOR

MONTPELIER PLANTATION, VIRGINIA

The winter sun rose over the snow-laden, rolling Piedmont hills, warming young Ralph Philip Taylor and his mother as they walked out the front door of their home into the surrounding hustle and bustle. Ralph's mother was a domestic slave, and she did not legally own their small, clapboard house. Still, he noticed that she spent much of her limited free time maintaining it. He often saw her and the other women bent over the clay yards in front of the cabins, sweeping them clean and barren, distinct from the green grass otherwise surrounding them and unlike the areas where men and women were busy working for the Madisons. But this morning his mother's time and labor was not her own, so Ralph watched as she made her way beyond the South Yard to begin her workday in the mansion.

Standing atop that mansion's second-floor terrace, James and Dolley surveyed the early activity. They were preparing, yet again, for visitors, whom the Madisons would welcome with one of their famed multicourse holiday meals. The South Yard laborers ensured that they and all their guests were well-fed and comfortable, that Montpelier lived up to its reputation as a place of great hospitality. The domestic service center therefore had to be near, but it could not be too closely associated with their own home. James had ordered that a grove of trees be planted between the two, a porous dividing line that allowed sights, sounds, smells, and people to waft through but that also provided a clear and necessary boundary.[1]

THE MADISON FAMILY had lived on this Orange County, Virginia, land for three generations, building various houses of their own and numerous structures for their growing enslaved population.[2] But in the first two decades of the nineteenth century, under the direction of James and Dolley, Montpelier took on a new, much grander form. The Madisons curated every element of their home, inside and out. They directed their slaves as the laborers expanded the mansion, cultivated the surrounding lawns and gardens, and built the domestic service center of the adjacent South Yard (fig. 1.1).[3] For the Madisons, this was where they, their white guests, and their Black laborers performed a carefully choreographed dance meant to demonstrate the owners' power, position, charm, grace, and intellect. This was, as archaeologists have suggested, the performative core of the plantation, and thus distinct from the rest of the estate.[4] The success of this performance hinged on maintaining a delicate balance of inclusion and exclusion, of incorporating enslaved laborers when and where they were needed, while hiding those working bodies and spaces when they were not. This extended even beyond the performative core to the rest of Montpelier's central agricultural complex, where dozens of individuals worked in the Stable Yard, the fields, and outlying areas.[5] These were not just workplaces, though; they were also home to generations of enslaved people.[6] Nothing on the plantation—the land, the buildings, their labor, their bodies—was legally theirs.[7] Yet this did not stop them from expressing claims over their world, not through legal documents but through material and spatial expressions undertaken through their own will.

The landscape, built environment, and material culture reveal how individuals forced to coexist embedded their own, often divergent, beliefs into the same land. For so long, visitors (whether in the past or present) tended to view the plantation as enslavers wanted them to see it—as a clear demonstration of the slave owners' beliefs and aesthetics, of their mastery and superiority, of Black labor and white home.[8] But enslavers did not have exclusive control over how the plantation was read and experienced, for enslaved residents held their own conceptions of and relationships to the physical world.[9] More than simply a demonstration of white *or* Black ideology, then, Montpelier's landscape is proof of the constant struggle between free and unfree to literally carve out a space of their own, distinct from the labor that defined so much of plantation life.[10]

Of course, homes were always sites of labor, but Montpelier's growth and transformation came at a time when many Americans began to think of home

FIGURE 1.1. Digital rendering of Montpelier's performative core looking east. The Madison mansion is at the center, with the South Yard to its right (south). To the right (south) of that, separated from the South Yard by a fence, is the Stable Quarter and Yard. To the north of the mansion is the Pine Allée and Temple. Courtesy of Montpelier, a National Trust Historic Site. Performative core constructed between 1808 and 1844.

and labor as separate spheres, not only ideologically but physically. Whether in rural or urban areas, in single rooms or grand mansions, home had been the site of most early Americans' labor, from the daily chores of a household to the production of goods for sale outside it.[11] But as industrialization and market-based capitalism flourished in the early nineteenth-century United States, particularly in the urban North, profit-driven labor in the public sphere became preferred and privileged.[12] American culture coded this labor and its spaces—factories, exchanges, offices—as male, aggressive, chaotic, and cut-throat. Home, in its ideal form, was to stand in opposition to the dirty, rowdy, greedy world that seemed to define the American public sphere. It was to be reserved for family, serenity, and happiness, not for work.[13] This separation was never complete or fully realized, even for elites. And for those without wealth, the unattainable ideal could become a source of considerable anxiety and even shame. Yet the ideology's power remained, even manifesting itself in alterations to the built environment, such as those reflected in architectural transformations in northern households.[14]

In fact, scholars usually associate the separation of work and home with northern and urban contexts.[15] But seeing how Montpelier residents transformed the landscape demonstrates that the desire to create domestic spaces separate from profit-driven workspaces was also present on Southern plantations. This may seem illogical, for the very purpose of plantations was to produce crops for profit, and work was everywhere. Black bodies labored ceaselessly and ubiquitously, toiling in fields, blacksmith shops, and kitchens as well as in mansions and slave cabins. Historians have thus argued that the separate spheres concept was impractical and impossible on plantations. The plantation household and the physical space it inhabited was, Thavolia Glymph argues, "a workplace, not a haven from the economic world."[16] Even domestic spaces were integral to the capitalistic endeavor, and thus any separation between the private and public—or homeplace and workplace— dissolved. This created what Stephanie Camp calls a kind of "twoness" in the slave quarters: simultaneous exploitative labor and home feeling.[17] Yet not all labor was exploitative, an assertion of domination and dehumanization meant to benefit enslavers only. Enslaved people also found moments and spaces separate from that kind of labor, separate from their enslavers, where they could willingly toil for *their own* good.[18] Laboring for themselves was not always easy or appealing; homemaking could be hard, difficult, aggravating work. But very often this labor for self, loved ones, and community took place in spaces, frequently domestic ones, that were intentionally made distinct from sites of coerced labor.[19]

This chapter treks across the Montpelier plantation landscape, illustrating how both enslaved and enslaving residents actively and materially defined their homes apart from various types and spaces of labor. We follow the undulating acres from the fields to the mansion and oscillate between the actions and ideas of Black and white residents. Starting in the fields, we move spatially northward, to the Stable Yard, then to the South Yard, and finally to the Madison mansion. In these various areas of the plantation, individuals drew lines on the ground, planted groves of trees, erected fences, stored objects, swept yards, and constructed buildings that would declare where, what, and who was (or was not) part of their home. They did so at the same time and in the same spaces in which other groups sought to impose their own ideas. This contested homemaking created a place with multiple layers of meaning where Black and white plantation residents were made to coexist.

Marking the Field Quarter as Worksite or Home

Approximately half a mile from the Madison mansion, fields of tobacco blanketed the ground, tended by dozens of enslaved laborers who lived in the nearby Field Quarter.[20] Physically distant and materially dissimilar from the plantation's performative core, James, Dolley, and their white guests associated this quarter with the fields that surrounded it. Yet enslaved residents appear to have held a more nuanced understanding. The Field Quarter evinced a village-style spatial arrangement, quite different from the quarters where James had a clear hand in the design. In creating a sheltered, communal space at the center of the Field Quarter, enslaved residents found a way to express that this was their home. Located far from the mansion, this distance enhanced enslaved people's claim over it, for as historian Henry Sharp has argued, such distance "shielded the [white] family's view not only from the appearance of the [slave quarter], but also from . . . its ownership."[21]

From the time James took over management of Montpelier from his father in 1790, we see his beliefs expressed in the plantation's built environment, including his attempts to associate Black bodies and Black spaces with labor.[22] Nineteenth-century Americans demonstrated an increasingly bifurcated understanding of mental and manual labor, a transformation reflected in the perspective of enslavers. While a slave owner's work (the business of slavery) was of the highest order, that of enslaved laborers was menial and even brutish.[23] By the end of the antebellum era, Joseph A. Turner—a Georgia enslaver and newspaper printer—proclaimed that the work of slaves was "menial service— for so far as real labor is concerned, I myself work harder than any negro on my plantation."[24] Enslavers like James Madison researched and innovated new agricultural and management techniques.[25] Virginia planters sought to be "crop masters," managing and overseeing the intricate workings of the entire plantation enterprise, which in Madison's case included several different farms, crops, and other products.[26] A new hierarchy of labor had evolved as capitalism cemented itself in American life, and increasingly the work that produced monetary profit or wages was regarded as more valuable than that which did not.[27] Of course, very rarely did those who gained the most actually provide the labor themselves. The work of enslavers like the Madisons was labor of the mind, an acceptable type of work for white elites, while physical labor was reserved for enslaved people. Dolley, for her part, was willing to let her housemaid Sukey "steal from me, to keep from labour myself."[28]

Enslavers always envisioned enslaved individuals as laborers first, a belief that shaped the plantation's built environment.[29] This is apparent in James Madison's 1790 instructions to Montpelier overseers. For example, he recommended that Lewis Collins "season the timber he gets by putting it in the lofts of the Negro Cabbins."[30] The lofts of one- or two-room slave cabins often functioned as sleeping spaces for children, but from James's perspective, these spaces were just as good for storing materials.[31] Slave cabins, like their inhabitants, could be used however slave owners and overseers thought best. James's directive implies an assumption about what the Field Quarter was for: another space for labor, where products could be stowed and human property sheltered at night. It was also for showing off: though the Field Quarter was on the opposite side of the property from the mansion, James would often invite guests to ride with him to see these outlying farms, thereby displaying his progressive farming practices as well as his position as a humane and efficient enslaver.[32] But by doing so, he also linked Black bodies with the fields near which they lived and the labor they performed.

When guests accompanied Madison to these quarters on the outskirts of the plantation, they found a world quite different from what they saw at its performative core. While textual and physical evidence is sparse, preliminary archaeological investigations have suggested that the Field Quarter contained log cabins with mud-and-stick chimneys (fig. 1.2).[33] Constructed without foundations or piers, these structures have left behind little architectural material. They likely looked much like those described by traveler John Finch, who visited Montpelier during his journey through Virginia and Maryland in the 1820s: "The negro huts are built of logs, and the interstices stopped with mud, of which material also the floor is composed. At one end is an enormous large chimney made of logs."[34] It is unclear whether these Field Quarter structures, like those described by Finch, had earthen floors or some kind of wood flooring directly on the ground, as has recently been proposed based on archaeological excavations.[35] Regardless, with log walls and open, glassless windows, inhabitants of these dwellings suffered through cold winters and hot summers. These types of houses, which appear to have been almost unfinished, show up frequently in travelers' writings about the US South. Unlike the Madisons' large, substantial, impressive mansion, and even unlike the seemingly better built slave dwellings of the South Yard, the Field Quarter cabins were basic and impermanent, meant only to provide the barest shelter for slaves, like a barn would for livestock.[36]

Yet within the material culture of these quarters, spaces that enslavers like James coded for labor, it is also possible to see enslaved people's subtle

FIGURE 1.2. Slave cabin (reconstruction) in Field Quarter at Montpelier. Courtesy of Montpelier, a National Trust Historic Site.

homemaking. As archaeologist Matthew Reeves has suggested, we should not assume that architectural choices in areas like the Field Quarter were made solely by plantation owners. In his comparison of assemblages recovered from field quarter sites in the Chesapeake and Jamaica, Reeves argues that since certain enslaved individuals had the resources to purchase window glass but chose instead to buy household goods (including ceramics), it is possible they placed higher value on portable items over immoveable ones like architectural improvements. This had a practice purpose: the former they could take with them if they were forcibly relocated to another site of slavery.[37] Enslaved people may have recognized the instability of their physical homes, and they adjusted their purchases accordingly.[38] That kind of choice—to *not* buy window glass, for example—was perhaps a mechanism to ensure their investment would not go to waste. While putting money into fixed architectural improvements may have seemed futile, they found other ways to invest in their homes. With severely strained resources, their living spaces would reflect a balance of what they desired and what was possible under slavery.

Other evidence suggests that enslaved people in the Montpelier Field Quarter may have spent time and energy on domestic material culture rooted to the ground. Dwellings at the outermost reaches of the plantation would have been arranged in ways quite different from those found elsewhere, like the South Yard. It is unclear if these distant quarters developed in an ad hoc manner, or perhaps the Madisons dictated the design. We do know, however, that Montpelier's slave housing changed from the barracks-style buildings of James's grandfather in the 1730s, to the small family or kin-oriented structures that dominated the Montpelier landscape by the time his father came to run it in the 1760s.[39] But it is also possible that field workers, far away from the Madison mansion, would have been left to their own devices to make such arrangements as they wished.[40] By 1807, Augustus John Foster described field quarters as "separate from the dwelling house [of the slave owner] both here and all over Virginia, and they form a kind of village as each Negro family would like, if they were allowed it, to live in a house by themselves."[41] The note of preference — "would like" — tells us much. Whether "allowed" to or not, enslaved people had preferences about their living situations.

It might be possible that the Field Quarter arrangement is reflective of their preferences, rather than those of James Madison. By the early nineteenth century, more enslavers adopted the technique of organizing slave cabins in parallel rows along a main road as a means of enhancing surveillance.[42] If it had been James's choice, this almost certainly would have been the cabin arrangement, as is clear from the layout of the South Yard, where the living and laboring buildings are set in parallel rows (see fig. 1.1). While Augustus John Foster might have imagined the Field Quarter as reminiscent of European villages, it was just as likely that enslaved people themselves decided to re-create a centralized village structure similar to that common in various areas of West Africa. Archaeologists of the region have argued that many peoples affected by the Atlantic slave trade shifted their spatial arrangements from more scattered households to nucleated village structures.[43] This was an obvious necessity during an era when slaving could rip apart families and communities. It also may have been one of the ways that enslaved men participated in homemaking, as construction work was most often performed by male artisans.[44] Scholars have shown how enslavement sapped enslaved men's domestic authority and their ability to protect their loved ones.[45] Perhaps by building a village-style community with a shared yard, Montpelier's enslaved men could provide a spatial arrangement that helped shield their people from prying eyes and hands. Creating such spaces of exclusion projected a belief that this was the enslaved inhabitants' space to decide what to do and who to include.

Enslaved people's domestic spatial arrangement may have helped create more of a home feeling in the Field Quarter by crafting a place distinct from the fields where they labored for their enslavers. Archaeologists have made clear the significance of outdoor spaces for African-descended people around the Atlantic world, both for socializing and for labor, such as in maintaining gardens, keeping pigs and chickens, and sweeping yards.[46] That work was (at least in part) for themselves, not for their enslavers, and material remains further support this. Borrow, or trash, pits found in Montpelier's Field Quarter include sewing materials like straight pins and beads, physical evidence that a seamstress or tailor likely lived and labored here.[47] While they would have performed much of their work in the service of the enslaver, the presence of beads in particular—objects often associated with meaningful African diasporic cultural practices—suggests the possibility that this labor supported the unfree community as well.[48] Creating this shared outdoor space and laboring within it could be, as archaeologist Garrett Fesler asserts, a kind of empowering domesticity.[49] This was the work of homemaking on plantations: carving out spaces where the enslaved held some authority amid the vast expanse of land where they held none.

Securing Barriers and Possessions in the Stable Yard

While some Montpelier guests like Augustus John Foster visited the Field Quarter, many visitors likely never saw the living and laboring of enslaved residents there. But there were slave quarters visible and walkable from the Madison mansion. North of the Field Quarter, past the blacksmith shop and the overseer's house, was the Stable Yard and Quarter, a workspace and home to enslaved artisans (fig. 1.3).[50] It was a short distance from the Madison mansion, "a pleasant walk" as Mary Cutts (niece of Dolley Madison) remembered it. In fact, family members and other visitors would take this short walk between the mansion and the Stable Quarter whenever they wanted, that Quarter being, as Cutts put it, "an object of interest."[51] The sights of enslaved labor and living may have fascinated some, but James Madison worked to demarcate these spaces as outside his domestic sphere. Those spaces and the people who inhabited them were his own and were necessary to maintain Montpelier's smooth operation, but that did not mean he wished them to be associated with his home. Closer to the mansion, and thus within its view James deemed it necessary to visually and physically disconnect this Black laboring space from the performative core. Even as these divisions were made, though, enslaved people found ways of establishing some authority over their own space.

Although individuals might walk freely between them, James utilized

FIGURE 1.3. Stable Quarter cabin (reconstruction) in foreground; South Yard and Madison mansion in background at Montpelier. Photograph by author, June 2018.

human-made structures and human-altered natural elements to mark off the Stable Yard and Quarter from the performative core and thus from the Madisons' home. These included barriers like fences and gates, which one traveler noted separated various parts of James's "rural domain."[52] This contradicted Madison's preferred English garden style of landscaping, which called for unobstructed lawns and rolling hills. Unlike the French formal style, these informal, sometimes asymmetrical gardens privileged the natural and were associated with freedom rather than with rigidity.[53] Madison, like Thomas Jefferson and George Washington, attempted to instill this eighteenth-century English ideal into his nineteenth-century American home. However, the necessities of slavery and the desire to isolate laboring spaces from his home led him to forego an uninterrupted picturesque landscape for the more practical procedure of dividing it with fences and other barriers.[54]

Just such a fence ran between the Stable and South Yards (see fig. 1.1). The two were mere steps away from one another, with the South Yard adjacent to the mansion and therefore north of the Stable Yard. Between these two areas of enslaved living and laboring, archaeologists have found evidence of a paling fence, a type of barrier similar to a picket fence that had both practical and symbolic functions.[55] Such a fence would help keep animals in the Stable Yard, thereby keeping the area to the north (including the mansion grounds) far cleaner.[56] But this fence, like those found on other plantation sites, was also a sturdy, solid boundary. The closely set stakes obscured the sightline between the South Yard and the Stable Yard and therefore differentiated the performative core—which included the white home—from enslaved work, or at least the kind of labor that did not directly support the Madison mansion.[57] The fence was erected, archaeologists estimate, between 1805 and the late 1820s, during the time when James oversaw (either from afar or directly) Montpelier's renovations.[58]

This paling fence, then, was likely a result of James's decisions, but it may not have been unique to his homemaking. Enslaved men most likely replaced the paling fence with a post-and-rail fence in the mid- to late 1830s, at a time when the Madisons were no longer at Montpelier. After James's death in 1836, Dolley relocated to Washington, DC, and though the fate of the plantation was in question, it appears that enslaved people living there still found reason to alter their world to better match their desires.[59] The new fence, which was visually more appealing than the old one, was oriented more toward the South Yard and allowed for greater movement across the various spaces in which enslaved people lived and labored. As archaeologist Terry Brock suggests, it may have been that "the community in the South Yard repurposed their labor to make modest improvements to their own homes" at a time when Montpelier's owners were absent.[60] Perhaps in this way, the enslaved men of the South Yard adapted an enslaver's homemaking practice for their own community's benefit.

But it was not only South Yard residents who made their homes on either side of the fence. The Stable Yard also contained a slave quarter, including an eighteenth-century log cabin that likely looked far more like the cabins of the distant Field Quarter than the whitewashed clapboard dwellings immediately to its north in the South Yard.[61] (See figs. 1.2 and 1.3.) It is possible that during the decades James oversaw Montpelier's operations, this or another nearby cabin served as home to three generations of a single enslaved family. Dolley's niece Mary Cutts, who wrote about walking through the Stable Yard, recalled in the mid-nineteenth century how the 104-year-old Granny Milly had lived with her daughter and granddaughter in a "residence in 'the Walnut Grove.'"[62] While no such location designation appears in Montpelier's textual or oral history sources, a traveler's account published in 1820 did chronicle that at "the rear [of the mansion] is another lawn, at the extremity of which . . . is a grove of the finest black walnuts."[63] As the rear lawn was near the Stable Quarter, it is possible that grove of black walnuts was "the Walnut Grove" that Cutts described, and thus that the Stable Yard log cabin was Granny Milly's and her progeny's. Three generations of Madisons had called Montpelier home; the same was true of Milly's family.

And though we know so little of Milly, she did leave behind small, subtle evidence of her life in the cabin. Milly apparently claimed at least some areas of her dwelling as her own, for in these spaces she dictated the sanctity and safety of her prized possessions. She kept those valued belongings in her residence, including a well-used copy of *Telemachus*, likely the novel *Les aventures de Télémaque*.[64] Though set in ancient times with mythical characters, this eighteenth-century book epitomized much of the philosophical thought of the time, rebuking the aristocracy and monarchy, encouraging more representative government, and pondering the meaning of liberty. At one point in the book, young Telemachus proclaims that freedom comes only when one lets go of fear and desire and submits to reason and the gods. A favorite of Enlightenment thinkers like Thomas Jefferson, scenes from the story even appeared in visual form as wallpaper in mansions on Southern plantations.[65] Apparently Milly would show the book to white visitors who strolled through the Stable Yard, including to another son of the Enlightenment, the Marquis de Lafayette, who visited Montpelier in 1826 and whose strong abolitionist beliefs may have been known even by enslaved residents.[66] It is unclear what James Madison would have thought of Milly's beloved book. Maybe he would have regarded it as an inappropriate possession for an enslaved person, or maybe he would have felt proud that he had prepared his laborers for freedom down the road, since James wrote during his life of the need to abolish slavery at some unknown point in the future.[67]

We also do not know what the book's story meant to Milly, who saw not only herself but multiple generations of her family enslaved by the kind of people who supported its principles. Whatever the narrative signified to her, the physical object itself was clearly significant. Whether she could read it or not, the book represented something quite different from the labor she and her children were forced to perform: it represented leisure.[68] Something far more associated with the enslaving family's home, a leisure activity like reading could have made the small log cabin feel like a whole different world from the plantation outside. The book could have been a portal to a different time and place, an experience that the three generations of women living in the house could share. This was therefore an object that Milly wanted to keep safe, and she kept it carefully tucked in "an old chest" in her cabin.[69] Even though white folks like Mary Cutts or the Madisons might intrude into her home at any time, the trunk may have been one way of establishing some sense of home, of control and ownership over her space, her things, and her life.

Sweeping Up Home in the South Yard

Just beyond the Stable Yard fence was the South Yard, the living and laboring space for Montpelier's domestic workers. It was located directly next to the Madison mansion, a typical arrangement for large plantations.[70] John Finch recognized this commonality while traveling through Virginia and Maryland, noting that "house servants live in detached dwellings sufficiently near to be within call."[71] Though right next to the Stable Yard, unlike it, the South Yard was part of the Madisons' performative core. As such, the Madisons took special interest and care in designing and overseeing the space, for they and their guests would be directly confronted with its sights, sounds, and smells. But even here, the enslaved residents strove to make this space feel like their own by creating visual and material distinctions between what they considered their homes and areas they were forced to labor.

The South Yard undoubtedly has James Madison's fingerprints all over it. It took form between 1809 and 1811, and though James was then in Washington, DC, he took time away from his presidential duties to make his demands clear to those overseeing the construction.[72] By the end of construction, six buildings composed the South Yard, including (moving from south to north) two double-pen dwellings on brick or stone piers, two square smokehouses, an additional dwelling, and one brick kitchen (fig. 1.4).[73] At least half these structures were explicitly meant for labor, culinary labor to be exact, where foodstuffs were smoked, cooked, and prepared. Food was an integral component of Southern hospitality, and much of the South Yard—from the enclosed kitchen and smokehouses to the open-air barbeque trench between them—existed to ensure its quantity and quality for those in the Madison mansion. Montpelier's famous barbeques and multicourse meals, which one writer described as a "perennial flow of feasting," took hours and hours of preparation.[74] Black bodies would have been constantly tending fires, basting meats, baking biscuits, cooking greens, and a host of other activities to pull off any one meal.[75] The sights, sounds, and smells of this around-the-clock labor,

FIGURE 1.4. Digital rendering of the South Yard looking north, with tree groves and the Madison mansion beyond it. Courtesy of Montpelier, a National Trust Historic Site.

performed to nourish and satisfy the white folks in the mansion, in many ways defined the South Yard.[76] But for Ralph Philip Taylor, his mother, and all who worked as enslaved domestic servants in the mansion, the Yard was much more than a space in the service of the Madisons' tastebuds.[77] Moments of relaxation and pleasure mingled with the quotidian tasks of homemaking, including the sweeping of the clay yards that extended from their front doors.

Archaeologists have found evidence in the South Yard of two such swept clay yards, one between the two double dwellings at the south end and one between the kitchen and north dwelling (fig. 1.5). These types of yards, which appear in historical and contemporary cases to be kept only around homesites, were consistently swept to maintain an open, clear space around a dwelling.[78] Swept yards have long been associated with Black residences in the Global South, but until recently few definitive slave-era examples from North America have been identified by archaeologists.[79] That might be because it is difficult to find them, as swept yards are identified in part by the *absence* of things in the archaeological record. If a plot attached to or near an identified homesite has a low density of common artifacts like bottle glass, ceramics, or other domestic trash, yet is surrounded by or near to areas with higher artifact densities, it may be an indication that this was a yard swept clean of debris.[80] Clearly, this landscaping required considerable labor. Keeping these sites nearly spotless was a difficult feat considering all the people, animals, and activity that ran through areas like the South Yard. These yards were literally swept with a broom on a frequent basis, but they were also carefully manicured to keep out flora, fauna, and trash. Enslaved people performed this labor with intention and purpose; it was a task they took on in addition to their many other duties.

A necessary component of this homemaking practice was a simple object often associated with housework: a broom, remnants of which were found during excavations of the South Yard dwellings.[81] The brooms used for sweeping a yard could be made of several different materials, including the "weed brush brooms" that one formerly enslaved woman living in Tennessee recalled using to sweep her yard clean.[82] It appears that women or children typically swept yards (fig. 1.6). Since the yard itself was an extension of the home, the labor there was usually gendered female.[83] Enslaved people did not always accept or adhere to white society's increasingly rigid gender norms and roles, but there appears to have been widespread acceptance of women's responsibility for certain domestic duties, from caring for children to cooking family meals to sweeping yards.[84] Though brooms are not gendered in their design or form, they would have been immediately associated with the work of women, whether in their own or in their enslavers' domestic spaces. Considering the variety of mass-produced brooms available by the early nineteenth century, South Yard residents may have had or have used several different brooms.[85] Perhaps they kept indoor and outdoor brooms for their own homemaking separate from the brooms they used as enslaved laborers in the Madison mansion.

This essential object in enslaved people's homemaking was also a crucial component in making families, as brooms were integral objects within slave wedding ceremonies.[86] The ritual known as "jumping the broom"—when a man and woman would literally leap across a broom that lay on the ground— has long been associated with African American weddings, and while the act has a much longer and more complicated history, it certainly held a place of importance for many slave couples. As historian Tyler Parry has demonstrated, enslaved Americans adapted this ritual that likely dates back to eighteenth-century Europe as a means of recognizing a union that the state refused to legally validate.[87] The details of the ritual have shifted and changed, but the one constant was a broom. Jumping the broom was the final act a man and woman performed before they were considered husband and wife. Even though they

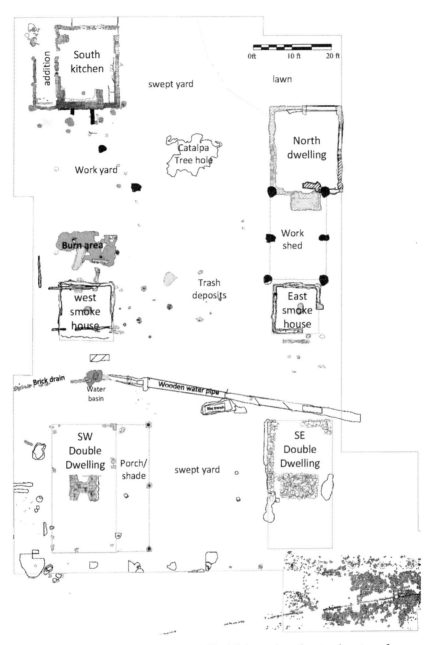

FIGURE 1.5. AutoCAD map of the South Yard, Montpelier, showing location of swept yards, buildings, and trash deposits. Courtesy of Montpelier, a National Trust Historic Site.

FIGURE 1.6. "Photograph of African-American Women with Brooms of Bambusa," September 29, 1899. Department of Agriculture, Office of Farm Management and Farm Economics. Courtesy of National Archives (83-F-B272).

lived in a world in which that marriage was not legal and in which their family and home stability was constantly threatened, this practice and the object at its center provided them the opportunity to physically realize their desire for connection and community.[88] The South Yard brooms, then, may have been used for multiple, meaningful purposes: sweeping yards in the quest to make a dwelling feel more like a home as well as consecrating unions in the face of perpetual uncertainty.[89]

Depending upon whether one lived in the South Yard or in the Madison mansion, though, visible outdoor spaces like yards and the activities that took place in such spaces were likely interpreted very differently. That enslavers like James Madison took active interest in designing spaces for their own purposes—particularly to reflect their benevolent management of enslaved laborers and to project power and status—does not discount the reality that enslaved people did not experience or give meaning to them in the same ways. In fact, even though James took such interest in the aesthetics and form of the South Yard, there is no evidence that the swept yards were a Madison-imposed idea. Certainly it is possible, perhaps probable, that both the enslaving Madisons and the enslaved South Yard residents desired the yards to be swept clean, for it eliminated bugs and rodents, nails and glass, and other undesirable objects from the landscape around the mansion.[90] But, as archaeologists like Whitney Battle-Baptiste have argued, sweeping a yard was about much more than cleanliness for enslaved people, for it excised bad spirits from the yard, thereby creating a protective barrier around the broader home of which it was a part.[91]

Earlier generations of enslaved Virginians, those recently arrived from West Africa, may have seen these swept yards as an "echo of home" that gave them strength to uphold their cultural identity.[92] Enslaved South Yard residents in the early nineteenth century, however, were not recent transplants from West Africa; they were descendants of families who had been enslaved for generations at Montpelier. Not only an echo of home, the yard *was* home, core to how South Yard residents made it their own. In fact, descendants of Montpelier's enslaved community remember their elders proclaiming that sweeping a yard is how you made it part of the home.[93] In this way, the ritual of yard sweeping may have been enslaved South Yard residents' way of creating a "cultural boundary" between what they considered their home and other parts of the plantation.[94] These were not impermeable barricades, for the presence of the nearby Madisons ensured that this space would be consistently interfered with and intruded into. But even where the Madisons had less design influence and less physical presence—in the Field Quarter, for example—evidence of a swept yard has been found, suggesting that enslaved people wielded this homemaking tactic regardless of an enslaver's desire for it.[95]

A swept yard, clear of debris and trash, could therefore distinguish their homeplace from the workplaces across the plantation, and it appears enslaved South Yard residents further asserted this through additional landscaping choices.[96] Archaeological remains indicate that enslaved residents discarded their trash—including bones, ceramics, and broken glass—away from their dwellings and outside the swept yards.[97] It was still common in nineteenth-century America to deposit garbage immediately outside one's dwelling door, either in the rear or at the front of a house; yet residents of the South Yard apparently did not do this.[98] The placement of trash away from the dwelling suggests the attempt to delineate that space as something separate from the function and activities of the surrounding area. Indeed, archaeological work at another Virginia plantation has shown how enslaved people tried to keep yard areas free from domestic trash, depositing it instead outside the fenced area.[99] At Montpelier, similar evidence of other trash middens were found outside the rail fence, beyond the official boundary of the South Yard and beyond the view from the mansion.[100] Again, this would have been a desirable choice for the Madisons, as they certainly did not wish to see or smell garbage from their house. But this does not negate the desires of enslaved people, first and foremost, to keep their *own* homes clear of refuse, for enslaved residents also deposited their trash closer to the mansion, near the smokehouses.[101] Additionally, evidence of this landscaping choice can be found far from the Madisons' eyes and noses in the Field Quarter, where enslaved residents likewise deposited their trash outside the swept yard, further enhancing the physical distinction between what they saw as their home and other areas of the plantation.[102]

Whether swept or not, yards were extensions of a dwelling.[103] Together a yard and house formed the "nucleus" of life; it was where enslaved people came together to socialize, to build community, and of course, to labor.[104] Like Milly in the Stable Quarter, South Yard residents found time and space for leisure, as evidenced by the discovery of clay tobacco pipe fragments.[105] Smoking may have taken place on porches that connected the duplexes to the swept yard, which archaeologist Terry Brock proposes were constructed by South Yard residents after James Madison's death and Dolley Madison's relocation in the mid-1830s. In this way, much like the post-and-rail fence, enslaved people may have taken advantage of the absence of their enslavers to construct homes that better reflected their desires, in this case by further extending their living space outside the dwelling.[106] Constructing a porch created a cooler, shaded area that connected the house with the swept yard, further integrating the two into a home and expanding the space enslaved residents could call their own. The labor to construct these porches, like that to keep a yard swept, was not like their nearby work for the Madisons, such as that in the smokehouses. These actions were undertaken to make and support their homes and the people in them.

Half-Veiling Labor from the Madison Mansion

With the South Yard so near to the main house, the Madisons and their visitors would have easily seen the buildings and activity of that place. Yet from the perspective of those in the mansion, the physical distinctions enslaved people made between home and labor were not worthy of notice or comment.

Mary Cutts simply remembered the South Yard as containing "the out builds so necessary to such an establishment."[107] That terminology is telling, for outbuilding was a term used to indicate a structure separate from and less important than a residence, and it often functioned as a catchall for a building where labor took place. The clapboard houses that enslaved people occupied in the South Yard were, according to white folks like Mary Cutts, like the worksites of the smokehouses.[108] The enslaved living quarters like those in the South Yard could exist so close to the Madison mansion because they were not perceived and treated as homes. They were spaces in which to sleep or eat, and their function was simply to shelter slaves like a barn shelters animals. Yet they were still within the performative core, the area that plantation guests would clearly see, walk through, and use to judge the Madisons. James and Dolley therefore struggled to maintain the delicate balance between hiding and exhibiting the South Yard and all its activities, creating distinctions between enslaved workspaces and their own home while not completely concealing the labor that made their hospitality possible.

Beyond the material comforts that the kitchen, smokehouses, and barbecue pit provided, the South Yard also supported the mansion's residents through its symbolic value. Unlike the slave dwellings at the outermost reaches of the plantation, the buildings in the South Yard were meant to be seen by the Madisons and their guests while they were at home. The Yard's arrangement and aesthetics functioned to display the enslaving family's wealth and character. Most Virginia slaveholding families owned fewer than five individuals, so the multiple family groups contained in the South Yard alone indicated the Madisons' elevated economic position.[109] More than just wealth, though, the display of slave quarters took on an ethical dimension. As American abolitionists aligned themselves with a burgeoning labor-reform movement across the Atlantic, enslavers, too, looked to ideas coming from England and Europe meant to improve the well-being and therefore the productivity of their workers, including improving workers' housing. And Madison was an early adopter of these ideas.[110] When the Madisons' guests peered into the South Yard, they would have observed orderly rows of well-built and well-maintained structures that reflected the trend in providing better housing for laborers as a means of displaying an owner's benevolent attitude toward those workers.[111]

The Madisons would have also wanted a visible South Yard to reassure visitors of the comfort and care they would experience at Montpelier. The famous "Southern hospitality" of plantations has been greatly exaggerated and romanticized, but that does not discount the accounts from travelers extolling the great hospitality of Montpelier.[112] This was well-known, and if someone traveled to Orange County, Virginia, they would expect a sumptuous table, flowing Madeira, and gracious hosts. One description of Montpelier declared, "Its business seemed but giving pleasure to its guests," and though "little was seen of the working machinery of the fine . . . estate, that poured forth its copious supplies to render possible all this lavish entertainment," carefully chosen moments and sightlines of slave spaces and enslaved bodies would show guests that Montpelier would live up to its reputation.[113] At the same time, however, white guests would not want to see too much enslaving, for they likely regarded Black bodies and spaces at best as eye sores and at worst detrimental to the moral and intellectual character of white people. Enslavers delicately balanced the exploitation, display, and exclusion of enslaved laborers within their homes, creating clear but penetrable dividing lines between them. George Mason, a Virginia contemporary of Madison's, sought to do just that on his plantation by planting two hundred cherry trees to separate what he and other enslavers considered the civilized world of the main house from the uncivilized in slave dwellings while still allowing surveillance of the latter.[114] An antebellum publication on the homes of American statesmen pinpointed the usefulness of this partial concealment, and it specifically addressed the Madisons' partial screening of the South Yard, saying,

> On either side [of the mansion] are irregular masses of these [trees] of different shapes and foliage . . . which thicken at places into a grove, and half screen those dependencies of a handsome establishment—stables, dairies and the like—which, left openly in sight, look very ill, and can be made to look no otherwise, even by trying to make them look genteel: for they are disagreeable objects, that call up (attire them as you will) ideas not dainty. As, therefore, the eye should not miss them altogether—for their absence would imply great discomfort and inconvenience—the best way is to half-veil them, as is done at Montpelier.[115]

The Madisons were able to "half-veil" the South Yard by directing laborers to plant groves of trees in front of the Yard, between it and the mansion, creating traversable but explicit barriers between the two (see fig. 1.4). Barriers between the mansion and the South Yard had been in place since the time of James's father. Brick and stone walls dating to the original 1765 Madison mansion extended out from the house toward each side, with formal front yard space visible to visitors, and with workspaces behind the walls shielded from view. The walls' curved pattern played a trick with the eye, making the mansion seem larger. They provided balance and symmetry, emphasizing the original house's Georgian aesthetic while reflecting a desire to control nature through order and reason.[116] They also provided a cover for slave spaces, in particular the blacksmith shop on the north side and a kitchen and outbuilding on the south.[117] Clearly, delineating between free and enslaved spaces, home and labor, took place at Montpelier before James took over. However, he would replace these stone and brick walls with clumps of trees.[118] A change had occurred in the *way* enslavers sought to distinguish different kinds of spaces: a shift from rigid walls to more permeable barriers, ones that would still show some of the laboring spaces.[119] When standing on the Madisons' front portico, John H. B. Latrobe could glimpse the plantation (i.e., the slave spaces) "to the left, peeping through the foliage near the house."[120] From the main entry, the South Yard would have been at least partially hidden behind a small grove of trees, though it would become increasingly visible as a visitor like Latrobe made his way farther into the house, first ascending the front portico then entering the mansion, exiting to the rear or ascending to the southern wing's terrace for a much clearer view.

In certain instances, permeable barriers like trees or fences between white and Black spaces may have been constructed with the purpose of shielding the reality of slavery's violence and inhumanity from observers.[121] This landscaping maneuver drew on attempts by British nobility to hide labor on their estates while emphasizing the natural quality of the landscape.[122] Enslavers cultivated the connection between their plantations and the estates of nobility across the Atlantic. The use of natural barriers, in particular, was noted as enhancing this comparison. As John Finch described of Montpelier, "Clumps of trees are left in various parts, and it has a great resemblance to an English nobleman's mansion."[123]

But Virginia was not England, and James Madison was not European nobility. He did not seek to completely hide enslaved spaces from view. While James's main goal in directing the renovations of Montpelier was to highlight the beauty and grandeur of the mansion, too much cover would block guests' view of labor.[124] The Yard's location was carefully chosen, and the Madisons would have known that guests would be able to hear, see, and smell what took place there. Its close proximity to the mansion suggests the Madisons may have wanted to ensure that visitors sensorily knew this was a house of hospitality. Only then could visitors be assured of their comfort and be impressed by the Madisons' wealth and progressive slave management.

FIGURE 1.7. Digital rendering of the South Yard looking south from the Madison mansion's south terrace. Courtesy of Montpelier, a National Trust Historic Site.

It would have been difficult to either completely conceal or simply ignore the presence of Black bodies and spaces while visiting Montpelier, not only because of the constant work in the mansion but also because of the straight sightlines to the South Yard. While the tree groves partially concealed the South Yard at various points along the winding road to the mansion, once a guest passed through the front gate, they could see the area from various parts of the house. We know, based on travelers' accounts, that guests used the flat roofs atop the house's wings to survey the landscape of Montpelier; this would have included using the south terrace that looked directly into the South Yard (fig. 1.7). The Baron de Montlezun-Labarthette, visiting Montpelier in 1816, recalled looking out "from my apartment, and particularly from the terrace which is attached to it" across the "vista" of forest, plain, and hill.[125] He does not remark here on the presence of enslaved people or slave dwellings and work buildings. Yet he would have been able to see them and hear them, just as enslaved inhabitants could have seen him. Surveillance, therefore, went two ways: white folks could monitor the activities and people in the South Yard, but enslaved people could likewise keep tabs on those in the mansion.

Idealized views of plantations, like Montlezun's writings, typically pictured them without Black bodies.[126] Most period paintings of Montpelier, including Anna Maria Thornton's 1802 watercolor, erased the labor and presence of enslaved people, while highlighting its hospitality, tranquility, and pastoral beauty (fig. 1.8).[127] But Thornton's painting is not simply an illustration of enslavers' exclusionary homemaking tactics; it is also evidence of the ways that guests (luxuriating in the house) similarly separated the reality of enslaved labor from their experience of the plantation. As a writer reflected upon his visit in 1820, visiting Montpelier allowed one to connect with nature through sight, sound, touch, and fresh air, to feel "the dignity of his nature, and the happiness of which he has been made susceptible." The writer asked, "Oh, rus! quando te aspiciam?" (O rural home: when shall I behold you!)[128] That was home: the vast picturesque landscape, the sights and sounds of unadulterated nature. But no mention of the sights and sounds of slavery, of the slave dwellings and worksites that were so evident in the Montpelier landscape. Maybe these were simply beneath the notice of or commentary by visitors; but that absence was still a choice.

Thornton's painting draws our eyes to yet another method that James Madison employed to dissociate his home from enslaved labor: the neoclassical temple. Located on the left-edge of the watercolor, the domed, columned temple was an iconic piece of the Montpelier landscape, and one that James very much wanted visible (see fig. 1.8). Guests would have taken in the front lawn's neoclassical layout as they rode up to the mansion or while sitting on the piazza, but Madison also wanted to see the temple while he was indoors. He therefore asked one of his carpenters to include windows in his library, which looked out toward the temple.[129] Madison also used a Pine Allée—twenty trees in parallel rows that were placed incrementally closer to one another the closer they got to the temple—to visually enhance the size and thus importance of the temple in the landscape (see fig. 1.1).[130]

This open-air structure was a material indication of James's political and philosophical beliefs, but it was also a cover for exploitation. Unlike Thomas Jefferson's Garden Pavilion, described as "a little Grecian temple" for reflection and reading, Madison's temple was a neoclassical façade for enslaved people's work.[131] As Mary Cutts remembered, "On the right hand a short walk from the house was a beautiful temple, surmounted by a structure of Liberty; it was built over the icehouse which made it very cool; close to it was an immense mulberry tree, this building was intended, but never used, for his

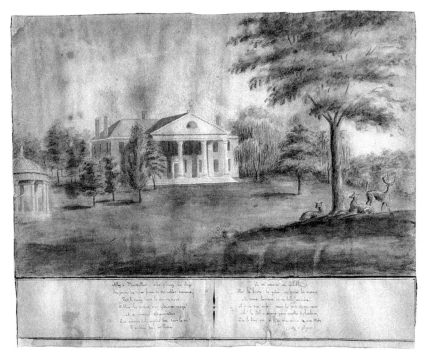

FIGURE 1.8. *View of Montpelier*, watercolor, by Anna Maria Thornton, ca. 1802. Courtesy of Montpelier, a National Trust Historic Site (MF2011.4.1). Purchase made possible through several generous Montpelier patrons, 2011.

study."[132] What Cutts does not mention is that the icehouse under the temple was a worksite where enslaved laborers stored harvested ice for the pleasure and comfort of the Madisons and their guests. James's use of a temple—a symbol of contemplation so associated with Greek ideas and appropriated by early Americans in their attempts to project themselves as both civilized and democratic—to mask the enslaved labor happening below points to his contradictory stance on slavery.[133] Enslavement was de rigeur for Southerners of the Madisons' elite status, but those of their position and generation still expressed unease, or ambivalence, over the institution's continuation even as they refused to stop participating in it.[134] Those who visited these men in their homes saw this up-close and personal. On a trip to Virginia in 1807, Augustus John Foster commented that Thomas Jefferson and James Madison "were notorious for their democratic tendencies . . . yet in their own houses were they surrounded with slaves."[135] Madison was willing to use his democratic and egalitarian convictions as a cover, literally, for the reality of his enslaving.

Enslaved laborers constructed the icehouse first, only later adding the temple atop it to mask the work that happened below. The icehouse, in fact, maintained a "secret" entrance that allowed enslaved workers to access the ice without disrupting the picturesque view.[136] This also meant that enslaved people might access this space at unauthorized times, with the Madisons unaware of their activities within. The temple-cum-icehouse may have thus unintentionally provided enslaved people a space of greater autonomy, a space where the Madisons and others could not overhear or oversee their conversations or actions. We know that enslaved Montpelier residents adapted other concealed laboring spaces on the plantation for their own purposes. A wide range of objects found in the mansion cellar rooms suggest their use for cooking, storage, and household chores but also for relaxation and transgressive activities like stealing wine or spiritual practices like conjuration.[137] Perhaps the icehouse functioned in similar ways, housing activities laborers did not want the Madisons to see. More simply, though, the icehouse would have been a desirable place to cool off in the hot Virginia summers. Conceivably, within the icehouse enslaved plantation residents found a space not just to labor for the Madisons but to take a moment for themselves, perhaps even engaging in talk and activities they wanted to keep private.

The icehouse construction process also involved harvesting the clay-fill to pave over an eighteenth-century blacksmith shop. It had previously stood close to the main house but was moved farther from it on James's orders the same year (1801) he inherited Montpelier from his father.[138] A blacksmith shop was apparently not the kind of enslaved labor he wanted within the performative core of his home. And so once again, James used natural barriers, including trees, to conceal this enslaved labor from view of the main house. While the Pine Allée was a clever ruse on his part to make the temple seem larger, it also obscured the view of more enslaved work buildings, this time those north of the mansion.[139] These strategically placed trees thus did double duty, emphasizing James's republicanism while also concealing what the antebellum publication *Homes of American Statesman* called "disagreeable objects"; that is, the work buildings so necessary to the operation of the plantation.[140] Interestingly, the engraving accompanying the book's chapter on Montpelier shows only the mansion, completely veiling these north-end worksites and the South Yard from the viewer, much like the Baron de Montlezun-Labarthette's 1816

MADISON.

FIGURE 1.9. "Montpelier,"
in *Homes of American Statesmen; with Anecdotical, Personal, and Descriptive Sketches*
(Hartford: O. D. Case,
1855), 181. Courtesy of Harry
Ransom Center, University
of Texas at Austin.

description of Montpelier had (fig. 1.9). Maybe the enslaved workers at these sites welcomed this veiling, however minimal or complete, for providing them at least some cover under which to live and labor.

AT MONTPELIER, the Madisons embedded their beliefs and desires into the landscape, physically defining their home against yet also among enslaved laboring spaces. The Field Quarter and Stable Quarter were more easily associated with the enslaved labor around it, though even here the Madisons imposed certain material boundaries as a means of segregating the landscape. This feat was more difficult within the South Yard, which was part of the enslavers' performative core. Slave spaces, from the viewpoint of the mansion, were spaces of labor, not of home. Whether observing the South Yard from atop the second-floor terrace or while seated next to James on a horse surveying the fields, a visitor would have seen the plantation as the Madisons did.

Yet theirs was never the sole or even the most widely held perspective of those who resided there. We can find enslaved Montpelier residents demarcating their homes across the plantation, whether through arranging the Field Quarter with a centralized communal space or by sweeping the ground in the

South Yard. They struggled to physically define a place of their own within the forced labor that defined much of the broader landscape, implementing ancestral and novel homemaking practices depending on where they resided on the large estate. In so doing, they embedded their own ideas into the land, claiming space as a means of claiming some control over their lives.

But Montpelier would not remain home for these enslaved or enslaving residents forever. When James Madison died in 1836, enslaved families were at the whim of Dolley, who found her choices dictated by economic, social, and personal factors. She finally sold Montpelier in 1844 and moved several enslaved people, including Ralph Philip Taylor, with her to Washington, DC.[141] But others remained on the estate, were sold to plantations near and far, or were transferred to Dolley's son, John Payne Todd.[142] At that point, many of the Montpelier slave dwellings were abandoned and left to decay, or they were demolished.[143] Only the Madisons' grand mansion, the core of their home, stood the test of time.[144]

Although their work had been erased from the landscape, enslaved people's homemaking at Montpelier left deep marks that eventually resurfaced through the work of dedicated archaeologists, public historians, and descendants.[145] Investigating the homemaking of Montpelier's residents helps us begin to unravel the struggle for home on Southern plantations, as Black and white residents sought to realize something more of the spaces in which they resided. In fact, within the South Yard, archaeologists have found more evidence of enslaved people's desires for spaces they could control: quartz and glass intentionally buried beneath dwellings to safeguard inhabitants, trunks and chests to keep their goods safe, locks and keys to keep unwanted persons out of their homes.[146] About two hundred miles south of Montpelier, enslaved North Carolinians likewise took advantage of hidden areas in their quest to create more private, protected domestic spaces. Homemaking did not always take place out in an open yard; sometimes, it was concealed behind closed doors, under a closed lid, or between two walls.

Chapter Two

CONCEALING FOR PRIVACY AND PROTECTION

STAGVILLE PLANTATION, NORTH CAROLINA

It was another cold morning in the North Carolina Piedmont as Ephram Hart surveyed his family's new home, the brick nogging of which had kept him and his family comparably warm during these late winter months. But the sound of horse hooves drumming up the frozen road stopped Ephram in his place. He fretted that Marse Paul—as folks called him—might be coming to order Ephram's family to relocate once again. They had been lucky last time, as the move to Horton Grove Quarter kept them at Stagville and close to places and people they loved. Yet so many others had been forced to leave for distant, unfamiliar lands. Ephram instinctually turned toward the house's rear wall. Within it, nailed to the brick nogging, were two seemingly unremarkable forked sticks, sticks he knew might help keep Paul out of his home and keep his family safe. Thankfully, he soon heard the horse hooves retreating from the quarter. He was able to breathe again, realizing that, at least on this trip, his enslaver would not disrupt his home.

As he trotted his horse away from Horton Grove, Paul Cameron once again felt proud of the time and energy he took to personally visit and inspect the slave quarters and worksites across his sprawling plantation, even on such chilly mornings as this. He wanted to ensure Stagville's efficiency and effectiveness, but Paul also needed to keep an eye on potentially nefarious or even murderous activity that could take place there. His own family had once been the target of such activity, when a plot by two enslaved men to poison his grandfather was discovered just in time. And that came just months after other enslaved men had been blamed for burning three white families' homes in the neighborhood. Paul knew that without proper surveillance of his slaves, his family and his own home could be at risk.[1]

BY 1860, STAGVILLE PLANTATION was one of the largest in the nation, having grown from just over twelve hundred acres in 1780 to an estimated thirty thousand acres eighty years later.[2] Paul, the third generation of Bennehan-Camerons to own and oversee the North Carolina estate, had likewise expanded the family's enslaved property, and by the start of the Civil War, Paul and his siblings owned nearly one thousand enslaved laborers.[3] Dozens of slave quarters dotted the Stagville complex, built to house this ever-increasing slave community.[4] Their labor for the Bennehan-Camerons took many different forms, as the estate included several farms, mills, stills, and shops, not to mention the domestic work required in the many houses owned by the family across the state.[5] But although Paul Cameron oversaw a profitable, diversified enterprise across an estate that spanned four North Carolina counties, he could not resist the pull of the Deep South and its promises of great profits. In the 1840s and 1850s, he purchased plantations in Alabama and Mississippi, forcibly relocating nearly two hundred individuals whose families had long called Stagville home. Although Paul vociferously argued that "no love of lucre shall ever induce me to be cruel" to his slaves, his actions and those of his predecessors—from the frequent intrusions into laborers' houses to ripping families from their homes—show otherwise.[6]

Paul Cameron insisted that his business's profitability and the privacy and safety of his own household necessitated such tactics. Absolute privacy was never possible within his or other enslavers' dwellings, nor was it for other nineteenth-century Americans, most of whom lived in houses crammed with people or in tightly knit communities where everyone knew everyone else's business.[7] But privacy was not about the absence of people or complete seclusion. To have privacy was to be able to decide when and where one was free from unwanted encroachment.[8] This ideal may never have been reality, but white Americans demanded the right to decide who watched, entered, and interfered with their domestic spaces. This was particularly important for white people living on plantations.[9] Marie Gordon Rice, for instance, thought back to her family's plantation roots and declared that "the old-time Virginian loved privacy" and would take measures to ensure his property, people, and home remained safe and secure from unwanted intrusions.[10] These measures included statewide restrictive racialized laws and county slave patrols, but enslavers were particularly attentive to their own plantations, enforcing stringent policies of surveillance, intrusion, and confinement of Black bodies and spaces.[11] Enslavers thus linked their own privacy and protection with enslaved people's lack of the same. As historian Thavolia Glymph rightly put it, "Freedom . . . meant privacy in the home."[12] Slavery, therefore, meant the lack of it.[13] And so enslaved people on plantations lived in a world where their bodies and spaces were not their own to protect and defend, not unless they were willing to risk retribution, likely violent retribution.[14] Unlike the homes of their enslavers, theirs were more akin to what Saidiya Hartman describes as a "threshold between the public and private rather than a fortified private sphere."[15]

Enslaved people faced surveillance, intrusion, violence, and familial disruption, so creating fortified private spaces on plantations was but a dream. Solomon Northup, for instance, related that enslaved people were careful even to talk of aspirations for "homes and families of their own, with none to disturb and oppress them," since "such conversations would have brought down the lash upon our backs."[16] But talk they did, for like freedom itself, home was something enslaved people not only dreamed of but actively sought.[17] Enslaved inhabitants knew that many, perhaps most, plantation spaces were surveilled spaces of captivity. Yet as scholars of slavery long ago showed, enslaved individuals sometimes escaped the gaze of enslavers, if only for a brief time, to pray or dance or simply be.[18] They could sometimes escape the plantation's geographies of containment and create, as historian Stephanie Camp describes it, their own rival geographies.[19] And even the most restrictive spaces—like Harriet Jacobs's famous hiding spot in her grandmother's small attic room—could be ones of resistance.[20] Enslaved people adapted spaces of captivity—large and small, fully hidden and partially concealed—for their own purposes, for activities and practices that they did not want watched or interfered with. In this way, though, more than simply resisting enslavement, they were trying to make something, to use and transform captive spaces to find a semblance of control over them. The struggle for home happened not only outdoors in swept yards but in captive, hidden spaces within dwellings across the plantation, where concealment could provide opportunities to act beyond an enslaver's knowledge.

At Stagville, enslaved residents took advantage of hidden domestic spaces to hide an assortment of objects, from sticks to shells. This was not unique to Stagville; enslaved people across the Americas concealed things in walls and foundations, under doorways and beneath floors, in locked trunks and in open lofts. Scholars have often framed these kinds of artifacts as demonstrating the preservation of West African traditions.[21] But they were more than retentions of tradition; the particularities of American slavery—and more specifically the multiple layers of context unique to the artifacts found at Stagville—shaped why and how individuals made and wielded them, including the adjustment of ancestral practices to better fit their needs and desires as enslaved individuals.[22] We do not know, and may never know, the names of the people who made, hid, or handled these artifacts.[23] Investigating the artifacts as products of Stagville's unique circumstances, rather than as decontextualized, isolated cultural examples, helps reveal more about the actual people who interacted with them, including what they hoped to achieve in the process.

To unravel those aspirations, this chapter begins by exploring Stagville's captivity, particularly the techniques adopted by the enslaving Bennehan-Camerons to confine and coerce their enslaved property. Even with such constraints, unfree residents still found ways to secure some of what they wanted out of their homes, including by manipulating out-of-sight spaces. We therefore investigate the materiality, spatiality, and temporality of four slave-era Stagville artifacts found within dwellings: a walking stick lodged in the walls of the slave owner's mansion in the 1790s, a cowrie shell left in a slave cabin in the 1830s or 1840s, and two forked sticks nailed to the brick nogging of a slave dwelling in the 1850s. One of these sites is not like the other, of course, but even an enslaver's house could be part of enslaved people's homemaking. And though these things may have been used for multiple purposes over time, by carefully considering the creation, use, and concealment of these domestically located objects, we may observe a hidden homemaking tactic deployed by enslaved people. Spaces of captivity, meant to constrain and limit their control, could also be adapted to call upon spirits or deposit charms that might facilitate the protection and privacy of their homes and people.[24] As the Bennehan-Cameron estate expanded over the first half of the nineteenth century, the possibility and reality of dislocation, surveillance, and violence increased for enslaved Stagville residents. They nonetheless sought to transform spaces of captivity into homes despite the restrictions that sought to make that endeavor impossible.

Securing and Controlling Stagville

Stagville's owners worked to ensure the security of themselves, their families, their homes, and their property through a series of common tactics adopted by enslavers around the Atlantic world, including surveillance, intrusion, containment, and other manipulative practices.[25] Beginning in the era of the early Republic, prison and asylum reformers imposed surveillance on inmates as part of their plans for a more humane and effective system.[26] Although surveillance was obviously antagonistic to the growing individualism taking hold in antebellum American society, the rights of the individual did not apply to prison inmates or, from the perspective of most white Southerners, to enslaved people.

Both prisons and slavery included surveillance as well as tactics of containment and intrusion. It is not surprising, then, that formerly enslaved people connected the two institutions in their writing.[27] Slavery, like the growing nineteenth-century prison system, was a panoptic institution characterized by the visibility, supervision, and judgment of individuals.[28] In all realms of life, owners desired to ensure that enslaved individuals were visible, that they knew they were being watched, and that the potential for punishment was ever-present. So enslavers built plantations to realize those desires. One enslaver, for instance, argued that with his design for slave dwellings, "a master may at night keep his slaves under the best control."[29] Cyrus Bellus recalled that at every moment his family members were not working outdoors, "they had to be found in their house."[30]

By the late eighteenth century, most planters had implemented landscape arrangements that allowed for and encouraged these monitoring tactics. This included the nucleated plantation village design, common throughout the Atlantic world, which placed service buildings and slave quarters in square or rectangular patterns near the landowner's or overseer's house.[31] The Bennehans employed this design in the Stagville home complex, arranging slave cabins at the top of what Paul Cameron called "a line of buildings" east of the mansion.[32] Placing these cabins along a "line," or street, facilitated surveillance, much like the South Yard at Montpelier. Planters therefore endeavored to maintain the often-competing imperatives of *privacy from* and *surveillance over* their enslaved property. By the nineteenth century, even enslavers who moved slave cabins away from their houses tended to arrange those dwellings along streets so as to more easily observe movement between them.[33]

White Stagville residents likely felt this was necessary as they experienced challenges to their mastery. The progenitor of the white family, Richard Bennehan, had moved from Virginia to North Carolina in 1768, seven years before the American Revolution erupted, and purchased the first parcel of land that would ultimately become Stagville in 1787. The Atlantic Age of Revolution

heightened enslavers' desire to embed protective forces into their worlds. Rebellion on a large and violent scale seemed particularly possible in the after-
math of the Haitian Revolution (1791–1804), and concerns over the security of
enslavers' homes increased with news of slave uprisings both far and near. But
attacks on one's own family caused the greatest fear. The attempted murder
of family members—as supposedly occurred in 1807, four years after the marriage of Richard Bennehan's daughter Rebecca to Duncan Cameron—surely
increased the desire to carefully watch enslaved laborers.[34]

Thus, along with the help of overseers and patrols, Stagville's owners mon-
itored enslaved people's dwellings and other spaces. As the family prospered
and the estate grew in size and population over the antebellum era, Paul
Cameron increased the intensity and severity of these control tactics. Cameron surveilled the quarters himself, traveling to the various plantations and
worksites on Sundays "to see what is going on & to break up any collection
of negroes from the neighborhood."[35] Paul was not the only intruder into
enslaved spaces, though. Morgan Latta recalled how, when he was enslaved
at Stagville in the 1850s, "the patrollers would come around and examine the
little children, and make them tell if there was any flour or sugar or spirits
in the house."[36] Not only did enslaved people have no authority to dictate
who entered their houses; they likewise could not leave them whenever they
wished. Latta related that "it was a crime for the slaves to be caught out of
their houses after half past seven o'clock at night; if they were caught out of
their houses after that time, the patrollers would call them in and give them
one hundred and fifty lashes."[37] Stagville-born Abner Jordan corroborated
this feeling of confinement, declaring that enslaved residents "couldn' leave
de plantation without Marse say dey could."[38]

The Bennehan-Camerons also used other manipulative tactics to control
their enslaved population, including promises to keep families intact. As historian Sydney Nathans has illustrated, Stagville's owners understood that familial maintenance was a powerful tool: if they worked to purchase and keep
Black families together, they could exert greater authority over their slaves.[39]
This could be simultaneously a blessing to enslaved mothers, fathers, and children and an instrument to manipulate them. But these promises may have
always sounded hollow to Stagville's enslaved residents, as the very business of
the slave trade happened at the plantation's store, where goods and people were
sold side by side.[40] Enslaved Stagville residents like Ned, Jim, and Joe—who
held skilled and high-ranking positions on the plantation—shopped at the
store and perhaps witnessed and conveyed to others information about the

slave auctions.⁴¹ Just down the road from where enslaved Stagville families were settled with promises of stability, other unfree individuals were bought and sold and taken from their kin.

Promises of familial security for enslaved residents became increasingly meaningless as Paul Cameron began rearranging the Stagville quarters in the 1830s, moving individuals to new areas and shattering families in the process.⁴² Indeed, Paul's decision to forcibly relocate hundreds of enslaved people to the Deep South in the 1840s and 1850s had its roots in these earlier trials at re-arranging and moving families. Cameron followed the latest scientific advice on plantation management, which argued that rearrangement would improve the health and well-being of his enslaved laborers.⁴³ We can see beneath this façade of paternalistic concern to the economic incentive.⁴⁴ Paul tested the waters of forced relocation, something that would expand and enhance his business, and in the process he bucked the Bennehan-Cameron tradition of maintaining families and homes. Paul Cameron regarded slave dwellings not as homes but rather like barns for sheltering livestock, calling the cabin of Faithy and her children a "hog pen."⁴⁵

Their dwelling might indeed have been insufficient and barely habitable, as many slave cabins were, but Faithy and the rest of Stagville's enslaved community may not have agreed with Paul's simplistic assessment of their residences.⁴⁶ Even a confining "pen" could offer more than bare shelter. In fact, within even the most degraded space of captivity, some enslaved people combated their enslavers' tactics of control, including the intraplantation and interstate migrations Paul Cameron forced upon their community. Several enslaved residents reimagined what they could do with out-of-sight spaces through the objects they concealed within them. By carefully choosing and placing artifacts within confined domestic spaces, enslaved Stagville residents may have been doing much more than storing items. Peeling back layers of meaning and context from four Stagville artifacts reveals the possible ways that enslaved residents used these objects as tools with which to create more privacy and protection in their world, including by seeking help from those beyond it.

The Walking Stick

Within the walls of the Bennehans' Stagville mansion, someone hid a walking stick (fig. 2.1). Little more than this is known: no documentation exists to tell us about the wooden cane, about who, when, why, and how it was made and

FIGURE 2.1. Walking stick recovered from wall of Bennehan house, unknown date. Courtesy of Stagville State Historic Site, North Carolina Department of Natural and Cultural Resources.

left hidden behind the enslaving family's house walls until it was discovered in the late twentieth century.[47] But the location and the object itself provide us with considerable information if we take the time to carefully follow the clues they provide. Piecing together the creation and design of the cane, the place and time it was deposited, and the contexts in which these acts occurred allows us to responsibly speculate that an enslaved man or men made and later hid the cane during a renovation of the mansion, perhaps for the purpose of using it as a conjuring stick without the Bennehans' knowledge. In using the cane as a conjuring stick, an object documented throughout the African diaspora to provide protection against foes, someone might have called upon those beyond this world to help keep the user safe from evil. By hiding the cane within the Bennehan house, rather than in a dwelling of his own, an enslaved man may have also meant to wield it against the white residents.

The cane itself reflects the time, energy, and skills invested by the person who crafted it. The maker would have had to search the nearby woods for a hickory tree, a particularly good choice for a cane because of the wood's strength, flexibility, and versatility. It is likely that the creator would have known how to identify hickory, as it was common to the Stagville area.[48] Once the maker found a straight branch or limb, twigs and leaves would then have been trimmed and the main branch cut to the right size. The maker would then have removed the bark, either through the repetitive process of whittling or by burning the tree limb in hot coals.[49] The stick then required further time to dry, between a few weeks and few months, to extract any remaining moisture and render it more durable. The final, cylindrical form has one rounder and one flatter end, the former more comfortable to hold and the latter meant to hit the ground upon walking. This thirty-six inches of solid hickory could

have supported the weight of a grown man as he ambled around the plantation. The time- and energy-consuming process of its creation resulted in a
strong cane with a smooth surface and slight sheen.

The walking stick's decorative motif suggests that its maker was enslaved.
Although not as ornate as later nineteenth-century examples of African
American walking sticks, such as a cane by Henry Gudgell (fig. 2.2), the
Stagville example does exhibit fine detailing, including a spiral along the top
two-thirds of the stick. The spiral mimics the natural curvature of a growing
vine, smoothed and debarked by human hands to emphasize the coil winding
up the stick (see fig. 2.1). This spiral design was used by other nineteenth-
century African American cane-makers, including on a walking stick crafted
to commemorate the Emancipation Proclamation (fig. 2.3). But it also reflects a long-standing tradition of snake motifs used by generations of African American cane-makers, including those at Stagville.[50] Lucille Peaks
Turner, who lived at Stagville and whose grandmother had been enslaved
by the Camerons, remembered that her father carved a snake into his maple
walking stick, the only one he owned.[51] If the walking stick found in the
Bennehan mansion was an early iteration of this tradition, it too would have
been crafted by a Black person, probably an enslaved resident of Stagville.

The walking stick was also likely made by a man, as was common in enslaved and later free Black communities.[52] Artisanal occupations, from black-
smithing to carpentry and construction, were most often held by enslaved
men, and the skills and tools required to craft this cane suggest that its maker
may have been an artisan of some kind at Stagville. The maker chose to spend
what little time he had to himself stealing away into the woods or whittling
away bark. His labor as a cane-maker, then, would have been different from
the labor Bennehan required of him; it would have been something he chose
to do. His skilled hands may have also helped construct houses across the
plantation, perhaps finding opportunities to create communal spaces, like
those in the Montpelier Field Quarter, for his people. But he would also have
likely been part of the crew renovating the Bennehans' house, which, like
the Madisons' mansion, required upgrades as the enslavers sought to better
project their social position on and off the plantation.

In 1799, a construction team completed a substantial two-story addition
onto the small one-and-a-half-story house that the Bennehans had occupied
since approximately 1788 (fig. 2.4).[53] For the white family, this newly renovated
and expanded house would make an ambitious statement, demonstrating their
rising wealth and status in the slave economy. The addition more than doubled

FIGURE 2.2. Cane, created by Henry Gudgell, Livingston County, Missouri, ca. 1867. Director's Purchase Fund, Yale University Art Gallery, New Haven, CT (1968.23).

FIGURE 2.3. Cane commemorating Emancipation Proclamation, ca. 1865–1900. Courtesy of Brooklyn Museum, Marie Bernice Bitzer Fund and A. Augustus Healy Fund (1996.179).

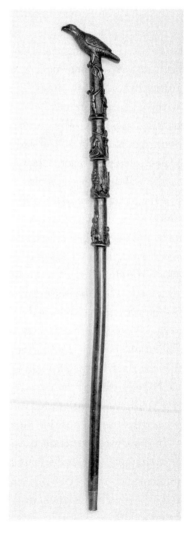

FIGURE 2.4. Bennehan house, Stagville, Durham County, NC, renovated and expanded ca. 1799. Courtesy of Stagville State Historic Site, North Carolina Department of Natural and Cultural Resources.

the available interior space, and while asymmetrical in its design, the overall structure otherwise exuded a late classical sensibility, with simple yet expertly crafted details throughout.[54] As Catherine Bishir has shown was typical of construction projects in antebellum North Carolina, the crew that constructed this architectural dream was likely a mix of free and enslaved laborers, both white and Black men.[55] It is also probable that Bennehan hired some of the labor, for few North Carolina planters owned enough slaves (including skilled artisans) to complete a house-build. Even the very wealthy Duncan Cameron, whose family merged with Richard Bennehan's following his marriage, hired free and enslaved laborers for his architectural undertakings.[56] Bennehan thus likely hired a carpenter, probably a white man, to oversee the renovations; and he likely hired enslaved or free artisans to work as sawyers, masons, and bricklayers.[57]

Not all or even most of the labor would be hired, however. Enslaved artisans resided at Stagville in the early nineteenth century, including Ned, the "smith," and Jim and Lewis, the coopers.[58] Additionally, other laborers—especially field hands—would have participated in many aspects of the building process. While it was essential to have or hire artisan labor, as Bishir notes, preparing materials and erecting a building in antebellum North Carolina also "involved laborers who carried or hauled heavy materials, lifted timbers or bricks," and the like.[59] And Richard Bennehan had the numbers: his enslaved property had increased from thirty-one in 1778 to forty-two in 1799.[60] It would have been common, and thus very probable, that Bennehan would have used his own enslaved laborers for some of this work, including raising the building frame, which needed strength more than skill.[61] After the addition's frame was erected, the lengthy process of finishing the house could begin—weatherboarding, roofing, laying floors, plastering walls, and installing doors, mantels, and trim—and the fine paneling and heavy woodwork on rooms such as the parlor indicate that this was the work of an experienced artisan. Whether that craftsman was free or not, hired or enslaved by Bennehan, is unclear. Still, Bennehan's own enslaved laborers would have performed at least some of labor required to finish the interior walls.[62]

This task would have provided someone the moment and opportunity to hide the walking stick between the former exterior wall of the old house and the new interior wall of the addition before permanently covering it with plaster and paint. The plasterer would have seen the cane, making it quite unlikely that its placement was accidental. And the moment when the object would have been placed—in the middle of construction—makes it likely that someone actually performing that construction placed it; thus it was probably placed there by an enslaved laborer. This kind of purposeful placement of meaningful objects within hidden spaces is part of a long Black tradition in the Atlantic world. Archaeologists and folklorists have shown how enslaved people took advantage of secluded or semisecluded spaces like subfloor pits, hearths, and walls in which to conceal spiritual and protective objects.[63]

The use of these objects harkened back to practices of West Africa, and they may reveal how unseen, untouchable things still had real meaning and purpose. Archaeologist Patricia Samford, for instance, interprets other Stagville artifacts—including a bottle holding a button, small cloth bags containing plant material, and an iron knife—as material evidence of the West African use of *nkisi* (plural, *minkisi*), which are objects (typically some type of container) that embody spiritual beings.[64] The physical and spatial context is important, as archaeologists found these objects concealed within the walls of Stagville's Eno Quarter and thus in a building that Black residents regarded (at least to a degree) as their domain. The walking stick, however, was found within the walls of the enslavers' house; yet even this was not unique to Stagville, as Samford has found similar artifacts within a white family's house.[65] Rather than storing *nkisi* within one's own home, the realities of slavery may have forced Black individuals to use it wherever they could, an ancestral practice retained yet adapted to American slavery.[66] For even hiding the *nkisi* within an enslaving household's walls could allow it to work in a conjuring ritual.

Conjuration, a form of magic work, involves invoking spirits for curative, protective, or defensive purposes.[67] This practice continued long after African peoples were forced to cross the Atlantic via the Middle Passage, and it appears in several nineteenth-century slave narratives.[68] Additionally, archaeologists have discovered object assemblages at US slave sites that resemble conjurer's kits in West Africa.[69] While those assemblages did not include large walking sticks, Albert Raboteau has argued that a conjurer's equipment often included a cane.[70] A conjuring cane might be used to heal, protect, or defend, as West African folklore suggests.[71] This tradition, recorded by anthropologist Allan Cardinall, tells of a "magic stick" that can kill slave traders and enemies by simply pointing "it at a man and that man fell dead."[72] Of course, the enslaved person could not have touched the hidden Stagville walking stick, but he would not have needed to.[73] As Alice Eley Jones has suggested, concealing such an object could be beneficial because it enabled the conjurer to call forth spirits no matter where the conjurer or stick were.[74] Not every ritual required physical contact, and calling for help from those beyond this world of captivity would limit the harm that could come to any who participated in the ritual, thereby enhancing the protective quality of the conjuring object and practice.

The Bennehan stick's snakelike spiral, a motif associated with African American canes, likewise suggests its use for protective purposes. Snakes appear throughout African and African American culture in folktales, spiritual practices, and material culture, although the connotations vary.[75] On the one hand, as Babtunde Lawal asserts, the snake is a symbol of Damballah, a god of healing for those practicing the African-derived Vodou religion.[76] On the other hand, African American narratives offer myriad examples of snakes as harbingers or literal incarnations of harm and evil. Andrew Boone, who lived in Northampton County, North Carolina, during slavery, directly connected snakes to the "Devil's work."[77] But there is further meaning: that of snakes bringing harm or evil to others as a means of protecting or empowering the self and community. Annie B. Boyd, who lived in Kentucky during and after slavery, declared that she could conquer an enemy by killing a snake.[78]

As had been the case for West Africans, those enemies included enslavers, and a snakelike conjuring cane hidden within an enslaving family's home might have been one way that Black plantation residents sought more protection from the enslavers in their world. Formerly enslaved people remembered using concealed objects and conjuring for just this purpose. Harre Quarls, who lived in both Missouri and Texas during slavery, remembered enslaved residents hiding a stick with notches under the front steps of their owner's house, which they used "to keep massa from bein' mean."[79] And Henry Bibb, writing about life in slavery, characterized the various conjuring tricks that enslaved people deployed within enslavers' dwellings as "all done for the purpose of defending themselves in some Peaceable manner."[80]

But it may not have been only peaceable. West African folklore described the specific use of conjuring sticks for protection against enslavers, calling up spirits to harm individuals who sought to capture and sell their people into the slave trade.[81] In this way, the concealment of the cane in the Bennehan mansion could have been a means of attacking enemies where they were most relaxed and where they believed themselves to be protected. Enslaved Americans' aggressive uses of hidden objects have been found elsewhere, including on Hume Plantation in South Carolina, where archaeologist Sharon Moses argues enslaved laborers intentionally placed a projectile point within the foundation beam of the overseer's cabin to "surreptitiously plant a spell in its construction to work on its occupant to cause harm or pain."[82] Placing the cane within the Bennehan mansion to target enslavers and thus keep the enslaved community safe, then, may have been another adaptation of an ancestral practice to American slavery. Enslaved people used captive spaces—indeed, spaces of their captors—for their own benefit. It may not have been their home, but imagining different ways of using it may have opened new ways of protecting their own spaces. Whether to shield or to harm, the hidden cane could have been used to call upon those beyond this world to help those held captive in this one.

The Cowrie Shell

Within a slave cabin behind the Bennehan mansion, a cowrie shell found its way beneath the floorboards to the ground below. There it remained for some 130 years before archaeologists discovered it among the rubble of the razed cabin in 1979.[83] Exactly how and why it came to be there is uncertain, but once again we can begin to piece together the story by exploring the object, its location, and its contexts. The shell had to have traveled across an ocean to get to Stagville, for the small snaillike creatures that inhabit cowrie shells originate far from Piedmont North Carolina. Someone took special care to keep the shell intact, undamaged, and without man-made alterations within the slave dwelling just a stone's throw from the Bennehan house. This space was quite different from the sealed wall that held the cane; although it had a door, this cabin was open to prying eyes and hands of Bennehan and others.[84] While it was one of many spaces of captivity for enslaved residents, it was also, at least to some degree, their own space. Slave cabins, even ones so close to the home of an enslaver, were semisecluded spaces; the dwellings could provide a degree of concealment that enslaved people could have used for their own benefit. The potential uses of the cowrie shell within the cabin are many, but diasporic traditions and the particularities of life under the purview of the Bennehans point to one reason enslaved people may have kept this unbroken cowrie shell in their dwelling: as a protective charm for their home and those within it.

The small cowrie shell, approximately 1¾ inches in length, fits in the palm of an adult's hand. Its two distinct faces can be distinguished by touch: a smooth, almost glossy dorsal face as opposed to the jagged "teeth" on the ventral face (figs. 2.5 and 2.6). Unlike the walking stick, the Stagville cowrie shell was not formed by human hands; it is an unaltered natural object brought from afar. It is lightweight and easily carried in the hand, pocket, apron, or satchel of its owner. It could therefore be transported long distances, moving with an individual as a symbol of or even as an artifact from one's home.

And this shell—like other examples of cowrie shells found in the Americas—at some point traveled across the Atlantic Ocean, in all probability from West Africa as a part of the transatlantic slave trade. Based on its small size, oval outline, yellowish color, and narrow aperture on the ventral face, the Stagville example is probably a *Cypraea moneta* or "money cowrie," the most abundant and widely dispersed species.[85] Humans have harvested this small, porcelain-like, glossy shell in waters from east of the Philippines to the East African coast. This particular kind of shell became widely used as a form of currency and circulated with changing trade routes. It may have made its way across the African continent in the trans-Saharan trade, but with the shift to maritime trade, it is also possible that the cowrie shell found its way to West Africa on a European ship, whether in the hands of a slave trader or hidden somewhere on a captive. Jan Hogendorn and Marion Johnson's study of the British and Dutch cartels that dominated the overseas routes tracked the movement of more than 25 million pounds of cowries (or over 10 billion individual shells) into West African ports between 1700 and 1790. In West Africa, cowrie shells functioned as a medium of exchange integral to slave-trading operations for

FIGURE 2.5. Dorsal face of a cowrie shell recovered from Stagville slave cabin, unknown date. Courtesy of Stagville State Historic Site, North Carolina Department of Natural and Cultural Resources.

FIGURE 2.6. Ventral face of a cowrie shell recovered from Stagville slave cabin, unknown date. Courtesy of Stagville State Historic Site, North Carolina Department of Natural and Cultural Resources.

both Europeans and Africans.[86] Beyond their use as currency, cowrie shells also served a range of sacred and secular functions for various African and African-descended societies across the diaspora, including in communication, divination, games, tools, food, medicine, and artistic and funerary practices.[87] The Stagville shell may have been used for one or more of these purposes at different points, and it may have been handled by many people before being buried in the rubble of the plantation's slave cabin. But this shell was almost certainly held and used by that cabin's enslaved residents, and the particularities of life within that house shaped the function and meaning of the shell for its residents.[88]

The Stagville example is not the only cowrie shell to have made its way across the Atlantic, however. Cowrie shells have been among the many small artifacts found on slave sites.[89] They have been discovered as elements of personal adornment for enslaved people, such as a necklace found at New York's Burial Ground and one at Newton Plantation in Barbados—the latter, archaeologists suggest, was connected to the practice of divination.[90] Cowrie shells also have been found in the US South, including examples excavated closer to Stagville.[91] In an extensive study of cowrie shells unearthed by ar-

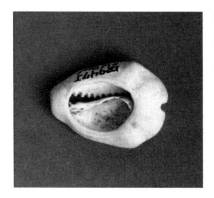

FIGURE 2.7. Cut dorsal face, cowrie shell recovered from slave cabin, Monticello, Virginia. © Thomas Jefferson Foundation at Monticello.

chaeologists in the Americas, Laurie Pearce analyzed these objects at thirteen sites, including several in Virginia at which enslaved people were present. Of those, one from Monticello was discovered in a slave cabin adjacent to the enslavers' house, just like at Stagville.[92] Unlike the Stagville example, however, the Monticello cowrie shell exhibits an intentional, man-made cut on its dorsal face (fig. 2.7; see also fig. 2.5). The physical and spatial context of the Monticello shell — found in a subfloor pit containing an assemblage of objects including crystals, a horn ring, pierced coins, and a game counter — also differ from that of the Stagville example.[93] Archaeologists have found comparable artifact assemblages of shells, crystals, beads, and other small items in similarly "restricted" spaces at the Charles Carroll house in Maryland.[94] Finding these types of concealed objects once again suggests the ritual of conjuring, of calling upon spirits to cure, protect, or defend, with the shell being just one element of the conjurer's kit.

But the details of the Stagville example do not point to exactly these same uses. While the Stagville shell was likewise found among a variety of objects, only the shell remained intact, surrounded by a seemingly random scattering of ceramic fragments as well as glass shards, broken wood, and rusty nails.[95] Conjuring kits typically include a range of objects, including shells, beads, and crystals, but not the types of architectural debris found at Stagville. Additionally, unlike the shells from Monticello and the Carroll house, it is less certain whether the Stagville shell was intentionally buried in the ground with these other artifacts, further reducing its likelihood as a component of a conjuring kit.[96] And unlike the New York, Barbadian, or Monticello examples, the Stagville shell is in no way altered by human touch; it lacks, for instance, the hole required to transform it into a piece of jewelry or adornment. Regardless, it appears that enslaved people kept cowrie shells in spaces over which they felt some degree of ownership and control, whether on a string around the neck, within a loved one's burial ground, placed within a cabin's subfloor pit, buried beneath the slave quarter, or stored inside a dwelling. Yet even the most concealed space was one where enslavers might interfere and intrude. Although not part of a full conjuring kit, the Stagville cowrie shell may nonetheless have been meant for something similar: to help the people and place that held it.

The proximity of the Stagville slave cabin to the Bennehan mansion further suggests this. When Richard Bennehan died in 1825, his son Thomas inherited eighty-eight enslaved individuals and 4,000 adjoining acres of land that Stagville comprised, which included slave cabins near the main house.[97] The younger Bennehan also inherited his father's expansionist mentality, working to diversify and develop the family's agricultural business. When he died unmarried and childless in 1847, Thomas Bennehan held 358 enslaved individuals and owned approximately 5,000 acres of land.[98] More people required more buildings to house them, so among his many construction projects, Thomas ordered another slave cabin be built close to the Bennehan house. While no documentary evidence of the construction exists, archaeologists have paired artifact dates with family records to estimate that the slave cabin was constructed between 1820 and 1850.[99] And based on the cabin's earliest layer of objects found during excavation, the cowrie shell came to rest beneath the cabin between 1830 and 1850.[100]

This cabin—like other slave dwellings—was not a fortified, private place; it was a captive space. Unlike slave quarters located near agricultural fields, this cabin stood immediately behind the Bennehan house and, like Montpelier's South Yard, it would have housed domestic workers.[101] Hypervisibility and close proximity to enslavers was not a common experience for enslaved Stagville residents, as few of the laborers lived immediately within the Bennehan and later Cameron home complexes. Even in distant quarters, however, slave owners had the ability to surveil their property. One man born enslaved in South Carolina recalled that the slave community there "expected their master at any hour, and were not surprised to have him present himself at their doors when he thought they were not looking for him."[102] While the threat of surveillance loomed large for all enslaved people, the nineteenth-century Bennehan house slave cabin was particularly vulnerable to this kind of intrusion and surveillance. As was often the case with plantation mansions, the Bennehan house stood at the highest elevation on the property, ensuring oversight of nearby buildings and activities.[103] Additionally, the forest that had formerly blanketed the area had been leveled, making way for fields and further augmenting Thomas Bennehan's surveillance capabilities.[104] The cabin could easily be seen and accessed from the enslaver's house by simply walking out the back door.[105]

Yet the physical building and material culture within it could still provide some decent cover. Household goods—such as trunks or storage containers—offered hidden spaces that could store anything from potentially subversive materials to ordinary objects. Granny Milly's trunk kept her beloved *Telemachus* safe at Montpelier, while on a Kentucky plantation Allen Allensworth "was allowed a plain candle box in which to keep his little belongings."[106] William Craft assembled furniture that he shared with his wife, Ellen, including a chest of drawers with locks that hid transgressive articles, like the disguise they used when escaping bondage. When locked away in the dresser, "No one about the premises knew that she had anything of the kind."[107] With its lock, this chest was more of a private space than any other that Ellen Craft knew in slavery. And though locks may seem a luxury unafforded to someone kept enslaved, locks appear on sites of slavery across the Atlantic world.[108] Even in the Stagville rubble, where the cowrie shell was found, archaeologists discovered pieces of a wooden lock.[109] While we do not know who affixed the lock and where—whether to the interior or exterior of the cabin—enslaved residents may have discovered that no matter the lock's intention—to keep unwanted people out or confine inhabitants within—a secluded and concealed space could still be beneficial.[110]

The cowrie shell, kept within this semiconcealed space of the slave cabin, might have provided a layer of protection for its inhabitants. Archaeologist Akinwumi Ogundiran has shown the widespread use in Africa of these small shells as protective charms for the health and well-being of individuals.[111] Enslaved individuals in North America also used natural and man-made objects as charms to protect, heal, or divine the future.[112] Black people's use of charms for protection was well known on both continents, so much so that even proslavery writers included this fact in their writing. Discussing the African uses of amulets and their continued use by African-descended peoples in the Americas, South Carolina planter and politician David James McCord described in 1854 how, "a chicken, a fish-bone, a stone, a feather, the skull of a monkey, the least *bagatelle*, becomes a Fetiche. Every negro has one upon his person, in his canoe, or in his cabin, and it passes as an heritage. They buy them at high prices from their priests. They are affixed to their doors, as a security to their houses against the intrusion of the devil and his imps, and against witchcraft. So, we have seen among superstitious negroes in America, old horse shoes nailed over doors with the same object."[113]

Though dripping with derision, McCord's words record the use of objects by both Africans and African Americans as charms against the "evil eye" and thus as a kind of protection.[114] Horseshoes, as indicated in McCord's article, were well-known charms for this purpose, too. Tom Hawkins, born into slavery in South Carolina, declared, "No witches or ghosties never bothered us, 'cause us kept a horseshoe over our cabin door."[115] Similarly, Laurie Pearce concluded her work on archaeological sites in Virginia by arguing that, "for the African, or his descendants . . . the cowrie shell also connoted great protective power which may be seen in its use as a charm to ward off evil and bring good fortune."[116] Enslaved people believed that charms of various sorts—from horseshoes to shells—could provide protection against harmful foes.

The shell's last known location in the Stagville slave cabin reminds us that otherworldly evil was not the only thing the residents needed protecting from. Enslaved people lived within a cruel system, one intimately associated with the individuals who surveilled them, intruded into their homes, and kept them enslaved, including the man who resided in the house just steps away from them, who kept an eye on them from the mansion's second window, and who likely walked out the back door with his whip in hand.[117] Like the walking stick, the shell may have been a charm against the present evils of Thomas Bennehan as much as a charm against potentially wicked spirits. By protecting their space and those within it, the cabin could be made to feel more like it was their own, like they controlled it. It is certainly possible these individuals took the cowrie shell out-of-doors at some point, but its final resting place within the cabin's remains and the lack of alterations to make it wearable suggest that the shell was kept safe within that dwelling by its inhabitants. By keeping it in the structure, the enslaved residents could ensure its continued presence as a charm, a kind of guardian over their home.

The Forked Sticks

Within a house at Stagville's Horton Grove Quarter, someone nailed two forked sticks to the brick nogging behind a wall. The wall had not been knocked down nor the nogging disturbed until a team found the sticks while restoring the slave house in the 1980s and 1990s.[118] The objects had clearly been placed there at the time the house was built; but why someone would nail these objects behind a wall, never to be seen or handled for nearly 150 years, is puzzling. At least, it is puzzling until we again seriously consider the artifacts themselves, their location, and the circumstances with which they may have been secreted away. For without careful inspection or context, the two forked sticks may just seem like branches, debris picked up from the wooded expanse around Stagville. But the smoothed exteriors with tapered ends reveal a pattern shared by sticks used for divining, whether for finding water and other resources, seeking out spiritual guidance, or foretelling the future. The extant Horton Grove dwelling provides physical evidence that these sticks were concealed inside the wall during a time of upheaval and change for Stagville's Black inhabitants. These forked sticks provide material traces of one more way that enslaved plantation residents may have struggled to use their captive spaces to secure protection and some privacy amid the uncertainties of slavery.

Like the walking stick found in the Bennehan house wall, human hands shaped the Horton Grove forked sticks into their current form. Since only certain tree branches would do, the maker first had to find two of the right shape, likely by scouring the woods around Stagville. The finished products (figs. 2.8 and 2.9) are long (14 and 10 inches, respectively), straight sticks with bifurcated ends. The maker then peeled them to a smooth surface and trimmed them to pointed ends. The process was not as involved as making the walking stick, nor were the end products as skillfully crafted. The rather rudimentary craftsmanship suggests that the sticks were not meant to be a gift. Even so, they would have required time and energy from the maker. The enslaved person or people who made them probably fashioned the sticks for themselves, though it is unclear whether they used them outside the walls of the cabin before they hid them within.

We do have evidence, though, that the sticks were purposefully nailed inside the house walls as enslaved laborers built the structure. As early as 1850, construction began on the Horton Grove dwellings, with workers stacking and firing some 100,000 bricks in October of that year.[119] These bricks were presumably manufactured to build the many Horton Grove chimneys and to make the brick nogging that would support the structure and provide insulation for the cabins' residents. The nogging was one of the many unique features that distinguished the Horton Grove slave houses from others around the US South (fig. 2.10).[120] Typical rural slave houses ranged in quality and size from small, dilapidated log cabins to sturdy plank double-pen (two-room) cabins, such as those in the yards of Montpelier (see fig. 1.4).[121] The Horton Grove houses, however, are two-story, four-room board-and-batten buildings, making them far larger and more substantial than most slave housing

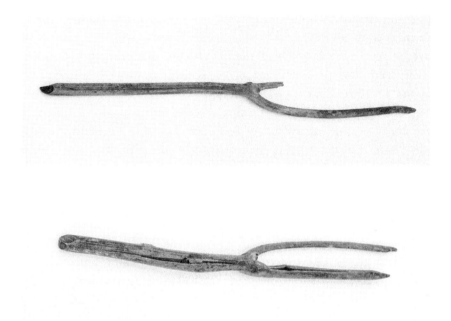

FIGURE 2.8. (*Top*) Forked stick (14 inches long) recovered from wall of slave house, Horton Grove quarter, Stagville, unknown date. The left tine of this forked stick appears to have been broken at some point; whether the break occurred before, during, or after it was nailed inside the house wall is unclear. Courtesy of Stagville State Historic Site, North Carolina Department of Natural and Cultural Resources.

FIGURE 2.9. (*Bottom*) Forked stick (10 inches long) recovered from wall of slave house, Horton Grove quarter, Stagville, unknown date. Both tines are intact. Courtesy of Stagville State Historic Site, North Carolina Department of Natural and Cultural Resources.

(fig. 2.11). They would have been built by a crew composed mostly of enslaved laborers, a common practice for slave dwelling–construction in antebellum North Carolina,[122] Their more complicated design may also have necessitated the involvement of one or more carpenters like Dandridge, an enslaved man so skilled in his craft that Paul Cameron's wife, Anne, wanted one of his wardrobes in their stately home at Fairntosh.[123]

In the late antebellum era, there were multiple large-scale, complicated architectural projects underway in the Horton Grove Quarter, including a monumental barn and stable that were completed in 1860.[124] It appears enslaved laborers finished the Horton Grove houses around that same time. Although

FIGURE 2.10. Brick nogging, interior wall of slave house, Horton Grove quarter, Stagville, built ca. 1850s. Courtesy of Stagville State Historic Site, North Carolina Department of Natural and Cultural Resources.

FIGURE 2.11. Horton Grove slave house, Stagville, built ca. 1850s. Courtesy of Stagville State Historic Site, North Carolina Department of Natural and Cultural Resources.

many of the materials had been gathered earlier in 1850, construction of the Horton Grove dwellings seems to have stalled until the end of the decade.[125] It was likely at this time, when the houses were being completed, that someone involved in the construction—probably an enslaved laborer, as they constituted the majority of individuals active in building slave housing—nailed the forked sticks to the brick nogging inside the wall of one of the dwellings. In fact, the late twentieth-century restoration team that discovered the sticks found the original mortar around them still intact, a material indication that the sticks were planted when the house was built.[126] But discerning *why* someone nailed these sticks to the nogging, hidden behind the house's wall, requires that we better understand this timing, including what was happening at Stagville that might have compelled this action.

As enslaved people made and hauled bricks, raised the timber framing, and filled the Horton Grove house walls with brick nogging, they were reeling from the cataclysmic changes wrought by the involuntary migration of nearly 200 enslaved Stagville residents. In 1844 and again in 1856, Paul Cameron tore apart families, ripped enslaved people from their homes, and forcibly moved them to the Deep South, to plantations in Alabama and Mississippi, far from their roots.[127] For the hundreds left behind in North Carolina, their future and their homes were in danger. Those in the Horton Grove Quarter, like all enslaved Stagville residents, still lived with the surveillance and intrusion of their owners. But the massive upheaval wrought by the two forced migrations traumatized enslaved families who feared that a third removal might be imminent. Anxiety and gossip would have spread around the plantation through the communication network that included enslaved couriers like Milton or waggoners like Pompey and Lewis, who delivered messages and goods (including illicit ones) throughout the plantation complex.[128] While Paul Cameron claimed in August 1850—the same year that preparations began for the construction of the Horton Grove slave houses—that "with but little exception the family of Negroes all keep well," he did not take into account the unease over familial separation and forced relocation rippling through the quarters.[129]

Amid the uncertainty wrought by these monumental changes, enslaved people at Stagville made concerted efforts to make their spaces feel more like their own. The Horton Grove Quarter, one of many throughout the Stagville estate, housed a large community, between 80 and 120 based on an estimate of 20 to 30 occupants in each of the four houses.[130] The extant buildings, with a central staircase flanked by two rooms on each level, suggest that a single family or other household unit lived in each of the four rooms.[131] Yet there was also likely communal domestic space in the shared outdoor areas. We know, for instance, that postbellum Horton Grove residents actively maintained swept yards, thus extending their homes outdoors.[132] It is certainly possible that antebellum occupants likewise swept the yards outside the Horton Grove dwellings, delineating their homes and claiming their space like residents of the Montpelier South Yard had. Though indoors and hidden from view, perhaps the forked sticks were likewise meant to help make this space feel more like the home residents wanted, a home that could provide not only a sense of ownership but also a sense of protection during the tumultuous 1850s at Stagville.

The forked sticks therefore take on greater meaning when placed in this context, which is not to say these sticks served only this one purpose. Forked sticks were often used by nineteenth-century Americans as divining rods or as dowsing sticks to find water, minerals, or other natural resources beneath the earth or in the sides of mountains or even to find stolen property.[133] For such uses, however, the sticks needed to be physically handled, with the user clutching a fork in each hand and moving the stick according to the "hidden power" within.[134] While the Horton Grove sticks may at some point have been used in this way, their physical and spatial context, nailed to the brick nogging, points us to a different or at least an additional function.

Perhaps their function within the Horton Grove house was more akin to that suggested by Alice Eley Jones: as ritual instruments or charms for protection.[135] Instead of a common divining rod, these forked sticks may have been *spiritual* divining rods, intended to help read the future and invoke ancestral spirits.[136] The sticks would therefore have been part of a long tradition at Stagville—going back to the walking stick—of enslaved people using concealed spaces and objects to conjure spirits for protection. Or perhaps the sticks were more like the cowrie shell, acting as talismans or charms against harmful external foes. And possibly the forks could have provided both services to whomever placed them there, once again adapting ancestral practices to realize greater protection for one's person and home. Formerly enslaved women and men recounted using forks and forked sticks to protect themselves from witches. Silvia Witherspoon, born enslaved on a plantation in Mississippi, still used forks in this manner in 1937: "I keeps a flour sifter an' a fork by my bed to keep de witches f'um ridin' me."[137]

During slavery, evil spirits were both ethereal and corporeal, as enslavers and overseers embodied such malevolence. Enslaved residents of Stagville lived with the routine intrusion and surveillance of their homes and spaces, but in the 1850s, they were also faced with the very real terror of separation from family and forced resettlement to the Deep South. They coped, grieved, and hoped for better during this fraught decade. They participated in "secret prayer meetings" in the 1850s when, as Morgan Latta recalled, Stagville's enslaved community "prayed to be delivered from slavery."[138] Others like Frank Walker simply left, fleeing the plantation in the spring of 1852. In time, other members of the Walker family followed, seeking out a place where they together could feel out of harm's way, or better yet, out of Paul Cameron's way.[139] The vast majority of enslaved Stagville residents stayed put, however, and attempted to transform the plantation's spaces of captivity into something more. Building more privacy and protection into one's home—to make spaces where those forced to live there might feel more authority over what happened— required the imaginative use of concealed spaces and objects. Like the cane, cowrie shell, and other ritualistic objects discovered concealed throughout Stagville, the Horton Grove forked sticks may have provided a sense of control over one's life, family, and home.

STAGVILLE WAS A site of subjugation, imprisonment, surveillance, and estrangement. Surviving and even counteracting that reality required careful and creative ways of circumventing the lack of privacy and protection provided by slave dwellings and experienced throughout the plantation. Enslaved people could not dictate who watched or entered their homes; it was not a place where they could keep themselves and their people safe, not without provoking retribution. If they wanted a modicum of privacy and protection in their homes, they had to make it themselves. It meant manipulating the spaces they had access to—whether their own dwellings or that of an enslaver—to embed material objects out of sight and out of reach, artifacts that might function as charms against evil of various sorts or as conduits to call for help from those beyond the watch and reach of slave owners.

Amid such violence, anxiety, and confinement, it may seem surprising that Stagville residents would have such deep, lasting connections to the place. Doc Edwards, born on the plantation in 1853, still lived on Cameron-owned land when he was interviewed by the Works Progress Administration (WPA) in 1937, arguing that "I'll stay right on in dat little house 'til de good Lawd calls me home."[140] But most formerly enslaved people would eventually leave Stagville, whether for higher-paying jobs in developing Durham and other

Southern cities, or for the North with the Great Migration. This did not mean they left home behind, though. Using portable homemaking tactics, including carrying material remains from the plantation, they made their homes elsewhere. Oral histories recount families using building materials from the dismantled Cameron Grove Baptist Church—founded at Stagville by people formerly enslaved there—to construct their houses in Durham.[141] Families thus embedded a sense of their former homes into their new ones.

Physically rooting material objects into an unknown place to create a sense of home was not a new tactic for free Black Americans. Finding ways to re-establish roots had been essential for people who lived in a system of forced migration. Over the course of nearly eight decades, perhaps as many as one thousand enslaved people lived at Stagville, but their homes existed within the captive spaces of the plantation, where they were forced or allowed to remain only as long as the Bennehan-Camerons permitted it. Nearly two hundred enslaved Stagville residents had no choice when they left North Carolina for the Deep South, forced from the place they and generations of their families had fought to build more private, protected lives. They were uprooted and compelled to find ways of reestablishing their roots in an unknown land, land where their people had not struggled, survived, and died. Hundreds of thousands of enslaved people would find themselves facing this same predicament, and in places they did not know. Some would turn, literally, to rooting their people in this new ground.

Chapter Three

ROOTING ONE'S PEOPLE

CHATHAM PLANTATION, ALABAMA

It was a muggy spring evening as the sun set across Chatham Plantation, slowly draping the woods where Cresy knelt in darkness. She could feel the hard Alabama soil beneath her, but she was motionless, fixated on the mound of dirt in front of her. She placed a stone atop it, marking the spot where her youngest child's body would now rest forever. A decade ago, she and dozens of others had been forced to walk for weeks before they arrived in this foreign land. Soon after, they created this burial place on the edge of the plantation, where trees provided cover and the water of the nearby Tombigbee River linked the living and the dead. Fields of cotton, which she would be busy picking in a few months, grew around the woods. But for now, Cresy mourned.

The warm air felt stuffy inside the mansion as Betsy Whitfield removed her wool shawl, lit a candle, and sat down at her writing desk to jot a letter to her husband, Nathan. Now more comfortable, she happily wrote of the health and well-being of their family, something she and Nathan did not take for granted. Just three years earlier they had lost three children to Yellow Fever, and they worried every day that another would be taken from them. The swamps that surrounded Chatham were deadly, a reality that prompted their move to the upper plantation at Gaineswood. All was well now, though—at least for her. She wrote on, noting that a slave's youngest child had died at Chatham, but she quickly transitioned to describing the many visitors to and temperate weather at Gaineswood.[1]

NATHAN BRYAN WHITFIELD had dreams of great cotton profits, and by 1835 he had forcibly moved Cresy and more than one hundred other enslaved people from their homes in North Carolina to the Alabama Black Belt. Over the next decade, the enslaved community established two plantations for the enslaving Whitfield family: Chatham, the lower plantation, and Gaineswood, the upper.[2] But Cresy did not choose to be uprooted from North Carolina, she did not choose the destination of Alabama, and she did not choose the site of Chatham, where the swampland threatened her and her loved ones. Yet in burying her child in this ground, she connected her people to it and laid claim to this place. Rooting her people in the land might make even this site of slavery feel more like a home.

Rootedness evokes one's people and also one's place. The image of a family tree connects kin to the ground beneath it, with ancestors closest to the roots. Although few enslaved people could document family trees like their free white neighbors, creating and remembering roots did not require pen and paper.[3] Where one's people are buried in the ground, their history is associated with that place. That is their ancestral land and home, and as such they have a claim to be and to belong there.[4] Free Black men in the North argued vehemently against colonization for this very reason, declaring, "This is our home, and this is our country. Beneath its sod lie the bones of our fathers."[5] So, too, did Uncle Smart Washington, a formerly enslaved man in South Carolina: "We parents' graves here; we donne oder country; dis yere our home."[6] In trying to make a plantation—a space of captivity and violence—feel like a home, enslaved people also looked outside traditional domestic spaces.

In death, enslaved people created moments and spaces of rootedness and belonging. Mortuary practices and burial spaces illustrate how, as historian Vincent Brown puts it, living and dying while enslaved produced a "productive peril . . . in which enslaved Africans and their descendants never ceased to pursue a politics of belonging, mourning, accounting, and regeneration."[7] Funerals and burial grounds demonstrated how enslaved people—people who sociologist Orlando Patterson declared were "socially dead"—used death to create and maintain social ties. As religious scholar Alexis Wells-Oghoghomeh has argued, death rituals provided enslaved people sites of "communal re-membrance" that connected people across space and time.[8] Through these rites, enslaved people could build, as Brown has shown, "ancestral connection to the land" where they were enslaved.[9] Archaeologist Grey Gundaker has likewise documented Black Americans' use of their burial grounds "to display connection to the dead" in order "to display one's roots in

FIGURE 3.1. "Gaineswood, Demopolis, Marengo County, Alabama," 1939. Photograph by Frances Benjamin Johnston. Courtesy of Library of Congress Prints and Photographs Division. Mansion constructed between 1843 and 1861.

a place." More than just a connection to a people and place, though, displaying roots was about how that connection provided special power. Through such display, Gundaker asserts, Black Americans communicated their *"rights* to inhabit and exert influence on the interpersonal, political, and practical activities that affect that homeplace."[10] Death became, as historian Jamie Warren asserts, "a time when the daily politics of slavery cracked open, allowing space to carve out new meaning," including the meaning of home on plantations.[11]

Unfortunately, we know very little about most plantation cemeteries, including those where Cresy and other Whitfield-owned laborers would have been buried. We know much about the Whitfields' home at Gaineswood, including the monumental Greek Revival mansion that still stands today (fig. 3.1).[12] Near the bustling town of Demopolis, Alabama, Gaineswood was a smaller plantation (roughly 1,400 acres) with all the necessary outbuildings to support it: stables, detached kitchen, slave quarters, smokehouse, and blacksmith shop.[13] Chatham, on the other hand, comprised more than 4,000 acres by 1860 and was a distant fifteen miles from urban sociability. Yet we know little else about it, including exactly where or how the enslaved community buried their friends and family on the plantation.

This is the case for the vast majority of antebellum plantation sites in the US South. As with nearly all aspects of life, we have far more and far better documentation of enslavers' cemeteries than of enslaved people's. Few known slave burial sites remain, whether in the archaeological or the textual archives, as ravages of time, encroaching development, and public apathy have led to the erasure of many Black cemeteries in the United States. Historic burial grounds, whether marked or not, are precarious; those of oppressed peoples, even more so.[14] Natural and man-made destruction continues to reduce the number of extant sites available for investigation. Grave markers deteriorate, land is repurposed, and family and local knowledge is ignored.

Scholars, by contrast, have been preoccupied with documenting African retentions in enslaved people's mortuary practices and material culture.[15] The focus on Africa underscores the enforced foreignness, the feeling of living as a "stranger" for enslaved people in the United States.[16] As a result, we have been left with too few explorations of how living in slavery shaped the practice and meaning of death. But when we attend to local context, we see enslaved people actively making claims and connection to *this* land, the place they built and maintained, the ground in which they buried their people. Indeed, we can ask how, through burial, they might have created a sense of rootedness and even belonging, transforming a strange space into a home.

But why try to understand the enslaved cemetery on a plantation when we have no direct evidence about it? The limitations, and opportunities, of the archive require it. Chatham, with its lack of archaeological and extant sources on burial practices, is far more typical than plantation sites with surviving cemeteries. Yet even if we don't have direct evidence of this rooting, Chatham's accounts of forced relocation expose the enslaved community's experiences of *up*rooting. This rich archive reveals the experiences and emotions that enslaved migrants brought with them to their new residences and documents the process of establishing their people there. The trauma of forced relocation would have haunted Chatham's enslaved community, and seriously considering that trauma opens avenues for exploring why and how they would have desired to be rooted once again, even if to a place of violent coercion. The absence of direct evidence of how Chatham residents actually *did* attempt to realize these feelings of home, though, requires that we utilize material culture techniques of speculation and contextualization. Thankfully, archaeologists, local historians, genealogists, and descendants have investigated and preserved slave cemeteries in Alabama and on other Southern plantations, allowing us to track local and regional practices to create a catalog of common material elements and spatial characteristics that we can reasonably apply to Chatham.[17]

This chapter, therefore, centers the enslaved community at Chatham within a broader discussion of how individuals rooted themselves through what we can interpret as another form of homemaking: the creation and maintenance of burial grounds. Doing so requires an understanding of the enslaved community at Chatham, in particular their uprooting and forced migration from North Carolina to Alabama, as well as careful speculation about their actions and beliefs based on logical comparisons to other plantations in Alabama and beyond. We start, as so many enslaved residents of Chatham did, at Shallowell Plantation in Lenoir County, North Carolina, to explore the particularities of their coerced move within the wider context of the Second Middle Passage.[18] We then attempt to rebuild the Chatham enslaved community's burial ground. Plantation cemeteries in Alabama and beyond demonstrate how people buried their kin in carefully chosen places and with specific objects—indeed, it was all these things together, the burial ground's assemblage, that gave it such power. Enslaved people knew their roots were tenuous; their forced migration made that reality undeniable.[19] As enslaved people sought to claim some sense of control over their spaces and their lives, burying the dead was another way of struggling to make a Southern plantation into their home.

Uprooting and Forced Migration

In the early antebellum era, a wave of migration—both voluntary and forced—brought more and more Americans to the area known as the Deep South.[20] The process began with and then accelerated the forced migration of Native peoples westward. Violent land dispossession, sanctioned and enacted by the federal government, allowed greater numbers of enslavers to establish monocrop cotton plantations in states like Mississippi and Alabama.[21] Enslaved people, themselves forced to move, provided the labor that transformed Indigenous homelands into the Cotton Kingdom, thereby developing the regional and national economy. The dozens of involuntary migrants to Chatham and Gaineswood plantations were part of this larger migration of enslaved and free Americans from the Upper South states like Virginia and North Carolina to those of the Deep South. As is often the case, we have far more evidence from free people who left one state for another. But within the letters, bills of sale, and contracts of white men like Nathan Whitfield, enslaved people's migration experiences appear, as they do in slave narratives. Examining the actions and words of enslaved and formerly enslaved people illustrates that many, though not all, felt a rootedness to the people and places from which they were removed. They held onto those roots with the knowledge that they were not in control of where their next home would be.

Nathan's decision to relocate his family to Alabama was, in the words of one historian, "a sound business decision," even if it caused "some emotional turmoil since it was difficult for the Whitfields to leave their home, family, and friends."[22] While the other Whitfield family members had little choice whether to migrate, they moved with the belief that this new place could become home, that they could, as Nathan's wife, Betsy, put it, "look forward when times will be more pleasant."[23] The enslaved laborers that the Whitfields forcibly relocated from Lenoir County, North Carolina, to Marengo County, Alabama, had neither Nathan's authority to decide where home would be nor Betsy's optimism about their future. Henry Goings, an enslaved man who had been forcibly moved to Alabama, described the disparity of feelings well: "The poor slave has not the hope which cheers toiling Anglo-Saxon emigrants, the hope of early independence."[24]

Forced migration was a consequential, life-altering process.[25] Between the American Revolution and the Civil War, more than one million enslaved people found themselves compelled to move from the Upper South to the Deep South.[26] Many had previously lived on plantations or farms with familial roots going back generations. Perhaps the Shallowell residents would have felt betrayed, like Frank and Peggy, an enslaved couple who also found themselves forced to relocate to Alabama. An enslaved man who traveled with the couple recalled that, upon hearing the news of the move, Frank and Peggy "were indignant at the word. Long and weary had they toiled. . . . Now they were growing aged and to be torn from the old place, and from all the friends in whose society the Sundays passed so pleasantly, seemed too hard a trial."[27] This Second Middle Passage would, like the first, uproot African-descended peoples from family, community, ancestors, and a place that some considered home.[28]

The idea of "going away to the South" distressed enslaved people, and many expressed a fear of moving. While enslavers like Nathan's brother James saw Alabama as "a better country" than North Carolina, enslaved people regarded Deep South states with "a great horror."[29] Harsh living and laboring conditions on large plantations in Louisiana, Mississippi, and Alabama were the stuff of nightmares, and rumors swirled through slave quarters as to "the desperate abuses" (as one formerly enslaved man put it) that people suffered there.[30] Enslaved people expected that the work would be more relentless and overseen by managers with particularly violent temperaments. Concerns over familial separation caused additional anxiety, as did the migration itself, as reports spread of the lack of clothing, food, and even shoes on the exhausting journey.[31] Regardless of exactly where they were going, enslaved migrants considered separation from home as a change of monumental significance.[32] Indeed, as historian Susan Eva O'Donovan asserts, forced relocation was "nothing short of catastrophic" for enslaved people.[33]

The enslaved community that eventually built and resided at Chatham experienced forced migration in stages rather than as a single event. Nathan Whitfield relocated groups of enslaved individuals to Alabama in waves, beginning in 1829. By 1832 he had sent forty-eight laborers to establish a foothold in the state and make him some money.[34] Within the next two years, he forced another twenty-eight from North Carolina to Alabama.[35] In April 1834, before the next wave of involuntary migrants completed their journey, their enslaver would finally buy 920 acres of Marengo County woodland "to settle the hands" and build his Alabama cotton plantation.[36] Within the year, Whitfield was ready to move himself, his family, and his home; but he still needed more labor to achieve the profits he desired.[37] In March and early April 1835, Whitfield purchased twenty-one enslaved laborers, some with families and others as individuals, from various enslavers or traders in North Carolina.[38] Those enslaved individuals purchased by Whitfield may have hoped that their sale would take them only a few miles from home, as some had previously been sold within the same county.[39] Many enslaved people recalled walking ten or more miles on a weekend to see family; so perhaps the individuals Whitfield bought imagined they would still be able to walk to see family or friends. Instead, they would find themselves walking hundreds of miles southwest, as part of Whitfield's last wave of involuntary migrants to Chatham.

Beginning in mid-April, within weeks or in some cases days of their purchase, these enslaved people began the long trek from North Carolina to Alabama. They traveled alongside the thirty-seven remaining enslaved residents of Shallowell and sixteen enslaved laborers owned by Gaius Whitfield, Nathan's cousin and brother-in-law.[40] Their experience would have been similar to the dozens who had already made the trek.[41] Henry Goings recalled that enslaved migrants ensured that "every means [was] adopted to make the journey agreeable and to drown in forgetfulness the friends and kindred left behind."[42] It is also possible that some of these migrants felt a sense of curiosity about the journey.[43] Few had probably traveled far from Shallowell, and the unknown offered all kinds of possibilities. But any novelty surely wore off during the punishing journey. Beyond the sheer distance walked on foot—some seven hundred miles—travel was slow, and for good reason: weather was unpredictable, roads were barely passable, baggage was heavy, and walking for weeks on end was nearly impossible.[44] Plus, there were no real directions for enslaved people to follow, which sometimes extended the time they spent trudging along bad roads in poor weather. Nathan complained to Betsy that they kept getting lost, even though he had hired Josiah Washington to guide them.[45]

The list recording the migrants' names and ages further suggests the grueling nature of this trek. David, age 1, appears on the list only to be, at some point, crossed off it. There is no indication whether he died before, during, or soon after the exhausting march. His age and position on the list indicate he was the son of Chloe, who—along with a woman named Jinny—demanded to ride in the cart rather than walk during the journey.[46] Perhaps the thirty-five-year-old woman would not walk because of the "rheumatism" that Nathan complained incapacitated her. Or perhaps Chloe's feet would not work because she was overwhelmed with the loss of her child.[47]

How could she grieve? If David's death occurred before or during the forced march, Chloe would never be able to visit her son's grave again. The possibility of forging connection to family through mortuary practices was not always possible, especially for those in the midst of uprooting. Burial could therefore be a marker of the fragility of one's roots, of unstable connections and vulnerable ties that many enslaved people experienced. That surely stayed with Chloe forever—the child she may not have been able to physically mourn, his body lost to her as she found herself uprooted to Alabama. The violent displacement of Chatham's residents would have shaped how they related to death and its customs, how they related to the place they were forced to leave and then to the place they were compelled to live, and how they may have sought to connect to it. But as historian Sydney Nathans writes about the enslaved migrants Paul Cameron forced to Alabama in 1844, "They had to make the best of where they were."[48]

Slave Burial Grounds at Chatham and Beyond

When the Shallowell migrants arrived in Alabama, they turned woodland into fields, planted and harvested crops, constructed houses and work buildings, and labored in countless other ways to turn the land into a plantation.

Those who arrived at Chatham knew what cotton cultivation required, as they had been performing that kind of work in North Carolina.[49] Yet things were different in Alabama, including the size and scale of the operation, which focused not only on cotton but also on corn, and which expanded quickly—from 900 acres in 1834 to over 5,500 acres at both Alabama plantations by 1860—thereby increasing the amount of labor to be done and prompting Whitfield's purchase of more slaves.[50] Labor and life were different in Alabama, a fact that Shallowell migrants soon knew. The land was also quite different. The enslaved migrants who arrived in 1834 would have found acres of uncultivated forests—marshy land with insects and animals carrying diseases like hookworm and malaria—that they drained, cleared, and prepared for planting, all while constructing the many buildings necessary to a functioning plantation.[51]

Surrounded by disease and likely death, the enslaved community needed to quickly establish a place where they could bury their people. Beyond the practical, cemeteries also provided a space for the liberatory possibilities of death. Watching his brother's burial at a Deep South plantation, Peter Stills mourned his loss while also believing that his kin now finally "sleeps sweetly. . . . The loud horn of the overseer reaches not his ear at dawn; the harsh tone of command and the bitter blasphemous curse break not his peaceful slumbers."[52] Death became a means of emancipating oneself, and heaven was the home one attained in that freedom. This idea is embedded in proverbs, sermons, and songs, including a well-known spiritual, "River Jordan deep and wide / I've got a home on the other side. / Lord I know I will fare better in that land / Lord I know I will fare better in that land."[53] In this way, rooting one's people in the ground provided them with the ability to leave this earthly home and reach their "ancestral spirit home."[54] This cosmology proclaimed that a more perfect home existed outside the grasp and machinations of enslavers, one that Black people could look forward to after death.

But cemeteries and mortuary practices were as much about the living as the dead, and home was as much about life here as in the beyond. A proper burial and its material culture allowed the deceased to move on to their spiritual home, something that also ensured they would not haunt those they left behind. "The moment when death claimed a life," historian Jason Young notes, "was a very dangerous and vulnerable time for the living; the passageways and portals connecting this world and the next were open during these times, allowing death to move about freely."[55] Enslaved and later free Black Americans believed that the dead could, and indeed did, return to earth, and that the death ritual had much to do with that.[56] The deceased lingered in an ambiguous state after burial, unable to ascend to heaven and able to meddle in human affairs, especially if the funeral was not performed correctly.[57] Additionally, the objects placed in and around graves, particularly things the deceased had owned or used, would appease the spirit and keep them from returning or wandering the earth. A Black Alabamian, interviewed in the early twentieth century, declared, "Unless you bury a person's things with him he will come back after them."[58] Enslaved people wanted to prevent harmful spirits from haunting their communities.

These ideas, and their ritual and material manifestations, assured positive connection with ancestors, a connection believed to provide protection and power for the living.[59] Spirits were said to directly influence life on earth and could be called upon—sometimes by using objects like the cane and forked sticks found at Stagville—to act as shields against evil spirits, keeping the living safe within the uncertain and violent reality of slavery.[60] Additionally, as the final resting place of those spirits, the presence and maintenance of ancestral cemeteries communicated enslaved people's values and their attempts to claim belonging.[61] As Grey Gundaker asserts, "Some of the rights of the living in a place, therefore, derive from proximity to the family dead."[62] The creation of sacred sites like burial grounds was a means of symbolizing, and also realizing, one's claim to a place.

These practices and spaces were not simply illustrations of enslaved people's agency, however much scholars have continually emphasized them as such. Scholars have searched for African retentions in enslaved people's funerals and burial grounds to the detriment of understanding how the context of slavery, including enslavers' demands for control over enslaved people's lives, shaped mortuary practices.[63] As archaeologist Ross Jamieson puts it, it appears true that funerals provided enslaved people a rare opportunity to "assume control of the symbolism around them, and thus create the dignity at death that negated the 'social death' of their slave status."[64] And yet others have argued that developments in slave management during the antebellum era—most especially the push to Christianize slaves and to improve sanitation in their spaces—encouraged slave owners to exert firmer control over enslaved people's mortuary practices and spaces.[65] Enslavers' control over this sacred practice could limit enslaved people's feelings of rootedness and belonging. As Orlando Patterson argues, this tool of control alienated enslaved people from one another and from a shared past, thereby elevating and prioritizing the master-slave relationship.[66]

Yet Patterson's contention, like those that overemphasize the agency of the enslaved, is too simplistic, for enslavers never held complete control over the plantation landscape, including slave burial grounds.[67] As William Faulkner wrote of Yoknapatawpha, a Southern Black cemetery contained "shards of pottery and broken bottles and old brick and other objects insignificant to sight but actually of a profound meaning and fatal to touch, which no white man could have read."[68] This was of course a description of a fictional town written by a white man long after the end of slavery, but even Faulkner recognized the power of these objects and places. Still, the language of postbellum writers relies on the antebellum ideas of proslavery writers, who advised enslavers and overseers to keep open spaces in, below, and around dwellings free of "filth." One enslaver from the Deep South maintained that all "filth and trash" stored by slaves underneath their raised houses should be frequently removed.[69] As Ywone Edwards has shown, however, these objects were not always "trash" to enslaved people, giving those artifacts a kind of power by virtue of enslavers' incomprehension of them.[70] Slave owners could never fully control slave burial grounds because they would never fully understand them.

Connection with kin, and the power derived from it, depended in part on the material world: the land, the sod, the bones of one's people. But enslavement broke connections to ancestors and kin. Forced migration forever separated Shallowell's residents from the place where their families lay buried. Phebe, an enslaved weaver who produced large quantities of cloth before her forced migration in 1835, had to leave behind the grave of a young daughter she lost to a horrific fire in 1826.[71] As a weaver, she probably made the shroud that she wrapped around her daughter before the body was laid in the North Carolina ground. Phebe's skilled labor was integral to the plantation's profitable operation, but she also likely used it for her own purposes as she said goodbye to her child, a child she would lose a second time upon her forced relocation to Alabama. Phebe was one of many compelled to leave the physical remains of those they loved. But if she continued to produce burial shrouds in Alabama, Phebe's handiwork was buried in this new place, too, with newly departed kin and her new community. Enslaved people like Phebe relied on the rituals of death—"settin' up" with the body, marching to the burial ground, the rites of the funeral—but also on spatial and material choices to demonstrate their connections to their people and place.[72] The living and dead together made this unchosen land more of their own.

The land of Chatham was not only unchosen but unknown, and it may not have seemed capable of providing such sacred, spiritual spaces. Vincent

Brown asserts that while enslaved people may have felt connection to certain places, particularly ones where they sensed a deeper "ancestral connection," such feelings did not extend to every parcel of land they inhabited; indeed, enslaved people taken to an unknown place "hesitated to encroach on new and perhaps spiritually perilous grounds where the unfamiliar dead, unplaced by ritual and ceremony, might be unwilling to countenance alien settlements."[73] Still others would find severe limitations on their time, resources, and land choice when determining how they could bury their people. Amid these and other constraints, enslaved people found ways of making meaning of this land and creating connections with their people (those dead and living, those nearby and far away).

Locating Slave Burial Grounds within the Plantation Landscape

A slave cemetery's location within the plantation landscape was not haphazard; it resulted from a push-and-pull between Black and white residents, both of whose desires are manifested in the choice. For enslaved people, the combination of West African cosmology, commemoration, and mortuary practices with those of American Christianity and the realities of slavery created a particular way of relating to death and the dead, including how they shaped the spaces of the dead.[74] They did so amid enslavers' continuous work to delineate white spaces from Black spaces in the plantation landscape. Enslavers appeared anxious about inhabiting a burial ground with bodies they had once enslaved.[75] So plantations typically maintained at least two burial grounds that were racially segregated and physically separated by distance or by barriers like fences or natural topography.[76] Additionally, separate burial grounds placed in precise locations reinforced the social hierarchy that enslavers imposed upon the plantation residents.[77] Yet enslaved people continued to make and comprehend their spaces in very different ways and for different purposes than their enslavers did.

Enslavers made some decisions about the location of slave burial grounds in the hope of further demonstrating authority and superiority. Most often they located the white enslaving family's cemetery near their residence, as was the case at North Carolina's Stagville plantation.[78] This was also the case at the Hickory Hill Plantation in Lauderdale County, in northern Alabama near the town of Florence. The enslaving Coffee family burial ground is located 150 feet west of their home, in clear view from the house (the brick wall that now surrounds the cemetery was not erected until the 1920s).[79] Enslaving families on plantations almost exclusively interred members of their immediate or extended family in their own burial grounds, although they did include enslaved individuals on rare occasions, such as at the Forks of Cypress Plantation near Hickory Hill.[80]

Within the enslaving Jackson family's cemetery at the Forks of Cypress, located near their mansion and enclosed by a large stone wall, two uninscribed limestone slabs rest near the rear of the enclosure. Family lore and oral tradition suggest that these slabs are grave markers for two enslaved men, more specifically, for jockeys for the Jacksons' horse racing.[81] Whether two enslaved men do, in fact, lie buried beneath the limestone slabs is unclear, undocumented, and unverified. That the story continued to be passed down through the white Jackson family suggests that the enslaved men's burial was not about those men at all but about the enslaving Jacksons and their descendants. On the surface, it reflects James Jackson's love of horse racing, but it also bolsters the Jacksons' belief in their ancestor's affection for and benevolence toward at least some of the eighty-five slaves he called "family."[82] At their most basic, though, these gravestones are visible signals of ownership and signs of Jackson's continued possession and control over his enslaved jockeys. These may have been deep and complicated relationships, yet the reality of enslavement influenced life *and* death. Given the presence of these gravestones in the white family cemetery, the two enslaved jockeys would continue to ride for the Jacksons even after their passing.

The vast majority of enslaved people, though, buried their kin and community members in their own burial ground, what Isaam Morgan, born enslaved in Alabama, called their "own special graveyard."[83] Still, enslavers usually had some influence over where that cemetery was located in the plantation landscape.[84] They wanted the slave sites isolated from the their homes; there was typically a quarter-mile to one mile between the two.[85] This put the slave burial ground beyond the enslaving family's (and their guests') view and clearly separated it from the white cemetery, which was located near the enslavers' home. At Montpelier Plantation, the walled Madison family cemetery was located within the old family complex at Mount Pleasant, while the slave cemetery was at the edge of the plantation property.[86] Beyond ensuring distance between the two burial spaces, enslavers also made sure that no productive land would be squandered for the benefit of enslaved people. Thus, as was the case at Montpelier, most often slave burial grounds were located on the margins of the property, on land deemed unproductive for agricultural or other money-making purposes.[87] At Alabama's Hickory Hill Plantation, the slave graveyard was near a steep ridge near the property's boundary, a location that had the additional effect of restricting the number and placement of individuals within the burial ground.[88]

Even if sites were chosen by enslavers, Black residents would have some control over the exact location of their burial grounds, so long as they were on the plantation's edge. These places were on the "margins" only if our understanding of plantations is centered around white homes; for enslaved people, the "margins" may have been central, a core part of Black homes, which could extend far beyond the walls of their dwellings.[89] But even so, slave burial grounds were often located much closer to slave quarters, such as the Black cemeteries near Stagville's Eno Quarter in North Carolina, which were set a distance from the plantation mansion.[90] Working on the "margins" of a plantation allowed for homemaking with less oversight. Making a burial ground on the property's edge provided distance between it and white homes, whether the enslaving family's house or an overseer's. White folks had less interest in and authority over nonproductive, marginal areas of the plantation. Black people knew these spaces far better and were better able to maneuver through them, whether in daylight or after dark.[91]

They also would have known exactly where they could place their burial ground to evoke the most meaning. We often find, for instance, that slave cemeteries are located on high ground, near water, or in wooded areas.[92] Burying a body above the water line was not always possible, particularly in low-lying areas on coasts, but higher ground would give enslaved people a greater chance of doing so. Choosing to place burial sites near water may therefore seem counterintuitive, but the symbolism of water as an intermediary between the living and the dead (part of some West African cosmologies) makes clear the meaning of such decisions.[93] Slave cemeteries also appear with frequency in tree-heavy areas, such as at the Montpelier Slave Cemetery and, closer to Chatham, at the Magby Slave Cemetery in Chambers County, Alabama.[94] It is possible that enslaved people intentionally chose these wooded sites for the cover they provided. With the natural canopy, these burial grounds became more private places of refuge where individuals had greater independence over their mortuary practices and materials.[95] This is not to say that white people were not present at slave burials. An 1860 painting by John Antrobus suggests that thickly wooded slave burial grounds were visited by white as well as by Black individuals (fig. 3.2). Two white figures can be seen on the right-hand side of the canvas between the trees, presumably the plantation owners come

FIGURE 3.2. *Plantation Burial*, by John Antrobus, ca. 1860. Historic New Orleans Collection, L. Kemper and Leila Moore Williams Founders Collection (1960.46).

to mourn or to monitor. On the left-hand side, the white man with arm slung over his horse is thought to be the artist himself, yet another outsider intruding upon this sacred scene. Of course, white people's routine surveillance and intrusion into enslaved people's spaces was a common occurrence, one that Black plantation residents were adept at circumventing or moderating.

Unlike highly manicured white cemeteries, the presence of natural tree formations, sometimes in thickly forested areas like that shown in Antrobus's painting, was another distinguishing factor of Black graveyards. By the antebellum era, wealthy white family and church cemeteries in the US began to take on a distinctive French aesthetic, with meticulously maintained and spacious grounds filled with romantic memorials like obelisks.[96] The dim, even dark wooded areas of many slave cemeteries provided a distinct contrast to those of their enslavers. A natural landscape does not signify an inadvertent one, though, for a ring of trees (a mortuary landscape often associated with enslaved people) indicates either the planting of trees in a circle or the removal of trees to form a ring, thereby denoting active and intentional landscaping.[97] The trees themselves may also have provided symbolic meaning of a people's roots in a place. As archaeologist Grey Gundaker contends, the presence of trees in burial grounds helps to visually connect heaven and earth, the trees' roots deep within it thereby connecting those above and those below.[98]

Considering the substantial size of the Whitfield-owned slave community—nearly 250 by 1860—it is likely they maintained their own separate burial grounds at Chatham.[99] There is no Whitfield family cemetery on the Gaineswood grounds; with the mansion located so close to Demopolis, the family chose instead to lay their kin in the more urban Riverside Cemetery.[100] But it is believed that a white family cemetery existed at Chatham, where the three Whitfield children who died in 1842 before the move to Gaineswood would have been buried. This family burial plot would have been located near the Whitfield's Chatham house, while Nathan likely commanded his slaves to locate their own burial ground away from his family's cabin, on the unproductive land at the edges of the plantation. When the Whitfields moved away from Chatham to take up residence at Gaineswood, an overseer probably moved into the family's cabin, thus maintaining white surveillance over Black activities. Yet the Black burial ground's distance from the Whitfield cabin would have continued to be a boon to enslaved people, allowing them to partake in their mortuary practices with greater privacy than otherwise possible. The plantation's periphery also provided forested land adjacent to the Tombigbee River, supplying enslaved people with both the trees and the water that many slave burial grounds contained. Away from white eyes, in a semisecluded space with symbolic links to ancestors and the afterlife, Chatham's enslaved community would have found an opportunity to lay their people to rest. For those like Phebe, whose uprooting severed their physical ties to the graves of their children, this new burial ground may have provided a place to forge a connection to family, both near and far. For those like Cresy, who lost children while enslaved at Chatham, this ground would have become theirs in part through the physical presence of their kin.

The Material Culture of Slave Burial Grounds

More than just the location, burial grounds became useful sites for growing roots and cultivating belonging through the objects that enslaved people used and deposited at their loved one's graves. Many of what white Americans would consider "traditional" funerary objects appear to be absent from slave cemeteries. Headstones and tombstones have long been studied by scholars seeking to understand a culture's relationship to death, including how people made meaning of burial places.[101] However, these types of grave markers—stone carved or otherwise marked with personal information, images, and other cultural signifiers like crosses—rarely appear in the textual, archaeological, or visual record of slave cemeteries. Plus, the ravages of time, urban development, and racist neglect have destroyed many Black cemeteries, leaving the remains incomplete. But imprints of slave burial grounds remain in text, image, and physical form, and so do simple fieldstones and broken ceramics.[102] Poor Black and white Southerners shared many funerary practices, including the use of handmade or local, natural objects as grave markers.[103] Yet these objects' context in the plantation landscape dramatically changed their meaning, making them particularly evocative of life under enslavement.[104] Along with the burial ground's placement in the plantation landscape, the things within it—the grave articles and markers as well as the bodies—suggest that enslaved residents attempted to connect to their people, past and present, and thereby connect their people to the place they were forced to inhabit.[105]

The material world was integral to the death rituals that would send the deceased to the next world, to mourn the family's and the community's loss, and to connect one's people to a place. Once an individual died, their body was washed, wrapped in a shroud, and laid on a board while the coffin was made.[106] The shroud, often reported to be white, would almost certainly have been made by an enslaved woman in the community.[107] The coffin, often described as painted black, would have been crafted by an enslaved man, likely a carpenter. Typically made of a soft wood like pine, poplar, or cedar, coffins were usually made from single planks, requiring less joining, and the side panels and lid were secured using nails.[108] People gave time, skills, and supplies— things enslaved people did not have in excess—to support the care of the dead and their community. After a wake or "settin' up," which often took place in the dwelling of the deceased's kin, the community would process to the burial ground, thereby connecting the traditional domestic space with the death space.[109] The objects of death—body, shroud, coffin—would be placed in the ground during the burial, another communal ritual. Each community member might throw a handful of dirt into the grave, allowing them, through the intermediary of the soil, to physically connect to the deceased one last time.[110] The burial pit was then filled, the body now a part of the land.

While not always the case, objects were sometimes placed atop a grave to mark the spot of the deceased, and these markers took a wide variety of forms. Textual, archaeological, and visual evidence suggests that small, seemingly utilitarian or quotidian objects were most common.[111] North of Chatham, the Old Prewitt Slave Cemetery in Tuscaloosa County, Alabama, contains the graves of an estimated three hundred to five hundred enslaved people and their descendants, some of whose burial plots are marked with hand-cut river stones and flat rocks.[112] Ceramic sherds are another grave article often associated with African American burial sites, both during and after slavery.[113] As an early twentieth-century folklorist noted about Alabama, "All through the Black Belt, broken crockery is used as the chief decoration for Negro graves."[114] Due to the fragility of the material and the frequent destruction of burial grounds, much of the evidence about the practice comes from postbellum sources.[115] Archaeologists have, however, found evidence of a blue shell-edged plate from the first two decades of the nineteenth century atop a burial site in South Carolina, evidence that more firmly links the practice to the era of slavery.[116]

Fieldstones and ceramics are just two of many artifact types, some of them intentionally broken, that have been found in cemeteries associated with enslaved people and their descendants.[117] Writing in 1891, Henry Carrington Bolton—a white Northerner, historian, and folklorist—described graves in a Black cemetery outside Columbia, South Carolina, as "decorated with a variety of objects . . . [which] include oyster-shells, white pebbles, fragments of crockery of every description, glass bottles, and nondescript bric-a-brac of a cheap sort."[118] A 1908 *Washington Post* article detailed a "negro cemetery" in northern Alabama, where atop a grave lay "shells, bits of broken, highly colored glass, and glistening stones." On others were bottles, including medicine bottles, and in almost every case a broken pitcher and lamp.[119] These things often had a purpose beyond simply marking the gravesite. They could help, as one formerly enslaved person recalled, "the spirits to feel at home."[120] Broken objects could also help stop death from coming for others, for as Rosa Sallins remembered: "If you don't break the things, then the others in the family will die too."[121] These included not only natural elements like shells but also man-made objects like water jugs and bottles.[122] The use of water-related objects as grave markers would have provided yet another method of linking the living and the dead, just as the presence of water in the funerary landscape did.

The majority of known grave markers in slave burial grounds are small, ordinary objects; but this is not to discount the possibility for tombstones or other inscribed grave markers.[123] At Hickory Hill Plantation, owned by John Coffee and later by his son Joshua, the slave burial ground contained just one known stone marker, the text of which is now unreadable. This single artifact is the only remnant of any marker for the approximately 140 individuals buried there.[124] It is also possible that many of Coffee's enslaved laborers identified through bills of sale—Sampson, Minda, Maria, Moses, Martin, Simon, Betty, Willis, Joanna, Jacob, Jerry, Alfred, Milly, Dennis, Webb—are also buried in the slave cemetery.[125] If their graves were ever marked it would have likely been with common fieldstones, though no such objects remain today.[126] This contrasts with the enslaving family's cemetery, which contains several different types of inscribed tomb markers, including a large obelisk monument dedicated to the family progenitor, John Coffee.[127] These many markers contain epitaphs, names, and important information on the individuals, and they differentiate individuals by the materials, design, and visuals used. This comparison between Black and white cemeteries would have been noted by contemporaries as well, as the two different cemeteries were physically closer to one another at Hickory Hill than at other Alabama plantations. A small path connected the enslaving and enslaved burial grounds, which stood just five hundred feet apart.[128] In the white family's cemetery, the inscribed, highly decorated, and often large monuments demonstrated the power of those who lay beneath, demonstrations made more potent by the slave burial ground, where few if any markers identified graves.

The slave cemetery located on another Alabama plantation owned by the Coffee family contains six tombstones, three of which include epitaphs.[129] Of those, two—for Martha Crawford and David Hutchins Smith—include lengthy textual inscriptions attesting to the loyalty and faithfulness of these "servants."[130] Where more "traditional" forms of tombstones do appear in slave cemeteries, archaeologist James Garman suggests that they are better understood as demonstrations of an enslaver's beliefs: their thoughts on "correct" slave behavior, their status above nonslaveholding white families, or their self-understood benevolent paternalism.[131] However, Alexander Donelson Coffee (the plantation owner and the son of John Coffee) did not erect these dedications as evidence of his mastery over the enslaved. Rather, his daughter, Mary Coffee Campbell, placed these tombstones decades after emancipation. Like the headstones of James Jackson's enslaved jockeys, these tombstones circulated a mythology meant to do much more than justify an enslaver's morality; the tombstones were intended to justify the entire institution of slavery, providing material vindication to those who, after abolition, wished to spout the new mythology. These were small monuments to the institution of slavery.

The material culture of a Black cemetery was obviously quite different from that of a white cemetery on a plantation, and it was made even more so by enslaved people's arrangement of those objects in the funerary landscape. As Henry Bolton noted about South Carolina's Black graveyards, mortuary objects were "sometimes arranged with careful symmetry, but more often placed around the margins without regard to order."[132] In contrast to the manicured, arranged, formal gardenlike landscaping of many white cemeteries, Black burial grounds maintained more natural landscaping. Additionally, based on ground depressions and probing, it also appears that many slave cemeteries did not exhibit the uniform nature of burials seen in white ones. Scholars determined to find African retentions have argued that the orientation of bodies in many slave cemeteries—with the body laid supine, head on the west side and feet on the east side—was meant to demonstrate enslaved people's continued orientation back to Africa, as if they might arise and start the trek back across the Atlantic.[133] Archaeologists have shown, however, that the majority of burials in Black and white cemeteries throughout the United States maintain this orientation, perhaps reflecting both African retentions and Christian adaptations.[134] Emmaline Heard, born enslaved in Georgia, was said to be a "firm believer in the practice of conjure," yet also declared that her people were "always buried so that . . . when judgment day come and Gabriel blow that trumpet every body will rise up facing the east."[135]

Enslaved people's mortuary decisions were not free of constraint: enslavers' oversight, lack of time and available supplies, and—particularly in relation to grave markers—illiteracy limited the spatial and material choices for their burial grounds. The Alabama Slave Code, amended after the Southampton Rebellion of 1831 led by Nat Turner, declared it a crime for any Black person, enslaved or free, to be taught reading and writing.[136] Throughout the region, the fear of slave rebellion escalated among white Southerners after this event, and the panic was particularly potent in places like Marengo County, where Black people far outnumbered whites: in 1850, enslaved people composed 80 percent of the county's entire population. Just one year after the last wave of Whitfield's slaves arrived in Alabama, copies of the abolitionist newspaper *The Liberator* were found some forty miles north of Chatham, in Greensboro. This, among other incidents, created what historian Marshall Rachleff calls a "crisis of fear" throughout the state in the three decades after the Southampton Rebellion, leading to the passage of increasingly harsh slave codes.[137] While laws like the 1831 antiliteracy mandate did not keep people from reading or writing, it is unlikely that many enslaved at Chatham or Gaineswood ever received instruction. Few, then, would have had the skills to inscribe tombstones with biographical information. Even so, we can find ways that enslaved people were able to express personal information about the deceased through material culture, using an individual's prized possessions or recently used objects to mark their grave.[138] Though not in textual form, this material evidence reflected something deeply personal about the individual, providing a glance into their life, just like a tombstone's inscription.

At the same time, the use of simple, unmarked stones could emphasize commonality over individuality, further distinguishing free and unfree burial grounds.[139] Indeed, as Lynn Rainville suggests, unlike white cemeteries, the burials in slave cemeteries seem to emphasize kinship and community over the individual.[140] We can see this at the Forks of Cypress Plantation cemeteries in northern Alabama, where the walled Jackson family graveyard is separated from the slave cemetery by a natural gully.[141] The white cemetery exhibits dozens of large tombstones, tablet stone markers, and obelisks that visually catch one's eye, emphasizing the individual while also placing them within the context of the enslaving family (figs. 3.3 and 3.4).[142] Whereas in the slave cemetery, located on the wooded edge of the property, only one uninscribed headstone and footstone emerges from the ground, while stones indicate burial sites of enslaved people and their descendants (fig. 3.5). Even more of the graves are unmarked; indeed, more than 250 individual graves have been identified based solely on ground depressions.[143] No particular groupings can be discerned from the extant Forks of Cypress slave cemetery. Perhaps it was less important to be buried within a particular plot than to be buried in the sacred place of your kin and wider community, regardless of who your body lay next to.[144]

We know that many enslaved individuals forced to migrate from Shallowell to Chatham came in family units, and the desire to remain together in life and death, even amid the threat of sale and further forced relocation, would have made these mortuary practices and objects a useful means of rooting themselves to their people and place. Perhaps Phebe continued to weave the shrouds that wrapped the bodies of Chatham's dead.[145] Perhaps Isaac, a carpenter, crafted the coffins in which those bodies would rest.[146] Isaac, like Phebe, had been forcibly relocated from North Carolina in the 1830s, and together their contributions to the rituals of death in Alabama would have made this unknown land feel more like a home.[147] They and the Chatham community would have walked from the slave quarter to the wooded burial ground near the river to bury an untold number from their community, maybe marking each lost member with a smooth fieldstone or pottery sherd. Certainly these grave markers looked nothing like the Whitfields' tombstones,

FIGURE 3.3. Jackson Family Cemetery, view from inside wall, Forks of Cypress Plantation, AL. Courtesy of the Alabama Historical Commission.

FIGURE 3.4. Jackson Family Cemetery, view from outside wall, Forks of Cypress Plantation, AL. Courtesy of the Alabama Historical Commission.

FIGURE 3.5. Slave burial ground, including stone markers, Forks of Cypress Plantation, AL. Courtesy of the Alabama Historical Commission.

FIGURE 3.6. Monument to Nathan Bryan Whitfield in Riverside Cemetery, Demopolis, AL. Photograph by Tim and Cindy Williams. Courtesy of Timothy Blair Williams.

especially not like the ornate monument that marks Nathan Whitfield's body in the Riverside Cemetery in Demopolis (fig. 3.6). But it may not have been as important, and it certainly was not as possible, for enslaved people to create a sacred landscape with towering monuments. Their mortuary landscape would have likely taken a far more natural look than the manicured and planned Riverside Cemetery. The entire burial ground and its material culture — from small grave objects to the physical bodies — could connect all those who lay within it to those who continued to live beyond it. The objects above and ground below might have created a sense of belonging to and in the land. The further use of material culture may have heightened this sense for enslaved people who lay something atop their kin.

Continuing to Root One's People in This Place

At several plantation sites in Alabama, the process of rooting one's people to the land continued long after slavery's demise. At the Forks of Cypress, many of the 87 individuals listed in James Jackson's 1840 will, as well as many of the 130 listed as living on the plantation or having a connection to the site in the 1870 census, are presumably buried in the slave graveyard.[148] We cannot say for certain if they were buried in familial plots or were generally spread throughout the site, but it is probable that more than two dozen Black families chose this sacred spot to bury their people.[149] Five individuals within these families—James Blue, Mariah Fern, Thomas Hawkins, Charles Jackson, and Mariah Jackson—are listed in both Jackson's 1840 will and the 1870 US Census as living in Lauderdale County, near the Forks of Cypress Plantation. The census also lists all of them as having been born outside the state of Alabama, meaning that all five of these individuals had been forcibly brought to the state during their enslavement, much like those at Chatham.[150] Whether held by connections to this land, or prevented from leaving by a postbellum legal regime that criminalized Black mobility, generations remained. Those who stayed continued to call the Forks of Cypress home, remaining rooted to the land and to one another through burial practices.

It is also believed that this cemetery holds the writer Alex Haley's great-grandmother, Queen Ester, who was owned by the Jacksons and was likely impregnated by James's son Joshua.[151] The Jacksons certainly were not her people, having enacted violence of too many kinds upon her. But she lies in the cemetery with her people and her community, rooted to the place that she did not choose but may have chosen to make her own. Haley would later seek out his great-grandmother, his roots, not only across the Atlantic but also in this overgrown Alabama slave cemetery.

Even after emancipation, formerly enslaved residents of Chatham and their descendants would have, like Alex Haley's ancestors at the Forks of Cypress, probably been buried in the plantation's slave burial ground. This was also the case at Hickory Hill, where individuals and families formerly enslaved there (and their descendants) continued to be buried near their kin and community. Webb Coffee, whom enslaver John Coffee purchased in 1823, continued after emancipation to live on or very near Hickory Hill Plantation.[152] In an 1874 Southern Claims Commission application, Webb asserted that he "resided 3 miles North of Florence Ala from the 14th of April, 1861 to the 1st of June, 1865. I was living on land rented from my former master, Joshua Coffee."[153] While the government denied Webb's request, he continued to live and later died on the land where he had once been enslaved. As Webb's obituary noted in 1881, he "died where he had lived for about 60 years, at the old Coffee homestead."[154] That homestead was almost certainly the Hickory Hill Plantation, and local historians argue that he and his mother, Nannie Jackson, both lay with their people in the Hickory Hill slave cemetery on Cloverdale Road.

These burial grounds may have been the only choice available, but their continued use after abolition allowed generations to stay connected. This includes Rebecca Coffee, whom John Coffee purchased in 1826 with her mother,

Judy, and who is believed to be buried at the Hickory Hill slave cemetery.[155] It is also assumed that Washington Coffee, his wife, Sally, and several family members (they had some sixteen children) were buried at either of the two Coffee slave burial grounds in northern Alabama.[156] Then there is John Kemper, who worked "plowing the gardens" at Hickory Hill, and who, after emancipation, remained near the plantation, likely close to the Black burial ground. In fact, local historians assert he lies buried at the Hickory Hill slave cemetery with his wife, Sarah.[157] Even Simon Jackson, who was born after the end of slavery and who died some seven decades after emancipation, likewise chose to be buried in the Hickory Hill plantation slave cemetery with his father and mother.[158] His people were a part of Hickory Hill, and Hickory Hill a part of his people.

Planting roots into the ground by burying one's people likely also continued at Chatham after emancipation. Names shared by several people formerly enslaved at Chatham appear in the 1870 and 1880 US Censuses of the Jefferson Beat (or subdivision) of Marengo County, close to the plantation. Ester Whitfield and Vinea Whitfield, for instance, were born in North Carolina, as were their parents. These women are probably Esther and Venus, who had been purchased by Nathan Whitfield at the same sale in 1827 and forced to move to Alabama eight years later.[159] They were also the daughters of Chloe and sisters of David, who lost his life around the time of their forced migration in 1835. Along with their younger sister Rony, Venus and Esther may have chosen to be buried with their mother in the Chatham burial ground. Connections to family members compelled some to keep burying their people on the same land where they had once been enslaved.

THE UNKNOWABILITY OF THE Chatham burial ground is, in many ways, a poignant metaphor for the anonymity of slave burials in our contemporary Southern landscape. But in the process of imagining the mortuary rituals of Chatham, we see how enslaved people more broadly sought to establish themselves and their people in a place they did not choose, thus creating a family history and remaking the land into a place they belonged. The ground, the body, the shroud, the coffin and laying-out planks, the grave markers, the natural landscape, the sky and heaven all together linked the dead and living, ancestors and descendants. In commemorating and honoring their dead, in establishing roots, enslaved people made sure their past—the past they could control, the past that had not been entirely stolen by their enslavers—was an integral part of their present. Struggling to create a sense of rootedness among the uprooting, they buried their people in the ground, declaring a connection between people and place. They belonged there; this place was their home.

With the rise of Black churches and the increased mobility of formerly enslaved people in the late nineteenth century, rural plantation cemeteries began to dwindle, sometimes forgotten by later generations. As people moved off plantations and into towns, or left the South altogether for the North or West, public burial grounds — usually around or connected to churches — increased in number and influence, creating additional spaces in which Black Americans could establish and maintain roots.[160] Despite this migration, though, ancestors and their material manifestations were never completely left behind.

In one remarkable case, a formerly enslaved man manifested his roots by keeping the actual wood that had been a part of his ancestors' burials. As the man's daughter, Cornelia Winfield, described in 1937: "All the planks eny of our family was laid out on, my father kep'. When he came to Augusta he brought all these planks and made this here wardrobe."[161] Cornelia's father, who supervised the plantation workshop during slavery, had managed to store pieces of wood that his family members had laid upon after death. It was with this wood — wood that had literally supported his people in death — that Cornelia's father made a wardrobe. He was, according to Cornelia, a man devoted to his enslaver's family, and he stayed on the old plantation even after abolition. This would be the kind of thing, like those gravestones to Jackson's enslaved jockeys, that white Southerners used as evidence that the enslaved were as much a part of the "family" as its white members. Yet this wardrobe tells a different story. He did not make the wardrobe from the planks upon which his enslavers lay. That would have represented *their* family history, not his own. Cornelia's father retained wood with the essence of *his* roots.

For generations, Black Southerners pointed to burial grounds, and to the rituals and objects within it, as sites where their families had created a sense of rootedness and belonging within the institution of slavery. There, outside the bounds of what we typically think of as the domestic sphere, enslaved people made the spaces they were forced to occupy into a home. Home was always more than the physical residence that enslaved people lived and ate and slept in. But Cornelia Winfield also placed significance in her physical house, where she displayed her father's treasured wardrobe, showing it to visitors as a manifestation of her family's survival. She connected the homemaking that her ancestors had performed in slavery, including the burial of their people in the ground, with her own homemaking in the twentieth century. Along with inspiring a sense of connection with long-lost family, the possessions and practices of home imbued certain individuals, particularly women, with power. Such power was not available to all, of course, as white society denied enslaved women their womanhood and domestic authority. Yet on slavery's frontier, where more and more white Southerners found themselves drawn in the antebellum era, one Black woman in Texas made claims on the real, though limited, power that the objects and practices of home gave to white ladies.

Chapter Four

PROJECTING DOMESTIC AUTHORITY

PATTON PLACE, TEXAS

The Texas summer sun was still scorching as Rachel sat down to dinner with Columbus. Perhaps it was too hot for her new, fashionable frock with multiple layers of fabric and lace, but she barely registered the discomfort as she glanced around the table, ensuring all was in order. There were no guests—as usual, his family had refused to join them—but the new table setting she had chosen had finally arrived at Patton Place, and it was as pretty as she had expected. She had been living in the mansion for several years, refusing the physical labor expected of someone of her color and commanding greater control over these kinds of household decisions, just like a lady should. She was even claiming authority over everyday activities on the plantation. This morning, in fact, she confidently gave orders to the overseer on how to better manage the laborers, taking the whip in her own hands.

Still, Rachel's conversation with Columbus earlier in the day made her pause: in a rage, face red and pouring with sweat, he had screamed that he would whip her. She was poised and controlled, daring him to try. He did not, but that could never take away the lingering reminder that he had the authority to commit any number of violent acts against her. This was not her only concern, of course. She had heard that Columbus had been fighting with his brother again, who was mortified by Rachel's role in the household. And she kept hearing talk that Columbus was acting a little oddly. Folks in town mentioned a "wild look" in his eyes. But she tried to put those thoughts aside, turning her attention back to the table and the lovely new dinner set.[1]

FOR A DECADE, Rachel—an enslaved woman—lived as "mistress of the Plantation" at Patton Place in Brazoria County, Texas.[2] She acted and purchased goods like the lady of the house; she also demanded respect like her, both on the plantation and in town. But the domestic influence she cultivated was tenuous at best. Although all available sources point to the fact that her relationship with the plantation's owner, Columbus R. Patton, was intimate—a term indicating carnality as well as closeness—it existed within the context of slavery's cruelty and constraints.[3] And as an enslaved woman, Rachel could not be legally married to anyone, including Columbus, even if observers asserted that the two "lived more like man and wife."[4] In fact, Columbus's relationship with Rachel and the power it gave her on the plantation was one of the three main pieces of evidence used by witnesses to successfully demonstrate the white man's insanity. Her domestic authority became fuel for the Pattons' court battles that resulted in Columbus's commitment to an asylum and the contestation of his secret will, both of which led to Rachel's loss of power and, eventually, to the loss of her home.[5] The Pattons tore Rachel from her position in the household, sending her to labor in the fields and live in the slave quarter before ultimately ordering her to leave Texas, claiming that her presence near the plantation was harmful to its operation.[6] She could, like any other enslaved individual, be temporarily or permanently uprooted from the place where she had once commanded authority. Her home, her body, her life was not her own.

Yet Rachel's domestic practices and possessions still held power for her. Even after losing so much, she continued to call upon the private and public acts that had demonstrated her domestic authority while she was lady of Patton Place. She sought the annuity and small but significant liberties accorded her in Columbus's will, which she may have helped the estate executors find in the mansion. She continued to purchase fine dresses but also bought ample dress-making materials, as her new circumstances demanded new kinds of labor. She used her knowledge of what provided white women power—their domestic roles, skills, and material culture—to grasp any iota of authority that she could, over both her own life and the lives of others. She deployed the very tools of patriarchal white supremacy in her efforts to make Patton Place, this site of slavery, into her home.

Rachel was, by definition, denied authority in the "woman's sphere" because she was enslaved. Slavery and capitalism defined the limits of domesticity and ladyhood, racialized who had legal and social access to womanhood and marriage, and dictated whose forced labor sustained the domestic ideal.[7]

These realities were bound up with each other; white women were meant to be domestic, dependent mothers, while Black women were meant to be unsexed/hypersexed laborers.[8] When enslaved women made claims to their own femininity and domesticity, they ran up against the racist limits of homemaking and confronted the violent precarity of bondage. Perhaps it is true that, as historian Anne Firor Scott has argued, many enslaved women in the antebellum South "were not much affected by role expectations," including the role of Southern lady.[9]

But Rachel's case offers a different perspective, one in which a Black woman was denied but nonetheless sought a position in the household. The unattainable ideal of the Southern lady was impossible for all women, but especially so for Rachel. She could never be submissive, gentle, meek, and, most importantly from society's view, white.[10] There were, however, other qualities of Southern ladyhood that Rachel could project: she managed the household and its laborers, she used domestic spaces and objects to her advantage, and she projected fashionable taste in the home.

These qualities of Southern ladyhood pertained not only in the home, however, for the pursuit of domestic power was never confined just to a house, or even to a plantation. Being lady of a household required performances outside as well as within, particularly those relating to self-presentation. Along with expert domestic skills, such as sewing samplers or preparing and serving tea, showing one's knowledge of and ability to purchase fashionable goods projected a woman's position as a refined (white) lady of the house.[11] Rachel seemed to know that the private and public spheres were never separate.[12] Her struggle for domestic power showcased how private life and gendered public authority were inextricable, for public presentations of self reiterated power held at home. At once remarkable and representative, Rachel's perspective exposes enslaved women's knowledge and ability to use white homemaking practices for their own purposes.[13]

As Rachel recognized, domestic authority was a pathway to power for antebellum white Southern women, which was perhaps why the white residents of Brazoria County worked so relentlessly to strip Rachel of her title as "mistress" of Patton Place. This was particularly true of Columbus's family, who initiated multiple lawsuits to revoke not only his own power on the plantation but Rachel's as well. While we rarely hear her voice within the hundreds of pages of court testimony—while enslaved, she could not testify in a Texas court—her actions emerge from these written records as evidence of her quest for domestic power.[14] Some of the witnesses in these cases were hostile to or held grudges against her.[15] Perhaps they exaggerated the extent of her control over Columbus and his plantation. Yet over and over, witnesses corroborated each other, and their antagonism exemplifies that Rachel acted in ways to anger them. If she had behaved in ways that fit what they expected of an enslaved woman, they would not have had reason to express their vitriol as they did.

And so we follow Rachel as her circumstances oscillated, beginning in the 1830s as she made her way with the Patton family from Kentucky to Texas, where she and dozens of other enslaved laborers made Patton Place into a flourishing plantation. Placed within the broader story of migration to and plantation-making in antebellum Texas, we can see how Rachel's intimate relationship with Columbus was at once atypical and familiar to Black and white Southerners.[16] It was within this relationship that Rachel began to establish domestic power in three ways: first, by controlling her own and others' labor on the plantation; second, by developing intimate practices and wielding material culture in racialized spaces; and third, by performing her domestic authority in public. In these ways, Rachel rejected white expectations of Black women. She labored, moved, shopped, and acted like the lady of Patton Place for a decade, from 1844 to 1854, until the Patton family and other white community members turned her life upside down. Yet still, amid the subsequent life-altering changes—forced migration from Texas, securing then losing her freedom papers, the Civil War, emancipation, and the possibilities and disappointments of Reconstruction—she struggled to wrest some control over her body, her living situation, and her life through the homemaking practices and possessions that had once defined her as lady of Patton Place. She continuously worked to find and make a place of her own.

Mistress of Patton Place

The large Patton family—which included Columbus and at least four of his brothers, two sisters, and parents—had made their way from Kentucky to Texas in the early 1830s, bringing with them at least three enslaved laborers.[17] This included a teenager named Rachel, whom a Kentucky slave owner had "left" with Columbus in 1833 before the family's long journey to the Mexican territory of Texas.[18] Over the next two decades, the Pattons expanded their slave labor force—which fluctuated between roughly fifty and eighty people—and transformed a small farm into a plantation.[19] Enslaved laborers produced considerable wealth for the Pattons by planting and harvesting

FIGURE 4.1. Patton Place mansion, built ca. 1835–56, with a detached kitchen and dining room to the left. Photograph ca. 1890. Courtesy of the Texas Historical Commission.

cotton, corn, and especially sugarcane.[20] They also constructed the Pattons' two-story mansion and detached kitchen/dining room along Varner Creek using handmade bricks (fig. 4.1).[21] During this time, Rachel established herself as "mistress of the Plantation" by demonstrating what historian Sean R. Kelley has called "domestic power."[22] To do this, she not only defined her own labor apart from the work expected of enslaved women but actively managed free and unfree laborers. Establishing these patterns took time, nerve, and the repeated performance of authority.

It was in the two-story mansion, completed in 1835 or 1836, that Rachel and Columbus later began to live "more like man and wife," as overseer Charles Grimm characterized them.[23] Yet there's no mention of children, and we do not know if Rachel ever called herself Columbus's wife, even if she could not have officially done so.[24] Enslaved people married all the time without legal sanction, and lots of white folks lived in common-law marriages, too.[25] But the coercion at the root of all enslaved-enslaver relationships may have prevented Rachel from claiming spousal status. As historian Tera Hunter has argued, "Marriage was ultimately a mutual exchange of affections and services. . . . A person could be forced to play the roles and abide by the form, but that did not make a marriage."[26] If any love or respect between the two developed over their twenty years together, it certainly did not come from a place of equality. Columbus did not even owe Rachel any legal or economic obligations, as a husband owed a wife.[27] The fact remained that Columbus never emancipated Rachel. Through the entirety of their relationship, he enslaved her.[28]

Yet the performance of wifely duties, specifically those associated with white Southern women's domestic practices, was in part how enslaved people identified a woman's position in the enslaver's home. Cases from Texas indicate that the broader enslaved community relied on quotidian domestic practices, rather than on any legal document, to track power in the home. John Clark maintained a long-term intimate relationship with an enslaved woman named Sobrina in antebellum Wharton County, and people enslaved on Clark's plantation testified that, although no priest had ever officiated a wedding, Sobrina was indeed John's wife. Clark not only explicitly declared this to his enslaved laborers; Sobrina's daily domestic labors plainly demonstrated to these observers that she was the "mistress of the plantation."[29] Individuals formerly enslaved on Patton Place likewise spoke of Rachel as Columbus's "wife." And while they knew that legal marriage between the two was impossible—Sarah Ford, who was born enslaved at Patton Place, insisted that she could not say if Rachel was "a real wife or not"—everyone could see that Rachel performed the role and duties of Columbus's spouse.[30]

A woman's role was to be nurturer, mother, sentimental companion, inculcator of morals, and comforter-in-chief, all of which took place within a so-called private sphere separated from the hustle and bustle of the public.[31] But women's domesticity also required that they organize and run a household, a role that required labor. To be lady of the household was, in part, to command the labor of others: to have people who performed the physical and menial work that allowed the mistress to labor in ways deemed more appropriate for a lady.[32] This was a fantasy for all women, of course. Yet real domestic authority was decidedly unexpected of enslaved women, something we hear from white witnesses in court testimony, which is where much of the information on Rachel's homemaking survives.[33] Over and over again, community members testified in the probate hearings to the "influence" Rachel held over Columbus and the household, unlike the other enslaved women at Patton Place.[34]

This domestic authority likely developed slowly as Columbus gained more control over the mansion and plantation at the expense of his siblings. By the mid-1840s, the deaths of Columbus's parents, plus the marriage of both sisters, left the mansion less crowded, affording Rachel more space and less scrutiny. Indeed, white Patton Place overseer George O. Jarvis recalled that after 1844, Rachel "had the entire swing of the place." But for years before, she faced resistance from Columbus's family as they challenged her increasing power in the domestic sphere. This "influence" in the household, for instance, caused "some difficulty" between parent and child. This was not a one-time dispute; Jarvis remembered that, in 1843 or 1844, Columbus complained that his mother "was bringing up that old matter again."[35] That Columbus was frustrated by his mother's frequent objections to Rachel suggests that, while some families and communities may have accepted (or at least tolerated) these intimate biracial relationships, they were not willing to allow a Black woman to play the lady.[36] Additionally, other family members continued to cycle on and off the plantation until after the Civil War, and they made sure to treat Rachel as an enslaved woman, not as the woman of the house.[37] Her attempts to define her own labor as well as to control that of others caused consistent "difficulties" between Columbus and his family, including with his brothers, Charles and St. Clair, and his nephew, Mat.[38]

Nineteenth-century ideals deemed domestic work to be part of women's duties, but divisions of race and class meant that these tasks were not the same for every woman. Household labor was racialized, gendered, and classed, but Rachel sought to define her own work as if she was a free white woman, not an enslaved Black one. Labor was a defining element of enslaved people's daily lives, and rarely did they actually choose what kind of work they performed and when.[39] Yet as John Adriance, administrator of Columbus's estate, recalled, "Rachel seems to be mistress of the place more than a servant."[40] Charles Grimm—who likewise referred to her as "mistress of the Plantation"— noted that Rachel "always had servants run for her & never done anything her self."[41] This was in contrast to enslaved field workers on Patton Place who, according to Sarah Ford, worked "from early mornin' till night . . . [and] in de field you better not lag none."[42] Unlike them, Rachel acted as if she had the right to determine when, where, and for whom she labored—and it provoked anger from those who disavowed her right to do so. When she refused on several occasions to pour coffee for a white worker named E. S. Jackson, he threatened to "break a chair over her"; but she remained steadfast.[43] This scene took place in front of Columbus at the dining table he and Rachel shared together, a table she took refuge behind to escape Jackson's violent threats. His vitriol clarifies just how unusual it was for an enslaved woman to deny a white man anything he desired, even if that white man was merely a worker on the plantation. Rachel would never be the lady of the house to Jackson. She was just another enslaved laborer whom he should have been able to command as such.

Yet she made a pattern of refusing him and other white folks at Patton Place, including those whose familial rank should have commanded her deference. After his father's death in 1840, Columbus became patriarch of the family, but as a bachelor, his mother, Annie, continued for a few years to serve as mistress of the plantation. Annie seemed to take her duties as lady of house seriously, managing the labor of enslaved domestic laborers, which she assumed included Rachel. But upon directing the enslaved woman to "churn up some butter or do some work about the Dairy," Rachel unequivocally refused: "She wheeled off and put her arm akimbo and paid no attention to her at all."[44] Not only did she defy the explicit directions of the supposed household manager; Rachel completely ignored her. Neither were actions that enslaved women were permitted to take.

To be more of the "mistress of the place . . . than a servant" required that Rachel, just like Annie, be the plantation's overseer of the domestic realm.[45] She therefore had to be able and willing to direct the labor that maintained the household. Though she did, as Charles Grimm put it, "wait about the house," this did not mean she sat still.[46] Rachel actively looked after and governed the household. She directed enslaved domestic laborers to fetch warm cakes and coffee when company was around, performing her role as lady and household overseer.[47] Though men like Grimm may not have recognized the work of household management as labor, and therefore did not remark upon it, it still required knowledge of and skill in a range of household duties.[48] Indeed, these tasks were commonplace enough for any woman on the Texas frontier to fulfill—even a woman of relative wealth—that others did not remark on it.[49] Whether she performed these duties herself or oversaw their completion by others, she had to know how to complete them and how to supervise them. Her responsibilities were apparently very like those of free wives as well as of the enslaved "wife" of John Clark, Sobrina, who "carried the keys and had management of everything."[50]

Managing labor on a plantation included using enslavement's brutal tactics. E. S. Jackson insisted that Rachel both compelled Columbus to whip enslaved laborers and took the lash in her own hands.[51] She seemingly did so by her own resolution. She managed them as she saw fit, even if this meant treating the workers "rough," as overseer George Jarvis recalled.[52] This use of aggressive force was, in fact, a marker of Southern white women's domestic power. As historian Stephanie Jones-Rogers asserts, white enslaving women used violent methods of control to maintain their authority in the plantation household. Rachel used the tools available to white women to declare her own domestic authority.[53]

Rachel made sure that her influence was, as George Jarvis put it, "observable."[54] She wanted those on the plantation—free and enslaved, white and Black, family and employee—to hear and see and feel her position. This meant managing more than just the mansion or the labor of other enslaved people. Charles Grimm, the white overseer on the site at various points in the late 1840s and early 1850s, left his position because of Rachel's interference with his management of field laborers. Grimm claimed to have been unwell in 1852 and thus inconsistent in waking early enough to oversee the morning field work. Rachel unambiguously expressed her discontent with this subpar supervision: "She came over to the quarters one morning about sun up & said the negroes were doing as they pleased and had no one to manage them & went on at a terrible rate & I don't know what she did not say. Mr. Patton was at the house . . . & she hallowed loud enough for him to hear her."[55] Rachel shouted her authority to every person on the plantation. And this was not the only time. Jarvis complained that Rachel "treated the overseer and workmen pretty rough," and that she made sure to "mutter and jaw at them where Mr Patton could hear her."[56]

Rachel used these managerial moments to underscore her position as mistress of the plantation instead of her status as an enslaved woman. E. S. Jackson recognized as much: "I could not say the woman Rachel occupied the position of a servant" because she "seemed to have charge of the house and premise."[57] Throughout the court testimony, observers of Rachel's behavior argued that she acted in ways that belied her skin color. "The negro woman Rachel," noted Charles Grimm, "occupied the position of a white woman as much as any I ever knew."[58]

Rachel inhabited the role of wife and lady of the house, and it appears Columbus recognized her as such. Witnesses testified that he never verbally or physically reprimanded Rachel for her declarations of domestic power, something that would have been expected of him as her enslaver. Jarvis remarked, "I never knew him, Mr. Patton, to do anything," though he did admit, "I have heard him & her have little spats frequently," Mr. Patton even threatening once to whip her.[59] Jarvis did not imply whether such a whipping ever occurred, but his statement foregrounds the possibility.

At the same time, Columbus did not perform his "husbandly duty" by

protecting her from others' threatened or actual violence. Two witnesses testified to having seen or heard rumors of Mat Patton, Columbus's nephew,
whipping Rachel.[60] Yet she evidently was not deterred; she continued to make
her authority and voice heard, for instance, scolding Mat "for every thing she
could lay her tongue to . . . at the residence of CR Patton."[61] She rebuked him
to the point that Mat left the plantation for a time, temporarily freeing herself of at least one injurious force.[62] Rachel's homemaking included decisions,
actions, and proclamations regarding work—both other's and her own. This
control over labor allowed her to establish and maintain power not only over
the inhabitants of Patton Place but also over her own space, her own body,
and her own life. At least for a time.

A Lady's Home

Domestic authority and one's position as mistress of the plantation was about
more than labor. Living as a lady necessitated that Rachel actually reside in
the plantation mansion—eating, conversing, and relaxing in rooms where
such actions were otherwise reserved for white people of a certain class.
The Patton Place mansion (like those throughout the antebellum plantation
South) is rarely if ever associated with enslaved Black individuals. If they are
mentioned in the history of the dwelling, it is as laborers, not as residents.[63]
And yet it appears that Rachel commanded authority in the mansion; she
made Patton Place her home. Rachel was probably not consulted about the
mansion's design, as she likely did not start living in the house until the 1840s,
almost a decade after its construction.[64] She would not have decided that the
house be built to encourage comfort amid an often brutally hot and humid
climate.[65] She would not have decided that the socializing rooms encompass
the first floor, while the second hold all the sleeping rooms. She would not
have decided that the kitchen and dining room be separated from the main
house in a two-story detached building.[66] She would, however, inhabit and use
these spaces and the material culture within them.

   Those with resources and capital in Brazoria County spent more on filling their homes with signs of their status than they did on updating or even
maintaining the structures. As Lucadia Pease wrote in 1851, Brazoria houses
may have been "shabby" but they "have much costly furniture."[67] Eliza Hill,
a Patton Place neighbor, possessed nearly $1,000 worth of furniture, lamps,
glassware, silverware, ceramics, and other material goods until her death in
the late 1840s. The inventory compiled at her death listed her many mahogany

furnishings, including one dozen chairs, and a silver set for eighteen.[68] Eliza had amassed such a large number of movable goods as she had twice been widowed, and according to Texas law, women were able to retain their own or communal property after their spouse's death.[69] Even on the Texas frontier, women demonstrated domestic power by acquiring expensive household goods.

Eliza's dozen chairs and massive silver set indicate the importance of both the parlor and dining room to American women's domestic practices and possessions in this era. The parlor was a gathering place for family and visitors, and it was to be both an elegant and a comfortable space that displayed a lady's tastes.[70] Furnishings, textiles, lighting, and prints needed to be tastefully arranged to encourage conversation. The dining room—a feature that began appearing in elite American homes by the Revolutionary era—was equally significant. At Patton Place, the dining room was connected to the detached kitchen, an unusual arrangement for the time. But regardless of its location, the dining room was a center of family and social life, a place to inculcate morals and good behavior, but also to display one's elegance, wealth, and status.[71] Ceramics, silver, glassware, and other dining implements were particularly important in demonstrating taste and style as well as class and status. By the early nineteenth century, as rooms became less multifunctional and privacy more desirable, these two domestic spaces were regarded as sites of sociability.[72] Yet ideals of domestic privacy restricted these more "public" dwelling areas to those deemed worthy. In homes across the United States, free or unfree laborers might clean, tidy, or serve a white family in the parlor or dining room, but they could not use them for their own purposes.

We have little direct evidence of the domestic goods in the Patton Place mansion during Rachel's occupation, but textual and material remains suggest an attention to objects that filled spaces of sociability like the dining room and parlor. It is probable that most, if not all, of the pieces listed in John D. Patton's 1840 inventory remained in the house after his death, including "1 dozen chairs, 3 folding leaf tables, 1 sopha, 2 setees, 1 side board."[73] Receipts for additional major furniture purchases have not yet been found, but Columbus's 1854 inventory recorded $450 worth of household furniture, kitchen equipment, and books.[74] Much of this furniture would have been placed in the public rooms, as pieces like sideboards and sofas were specifically associated with the dining room and parlor, respectively.[75] This furniture allowed inhabitants and guests to comfortably sit and converse with one another under the purview of the plantation mistress.

These domestic spaces, objects, and acts were considered private and intimate, by invitation only, and thus reserved for the white family and their company. By all accounts, though, Rachel took part. It was likely on the parlor sofa and at the dining room table that George Jarvis saw "Rachel sit down in the room with Mr Patton & converse with him often."[76] E. S. Jackson likewise remarked that he had "seen them in conversation together."[77] Rachel had evidently established a pattern of chatting with Columbus in rooms that were at once open to observation yet closed to those deemed unworthy of relaxing on the furniture. Enslaved domestic laborers who attended to Rachel and Columbus in the parlor were not allowed to sit on the sofa themselves, let alone to do so and speak with their enslaver on literally the same level.

To sit and talk in these rooms was an act of intimacy for an enslaved woman and an enslaving man, just as it was for a wife and her husband.[78] In another Texas case, witnesses argued that it was, in part, the act of close conversation that proved Sobrina was her enslaver's wife.[79] So too did the fact that they and their children ate at the same table together.[80] Rachel also evidently shared food and drink with Columbus at the dining room table, another intimate act that enslavers of the Pattons' status did not partake in with just anyone.[81] In the nineteenth century, wives were never regarded as truly equal to their husbands, but the demonstration of such close acts between couples did signify the woman's role in the relationship and thus in the home, a role that provided her a modicum of authority and power.

Along with the domestic practices Rachel performed in the parlor and dining room, she also would have used the material culture of these rooms as a means of showing her sense of taste and style and, thus, her position as lady of Patton Place. Archaeological excavations near the mansion and dining room/kitchen building uncovered dozens of ceramic sherds, including at least nine different transfer print patterns and one hand-painted pattern, all of which date to the antebellum era (fig. 4.2).[82] With so much of the ceramic assemblage around the main house and dining room/kitchen dating to this period, it is likely that they were purchased and used during the Patton residency. Rachel is one of the few women who lived in the mansion full time, from approximately 1844 to 1854, a decade that saw Columbus Patton's wealth grow, Rachel's domestic authority increase, and the production of several ceramic patterns found by archaeologists near the mansion. The concurrent timing of her residency in the mansion and the production and likely purchase of these ceramics suggest that Rachel chose the particular patterns that graced the Patton Place dining table, the same table around which she would have

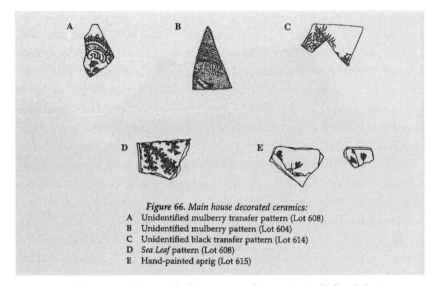

Figure 66. Main house decorated ceramics:
A   Unidentified mulberry transfer pattern (Lot 608)
B   Unidentified mulberry pattern (Lot 604)
C   Unidentified black transfer pattern (Lot 614)
D   Sea Leaf pattern (Lot 608)
E   Hand-painted sprig (Lot 615)

FIGURE 4.2. Drawings of five antebellum patterned ceramic sherds found during excavation of the Patton Place main house and detached kitchen/dining room. Amy C. Earls and Mary Beth S. Tomka, "Historic and Prehistoric Archaeological Excavations at Varner-Hogg Plantation State Historical Park Brazoria County, Texas" (October 1994), 87, Varner-Hogg Plantation State Historic Site. Courtesy of the Texas Historical Commission.

dined and conversed with Columbus.[83] If so, her choice would have been a material demonstration not only of her aesthetics but also of her intimacy with Columbus and her authority in the home.

A Lady in Public

Rachel's performance as a Southern plantation mistress extended beyond the confines of the private sphere, as these actions needed to be observed by others to have their greatest impact. Although Brazoria County plantations appeared secluded to outsiders like the Ohioan Rutherford B. Hayes, who remarked on their remoteness and "wildness" while visiting in the 1840s, Rachel and other plantation residents did not live isolated lives.[84] Neighbors visited for social or business calls, and they met one another in the bustling towns dotted along the Brazos River, including Columbia, which was located a couple miles from Patton Place.[85] This was still a small town, though, small enough that everyone knew everyone else (and knew all their business, too).[86] People shopped and sold goods, socialized and worshipped, gossiped and watched each other. Enslaved women, men, and children also milled about the town. Despite restrictions on their mobility, enslaved people were never fully confined to plantations.[87] The same was true for Rachel, and while in public, she displayed a mastery over herself through her mobility, purchasing power, and keen fashion sense. These public displays of power reinforced her position at home on the plantation, even as white community members balked at these demonstrations.

Rachel exercised a relative freedom of movement beyond that of most enslaved Southerners. Columbus may have preferred that she solicit his presence or permission when she left the plantation, but it appears he nevertheless provided Rachel with the tools to move about autonomously, including a horse that would quickly transport her the couple miles to Columbia.[88] Rachel also likely traveled to town in a buggy, which in the late 1840s was upgraded after Columbus hired Liam and Adam to paint, repair, clean, and equip the vehicle with new cushions and bolster.[89] The Patton buggy would have been recognizable, as only the wealthiest families in the county could have afforded such a luxury. Whether she made her way to town on horseback or by buggy, Rachel would have certainly been visible — if not hypervisible — to any observer, bonded or free.

Once in town, Rachel shopped both for the household and herself, and appeared to do so on her own. As lady of the household, she procured goods necessary to running it. John Adriance, who owned a large mercantile business until 1852, asserted that Rachel "frequently purchased family supplies which were charged to Col. Patton." And Adriance's was not the only establishment she frequented, for he reported that "she dealt also in Columbia at other stores."[90] Rachel had access to capital that allowed her to perform the role of mistress of the plantation in public, for as historian Stephanie Jones-Rogers asserts, "mistress" was one who not only governed but was a "'woman who ha[d] something in [her] possession,' . . . that something was capital."[91] Rachel was well-versed in the many possible purchase methods available in antebellum Texas. She sometimes paid Adriance in cash, "as high as twenty five or thirty dollars," while at other times she paid "in meal and meat from the plantation." She bought on Columbus's account while also keeping her own, and regardless of how she paid Adriance, she did not limit her purchases to household necessities, as "her bills with me judging from her accounts were at least one hundred and fifty dollars a year, mostly fine dresses."[92] Fashionable clothing was key to a Southern lady's self-presentation, a fact Rachel knew, and so she purchased exactly what she wanted for herself, including elegant frocks.[93]

This attention to fashion was not limited to Rachel, for enslaved people often spent what little they had augmenting their attire. In Black communities around the Atlantic world, individuals made, bought, bartered, traded, or stole dresses, hats, shoes, and other items.[94] As Lucy Lewis of Brazoria County remembered, "When we-all real good, Marse John used to give us small money to buy with. I spent mos' of mine to buy clothes."[95] Sarah Ford's father, Mike, who frequently ran away from Patton Place, even risked capture by returning to the plantation with dresses for his daughter and wife.[96] Enslavement denied Mike patriarchal authority in his home, but perhaps these gifts functioned as material attempts to establish some semblance of his paternal role.[97]

Enslaved people often focused their material acquisitions on easily transportable and concealable goods, like clothing, rather than on investments in materials for architectural improvements or new furniture.[98] They creatively repurposed old pieces but also actively participated in the purchase of new consumer goods. These goods were the most public of enslaved people's material culture, worn during social events like church services and dances rather than solely at home. They also happened to be vehicles of communicating a sense of self and individuality amid the demeaning restrictions of slavery. So often, enslaved people were forced to wear "negro cloth," clothing supplied to them once or twice a year by their enslavers. The lowest quality fabric available, "negro cloth" was often itchy, uncomfortable, and exceedingly plain. It was, in many ways, a material marker of one's enslavement.[99] Fashion, then, was not merely about vanity. It was a means of claiming some scrap of freedom.

In a world where so much was dependent upon and circumscribed by enslavers, enslaved people relished opportunities to express themselves.[100] Indeed, as historian Stephanie Camp argues, "dress was an especially important dimension" of bodily pleasure for enslaved women.[101] Of course fashion, including clothing, can be difficult to interpret; as Elizabeth Wilson maintains, "Fashion is ambivalent—for when we dress we wear inscribed upon our bodies the often obscure relationship of art, personal psychology and the social order."[102] Yet it is in those multiple layers—and in the 1840 and 1850s, there were *many* layers of fabric in a lady's dress—that we can discern individual and communal ideas, particularly for someone who left behind very little in the traditional historical record.

No wonder Rachel might have sought to communicate her position and power through clothing, both through the dresses themselves and through the act of purchasing them. "When ever there were any new goods brought to town & the young ladies would purchase dresses," George Jarvis proclaimed, "Rachel was sure to go and purchase some just like them."[103] This was not a one-time occurrence; John Adriance spoke about her "habit" of "buying more fine dresses than any lady in the community."[104] This was not a private action. Other folks in the community witnessed Rachel using her buying power; as Thomas Cayce, a white Brazoria resident, declared, "I saw her Rachel standing at Mr Adriances counter in Columbia buying a great many fine goods, and heard her tell Mr Adriance to charge them to old Columbus."[105] While Adriance may have been surprised that Rachel bought so many fine dresses, he accepted her authority to charge such substantial purchases to Columbus's account. Rachel thereby publicly demonstrated her economic power and, thus, her position as lady of Patton Place.

Of course, Rachel did not just buy these dresses; she wore them openly, wanting others to see her in them. This was a bold move, and it rankled white folks. As historian Elizabeth Fox-Genovese argues, "Whether in the world or in retirement [at home], the lady relied upon fashion, upon dress, to demarcate her class position." Indeed, even in the extravagant styles of the late antebellum era, a Southern lady needed to know the difference between good taste and unnecessary showiness.[106] Perhaps Rachel knew exactly how to toe the line.

The au courant ladies' fashions of the 1840s and 1850s included large hoop skirts, ample fabric and decoration, and an overall excess of material (fig. 4.3).[107] This may have been the type of dress that Rachel wore to church and that finally inspired backlash from white parishioners. She had been in the habit of sitting with the white ladies at the Methodist Church in Columbia, but on one occasion, she "took up more room than usual," perhaps because of her elaborate early-Victorian-style dress.[108] Her brazen expression of power—the purchasing power to buy such a dress, the domestic power to have the capital to do so—in a space clearly meant for white churchgoers appears to have been the last straw. Such seats and such clothes were not appropriate for an enslaved woman. Social norms dictated that her black skin should have excluded her from participating in such fashionability.[109] At the same time that elegant clothing was to be reserved for wealthy, white wearers, Southern women were also warned to not be *too* fashionable, for such luxuries could

FIGURE 4.3. "Women in dresses and seven bonnets, United States, 1853," *Godey's Lady's Book*, 1853. Courtesy of Wallach Division Picture Collection, New York Public Library.

corrupt.[110] When Rachel wore au courant dresses, then, she flaunted multiple social norms; dressing outside her status symbolized the dangers of such frivolous fashion.[111] The white parishioners agreed that they no longer would accept Rachel's public demonstrations; they finally demanded that Columbus "speak to her and let her know which seats [in the church] was intended for slaves."[112]

But Rachel continued to wear her dresses where she wanted, particularly in places off and on the plantation where her fashion made a powerful statement. Family members, friends, enslaved and free laborers, business partners, and neighbors saw Rachel's public declarations of power underscored in the domestic sphere when she wore her "fine dresses" while acting as mistress of Patton Place. George Jarvis remembered that Rachel "wore those dresses on the Plantation where the young ladies were."[113] Such young, white women would not have engaged in the manual labor or physical activity associated with enslaved people; their constricting and ornate dresses would not have allowed it. Rachel clearly knew the power of such clothing to reflect one's relationship to labor, and she broadcast her own position as lady of the household by parading her exquisite attire in front of those who inherently (as wealthy white women) held the status of "ladies."

Her actions off the plantation—especially her buying power and fashion statements—made public her private, intimate patterns of domestic life; but they also reinforced her demands for greater control. It is uncertain whether she made such declarations in other contexts, including parties at Patton Place or on other Brazoria County plantations she might have visited with Columbus. She may never have mingled with white enslaving women or danced with Columbus in front of them. As historian Dale Baum asserts, bachelor enslavers like Columbus who lived with enslaved women were "governed by a set of obligatory social rules. In the mixed company of whites, he could neither flaunt his illicit affair with a slave woman nor boast about having a slave mistress. If he had, his relatives would have accused him of insanity or alcoholism."[114] In fact, Columbus's family accused him of both because not only did the whole town know about his relationship with Rachel, they also knew about the power and influence she held—at least, for as long as fortune allowed.

A Lady's Change in Circumstance

Rachel's life dramatically changed just a decade after she became known as the lady of Patton Place. As her power appeared to increase, that of the Patton siblings decreased, a reality that by 1854 the family deemed unbearable, and they lashed out. In November of that year, Charles Patton filed a petition to the Brazoria County Court that his brother, Columbus, was incapable of managing his affairs and should be deemed non compos mentis. At the core of Charles's concern was the profitability of Patton Place, the "large estate situated in Brazoria County" that was the center of the Pattons' wealth and prestige.[115] One day later, a jury found Columbus Patton "not of sound mind" and ordered that he be removed to "some proper asylum for the care of the insane." The court named Charles the guardian of Columbus's person, and they appointed John Adriance as guardian of Columbus's estate. Adriance did not move onto the plantation or deal with its everyday management; his role was to manage the money, hire a competent overseer, and make sure the entire operation did not fold.[116] Charles Patton, on the other hand, directly controlled Columbus's fate. Within the month, Columbus was in an asylum in South Carolina.[117] He had lost both Patton Place and Rachel.

Rachel also lost much. As Sarah Ford recalled in a 1937 interview, once the court ordered Columbus to the asylum, Charles took Rachel from the mansion and "puts her to work in de field."[118] Laboring in the field certainly included a change in living situation; field hands did not sleep in the mansion or even in the adjacent domestic laborers' cabins. They certainly did not wear fashionable dresses. Her work, her home, and her identity shifted instantaneously from the mansion complex to the fields. This was a seismic change, one that Sarah expressed as "iffen a bird fly up in de sky it mus' come down sometime, and Rachel jus' like dat bird."[119] After a decade living as the lady of Patton Place, Rachel had established certain patterns of domestic and public life that gave her some semblance of authority and autonomy. Charles snatched that away, forcing her into the fields to toil beneath the sun and, in all probability, to reside in the slave quarter. While the changes to her material comfort were certainly palpable and likely deeply felt, Rachel's fall from power left her vulnerable in far more significant ways, including to the many men and women she had angered on the plantation and in the community.[120] When Columbus's family stripped away his domestic power, Rachel's disappeared, too, and she was confronted with the full reality of her legal dehumanization.

Yet Rachel continued to seek domestic power. In fact, she may have helped the right people find the very thing that would give it back to her: Columbus's last will and testament. When Columbus died in the South Carolina asylum in September 1856, no will had yet been filed with the court; and without children, Columbus's large estate would have passed to Charles, his sisters, and his nephew. However, while examining papers in the Patton Place mansion, John Adriance found a will dated June 1853 that had never been officially submitted to the court. Adriance did just that in January 1857.[121] None of the assumed Patton inheritors were even mentioned in the will; instead, the bulk of the estate went to Columbus's niece, Mary Hester Aldridge, who was just a child at the time he wrote the will.[122] This document went against everything the Pattons expected, drastically altering the inheritance plan.[123]

Charles, his nephew Mat, and his sisters, America and Margaretta, were incensed. They contested the will, proclaiming that Columbus had been insane and that the will had been "extorted from him by . . . [a] certain negro woman slave named Rachel with whom the said C R Patton lived in disgraceful intimacy." The Pattons believed that Rachel had manipulated Columbus into making herself "one of the legates named in the said will, being allowed one hundred dollars for annum and in effect set free."[124] Indeed, Columbus's will dictated that his enslaved laborers Jake, Solomon, and his "house women" Maria and Rachel were "to live with whom they wish without hire," with $100 per year given to the women "so long as they live."[125] They were not "in effect set free," as the disinherited heirs argued, but these enslaved individuals would have far more autonomy than before, and the women would have a measure of financial security.

Rachel may or may not have actively participated in the creation of the will, but it seems that Columbus at least had shared its contents with her. In his testimony, Charles Grimm claimed that Rachel knew everything about the document immediately after it was found at Patton Place, even though she was illiterate. She seemed quite pleased that Columbus's nephew Mat received nothing in the will: "She saw the reason Mat did not get anything that he was always pounding her & beating her & that was the reason he did not get anything."[126] She would later confirm, in an 1870 court case, that she knew what Columbus had intended for her after his death.[127] Rachel's intimate patterns of domestic life had created a bond between her and Columbus that resulted in his giving her more than he gave to Mat, his own family.[128] Her domestic authority gave her knowledge of the will and the ability to, perhaps, relay where it was to be found. In July 1857, soon after filing a petition claiming that Rachel's "undue influence" negated the will, the Patton siblings agreed to provide her with what Columbus had promised.[129] Rachel may have known she would never receive her freedom from Columbus or his family, but she was able to get something from them that improved her everyday life: to be provided, as Rachel herself declared in that 1870 court case, "with a home and one hundred dollars in coin to be paid to her annually during her natural life."[130]

By 1858, Rachel could "choose for herself the place where or family in which she should live"; but it is uncertain exactly where and with whom she chose to reside.[131] She may have remained on the plantation through the year, as a court document filed by John Adriance intimates.[132] Sarah Ford also remembered that after Charles tore Rachel from her privileged position as lady of the household, "she don't stay in de field long, 'cause Massa Charles puts her in a house by herself and she don't work no more."[133] The records do not tell us where this house was or how long she stayed there, but in February 1858, just one month after Rachel gained the privilege of choosing her own living situation, Charles Patton moved into Patton Place and brought his enslaved laborers, including Deenie, an enslaved woman with whom he had an intimate relationship.[134] Perhaps conflict between Charles and Rachel simmered again, as she may have left Patton Place by 1859. That year, a doctor recorded the night-time treatment of Rachel at the house of "Mr. Hayr," likely James Hayr living in the nearby town of Columbia.[135] His name appears again on a receipt for goods she purchased in 1858 and 1859, indicating she may have been running Hayr's household by this time.[136] Additionally, a March 1860 statement from Adriance noted Rachel was "near," but not necessarily on, the plantation.[137]

After being stripped of her domestic authority at Patton Place, Rachel's homemaking tactics had to change. No longer could she seek to demonstrate her power and position on the plantation. Still, she used her purchasing power and her sartorial statements to demonstrate her desire for autonomy. She continued to buy an abundance of material goods, making ten visits in 1859 to A. Underwood & Co.'s shop, where she spent $79.65 (fig. 4.4).[138] She bought garments for both public and private uses, including a fine dress and a robe dress, the latter an object that a lady wore while relaxing at home. But her shopping also included objects like a silver thimble, a decorative yet practical tool for performing domestic work and, perhaps, for making her own dresses.[139] In those few months, Rachel bought thirty-five yards of fabric—including muslin, gingham, and cambric—enough to make several dresses in the extravagant style of the late 1850s and early 1860s (fig. 4.5).[140] She also purchased several different embellishments, from popular fringe trimmings to beads to a silk cord, all of which could have adorned a new dress, bag, or cap.[141] Any of these decorative elements may also have been used to update an older item of clothing, or perhaps even the new hat she bought at the store, as headwear fashions changed rapidly in the nineteenth century.[142] She also acquired the necessary structure to make this an outfit for a lady: a hoop skirt, an impossibly large undergarment that made doing nearly anything impossible. Adding to her purchases a bottle of cologne, a fan, handkerchiefs, and a cotton umbrella, she was ready to maintain elegance despite the Texas heat. Three bars of soap allowed her to keep this ensemble impeccably clean and to present herself as a member of the leisure class, even if she performed the labor herself.[143] She may have been forced from her position at Patton Place, but Rachel persisted in publicly performing authority over her style and her body.

But the white population struck at Rachel again. By March 29, 1860—barely two years after granting Rachel the privileges Columbus's will had promised—the Patton family declared that she had become a threat to the stability of Patton Place. As John Adriance wrote in a statement to the court, "Her presence near the plantation and slaves belonging to said Estate was believed to have become exceedingly injurious to the interests of said Estate and perhaps dangerous."[144] This language was also used to describe another enslaved person at Patton Place, Adam, whom Adriance wanted to sell because of his "troublesome" and "insubordinate" nature.[145] Rachel was clearly

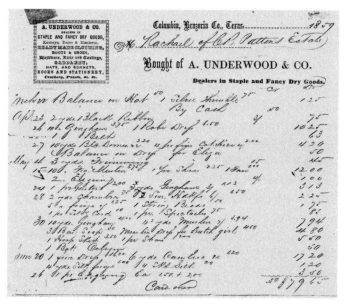

FIGURE 4.4. Receipt listing Rachel's many purchases at A. Under-
wood & Co. in 1859. Case #690, Probate Records, File 4, Varner-
Hogg Plantation State Historic Site (originals in the Brazoria County
Court). Courtesy of the Texas Historical Commission.

FIGURE 4.5. "Fashions for May," *Godey's Lady's Book*, 1860. Courtesy of Wallach
Division Picture Collection, New York Public Library.

also making trouble at Patton Place, and the mention of her proximity to the space of the plantation and its people suggests that her physical presence— her body, dressed in fashionable clothing, moving on and off the plantation —threatened the enslaving family's authority.[146] So they "deemed [it] not only best but necessary to procure her removal . . . to Cincinnati."[147] Rachel later claimed she had not wanted to leave her Texas home, not even for the possibilities of a free life in the North.[148] Obviously the long simmering resentment, conflict, and anger at her had not died with the resolution of the will, nor had Rachel's deep connection to Patton Place abated.

These disagreements went beyond the Pattons, it seems, for Rachel declared in an 1870 court case that it was in fact John Adriance who had concocted this scheme to remove her from Texas. He had apparently not been providing Rachel with the annual $100 legacy she was due from Columbus's estate, providing instead just "small and trifling sums of money paid occasionally." Why Adriance, who otherwise took such pains to execute his duties for Columbus's estate, did not fulfill this particular aspect of the will is not immediately clear. Rachel, however, said it was part of a pattern of cruel punishment. While in Cincinnati, she procured her freedom papers, and with the assurance these papers provided, she quickly returned to Texas "and to her old home on the Patton Estate," likely thinking she would live as a free woman in the place she called home. But Adriance "unjustly detained" Rachel's freedom papers, reducing her once again, in her own words, "to hard and rigorous slavery and compelled to labour on the estate of CR Patton for several years as a regular field hand until slavery was abolished in the year 1865." She clearly felt a connection to Patton Place, though that connection was complicated: it was there she had commanded authority and lived like a lady, and it was there she had also been enslaved, re-enslaved, and compelled to labor. But even after abolition, Rachel proclaimed that, because of John Adriance, she was "not allowed a home on the Estate of CR Patton but had been compelled to rent a house" elsewhere.[149] She did not just want a *house*; she wanted to make her *home* once again at Patton Place.

Despite the limitations of emancipation, Rachel found ways to continue partaking in domestic practices and wielding possessions that offered her some control over her life. By August 1867, she was once again exercising her purchasing power in Columbia. She spent $215.64 with W. F. Swain over the next several months, buying household essentials like milk, sugar, and coffee, as well as buttons, thread, scissors, linen, silk, velvet, and jaconet (a kind of lightweight cotton).[150] Perhaps she had gone into business herself, making

clothing for Black or white Brazoria County residents.[151] In this way, she could
once again have controlled her own labor, this time making money for herself
instead of managing laborers for the profit of her enslaver or being compelled
to the hard physical labor of the fields. Knowing her penchant for fashion
and her purchase of sewing materials, she surely made clothing for herself,
determined to maintain a particular look amid the changes in circumstance
she was once again experiencing.

By the time the 1880 US Census rolled around, Rachel was not laboring
outside of the home. She was "keeping house," though not at Patton Place,
as the plantation had been sold out of the family in the late 1870s. But Rachel
maintained connection to the Pattons by adopting her former enslaver's last
name. This was a recent change; when she had sued John Adriance in the early
1870s, she used the last name of Bartlett.[152] She may have married a man in
Ohio or Texas or elsewhere, only to lose him, for the 1880 US Census lists her
as a widow.[153] We do not have a written declaration or record of a verbal one
of why she then took her enslaver's surname decades after their relationship
ended and presumably after her marriage to another man. Perhaps she felt
she had earned it after nearly a decade managing the Patton family home.
And now that she received her annual allowance, she could finally fulfill her
ambition for domestic autonomy, a dream she claimed Columbus had also
shared.[154] She could finally focus her energies on "keeping house," on making
a home. But not on the land she had struggled for so long to make her own.

FOR THOSE LIKE RACHEL who found themselves (or who worked to make
themselves) the wifely figure in an enslaver's household, domestic practices
and possessions could provide them with a sense of authority both on and off
the plantation. Rachel seemed to recognize how powerful her domestic power
was, how it could provide her some control in a world that otherwise sought
to deny it to women like her. This is not to say that her intimate relationship
with Columbus somehow liberated her; she remained enslaved, constantly
vulnerable to violence and instability. Whatever authority she felt or extracted
was tenuous. Rachel ultimately lost her power at Patton Place, but she continued to display autonomy after her fall, and she continued to call (or want
to call) that place her home. Through her domestic practices and possessions,
she found a measure of control within an institution that sought to deny any
that she claimed.

Even after emancipation, Black women continued to live in a racist, patriarchal society. Yet Rachel's time moving through white society, despite resistance, had given her keen insight into the mechanisms of power, including into newly available channels to justice. In April 1868, she brought a complaint to the Freedmen's Bureau after a man named D. C. Roberts assaulted her.[155] Both parties compromised and Rachel received $5.00 in compensation. This incident underscores that the violence that loomed around her during slavery did not suddenly cease with the institution's demise; but it also suggests her knowledge and willingness to use the system to her advantage.[156] And she would do so again in 1870, when she sued John Adriance for $3,325 and laid out his deceitful actions: withholding her yearly bequest, forcing her to Cincinnati, taking her freedom papers and re-enslaving her upon return to Texas, and refusing her the right to make her home at Patton Place. These abuses, she declared, demanded compensation; the court agreed.[157]

Rachel struggled to exert control over her home, over her labor, over her life. We cannot forget that this struggle took place against an enslaving family and a white society that found her power increasingly unacceptable. Witnesses were wary of the influence Rachel held at Patton Place. White Southerners believed that Black female sexuality was powerful and dangerous, and testimony from neighbors and employees suggest it was this fear that underlay their concerns about Rachel, whom they described as "shrewd" and "cunning."[158] Enslaved women had to contend with enslavers' expectations of their sexual and reproductive labor at the same time as society assumed their sexuality was somehow flawed because of it.

Yet if enslaved women gave birth to the children of their enslavers, those babies would rarely be considered part of their father's family. Enslavers actively sabotaged enslaved homes and families—including those they helped produce—from a desire to build a legacy that would create a future for their own (white) families; for the stability of an enslaving family lay in the stability of slavery itself. Crafting material manifestations of that steadfastness became even more important as the sectional crisis ramped up in the 1850s, during which one vehemently proslavery South Carolinian endeavored to make his home into a monument to white supremacy and slavery. But generations of Black residents would ensure that the plantation is remembered for more than that. Their own attempts to make stable homes and create a legacy for future generations would likewise be written into the landscape.

Chapter Five

BUILDING STABILITY AND LEGACY

REDCLIFFE PLANTATION, SOUTH CAROLINA

On a clear winter day, the morning sun began to warm the red clay bluffs looming above the Savannah River as Sullivan and Ben climbed to their top. The pair, seasoned carpenters, were glad for the warmth, as they had plenty of work to do inspecting the recent additions to James Henry Hammond's new house at Redcliffe Plantation, which had been under construction for years at this point. Hammond had blamed the delays on the workers, but Sullivan and Ben knew the setbacks resulted from their owner's over-the-top design and overbearing management. But with Hammond finally away in Washington, DC, and no longer incessantly meddling, Sullivan and Ben could see their work finally paying off. The pair admired the building, knowing its mudsill was expertly affixed to the foundation. The legacy of their skilled craftsmanship would last for generations.

In Washington, DC, the fireplace blazed in Hammond's Senate office as he paced around it. His twin obsessions, architecture and enslavement, suddenly and surprisingly came together as he found the theme for his forthcoming speech before his fellow congressmen. Hammond would argue that the natural position of Black Americans was to labor for the benefit of their white owners. No other labor arrangement would, in his view, create lasting stability. And he finally identified the perfect metaphor: enslaved laborers were society's "mud-sill," the integral layer between a house's foundation and the structure atop it. With the sound structure of slavery permanently affixed to American life, Hammond believed that the Republic would endure indefinitely.[1]

AS SECTIONAL TENSIONS GREW in the 1850s and enslavers simultaneously fretted about slavery's future and boasted of its superiority, James Henry Hammond purchased the property he would call Redcliffe.[2] The house that workers like Sullivan and Ben built there was to serve as the Hammond family seat. And it would one day be owned by James's children, as would the hundreds of enslaved people whose labor had enabled such extravagance. Completed in 1859, the Redcliffe mansion and plantation was to be an enduring monument to white supremacy and slavery, thereby further securing the Hammond legacy.[3] By this time, James had once again uprooted and relocated several enslaved families—the Smiths, the Henleys, and others—to the Redcliffe Yard behind the mansion. As reflected in his 1858 Senate speech, Redcliffe was to make clear slavery's permanence and naturalness in this world.

Just six years after Redcliffe's completion, though, chattel slavery was dead, and the Black Southerners who had previously composed a majority of the Hammonds' inheritance could establish their own homes where their families might grow and thrive together. After making and remaking their homes in slavery, they would do so again in freedom. With emancipation, millions of people formerly enslaved in the South faced a dilemma: would they make those homes here or elsewhere? Would they remain close to the world they knew, despite its proximity to legacies of abuse, or would they risk new opportunities and new horrors in a world seemingly bent on their continued subjection? Hundreds of thousands of enslaved Southerners fled the region's plantations during the war, and more would promptly do so after hearing of their legal freedom. Yet in the first few decades after the Civil War's end, large numbers of now free Black Southerners stayed right where they were.[4] This was not because of some fabricated Lost Cause myth that they loved their enslavers and could not bear to leave them. Their reasons were many: lack of money, potential retribution by white employers, few opportunities elsewhere. But some also stayed because this place was what they knew, because some of their family or community was there, and because they hoped they could finally live without the disruption of an enslaver's demands. Slavery's scars marked the landscape, but so too did enslaved people's attempts to make their home there. Free Black Southerners would continue that work, seeking the dependable, stable legacies of home for themselves and their families on the plantations where they were still exploited.

Home was to provide continuity amid disruption, a place to which people might return and on which they might depend regardless of life's uncertainties.[5] At a time when not only the present but the future seemed so uncertain,

Black and white Southerners craved this stability. Nineteenth-century Americans were certainly interested in what that future would hold, and some anticipated a progressive future while others held more fatalistic, catastrophic views.[6] Despite the many transformations of war and emancipation, we find continuity in the hopes of many Southerners. Connecting the eras of slavery and emancipation can therefore give us further insight into the priorities not only of freed people but also of those in slavery.

And we can see these desires for a more certain, stable future expressed through decisions about home, whether its physical form, its material culture, or its location on a plantation. For instance, plantation architecture—particularly the mansion—communicated many messages about enslavers' social, political, and economic aspirations for themselves.[7] Such enduring architecture was not just for the present. It was a testament, a monument in fact, to the person and society that built it. It was also a testament to future generations, built for the benefit of their family and people *like them*: white people with power. Enslavers like James Henry Hammond embedded their racist convictions in the Southern landscape through monumental architecture, thereby fixing their beliefs in the ground as a means of inscribing them into society.[8] In many ways this worked: for centuries, the plantation landscape has overwhelmingly been interpreted as slave owners wanted it to be.[9] But it was never *just* what they desired. Redcliffe was a home and monument to the enduring strength of more than just the Hammond family.

This chapter follows individuals and families, Black and white, as they struggled to create stable homes amid upheaval. We start by exploring first how James Henry Hammond's acquisition of Silver Bluff Plantation in 1831 forever altered the lives and labor of enslaved people there. Over the course of three decades, his profit-driven pursuits shaped where and how enslaved residents could make their homes. Brutal work, increasing sickness and mortality, and frequent relocation fractured families and transformed enslaved residents' homes. Looking particularly at one enslaved family, the Johnsons, we see how they found themselves uprooted and distressed through Hammond's interference; but we also see how they nonetheless pursued homemaking both before and after emancipation.

We then move to Hammond's acquisition of Redcliffe, where in the mid- to late 1850s his desires to leave his own legacy, one he hoped would forever demonstrate the righteousness of his ideas, propelled the construction of his ideal home. Hammond designed Redcliffe as a monument to slavery and to white supremacy, but in the process the plantation also became a monument to the persistence of Black Southerners in providing a place of stability and permanence for their families. This continued as emancipation offered the hope of establishing home in a place of their choosing. Long after the institution of slavery crumbled, we find free Black families like the Johnsons, the Smiths/Wigfalls, and the Henleys making their homes near their kin and leaving their mark—sometimes literally—on the Southern landscape for generations to come.

Disrupting Life, Labor, and Home

James Henry Hammond's great ambitions required money and status he could acquire only through marriage. And indeed, the property in his wife's inheritance became the basis of his fortune. Hammond acquired Silver Bluff Plantation, located twelve miles south of Augusta, Georgia, on the South Carolina side of the Savannah River, after his marriage to Catherine Fitzsimons in 1831.[10] At the time, the cotton plantation included a rather lowly house that James would quickly replace with a larger home he called Silverton, a process he would replicate following his purchase of the Redcliffe property, almost fifteen years later. Catherine's inheritance also included nearly 7,500 acres, ample livestock, many outbuildings, and 147 enslaved laborers.[11] Silver Bluff was home to generations of enslaved families who had resided there before Hammond ever arrived.[12] Plantation records are riddled with the surnames Smith, Shubrick, Grant, Campbell, Goodwin, Glaze, and Fuller indicating large, extended kin networks. It appears that the plantation had thus far provided some modicum of stability for building family networks, though the inherent instability of slavery—the possibility for forced relocation or sale away from family—always loomed.[13]

Once he was in possession of Silver Bluff, Hammond immediately sought to "improve" the plantation, a process that meant altering and upsetting the lives of these longtime enslaved residents. From the beginning, James believed that his role as paterfamilias necessitated that he regulate almost every aspect of the plantation.[14] He found his enslaved laborers less than eager to follow his directions, and he complained that they were "trying me at every step."[15] He instituted harsh punishments, so harsh that he quickly fired a recently hired overseer who claimed that Hammond was too strict.[16] He instituted a brutal work regimen for men and women, including pregnant women and nursing mothers, that caused sickness and death at shocking rates, even as he adopted other management practices designed to improve their health and housing.[17]

Mothers and fathers, like Rose and Jack Smith, watched as nine out of their ten children died in infancy or childhood. Hannah Shubrick had six children between 1822 and 1838, all but two of whom died in infancy.[18] Hannah passed away while giving birth to her seventh child, who had in fact died in her womb days before her labor began.[19] Her two girls—Elizabeth and Mary, both of whom were born before Hammond acquired the plantation—were left motherless after also having lost brothers and sisters.[20]

This loss of life deeply affected the Black Silver Bluff community, shaping even their living quarters. Within the first decade of Hammond's ownership, more than eighty enslaved people had died and more than a dozen had attempted to run away. Rather than consider whether his exploitation and mistreatment had anything to do with it, James instead mused over whether the location of their housing might be to blame.[21] Hammond's dreams of economic prosperity would dissolve if he could not maintain his workforce, and so he purchased a new slave settlement, one that was located away from the swampland and the river that tempted escape by paddleboat.[22] Additionally, he still had problems with disobedient workers who, he reported, often complained of sickness, stole, got drunk, and refused to live with their spouses.[23] Moving his slaves to a more healthful location and forestalling escapes, James hoped, would decrease the number of laborers he lost every year.

Hammond's motivations and decisions were clearly influenced by a growing preoccupation with refining the "best" enslavement practices, practices that he claimed would result in the "increase in number & improvement in condition & value of negroes."[24] To realize these desires, slave owners like Hammond developed scientific methods of enslavement. By the 1830s, enslavers were taking a more active role in planning slave quarters and comparing notes on labor regimens, clothing, food, and housing.[25] They sought healthful locations and cabin designs, and they planned layouts that facilitated surveillance. Some of these tactics were not new—James Madison had implemented many in the design of Montpelier's South Yard in the first decade of the nineteenth century—but high-profile slave revolts and a louder, more radical abolitionist movement emerging in the 1830s increased the pressure on slave management.[26] Much like Paul Cameron's rearrangement of the slave quarters at Stagville, we can peel away this façade of paternalistic concern for the "comfort of the occupants" to see the economic incentive and desire for control that lurked behind it. Better housing, slave owners believed, promised better health and more amenable laborers, leading to more efficient work and thus more profit.[27] The goal was always the same. And although specifics varied, broadly speaking, enslavers relocated slave quarters closer to their own homes, arranged dwellings in easily surveillable designs, and required more durable and spacious cabins for their laborers.

The new Silver Bluff slave settlement did all of the above. James established the new slave quarter closer to his Silverton house, which was located on a slight rise and gave him good views of the surrounding buildings, people, and activities.[28] He planned for several new slave dwellings to dot the landscape, adding a matching cabin to that which already existed in the Silverton backyard, plus two lines of four houses each, extending toward and along the nearby creek. The houses were to be thirty-two feet wide, large enough to split each building into two units using a double-pen design.[29] The cabins were then to be built at thirty-foot intervals, creating two long rows set at right angles to one another. According to one of the Hammonds' visitors, this was regarded as a "wise arrangement," where the "house of the overseer is in the midst of a grove of live oaks, and in each street are a certain number of cabins."[30]

The new planned settlement changed where and how enslaved people lived. The original Silver Bluff slave settlement had been home to families like the Smiths and the Shubricks for years, if not decades. At the whim of their enslaver, some fifty to one hundred people were forced to remake their homes in this new slave quarter.[31] Their dwellings were now in a location nearer to Hammond, within close proximity of the overseer, and farther from the cemetery where many of their people were rooted.[32] The quarter's clear-cut, right-angle arrangement provided a communal yet easily observable yard for enslaved residents. This new homesite therefore left them even less privacy than they had previously experienced when living a distance from Silverton.

Throughout his thousands of pages of writing, Hammond evinced little concern for what changing enslaved people's living quarters would mean for them. He was aware, though, that separating families could negatively affect the working habits of enslaved women and men. When Hammond purchased Green Valley Plantation in November 1839, he moved several families to the new site, including Rose and Jack Smith and their one surviving child, Sallie.[33] Yet in removing them from Silver Bluff, Hammond took this part of the Smith family away from their extended kin, as he did with several Shubrick branches as well. Hammond preserved many nuclear families but removed them from larger networks that had been maintained for generations.[34] Families like the Smiths would demonstrate their desire to live with or near multiple generations of their kin after emancipation, but for now they endured separation.

The individuals and families that Hammond moved around his estate like pawns on a chessboard did not always have deep roots like the Smiths or Shubricks. Hoping to supplement the present and future workforce lost through illness and death, Hammond began purchasing enslaved people in the late 1830s, including Sally Johnson and her one-year-old daughter, Louisa. The mother and daughter arrived at Silver Bluff in January 1839, and over the next two and a half decades they would be required to move their residence again and again.[35]

This frequent movement resulted in part from James Henry Hammond's sexual pursuits of both mother and daughter. It is likely that Sally and Louisa lived near Hammond's Silverton house throughout much of the 1840s. The newly built Silver Bluff slave settlement offered Hammond easier access to their bodies.[36] By 1845, Sally had a child, Henderson, whom she boldly claimed was James's.[37] She openly spoke of this, insinuating in the process that Hammond held additional responsibility for him than for his other enslaved laborers. Even though James was unsure of the boy's parentage—"It is possible, but I do not believe it"—he still directed his white son Harry to "act on her's rather than my opinion."[38] Considering his mother's actions and his very name (Henderson is Scottish for Henry's child or for Henry), it is likely the child knew his parentage.[39] Perhaps Henderson found himself alienated, not fully a part of either Black or white family.[40] Yet, since the Johnsons *all* had light brown skin—evidence that such sexual violence went far back in their family history—perhaps they all experienced this tension together.[41] Still, Sally wanted James Henry Hammond to recognize Henderson as his son, maybe hoping that in the process, her son and her family might gain something by it.

Instead, Sally found her family further targeted by Hammond's abuse, as his sexual assault expanded beyond herself to her daughter, Louisa. By the time Louisa was thirteen years old, Hammond had forced a sexual relationship upon her. When Catherine, James's wife, discovered this, she left their home with their two daughters. Catherine demanded that Sally and Louisa be sold; Hammond refused.[42] So Catherine countered with a declaration that she would return only if Louisa were sent away. In 1852, Hammond begrudgingly removed Louisa from Silver Bluff and sent her to his mother-in-law in Charleston, on the opposite side of the state.[43] James's sexual predation had broken Sally's family apart. As the formerly enslaved writer Henry Bibb described of this all too common process, "licentious white men, can and do, enter at night or day the lodging places of slaves; break up the bonds of affection in families; destroy all their domestic and social union for life."[44] White Southerners degraded the sanctity of the Black home just as they degraded the autonomy of Black women's bodies.

While in Charleston, Louisa surely missed her family, though she apparently fulfilled her duties in the Fitzsimons household well. She impressed Hammond's mother-in-law, who reportedly had "no doubt but what she will find her a very usefull servant."[45] Louisa may have even taken advantage of the possibilities offered by a bustling city like Charleston, where she might be (as Hammond worried) allowed to roam "loose on the town."[46] She was also probably grateful for the physical space between herself and Hammond. And yet still, Louisa was, for what appears to be the first time in her life, separated from her mother and from the only place she had ever known. She had lived at Silver Bluff since she was one, and despite the disruption of relocation to the new slave quarter in the early 1840s, she at least had her mother. But now at fourteen years of age, Louisa found herself alone in a new place—an urban rather than rural space, surrounding by people who were not her own and unaware if or when she could return to the family and home she knew.

Within months, though, Louisa was back with her mother and thus back in proximity to Hammond's sexual exploitation.[47] It is not clear why Louisa's relocation was only temporary, given Catherine's demands.[48] Hammond, as paterfamilias, may simply have demanded that it was his right to do with the women what he wanted, his wife's opinions be damned. Indeed, his opinions on women were clear: as he wrote to his son Harry, women were "made to breed" and to serve as "toys for recreation."[49] Hammond had chosen Sally and Louisa to serve both purposes, forcing them to grow his enslaved labor force while also satisfying his sexual desires.[50] And he continued to do both with little to no reservation, noting in 1852 that, "I never in my life did any thing I thought unjust or wrong. . . . I can recall but few acts for which I can reproach myself, & these not important."[51] Just the next year, at the age of fifteen, Louisa gave birth to her first child, Sarah, whom Hammond later admitted "*may* be mine."[52] Clearly he returned to sexually assaulting Louisa upon her return from Charleston, and he would not stop for years, fathering at least one more child, Edmund, by Louisa in 1855.[53] Louisa's comfort in returning to her family and her home also meant she was returned to her abuser. She likely never felt a sense of privacy and protection in the place she was forced to reside. Yet her family was there, conceivably providing them some sense of stability despite the vicious cycle of sexual assault plaguing their household.

Over the next ten years, the Johnson family struggled to stay together even as Hammond relocated them. By the early 1850s, Hammond had developed two additional plantations, Cathwood and Cowden, both of which were contiguous with his existing property.[54] These sites required more laborers, for without them, Hammond believed his land was "useless."[55] So by the mid-1850s, he owned nearly 300 enslaved people who found themselves relocated to the multiple plantation sites owned by Hammond.[56] This included three generations of the Johnson family, who were living at Cowden by the mid-1850s.[57] Yet James had once again separated child from mother when he sent Sally's son Henderson to Augusta, first to work with a horticulturist in 1857 and then, two years later, to the more formal position of apprentice to a German viticulturist, with whom he was to have four years of training with no other labor required of him.[58] While some scholars have seen this decision as reflective of Hammond's care for and feelings of obligation toward his enslaved son, this analysis does not consider Henderson's feelings, regardless of the "special treatment and opportunities" of an apprenticeship.[59] The fact that Henderson soon ran away suggests his yearning for family and home, or perhaps freedom.[60] But this was not the last time Hammond's decisions would alter a Johnson's living situation. By December 1856, Hammond had resolved to move the family from Cowden back to the Silver Bluff slave quarter, only to be relocated again, this time to the Silverton house in January 1862.[61] Hammond no longer lived there, though he did visit the house in 1862, perhaps to see one or both Johnson women.[62]

Although they were James's progeny, Henderson and several other Johnson children experienced the same relocations and separations plaguing other enslaved families on the Hammond estate. Bearing James's children did not provide Sally or Louisa with more stability, although it did assure their continued enslavement. Hammond pressed his white son Harry to "take care" of his enslaved siblings and Louisa and to provide them with "indulgences." But for James, care and compassion for his Black family members meant their eternal enslavement: "Do not let Louisa or any of my children or possible children be the Slaves of Strangers. Slavery *in the family* will be their happiest earthly condition." To manumit them, he noted, "would be cruelty to them."[63] Hammond recognized a biological connection to Sally and Louisa's family, and to his own Black children, but he was unwilling to give them freedom. Hammond's paternalist claims on enslaved people's bodies, homes, and families afforded him the pretext to continually undercut these very same things, a proslavery process wherein family and humanity were used to justify the system that ripped apart families and dehumanized individuals. He may have truly believed in the faulty logic of paternalism, or perhaps he just privileged their existence as his property over their existence as his blood kin.[64] Regardless, his biological Black children would be part of the legacy he left to his white children, the inheritance with which the white Hammonds would build stability for their own families and homes.[65]

A Monument to Mastery

It was with this legacy—his enslaved workforce—that Hammond built his ideal home, Redcliffe, in the mid- to late 1850s. This was to be where generations of his family would demonstrate their wealth, status, and lineage. "I have gathered up the fruits of my life's labor here," James wrote, "in the hope that we should all dwell together & I might die among my children."[66] Redcliffe would be, he hoped, an enduring symbol of his intelligence and tenacity, passed down to his children who would maintain the homestead and continue his work.[67] But the security of Hammond's legacy—his slaveholdings, his properties, his new family home—depended upon the security of slavery. Redcliffe thus became a monument not only to Hammond but to the institution that made him rich. It would be a monument to mastery.

The Redcliffe property, which Hammond purchased in 1855, was located just north of his Silver Bluff plantation.[68] And like at Silver Bluff, while a fine house already existed on the Redcliffe property, Hammond desired a much grander home.[69] He of course wanted a house that would be aesthetically pleasing; his friends would later say that the Redcliffe mansion "looks elegantly" and is a "splendid building."[70] Yet there was more to architecture and the plantation landscape for James. He wanted Redcliffe to be a place for his family to rest, but he also wanted to continue the work he had dedicated his life to—agricultural innovation in a profit-driven plantation industry built on the labor of enslaved people.

In the late eighteenth and early nineteenth centuries, many Americans (including enslavers like James Madison) had argued that slavery's demise was inevitable.[71] But their successors, like James Henry Hammond, loudly and persistently proclaimed that slavery was a permanent American institution. "The idea of successfully abolishing African Slavery anywhere," Hammond asserted, "is simply absurd."[72] Slavery, white supremacy, and the nation's founding principles were inextricably intertwined: "It is equally absurd to suppose that the principles of free government forever established by our ancestors can go down. Happily they are in exact conformity with the subordination of an inferior and menial Race."[73] Hammond was convinced that slavery must be protected.

In newspapers, speeches, and letters, enslavers defended slavery's economic, social, religious, scientific, and moral righteousness.[74] Yet Hammond's brazen confidence in the institution of slavery belied his anxiety over its future and his own success.[75] Within his personal writings, Hammond constantly complained about and worried over the present and future productivity and profitability of his plantations, frequently lashing out at God for unfairly targeting him with unfavorable weather and other perceived injustices.[76] His writing evinced a parallel concern over slavery's stability; although he boasted of abolition's absurdity, he and other slave owners were paranoid. Enslavers sought to safeguard the institution amid increasing calls for its destruction, even though slavery remained firmly ensconced in and supported by the American system.[77] Hammond's circle of friends and colleagues expressed concern over the work of abolitionists, whose publications were a "deep cause of anxiety" for them.[78]

Like other enslavers whose wealth was directly tied to their enslaved property, Hammond believed that the security of his white family depended upon the maintenance of slavery. James was "looking . . . to laying a foundation for my children" that would give them a sense of stability.[79] And it was his enslaved property that constituted this foundation, or, as he phrased it in his 1858 speech to Congress, that constituted the "mud-sill." The use of the term implied that Black people were the base upon which white society was built. As Hammond put it, "you might as well attempt to build a house in the air . . . except on this mud-sill."[80]

That Hammond would use an architectural metaphor was no coincidence. "I must build & I will build," he wrote of his Redcliffe mansion, which, along with wine making, had become his preoccupation in the mid-1850s.[81] Hammond had long shown an interest in architecture, adding several volumes on the subject to his library over the years, and he took an active role in the design of the house and its surrounding built environment.[82] Even as he rekindled his political career, he continued to direct the mansion's construction.[83] James had put his sons in charge of the everyday management while he was in Washington, DC, but he wrote frequently to the contractor in South Carolina seeking to ensure the perfect execution of his design.[84] As Hammond spoke to Congress about his theory of the social mudsill, enslaved carpenters like Sullivan and Ben built the actual mudsill and other architectural elements of Redcliffe, while the entire enslaved workforce provided the capital for Hammond to make the extravagant expenditure possible.[85] As "slavery is an established and inevitable condition to human society," so too would Redcliffe remain an established monument to prove such a position to future generations.[86]

Hammond's Redcliffe mansion was to be a private monument, distinct from those in public spaces like parks and cemeteries, yet in many ways built for similar purposes. A monument is erected to be a permanent and enduring part of the landscape, one that will communicate (through symbolic messaging) collective memory. "The impulse behind the public monument," art historian Kirk Savage argues, "was an impulse to mold history into its rightful pattern." Of course, the reality is far from this, often creating conflict over history instead of consensus.[87] Even so, the intentions of the monument-makers tell us much about how they wanted the past to be remembered and how they sought to use that history for their own purposes.

Hammond was adamant that his mansion "must face South or SW," a symbolic choice that oriented his home both toward the firmly entrenched slaveholding South and toward the area of the country where the institution still had room to grow.[88] But his home would materially demonstrate the place of slavery in the Southern landscape through the popular, though increasingly passé, Greek Revival architectural movement.[89] "My house will be large," Hammond wrote to a friend in 1855, with "three stories including basement . . . [and] Piazza all round."[90] The piazzas wrapped around the house and provided ample covered outdoor space on both the ground floor and second stories, but they also necessitated the use of supporting structures, in this case simple fluted columns. These columns, along with its bright white paint and a tendency toward the symmetrical, marked Redcliffe mansion as a Greek Revival structure (fig. 5.1).[91]

If there ever was an architectural movement that seized the attention and admiration of the nineteenth-century American populace, it was Greek Revival.[92] In adopting the Greek Revival style, Americans were, as one architectural historian put it, "asserting that they felt themselves to be worthy successors to the republicans of Athens."[93] Hammond, ever the classics-obsessed patrician, certainly saw himself as such.[94] The architectural movement saw public and private buildings imitating, to varying degrees, Grecian temples built to house deity statues, which Americans associated with their beloved republican virtues. Hammond's home adopted elements of these temples—weighty proportions, simplicity, monumental size, symmetrical tendencies, a colonnaded

FIGURE 5.1. Hammond mansion, built ca. late 1850s, Redcliffe Plantation, SC. Photograph by author, 2018.

portico, and a dazzling white façade—thereby mimicking their use as monuments not only to the gods that lived within but to the very society that created them. Greek Revival was not a purely Southern architectural movement. But some proslavery Southerners saw a connection between their ideology and Greek Revival, maintaining that the style demonstrated how ideals of liberty and equality naturally existed alongside slavery, as they had in Greece.[95] Hammond did not believe that slavery needed to be purified, unlike the enslavers discussed in Kenneth Stevens's history of Southern architecture who felt that slavery might be "exonerated through associations with classical iniquity."[96] For Hammond, Greek Revival plantation architecture would celebrate the connections between the world's first Republic and the US South, especially their shared reliance on slavery.

But even as slavery was teetering on the edge of an abyss and the nation devolved into civil war, Hammond's thoughts in early 1861 were squarely on building a stable, self-sufficient legacy for his children: "My only earthly ambition and desire is to secure Redcliffe as a family residence to my children."[97] He meant self-supporting with the use of enslaved labor, of course. Hammond had by this time apprenticed fourteen-year-old Henderson, his son with

FIGURE 5.2. Slave cabin in the Redcliffe Yard, built ca. late 1850s. Photograph by author, 2018

Sally Johnson, to learn "vine culture and wine making," ostensibly with plans to bring him back to Redcliffe to work.[98]

Before he was sent to Augusta, Henderson may have been one of several enslaved people that Hammond moved to Redcliffe in the late 1850s, relocating them from other areas of his sprawling estate to a yard immediately behind the new mansion.[99] There, enslaved carpenters had built double-pen cabins, a kitchen, and various other outbuildings that aesthetically melded with the mansion's style but that clearly functioned as enslaved living and labor spaces (fig. 5.2). The large, imposing mansion dwarfed the small cabins, even as those dwellings supported the aesthetic goals of Hammond's home. James believed firmly in "the immense disparity in the races of man," a disparity that took material form in the architecture and landscape of Redcliffe.[100] Plantation landscapes were meant to reflect and support the social structure of slavery, with enslavers' homes at the top, dominating the landscape, and flanked by the dependencies that housed those deemed dependent.[101] Hammond situated the Redcliffe mansion at the highest elevation on the property, which provided magnificent views of the surrounding countryside.[102] Just as he had moved up the social and economic ladder, so too did his home, which was located at a higher elevation than even his Silverton mansion at Silver Bluff. Redcliffe reinforced Hammond's position at the top of the hierarchy and the plantation's wider "family." Enslaved people's cabins mimicked the mansion's aesthetic but were far smaller, thereby materially projecting Hammond's fantasies of paternalism and mastery.

At the same time, the aesthetic unity of Redcliffe's built environment demonstrated how slavery was naturally a part of the homes and lives of white Southerners. In Virginia, for instance, Philip St. George Cocke and his architect, A. J. Davis, wanted to visually unite the natural land with both white and Black plantation spaces. By adopting a unifying picturesque aesthetic, Cocke meant to demonstrate enslaved people's acceptance of their natural place in the plantation hierarchy as well as slavery's own natural place within the United States.[103] Similarly, as a legacy for Hammond's white children and a monument to mastery, Redcliffe's built environment could not ignore or obfuscate enslaved living and laboring; it needed to embrace it. While James and Dolley Madison's Montpelier sought to partially conceal enslaved living and laboring, Hammond's Redcliffe more fully embraced it to transform his plantation into a monument to mastery.

Redcliffe's buildings were an aesthetically cohesive set, reflecting the paternalist fantasy of one plantation family, even as the size and construction differences reiterated the hierarchy at the root of Southern paternalism. Hammond was not interested in covering up the harsh realities of slavery, for he believed firmly that benevolent paternalism made for good lives for his "Black family."[104] These slave dwellings were indeed well-built and stable, far more permanent than many other slave cabins. Redcliffe's double-pen cabins were made of planks instead of logs, and they were whitewashed to maintain Hammond's strict standards of cleanliness. They were set on piers with wood floors, a practice that enslavers like Hammond believed allowed for better airflow and healthier living conditions, not to mention cleaner than those with floors of packed dirt (fig. 5.3).[105] These architectural decisions reinforced enslaved people's position in the hierarchy and also set them as more enduring features of the landscape. Their permanence would be as laborers, as the mudsill upon which all else was built.

James's enduring quest to secure the future of slavery, and thus his wealth, family, and home, once again changed enslaved people's homes. As he had with the new Silver Bluff slave settlement in 1842, Hammond relocated enslaved individuals and families and set them within yet another surveillance landscape, taking them away from extended kin and whatever (limited)

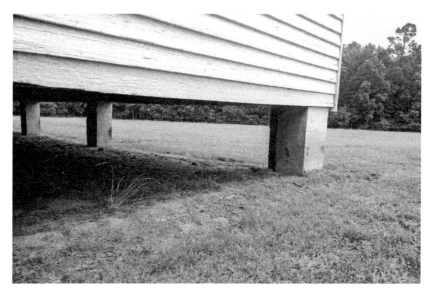

FIGURE 5.3. Notice both the plank and raised-pier construction on the Redcliffe Yard slave cabin. Photograph by author, 2018.

security that family might have provided.[106] The Redcliffe Yard was just feet behind the Hammond house, physically close but also clearly observable from the piazzas as well as from the cupola that perched atop the mansion. Its layout was not in rows, as many proslavery writers contended was the best arrangement possible, but once again (like the Silver Bluff settlement) the cabins were set at right angles (fig. 5.4). This formed a central yard to the rear of the mansion where enslaved living and laboring could be surveilled. The cabin entrances were oriented toward the Yard itself, a layout that suggested enslaved laborers' focus would be on their work in the yard and in the mansion ahead of them. This, of course, also allowed for the monitoring of activities and of movement into and out of cabins.[107] Additionally, the technique of setting cabins atop piers discouraged privacy by eliminating the possibility for subfloor pits; with buildings hovering above the ground, residents could not dig pits inside their homes without them being clearly visible from the outside (see fig. 5.3). With this and other regulations, including forbidding the use of loft spaces, Hammond limited the number of concealed interior spaces and increased the likelihood for surveillance of enslaved people's activities.[108] James subscribed to the belief of other enslavers that laborers should have "no

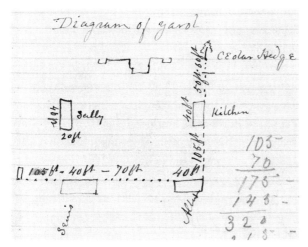

FIGURE 5.4. Diagram of Redcliffe Yard, 1873, Harry Hammond Account Book. The rear of Redcliffe is shown at the top of the diagram, with the Yard buildings behind it. From Harry Hammond Papers, South Caroliniana Library, University of South Carolina, Columbia.

place to stow away anything" in their dwellings.[109] Hammond demanded that the Yard be kept spotless, which included the stipulation that nursing mothers (who supposedly had more free time) must "clean the entire yard from time to time, & always remove all litter & trash."[110] The archaeological record suggests that this regulation was followed at Redcliffe, where indications of a swept yard between the slave cabins remain.[111]

Yet the presence of a swept yard encourages a reexamination of the Redcliffe Yard from the perspective of those who actually lived there. Hammond had control over the spatial and material form it took, but enslaved Redcliffe residents did not necessarily comprehend or experience the Yard in the way he did. Perhaps they welcomed the material comforts created by the sturdily constructed cabins, or perhaps they appreciated the physical changes that plank pier-raised floors brought to their homes. They may have constantly felt the reality and potential of surveillance, but that did not prevent the creation and use of hidden spaces within the cabins that Hammond simply had not thought of, much like enslaved Stagville residents had. And like the swept yards of Montpelier's South Yard and Stagville's Horton Grove, Redcliffe's swept yard may also have been a means of establishing a sense of ownership and meaning even in a place so surveilled.[112] Rather than simply an enslaver's demand, yard sweeping was a homemaking tactic passed down through generations of Black Southerners, a practice across time and space that suggests stability. Hammond, of course, would not have recognized it as such, nor would he have regarded the Yard as part of a Black home. The buildings, landscape, and labor at Redcliffe constituted *his* home, *his* legacy for his white children and for generations of enslavers to come.

Or so he thought. As the Civil War raged around him, Hammond stayed focused on Redcliffe and his wine, on his land and his laborers, on his white children and on the future of slavery. Though he publicly supported the Confederacy, in private he expressed grave fears and resentments. His certainty in the justification for secession—"because of these insupportable invasions of all our rights and property of our peace, and of our firesides . . . we would secede from this union"—did not waver.[113] The righteousness of defending home, slavery, and white supremacy (all three of which were inextricable for him) remained strong. But he sincerely doubted the Confederate leadership and its execution of the war, especially the sacrifices he made to support it: his three white sons on the battlefield to man the war effort, crops and foodstuffs from his plantation to provision it, the purchase of large bonds to finance it.[114]

The war affected more than just Hammond's family and home. As early as January 1861, enslaved people could hear the Union army firing on Savannah, and from that point on, they appeared to Hammond to be worried, though as he noted in his journal, he could not tell "which side" they were anxious for.[115] By 1863, which side enslaved people were rooting for was clear, as Hammond noted that a recent Union defeat had made them "seem utterly subdued as if by blasted hopes. . . . I have no doubt they have all along been well apprised with the Abolition version, of what is going on, & may thus shut up their faces & cease their cheerful greetings in view of the future, not the past."[116] Enslaved people living on the large Hammond estate were holding on to hope, looking forward to a potential future of freedom rather than to their past of slavery; yet, in the depths of the war, that future in no way seemed certain. Clearly, they were kept apprised of battlefield victories and losses, as they evinced dread after major Union defeats and cheered Union successes. Most apparently stayed put in their homes on the Hammond estate, waffling between optimism and fear, though at least one man—a Black driver named Frank—did escape, potentially seeking freedom at Union lines.[117] Almost half a million enslaved people across the Confederacy would do so, leaving their homes in slavery in the hope of finding a place of freedom. It was in the physical shelters they built in refugee camps—whether simple tents or more substantial cabins—that they set down, as historian Amy Murrell Taylor argues, "a physical toehold in Union lines and, therefore, in the promise of freedom."[118] Enslaved people knew the power of making their homes—of transforming residential space into a meaningful place—wherever they could, whether by fleeing from or staying on the plantations they were forced to inhabit.

As the war progressed and the Confederate cause grew increasingly dire, Hammond grew increasingly ill and bitter, writing condescendingly of the excitement and hopefulness of the hundreds of enslaved people on his estate.[119] When James died in November 1864, his funeral was held at Redcliffe. Family history relates that slaves filed by his casket with great solemnity and sadness, nearly despondent in losing their "defender."[120] Of course, they might have been equally anxious about what his death meant for their families and homes. Would they be sent to his son's house down the road, or perhaps all the way to another son's Mississippi plantation, or to any buyer who would pay enough?[121]

Finding Stability in Free Homes

Within six months of James Henry Hammond's death, the war was over and the majority of his 300 formerly enslaved laborers were still living and laboring on the estate.[122] Hammond had separated families and destabilized homes, but free Black Southerners made clear their determination to make real on the promises of emancipation, including the ability to establish their homes where they wanted. Certainly, some formerly enslaved people felt compelled to stay, though perhaps for different reasons, such as the continuing power of former enslavers, including the passage of strict Black Codes in South Carolina; the uncertainty of income or food elsewhere; or the presence of family members nearby.[123] Others evinced an emotional connection to the land that made them stay. Betty Farrow told a WPA interviewer that she and her family "stayed right dere en de farm" after emancipation "cause it was de only home we knew and no reason to go."[124]

But things on plantations were not static after the end of chattel slavery. As sites transitioned from enslaved labor to tenant farming, much of the plantation landscape transitioned as well. The arrangement of slave housing in condensed, village-like quarters gave way to more dispersed housing on individual plots of land.[125] In sharecropping or tenant farming, Black families rented or were provided cabins as part of their contracts with white landowners. The dispersal of dwellings, then, may have been a choice of the landowners rather than the laborers. Still, moving away from a centralized location provided Black families more privacy and control over their homes. This dispersed settlement pattern, however, maintained a focus on kinship and community, as family members were often found on neighboring fields just a third- or a half-mile from one another. Archaeologists found this familial proximity across dispersed settlements in the twentieth-century Savannah River Site, the northernmost area of which encompasses part of Hammond's former landholdings.[126] Whether raising a barn, bringing in crops, or supplementing a poor harvest with neighbors' produce, having family nearby provided physical and emotional support necessary to rebuilding lives after emancipation. Although postbellum homes often included multiple generations of one family or extended kin networks, they were not the shared dwellings of slavery.[127] Mothers and husbands, daughters and sons, could choose to live with or near one another.

This was the case for several families who had been owned by the Hammonds, including two who had direct connections to their former enslavers: Sally and Louisa Johnson. By 1870, Sally had a house in the Silverton Township, where she and four of her children farmed on land leased from the Hammonds.[128] Silverton Township included Cowden and Silver Bluff Plantations where Sally and her family had been enslaved.[129] The 1870 census taker noted that the "lady farms on lease," an unusual phrase that reiterates her unusual position as a woman working directly with the landowner. Most other heads of household leasing land around her were men. But Sally had a decent support system to help her work the land, including—in all likelihood—the family of her daughter Louisa, who lived the next dwelling over.[130] Together with two of her other children, Sally would have had seven workers ages thirteen and up. Thus, three generations of Johnsons lived just a short walk from each other, a physical closeness documented by their consecutive entries in the 1870 US Census.[131] Hammond's desires had once led to Sally and Louisa's separation; no longer would they be subject to James's whims.

Neither Sally nor Louisa owned the land they lived and labored on; they leased it, like so many other formerly enslaved people living in the area, and they worked it according to the parameters set by Harry Hammond, one of James's sons. The arrangement included a house, water, firewood, rations, and loan of a mule and plow for each worker, plus $15 cash at the end of the crop year.[132] Though these terms were typical, they did not leave much room for building wealth. For many Black Southerners, one of the continuities between enslavement and freedom was the lack of access to property ownership and any means of wealth accumulation.[133] Some even continued living in the same dwellings they had formerly inhabited while enslaved, making the persistence of bondage all too real.

Plus, white Southerners' practices of inspecting, intruding, and surveilling Black domestic spaces did not cease with emancipation. Harry Hammond likely included stipulations similar to those of South Carolinian J. Rhett Mott, who in 1867 hired twenty-eight freed people with the requirement that "they agree to keep their houses & garden plots in a neat & orderly manner, & subject to the inspection of the employer or his agent at any time."[134] Such language is reminiscent of advice given to slave owners by plantation management advocates, including the belief that "the interior of their [slave] dwellings should be frequently inspected by the master or overseer to see that all is right within—that they keep a clean house."[135] Ignoring the momentous change in the Southern economy and social system that emancipation initiated, former enslavers like the Hammonds demanded that their now free Black laborers withstand the same encroachment into their bodily and domestic privacy they had experienced under slavery.

Even with such drawbacks, farming on leased land was a logical choice for many Black Southerners, for while most could not purchase land, many already possessed the agricultural skills and knowledge to make it productive. Yet it was not necessarily the obvious choice for Sally Johnson, who had been a seamstress in 1839 when James Henry Hammond purchased her. She did not take up this occupation after emancipation, even though this skill could have offered her more money and less hard labor. Sally was fifty years old in 1870, not an old woman but certainly old enough to feel the many years of physical labor. She had been required to work as a domestic laborer for Hammond, as his records show.[136] But, once free, Sally chose to farm instead. Perhaps it was the only viable option available to her. But it is also possible that such a choice was more desirable because it allowed her extended family to remain close to one another and close to the place that she had struggled to make her home over the past several decades.

The Johnsons did much more than just work together, though. One can imagine the meals they cooked, the prayers they shared, the arguments they had, the quilts they made, the holidays they celebrated. These were not new activities; Hammond's own plantation records note that families like the Johnsons did all these activities together while enslaved, too. But now they were in homes that they had some degree of choice in and authority over. Though they lived in separate households, they were near one another, providing their growing extended family with support and stability.

For the Johnsons, this meant staying on the land they had lived and labored on as enslaved people and taking advantage of the options, though limited,

now afforded to them by freedom.[137] The house that Harry Hammond provided them was probably not the dwelling they desired; it is not clear what this
assigned housing was like, though the structures were probably quite similar
to if not just like the cabins Black residents had lived in while enslaved.[138]
Landowners rarely kept up with the housing on these postbellum plantations;
as W. E. B. Du Bois later noted, "The homes were even worse than before on
account of the deterioration of the old slave quarters and the failure to repair
them."[139] But there is clear evidence that many formerly enslaved families
sought to improve their homes, however much or little their resources, time,
and energy allowed. Sharecroppers utilized the skill of improvisation, or
"making do" as historian George McDaniel puts it, that so many had acquired
during slavery to improve their lives in freedom.[140]

   We can see this at Redcliffe, where an 1890 photograph of a cabin shows a
postbellum architectural development: the addition of a "lean-to" attached to
the rear of the structure (fig. 5.5). This double-pen structure, with two separate
one-room dwellings on each side of the central chimney, was commonplace
on the Hammond estate; we know at least two of them stood (and still stand
to this day) in the Redcliffe Yard (see fig. 5.2). But unlike the typical slave
dwelling form, the sharecropper's cabin includes an addition, extending the
roof line downward and adding a significant amount of square footage, plus
another window to each side of the house. The large family pictured in front
of the cabin likely found this lean-to addition practical and pleasant, as it gave
them more room and let in more light, and possibly allowed them to catch a
breeze and cool the house down.[141]

   In slight but important ways, then, free houses were distinct from slave
dwellings. In the all-Black town of Mitchelville, South Carolina, which was
founded while the Civil War still raged, recently enslaved individuals took
pains to craft homes that were not only more practical but reflective of their
aesthetics. The exteriors of Mitchelville's dwellings were quite different from
one another, as some residents utilized weatherboarding, while others used
board-and-batten siding or flush-board siding. Some put their money into
glass windows, while others settled on wooden shutters, perhaps painted in
the color that most suited them. Other decorative elements were also present:
some front doors even included knobs made of agateware, a type of pottery
decorated with contrasting colors of clay.[142] The Johnsons probably made similar types of improvements to their cabin, imbuing some of themselves — their
needs, tastes, desires — into where they lived.

FIGURE 5.5. "A Happy Family, Redcliffe, SC," ca. 1890. Scrapbook from the John Shaw Billings Papers, Accession no. 7108, Photo Album 3, held at South Caroliniana, University of South Carolina, Columbia.

Others believed that more opportunities were available away from the presence of those who had legally owned them. Emmaline Heard, who had been enslaved in central Georgia, recalled that her mother and father "thought they might fare better elsewhere and hired out to a plantation owner in an adjoining county."[143] Some moved within the state, some within the same county. Some established settlements and towns, imbuing them with their own ideas, identities, and names.[144] Others left for nearby urban areas, including Anson Harp, who had been enslaved on the Hammond estate and who moved to Columbia, South Carolina, almost immediately after emancipation.[145] In fact, most Black individuals and families who migrated in the late nineteenth century moved from rural to urban areas.[146] But even in these cases, migration was often impermanent. Movement was certainly frequent, and it appears to have taken place most often within the small territory known by the individual or family.[147] For many, economics limited their mobility. For most, though, proximity to family was likely a major motivator in their decisions, for with family there was more protection, more support, more stability.

While Anson Harp and others left the Hammond estate, many formerly enslaved families of Hammond's moved within or stayed put in the Silverton and Hammond townships that had formerly been Silver Bluff, Cowden, Cathwood, and Redcliffe Plantations. This included Sallie Smith, daughter of Rose and Jack Smith, who by 1870 was going by the name Sallie Wigfall.[148] Sallie had lived in the Redcliffe Yard since at least 1857 and remained there with her growing family for decades after emancipation.[149] Unlike her parents, who had seen nine children born and die in slavery, Sallie witnessed two daughters and a son survive to emancipation, and another three born after. Sallie and her husband, John Wigfall, continued their pre-emancipation work as domestic servants in the Redcliffe mansion, a position that their daughter Ella would take up by 1880. Ella, who had been born at Redcliffe, would also build her family and home there, in the same place her mother had.[150] Sallie remained in the Redcliffe Yard near Ella, though with a new husband, John Bruce, and a blended family.[151] Once again, we see three generations of one family making their homes next door to one another.

Sallie and Ella lived at Redcliffe for decades, in the process creating a place for their families to come back to. The cabins they inhabited during slavery continued to serve as their homes, and the yard continued to be a central living and laboring space. Unlike other slave quarters across the region, which dispersed across many acres into individual tenant farms, the Redcliffe Yard maintained its arrangement after emancipation.[152] An 1873 diagram of the Redcliffe Yard shows the cabin of "Sally" immediately behind the mansion (see fig. 5.4).[153] Ella's family may have lived in the adjoining room in the cabin, the other "pen" in the double-pen cabin.[154] Sallie's and Ella's children ultimately left Redcliffe, seeking out new opportunities and new places, but the Redcliffe Yard continued to be home to Black individuals and families working for the Hammonds through the mid-1970s.[155]

Most Black families after emancipation were, in fact, highly mobile, even if their movements were often within overlapping neighborhoods of the old homes. With each move, they took the physical elements of their homes — their possessions and their people—with them, each time remaking their homes in a new place. Enslavement had required this kind of adaptability; frequent forced migration, whether across thousands of miles or across a single enslaver's estate, had forced a kind of malleability, the ability to make a home when and where and with whom one could. Many would find themselves continuing to rely on this skill, creating homes in new spaces, near and far.

But for those formerly enslaved people who remained on plantations for years or even generations, like the several families residing in the Redcliffe Yard, their material culture illustrates something else: not disruption but continuity—a physical continuity of Black families and homes across slavery and freedom.[156] A nineteenth-century clear glazed porcelain vase, believed to have been part of a hope or dowry chest, speaks to a young woman's expectations about her marriage and her future. Pieces of a fragile china doll, dating to the 1860s or 1870s, documents the presence of children in the Yard. More than that, though, the doll suggests the joyful play that a child engaged in and the doting parents who would have given the child such a toy. The high number of postbellum ceramics found near the cabins suggests an increase in the size of families who lived in or visited these homes to share meals together.[157] At some point, all these meaningful objects were discarded. The vase broke, the doll fell apart, the dinnerware chipped, and they found their way into trash middens under and near the cabins. There they lay for nearly 150 years, not worthless trash but instead material reminders of the Black homemaking and family-making that took place in the Yard.

UNLIKE HIS OTHER PLANTATIONS, James Henry Hammond's Redcliffe remains to this day, its mansion and Yard open to visitors who wish to peek into the past. He would likely have been pleased to see the house and its dependencies still stark white against the green grass and trees, a monument to all he had worked to achieve and maintain: his family's stability and white supremacy. His son Harry was able to preserve his father's legacy, keeping most of the estate in family hands for a time.[158] Slavery, of course, ceased to exist legally within a year of Hammond's death, but in many ways, the essence of his mudsill theory lived on. The vitriolic racism at the root of Hammond's convictions continued, preserved in law and social norms for generations in South Carolina and beyond. While his side may have lost the war, so much of what he believed in, what he wanted to preserve through secession, remains: his fireside and the belief in white supremacy. Redcliffe's built environment was to represent the stability of Hammond's family and the institution of slavery, not that of Sallie and Ella or other enslaved families at Redcliffe.

Yet the physical remains in the Yard—whether the indications of a swept yard or the cabins that have withstood the ravages of time or the material culture that lay for nearly 150 years in the trash middens beneath and around them—tell a more complicated story. In those dwellings, in that shared space of the Yard, formerly enslaved people continued their struggle to make their homes. Two of the original white-washed cabins still stand in the Redcliffe Yard, monuments to the enduring work of Black Southerners to make homes for themselves, even as those in the nearby mansion sought to deny the possibility to them. James Henry Hammond's fixation on improving his business and proving his power continually fractured the families he enslaved, relocating them on a whim and disconnecting them from people and place. Enslavement meant a life of uncertainty and change. But houses like those in the Redcliffe Yard remain today as architectural embodiments of the families who lived within them.

We need more public memorials and monuments to the enslaved people who literally built this nation. Their histories, their lives, their contributions have rarely been recognized in stone or bronze or in monumental architecture, limiting the possibility of creating a commemorative landscape that actually grapples with the crime of slavery and the continuing crime of white supremacy.[159] Writer Clint Smith's observation after touring Thomas Jefferson's Monticello applies to dozens of historic plantation sites today: "As much as this land illuminates the contradictions of Jefferson's legacy, it also serves as a reminder of the hundreds of Black people who made a home there. Their lives are also worthy of remembrance, and commemoration."[160] Beyond erecting new memorials to commemorate and remember those individuals, we should also work to shift our perspective and understanding of the extant built environment of these places. Plantation buildings and landscapes are not just monuments to the enslavers who lived in the mansion. They are monuments to those enslaved there, those who (in far greater numbers than the white families) built, sustained, resided, and died there.[161] Re-directing focus toward the Black families who, for more than a century, made their homes at Redcliffe allows us to see how the built environment and landscape of the past and present is as much a monument to them as to the Hammonds.[162]

As much as James Henry Hammond wanted this place to be a legacy for his white family, Redcliffe has also become a legacy for the descendants of his Black "family." The very last Black family to live in the Redcliffe Yard, the Henleys, had made that place their home for four generations.[163] In May 2021, Breanna Henley, a descendant of Lucy and Anthony Henley (whom Hammond legally owned and forcibly relocated to the Redcliffe Yard in 1857), took her dental school graduation photographs in front of one of the remaining slave cabins behind the mansion. When asked why she chose this as a background, she noted the sense of immediate "attachment" and "belonging" she felt in this place.[164] Captioning a photograph of herself walking proudly with a graduation cap atop her head and a Redcliffe Yard cabin behind her (fig. 5.6), Dr. Henley wrote: "I stand tall on the soil of MY ancestors. I stand directly

doctorbreezy_ · Follow
Redcliffe Plantation State Historic Site

doctorbreezy_ I stand tall on the shoulders of my ancestors. I stand tall on the soil of MY ancestors. I stand directly where the Henley family legacy began out of sacrifice and perseverance.

It's not lost on me that in 4 days, I will be Dr. Breanna Richelle Henley as a direct result of their resilience.

I AM my ancestors' wildest dreams. ✨

📷: @becoming_dr_chew

#dentist #dentalschool #dentalstudent #blackdoctors #classof2021 #graduation #blackgirlsgraduate #tsrgradz #watchtheyardgrads #alphakappaalpha #blackx #gradszn #whitecoatblackdoctor #blackgirlmagic #melaninpoppin #melanin #slavequarters #slavehouse #ancestorswildestdreams
Edited · 67w

886 likes
MAY 11, 2021

FIGURE 5.6. Instagram post and photograph with Redcliffe Yard cabin in background, by Breanna Henley, May 11, 2021. Courtesy of Breanna Henley.

where the Henley family legacy began out of sacrifice and perseverance."[165] This was the land and the home of her people, something that while they had not legally owned was passed down to her as her legacy.

With the abolition of slavery, Black Southern families like the Henleys, the Smiths/Wigfalls, and the Johnsons seized on the opportunities to make their homes without the constraints enslavers had placed upon them. There were many obstacles to making that reality: lack of money and resources, families separated by sale and forced migration, the continual oppression and violence of white Southerners, and the simple but real anxiety of what day-to-day life would actually look like. Enslaved Southerners had struggled for generations, and that struggle would continue after emancipation. Yet with freedom came the possibility of using one's home—as white Americans long had—as a means of maintaining liberty and securing the rights that should be theirs. As the harsh realities of Jim Crow replaced the promises of Reconstruction, still Black Southerners continued their long struggle to make the homes they wanted and knew they deserved.

HOME IN FREEDOM

George Gilmore looked out the window at the snow and prayed for warmer weather, something he knew was a prerequisite if he was to begin building soon. Unlike so many times before, though, this particular construction project would be for *his* family. Born enslaved at Montpelier Plantation in 1810, he had spent more than half a century laboring—field work, saddle-making, and carpentry—for the wealth and well-being of white families and homes. As news of emancipation spread to Montpelier, though, George focused on his own family and home, quickly assembling a new residence out of the nearby ruins of a Confederate camp. But George had always known this was just temporary, and his current construction project would create something more permanent, something to give his wife and children what they deserved: a private, secure home where Gilmore roots would run deep, where they could control their domestic space, feel a sense of stability, and create a legacy for future generations.[1]

BY THE EARLY 1870s, George Gilmore had done just that. He had built a log farmhouse that stands to this day in Orange County, Virginia, across from the entrance to what is now the Montpelier Plantation historic site (fig. C.1).[2] The Gilmore Cabin, as it is known today, is one of the many material legacies of Black homemaking that endures in the contemporary Southern landscape. The descendants of Gilmore and others formerly enslaved at Montpelier have worked for decades to ensure that the history of their ancestors is preserved, including buildings like the Gilmore Cabin.[3] Indeed, the cabin's continued

FIGURE C.I. Gilmore Cabin, Montpelier, VA, built ca. early 1870s. Courtesy of
Montpelier, a National Trust Historic Site.

existence—not far from Montpelier's South Yard cabins—tells the story of
home for Black families both during and after slavery.

Black Southerners had long sought to make spaces of slavery into homes.
They actively and intentionally used the physical world around them to transform where they were forced to reside into something more. They swept yards,
hid objects in walls, preserved burial grounds, engaged in intimate activities,
and maintained their families amid the uncertainty and constraints of enslavement. But making a home on a plantation was a perennial contest that
pitted enslavers' homemaking—which they believed could be realized only
through the control and surveillance of their human property—against that
of the enslaved. Sometimes this contest set enslaved people against one another; at other times, it cemented familial or community bonds. Sometimes
it followed long and widely held traditions of homemaking; at others, it was
intimately bound up in the particularities of a time and place. On sites of

enslavement, Black Americans engaged in the struggle not only to survive but also to find meaning, and as part of that quest they continuously proclaimed and demonstrated, "this is our home."

This struggle did not end with emancipation. Formerly enslaved people sought homes unencumbered by the limitations that enslavers and Southern society had long placed upon them. They wanted homes of their own and to maintain their freedom and secure their rights, even in the face of new systems of violent oppression. Across the region, Black and white Southerners continued to clash over the appearance, function, and meaning of home. Elements of this conflict looked similar, both before and after emancipation—one of the many consequences of a deeply entrenched, racist system that not even a civil war could destroy—but freedom did alter the possibilities for Black homemaking in the postbellum South.

Black men and women vociferously argued that homemaking was a pivotal part of their continued struggle for freedom. As one Black newspaper in Louisiana argued in 1869, "Without homes, without any right in the soil, what freedom our people have, must be gradually reduced."[4] If liberty was to be preserved, homemaking had to be promoted. "The very first thing every colored man should do is to get a home," a Black newspaper in neighboring Texas asserted in 1869. That was because Black Southerners believed that with freedom, they could realize the homes they had struggled for in slavery. "What we mean by a home," the Texas newspaper continued,

> is a piece of land, large or small, with a house upon it, large or small. A place you can call your own. . . . It will be a home—a home for you and your children. It will be a place where you can rest in peace without fear of being molested or being made afraid by a hungry landlord. In the eye of the law it will be your castle, as sacred to you as the palace to a king. No man has a right to tear you from it, or to molest it. You have a right to defend it against every intruder.[5]

Home was a dwelling and the land upon which it stood, but it was also a place of privacy, domestic authority, familial roots, safety, security, and stability. Only when you had a place of your own could you fully realize these; only then could you really call yourself free.

Whether freed people stayed on the same plantations where they had been enslaved or whether they searched for homes elsewhere, they sought something of their own, even if they could not legally own it. On the South Carolina coast, newly freed people immediately commenced building "with all their heart," for "nothing has ever taken such hold of them as this hope—the first they have ever had—of having homes of their own."[6] Back in Virginia, Selina Grey boldly told her former enslaver—the family of Confederate general Robert E. Lee—that, "I am very happy that I have got a comfortable home of my own now."[7] Establishing a home of one's own, however, was neither easy nor automatic. Margrett Nillin, who had been enslaved in Texas, insisted as much, noting, "In slavery I owns nothin' and never owns nothin'. In freedom I's own de home and raise de family. All dat cause me worryment and in slavery I has no worryment." Even so, for Margarett, it was worth it: "I takes de freedom."[8]

Many Black writers, politicians, ministers, and other public figures argued that the acquisition of land was the most important aspect of homemaking for realizing emancipation's promises. Francis Ellen Watkins Harper encouraged a crowd of freedmen in Mobile, Alabama, to "get land, every one that can, and as fast as you can. A landless people must be dependent upon the landed people. A few acres to till for food and a roof, however humble, over your head, are the castle of your independence, and when you have it you are fortified to act and vote independently whenever your interests are at stake."[9] Black activists believed that the desire to own property was an American virtue that recently enslaved people (having so long been legally barred from it) needed to demonstrate.[10] Landownership was, W. E. B. Du Bois argued, the "most pressing of his problems," for land was the "absolutely fundamental and essential thing to any real emancipation of the slaves."[11]

Owning land was not enough, however. Black Americans needed homes. Activists argued that the home was a crucial site of individual and communal uplift, a place where civil rights would be fostered and defended.[12] As Senator Blanche K. Bruce, one of the nation's first Black senators, declared in 1880, "We cannot adequately conceive of American citizenship apart from American homes. . . . If we, as a people, would acquire the self-respectful, independent, conservative, resolute qualities that distinguish American citizens from all others, we must find the nursery of such qualities in American homes."[13]

Yet by the turn of the twentieth century, W. E. B. Du Bois would note that while "emancipation meant more or less of a change in home life for the freedmen," it still was "not violent change." In fact, in many free Black homes, "the change was scarcely noticeable."[14] This was in part because of new labor arrangements that replaced slavery on plantations throughout the South. These arrangements included sharecropping and convict leasing, both deeply inequitable systems that denied wages for labor and kept individuals and families in cycles of poverty and imprisonment.[15] And while each allowed for different degrees of control and freedom for laborers, in both cases, white landowners remained responsible for providing housing to Black workers. Many simply reused slave cabins with little to no improvements to the residences.[16] This was true at Patton Place, where the plantation's new owners (like those across the region) relied on Texas's system of convict leasing to fulfill their labor needs.[17] Men who had been enslaved on plantations across Brazoria County were forced—once again—to labor in the fields for no pay and live in the same dwellings they had inhabited in slavery.[18] From the perspective of many Black Southerners, post-emancipation labor and economic systems had not fundamentally changed since the era of slavery, and neither had their homes.

Just as in slavery, though, Black Southerners used the physical world—including the objects they purchased and displayed in their residences—to realize more from the places they lived. Not far from George Gilmore's cabin near Montpelier, Frank and Polly May Ellis pursued their aspirations of home, filling their Orange County, Virginia, farmhouse with furniture and domestic wares. A ceramic pitcher and washbowl suggest Polly's desire to exert domestic authority (fig. C.2). By 1880, Polly—much like Sally and Louisa Johnson in South Carolina and Rachel Patton in Texas—told census takers that her occupation was keeping her own house, fulfilling what could only have been a dream for Black women before emancipation.[19] Even in freedom, most Black women would be compelled by economic necessity to take jobs outside the home, including working in white women's houses.[20] Some Black women like Polly, who could dedicate their labor to their own homes, proudly demonstrated domestic virtues like cleanliness and refinement.[21]

Free Black women and men also persisted in pursuing greater domestic protection and privacy, declaring, "We want peaceful homes and quiet firesides; no one to disturb us or turn us out."[22] The law and the promised protection of government often failed them in this quest.[23] Yet they sustained certain home-making practices and acquired possessions meant to safeguard their spaces, such as a cowrie shell hidden in the wall of a former slave cabin at Magnolia Grove Plantation, some twenty miles northeast of Gaineswood Plantation. Constructed in the 1840s, the Magnolia Grove slave cabin is a small one-room, weather-boarded dwelling immediately behind the mansion of Isaac Croom, an enslaver who—like Nathan Whitfield and Paul Cameron—had moved enslaved families from North Carolina to Alabama in the rush to

FIGURE C.2. S. Bridgwood and Son, white and pink pitcher and washbowl owned by members of the Ellis family, ca. late nineteenth–early twentieth century. Courtesy of the Smithsonian National Museum of African American History and Culture. Gift of Clara Ellis Payne.

establish profitable cotton plantations in the fertile Black Belt (fig. C.3).[24] The cabin contains only one window, set in the north wall, looking toward the back of Croom's house; and it was near this window that an individual embedded a cowrie shell during repairs made to the dwelling.[25] An 1870s cologne bottle lodged in the wall next to the cowrie shell indicates that the objects were concealed together after emancipation.[26] Intentionally hidden near the window that looked toward the former enslaver's house, perhaps this cowrie shell, like that found at Stagville Plantation in North Carolina, was part of a homemaking tradition meant to protect Black homes and families.

But white Southerners' practices of limiting the domestic aspirations of Black plantation residents also continued. Almost immediately after emancipation, Elijah and Lucy—who had been sold in 1859—attempted to make their way back to Stagville.[27] Once they had the choice, they chose to return to the place they had called home, even if it had been a place of forced residence. Their former owners, however, did not welcome such homecoming. Writing

FIGURE C.3. Magnolia Grove slave cabin, built ca. 1840s. Photograph, December 26, 1934. Item 14 in series, "Magnolia Grove, 1002 Hobson Street, Greensboro, Hale County, AL," Historic American Buildings Survey. Courtesy of Library of Congress Prints and Photographs Division.

to his brother-in-law George Mordecai, Paul Cameron warned that Elijah "and his wife and all their children" were "on foot & without means" walking back to the Bennehan-Cameron property. Paul advised George, "You would at least do well to have an order at the plantation to prevent him taking up his quarters. My fear is that the negroes will like the cat return to their old houses & will build huts all over our lands & make a large & most unpleasant colony. At any rate we should do our upmost to guard against it."[28] Elijah and his wife wanted to return home, but Cameron denied that the roots they had created there held meaning or power. Only he would decide where Black laborers would live on what he considered his familial homeland.

White Southerners also turned to terrorism. Free Black homes represented the economic and social progress of formerly enslaved people and were therefore targets of violence. White terrorists saw Black homes not as domestic private spaces but as public battlefields for white supremacy. With the support of a broad swathe of white Southern society, these men argued that surveillance and intrusion into Black dwellings was necessary to defend white homes.[29] In their view, such action was also essential in maintaining the Southern status quo, for attacks on Black homes were meant as deterrents to Black voting. A federal order recognized as much, noting that vigilantes used "violence and intimidation, to alarm and overawe a large part of the population, and by this means affect the results of pending elections."[30] Targeting homes was thus a purposeful tactic meant to hit Black Southerners and their white allies in particularly vulnerable places.[31] In Smith County, Texas, Klansmen attacked and robbed the homes of the area's freed people nearly every night for months.[32] Similar violence hit Black homes and neighborhoods across the South, including in Raleigh, North Carolina, where Black citizens were left feeling "perfectly terror stricken, afraid to lisp a word or leave their cabins, & may have not had a quiet nights rest for weeks."[33]

Black Southerners had hoped that with freedom, their homes would no longer be subject to unwanted surveillance and intrusion, that their lives would be free from targeted racial violence, and that their rights would be secured and upheld. But the promises of emancipation failed them. By displaying continued control over Black spaces and bodies in freedom, white Southerners preserved the racialized, gendered, and classed system from which they derived their power. The belief that home was a privilege reserved for white Americans, one that should be defended with violence and cruelty, continued after abolition. As W. E. B. Du Bois deftly put it, "the Big House and the slave quarters remained" long after slavery was dead.[34] This racialized ideology of home shaped US laws, US banks, and US cities.[35] Contests over segregation, equitable access to home ownership, and surveillance of Black houses and bodies were fundamental issues at the center of the twentieth-century's long Civil Rights Movement.[36] And they remain unsolved problems in the nation today.[37] Who gets to make this place their home remains a perennial struggle.

Clearly, this history is not in the past. The violence, pain, and trauma of slavery still haunt the South, leaving what Jessica Adams has called "scars" on the landscape.[38] But so, too, have Black love, Black perseverance, Black joy, Black family-making, and Black homemaking left marks. Today across the South—in the houses, in the ground, in the family histories, in our memories—stand testaments to Black Americans' steadfast efforts to make meaning of their lives amid a torrent of ruthless obstacles. Dedicated staff and volunteers of historic plantation sites across the region are working tirelessly to tell the complicated, difficult, real history of these places.[39]

Indispensable to this historical reframing are the individuals whose ancestors were enslaved on these plantations, including the great-granddaughter of

George Gilmore. At the turn of the twenty-first century, as The Montpelier Foundation worked to raise millions of dollars to restore James Madison's mansion, Rebecca Gilmore Coleman asked the simple question: Why not preserve Black homes, too? Descendants like Coleman made clear the necessity of this work and convinced Montpelier to conserve the Gilmore Cabin and incorporate it into a Montpelier tour.[40] Coleman's work preserved a legacy of Black homemaking in the plantation landscape. Coleman's work, like that of her ancestors, kept a Black home safe, rooted in the land of her people, a stable force for future generations. This is their home.

Appendix

WHY, WHAT, AND HOW

A NOTE ON MATERIAL CULTURE THEORY, SOURCES, AND METHOD

What intellect restores to us under the name of the past, is not the past. In reality, as soon as each hour of one's life has died, it embodies itself in some material object, as do the souls of the dead in certain folk-stories, and hides there. There it remains captive, captive forever, unless we should happen upon the object, recognise what lies within, call it by its name, and so set it free.
—Marcel Proust, *Contre Sainte-Beuve*, ca. 1895–1900

IN THE SUMMER OF 2012, I spent four sweltering weeks rummaging through privately owned antebellum mansions in Mississippi and Louisiana. That month changed my scholarly identity. Our team of four field researchers for the Decorative Arts of the Gulf South found, described, cataloged, and photographed material culture of the Old South, items like furniture, ceramics, carpets, tools, and clothing.[1] My three colleagues—Lydia Blackmore, Caryne Eskridge, and Maria Shevzov—expertly identified the materials, style, and quality of objects using their decorative arts training, or "connoisseurship." This skill was not one I was acquainted with, having just finished the first year of a conventional history PhD program. But the many hours spent in dining rooms and bedrooms, attics and basements, provided a crash course in analyzing material culture that expanded my historical skill set and allowed me ample opportunities to perform my role as historian. My task was first and foremost to put all the things we found into context. Doing so included recognizing the presence of enslaved people in these homes and acknowledging the fact that slavery suffused every inch of them, even if their white owners rarely mentioned it. Efforts to contextualize slavery seemed doubly necessary as we toured historic plantations along the Mississippi River. At these sites, slavery was rarely alluded to; enslaved individuals, although they made up the majority of residents on these large plantations, were virtually absent from the interpretive programming.[2] In the rare moments when a tour guide mentioned enslaved people, it was only as laborers, whether in the mansion, in the fields, in the kitchen, in the blacksmith shop, or even in slave cabins. Most of those cabins were either gone from the landscape or retrofitted into gift shops, in contrast to the white home that remained standing in its antebellum glory. The tours presented a racialized dichotomy: labor was Black, home was white. Yet for enslaved laborers, the historical reality was different. These spaces were theirs, too. Home was Black as well as white. This book is my attempt to understand why, despite this fact, we nevertheless grant enslavers the right to have homes on plantations yet rarely do so for the enslaved people who lived there, too.

That summer of researching artifacts and touring the Southern landscape demonstrated the power and possibilities of material culture to me. Scholars of slavery have long been vexed by the limitations of the archive, namely, the seeming lack of sources that truthfully represent the enslaved perspective.[3] But when we reconsider what constitutes the archive itself—not just textual sources held in libraries, historical societies, or government buildings but material culture, as well—we open new source bases to explore and interpret. Material culture offers theories, source bases, and methodologies that center the tangible in humanistic investigations and interpretations.[4] It is particularly valuable when exploring people, places, and cultures with sparse written evidence, and it can also be incredibly useful in corroborating, challenging, or complicating other forms of primary sources.[5]

Central to material culture theory is the assertion that the material world reveals much: it can tell us about individuals, relationships, communities, beliefs, values, and institutions. Sometimes objects, buildings, and landscapes are powerful because they are representative, acting as physical evidence of some widely held idea or experience. Other times they are significant because they are remarkable, functioning as unique proof of exceptional moments or people. Material culture therefore illuminates both the personal and the social, displaying "outward signs and symbols of particular ideas in the mind" as well as "mirror[ing] a society's values as accurately as its great monuments."[6] But artifacts and the built environment are not simply reflections; they create who we are.[7] Objects, notes architectural historian Dell Upton, "are part of the symbolic process that continually recreates the world by imposing meaning and order on it."[8] Material culture, therefore, suggests that the physical remains of the past can help us better understand the people in it, their actions and beliefs, and how they made meaning of their world.

Material culture is both an approach to the past and the evidence used to analyze it. The "stuff" of material culture is anything made, modified, used, or consumed by humans. This stuff can be found anywhere and everywhere, from manmade objects like a spoon to landscapes modified by humans like a burial ground. Unfortunately, we do not have nearly as many surviving buildings, well-preserved objects, or maintained landscapes relating to enslaved Black Americans as we have of elite white families. For communities that have been oppressed or marginalized, so much of the material past has been lost because their history has for so long been seen as unworthy of preservation by white-dominated historical associations and museums.[9] Yet archaeologists are constantly unearthing artifacts of the enslaved; more curators are exhibiting objects long held in storage; families of African descent are finding and donating boxes and boxes of forgotten heirlooms.[10] Exploring the lives of enslaved people through material culture requires also delving into an array of textual and visual sources that further illuminate the material world: archaeology reports, museum catalogs, paintings, blueprints, field sketches, family stories, and oral histories. Together, these many items constitute assemblages, or networks, of various evidentiary forms that support or even reveal new interpretations of the past.[11]

Through these additional archives and approaches, historians' source base—and thus understanding of the past—can expand. Despite tour guides who focused on the stories of elite white families, the homes I visited in 2012 actually contained ample material evidence of enslaved people's lives and homes: the punkah fan found in the attic of Green Leaves in Natchez; the ladder-back slave-made chairs discovered in the basement of Richmond Plantation, outside the Bluff City; the ramshackle sharecropper cabin (and likely former slave dwelling) seen standing alone amid acres of open fields in St. Francisville. It just took embracing material culture studies, along with patience, time, curiosity, dedication, and listening to archaeologists, public historians, local historians, and descendants, to see it.[12]

While many historians now recognize the legitimacy of utilizing objects as sources, some continue to push back against what material culture scholars actually do: speculate about what the physical remains of the past meant and represented then, and what they now demonstrate to us about individuals and communities.[13] It is that word—speculate—that raises concern. Some fear that speculation is purely subjective and thus a careless humanistic endeavor.

But speculation is legitimate and essential to historical research and writing, especially for people historically marginalized in or excluded from traditional archives.[14] And speculation is just one of the many skills and steps of material culture methodologies that rely upon rigorous research.

So how do you actually do material culture? No single process is codified as *the* material culture method, yet my survey of foundational and recent works from a range of practitioners across disciplines reveals five commonly shared steps: observation, description, deduction, speculation, and contextualization.[15] The goal is to take each step in order, allowing for interpretation to develop from the object itself rather than from your assumptions about them.[16] Much like with a text, the analytical process therefore goes from what is obvious to what is not: it starts with seeing what is in front of you (the object's basic physical characteristics) to contemplating what it can tell you about the past (the potential meanings of the object).

Following this process begins by observing and inspecting the object from all possible angles, from different distances, in every nook and cranny. Then you describe what you see; that is, describe only the object's physicality. Let's take, for example, the Stagville walking stick: *a long, thin piece of solid wood with a carved spiral down its body and one end slightly thicker and rounder than the other.* (See fig. 2.1.) In these early stages, you must not jump to conclusions about what the thing is or does or means. You then engage in deduction, a process wherein you interact and respond to the object with your intellect (e.g., How is it used? How does the object interact with human bodies? How is it oriented?), with your senses (e.g., How do your senses of sight, touch, smell, taste, and sound react or engage with the object?), and with your emotions (e.g., What emotions does the object evoke for you, and what precisely about the materiality of the object brings those feelings out?). *The piece of wood looks like a staff or cane (in its length, width, and form), and a human hand would hold the thicker, rounded end, while the flatter end would hit the ground upon walking. It is smooth to the touch and almost shiny with a rich brown color, suggesting extensive time taken to peel or polish it. For me, the object conveys feelings of relief, support, and assistance, of the artifact being used to help someone.* The last of these deductions is likely the most unusual for scholars: one's emotional response is the opposite of objectivity; it is pure subjectivity. But in recognizing and articulating your own personal response to the object, you can confront and challenge that subjectivity by contemplating its meaning for people different from yourself, for those who lived in the past. *Perhaps the walking stick did more than just assist someone in walking.*

After focusing on the materiality of the object—including what you as a viewer perceive and how you respond to it—you move on to consider the artifact as historical evidence through the steps of contextualization and speculation. Objects rarely communicate their significance outright; you have to ask questions about its meaning and use for people in the past. Additionally, as an object's meaning changes over time and from person-to-person, you must put it in its multiple layers of context to grapple with its value for individuals, groups, and cultures.[17] Once again, start with the object first. Compile the object's biography, even if you cannot answer all the questions yet: who made it, where and when, was it passed down or sold or thrown away, where was it later discovered, and by whom? *I don't have documentation of who made the stick, when, and exactly where, but I know it was concealed inside the wall of the Bennehan house, where it was discovered in the late twentieth century by Stagville staff.* Then seek to understand the object in the context of other objects like it, assembling a supporting cast of similar artifacts that will give you even more material with which to work. These choices should be made thoughtfully. The goal is to find objects of similar, though often not identical, contexts. *Canes made by Southerners before the twentieth century provide comparisons for the Stagville example.*

Much as an archaeological dig investigates and records artifacts, soil stratum, faunal elements, and horizon, material culture scholars dig into additional historical evidence to establish the political, economic, and social contexts within which the object existed, was used, and was given meaning.[18] Contextualization therefore requires extensive research to provide the supporting evidence (material, visual, and textual) with which to reasonably speculate what the object might have signified to the various people who made, used, interacted with, destroyed, or discarded the object. *Based on research into Black artisans and cane-making, into common symbols and signs used within African diasporic craftsmanship, into building practices on Southern plantations, and into other archaeological evidence and the interpretation of "wall finds," I hypothesize that the stick was made by an enslaved man who intentionally carved a spiral to mimic a snake. Then he or another enslaved man later placed it in the Bennehan house as it was being constructed in 1799, likely for the purpose of using the cane for conjuration.*

Speculation involves not only creative thinking but corroborating evidence: open yourself to multiple possibilities, but always test those hypotheses. *It is possible, for instance, that the cane was simply lost or forgotten behind a wall. Yet based on research into building practices, a worker would have clearly seen the stick as the walls were erected and plastered, suggesting that the cane was placed and left there intentionally.* As art historian Jules David Prown rightly notes, "It is impossible to respond to and interpret the object in exactly the same way as did the fabricating society," and no historical interpretation can claim absolute, complete precision.[19] I, like other material culture scholars, do not attempt to hide from the multiplicity of meanings but instead signal various levels of possibility with words such as "perhaps" or "likely." This acknowledgment is not prevarication; rather, it is approaching the past (and our attempts to pull meaning out of it) with caution, care, and rigor.

By uncovering the significance and function of the objects and environments created and used by people in the past, historians can uncover something about those people as well as about the relationships between those people and the society in which they lived. The process of unearthing and analyzing the physical remains of slavery is not confined to the academy. In fact, some of the most exciting work is happening at historic plantation sites, more of which are overturning the mythological, racialized history I often encountered a decade ago.[20] Academic historians, historic site staff and volunteers, archaeologists, activists, and descendants are working together to present a fuller story of slavery to the public. Artifacts do not speak on their own, but material culture methodology and sources allow us to discover and present a more honest history, one rooted in the material conditions of everyday life. I hope more historians—academic, public, local, and family—will pursue these truths, will seek (as Marcel Proust so eloquently stated more than a century ago) to find what lies within and set it free. Doing so will help us reimagine the past and how it is presented today. It will allow us to see that millions of enslaved Americans not only labored on plantations but also declared through their objects, built environments, and domestic practices—through their material culture—that these plantations were home.

NOTES

Abbreviations

BCC   Brazoria County Court, Angleton, TX

CFP   Cameron Family Papers #133, Southern Historical Collection, Wilson Library, University of North Carolina at Chapel Hill

FWP-WPA   Federal Writer's Project, Work Projects Administration

JHHP, LC   James Henry Hammond Papers, Library of Congress, microfilm

JHHP, SCL   James Henry Hammond Papers, South Caroliniana Library, University of South Carolina, microfilm, *Records of the Ante-bellum Southern Plantations from the Revolution through the Civil War Series A, Part I*

MAD-MF, JMM   Montpelier Archaeology Department, The Montpelier Foundation, James Madison's Montpelier, Orange County, VA

NMAAHC   National Museum of African American History and Culture, Washington, DC

NRHP   National Register of Historic Places and National Historic Landmarks Program Records, Record Group 79: Records of the National Park Service, National Archives and Records Administration, College Park, MD

RPSHS   Redcliffe Plantation State Historic Site, Beech Island, SC

SHC   Southern Historical Collection, Wilson Library, University of North Carolina

SSHS   Stagville State Historic Site, Durham, NC

V-HP   Varner-Hogg Plantation State Historic Site, West Columbia, TX

WFP   Whitfield Family Papers, Auburn University Special Collections and Archives, Auburn, AL

Note on Terminology

1. Holden, "'I Was Born a Slave.'"

2. Harris, "Names, Terms, and Politics."

3. Bauer and Ellis, "Indigenous, Native American, or American Indian?"; Mitchell, "Black and African American"; W. Stewart, "White/white."

4. C. Stewart, *Long Past Slavery*, quotes from 5–7. See also Tilton, "Race and Place."

Introduction

1. Vignettes based on primary sources open the introduction, the five chapters, and the conclusion and are boldfaced to differentiate them from the text that follows. Sources for this vignette include a letter from Henry Bram et al. to the President of these United States, October 28, 1865, in Hahn et al., *Land and Labor, 1865*, 442–44. Though the petition appears to be in Bram's handwriting, each committee member signed his own name. In his seminal work on plantation architecture and landscapes, John Michael

Vlach described the perspective of these letter writers as "a decidedly African-American view of land tenure," which is a "rooted in a firm sense of place . . . they wanted land that was familiar to them, plantation land with which they had developed a personal bond." Vlach, *Back of the Big House*, x. For more on enslaved people's complex conceptions of property and ownership, see Penningroth, *Claims of Kinfolk*. For more on the history of Black placemaking on Edisto Island, see Elliott, "Legacies of Place."

2. Plantations were, of course, only one of many sites of enslavement across the South. Slavery could as easily be found in crowded seaports, in frontier towns, and on secluded yeoman farms. But visions of sprawling Southern plantations, with their sometimes large and spectacular mansions, are what most people conjure when they think about American slavery, and for good reason. As Jessica Adams has argued, plantations were the "epicenter and emblem of slavery in the Americas and a primal scene in the emergence of the United States." Adams, *Wounds of Returning*, 4. While the oft-cited statistic that only 25 percent of white households in 1860 owned slaves is true, as is the similarly repeated fact that most (approximately 75 percent) of those households enslaved fewer than five individuals, we must look at the past not only from the white perspective. From the outlook of enslaved people, the plantation—whether a smaller site of some twenty laborers or one of the massive estates with hundreds of enslaved residents—was the more common experience. In other words, a great number of the four million people enslaved in the United States at the outset of the Civil War had lived and labored on the kinds of plantations that tourists still visit today. Boles, *Black Southerners, 1619–1869*, 75, 113. John Michael Vlach estimates that some 5,000 of the more than 46,000 plantations in the United States in 1860 exhibited the abundant land, architectural grandeur, and careful landscaping design that we associate with plantations today. Vlach, *Planter's Prospect*, 5.

3. These historical explanations can be traced across the twentieth century to the work of influential scholars including U. B. Phillips, Stanley Elkins, E. Franklin Frazier, Kenneth Stampp, Eugene D. Genovese, John W. Blassingame, and Walter Johnson.

4. When we focus only on resistance and not on the violent and oppressive conditions that necessitated that resistance, for instance, we are left with only part of the story, for as historian Jennifer Morgan notes, "in the vacuum of perpetual resistance, there is no pain, no suffering, no wounds." Morgan, *Laboring Women*, 167.

5. V. Brown, "Social Death and Political Life," 1246, 1248.

6. They were also, of course, Native homes. Colonization and displacement shaped the possibility (and impossibility) of home for all nonwhite Southerners, though in different ways. These processes, enacted through the violence of individuals and governments, forced Indigenous people from their ancestral homes in the South, unwillingly transported Black individuals and families from their homes in the Upper South to unknown lands in the Deep South, and made possible the establishment of new homes for white Americans. Scholars have shown how deeply intertwined the histories of colonization, slavery, and forced migration are in this nation's history. See, for instance, Rothman, *Slave Country*; Guyatt, "'Outskirts of Our Happiness'"; W. Warren, *New England Bound*; and Saunt, *Unworthy Republic*. Alaina Roberts's recent work has shown how these intertwined processes continued even after the Civil War, shaping the struggle for Black freedom after the abolition of slavery. Roberts, *I've Been Here All the While*.

7. Gallagher and Nolan, *Myth of the Lost Cause*. The Lost Cause took root in the Southern landscape most notably in Confederate monuments erected by ladies' and veterans' associations. See Mills and Simpson, *Lost Cause*.

8. Eichstedt and Small, *Representations of Slavery.*

9. Antislavery activists, both Black and white, often depicted plantation slave dwellings as cramped, unclean, and dilapidated spaces that could never provide the comfort, security, and virtue of ideal homes. Theodore Dwight Weld's *Slavery as It Is,* for instance, contained a large chart—titled "DWELLINGS. THE SLAVES ARE WRETCHEDLY SHELTERED AND LODGED"—with twelve different descriptions of the horrid living conditions of enslaved people throughout the South. Weld, *Slavery as It Is,* 43–44.

10. For more on the racialization of home in the antebellum South, see Stewart, "Racialized Politics of Home."

11. Dedicated descendants and public historians have for decades pushed for more nuanced, complicated narratives of plantation life that center enslaved people. The Montpelier Descendants Committee is a prime example of the power that descendants can and should have at historic plantation sites. Over the past several years, public historians have become more vocal in advocating for this kind of reinterpretation. One of the best guides on how to actually bring about such change is the American Association for State and Local History's Interpreting History Series.

12. As Thavolia Glymph notes, "It is only by looking at the two," both Black and white plantation residents, "separate and together . . . that we can begin to understand what the sources tell us." Glymph, *Out of the House of Bondage,* 17.

13. For more on ideas and physical manifestations of home, particularly the philosophic underpinnings of both, see Barrie, *House and Home.*

14. I am using theories of place and placemaking to define home. Geographer Yi-Fu Tuan argues that the difference between space and place lies in the meaning that humans physically embed in or symbolically attach to a location, with space having none or little and place being contingent upon it. In other words, humans make meaning out of space (an area devoid of meaning) by creating place (an area defined by a human's connection to it). Tuan, *Space and Place.*

15. I describe homemaking practices similarly to what philosopher Mariana Ortega calls "hometactics," strategies that help in "the production of a sense of familiarity in midst of an environment or world in which one cannot fully belong." Ortega, *In-Between,* 203.

16. For a broad overview of the nineteenth-century ideal of home and how it shaped many different Americans' lives, see Richter, *At Home in Nineteenth-Century America.*

17. See the articles included in the AHR Roundtable: Unsettling Domesticities: New Histories of Home in Global Contexts, featured in *American Historical Review* 124, no. 4 (October 2019), esp. Sklar, "Reconsidering Domesticity." As Abigail McGowan has shown, material culture can help us bridge the divide between ideal and reality when it comes to domesticity and homelife, including for those who, because of their race, class, or status, were barred from truly attaining the ideals at the center of nineteenth-century domestic literature. McGowan, "Materials of Home."

18. The number of manuals, poems, short stories, novels, drawings, magazine articles, speeches, sermons, and other cultural products focused on home is astounding. At the American Antiquarian Society in Worcester, Massachusetts, one of the most complete archives of printed materials from the era, the number of texts is overwhelming, offering thousands of relevant search results from their holdings alone.

19. Lasch, *Haven in a Heartless World.* These expectations were not stagnant, as they shifted over the nineteenth century. See, for example, Grier, *Culture and Comfort.*

20. The scholarship on changing domestic ideals and growing "separate spheres" in the long nineteenth century is extensive and includes Welter, "Cult of True Womanhood"; Cott, *Bonds of Womanhood*; Boydston, *Home and Work*.

21. The texts of architect and landscape designer Andrew Jackson Downing were particularly influential in spreading the belief that the physical form of a home revealed much about the morality and character of its inhabitants. See Twombly, *Andrew Jackson Downing*.

22. A. Kaplan, "Manifest Domesticity."

23. For enslaved people, abuse and cruelty could come from all corners, as domestic violence on plantations was not confined to the master-slave relationship. As Christopher Morris has shown, enslaved individuals had to contend with physical abuse within their own families as well as that imposed upon them as part of the enslaver's "family, black and white." Their own domestic spaces were thus open to multiple types of violence, further reinforcing the lack of bodily autonomy and safety within them. Morris, "Within the Slave Cabin."

24. Glymph, *Women's Fight*, 14.

25. As Orlando Patterson maintains, "The slave was utterly kinless, which is to say, homeless." Because of this lack of kin and home, Patterson goes on to say, enslavers had "absolute powers of life and death over her or him." Patterson, "Slavery, Alienation, and the Female Discovery of Personal Freedom," 163–64. Saidiya Hartman has likewise declared, "The slave is always the stranger who resides in one place and belongs to another. The slave is always the one missing from home." Hartman, *Lose Your Mother*, 87. Thavolia Glymph has likewise argued that it was not until emancipation that Black Americans could begin to seek home. Glymph, *Out of the House of Bondage*, 1–2.

26. W. Brown, *Narrative of William W. Brown*, 52; C. Ball, *Fifty Years in Chains*, 402. Other formerly enslaved people focused on poor material conditions of enslaved housing; Josiah Henson, for one, called slave quarters "wretched hovels." Henson, *Uncle Tom's Story of His Life*, 23. As archaeologist Charles E. Orser Jr., argues, "slaves remembered their cabins for what they were: primitive shelters for use at the end of a long work day." Orser, *Material Basis of the Postbellum Tenant Plantation*, 15. To be fair, even the writings of former slaves, many of whom were antislavery activists, are imbued with the nineteenth-century ideal of home (a means of appealing to their mostly white, middle-class audiences). See E. Ball, *To Live an Antislavery Life*.

27. Elizabeth Fox-Genovese, for instance, refuses to use the term because home, as she describes it, "is a modern and ideologically charged term." From her perspective, home elicits a bourgeois space separate from production, while she understands the plantation household to be a unit of production. Fox-Genovese, *Within the Plantation Household*, 31. Other historians of slavery have been equally wary. In ways similar to Fox-Genovese, Thavolia Glymph contends that the constant, coerced violence and labor of the plantation household made it a site of production rather than a home; it was public and political, rather than private and domestic. Glymph, *Out of the House of Bondage*, esp. the introduction. This is not to say that historians have not referred to slave quarters and cabins as home. The tendency is fairly common; but within these studies, the idea and reality of an enslaved person's "home" has rarely been deeply interrogated or analyzed. Archaeologists have been more open to considering slave or later free Black domestic spaces as home, and especially influential in this (and for my own work) is McDaniel,

Hearth and Home. It should also be noted that this does not take into account other types of writing, especially autobiography and fiction, in which home plays a critical role, including in the work of twentieth-century Black writers like Maya Angelou, Toni Morrison, Ralph Ellison, and others. See Prince, *Burnin' Down the House.*

28. This includes those investigating the intersection of slavery and capitalism, including Baptist, *Half Has Never Been Told*; Beckert, *Empire of Cotton*; W. Johnson, *River of Dark Dreams.* Many of these scholars have pushed against the 1990s attention to agency in slavery studies, thus swinging the pendulum to stress both the micro- and macro-oppressions of the peculiar institution. Walter Johnson most overtly discusses this in his 2003 article, "On Agency," but four years earlier Deborah Gray White explored this issue in the second edition of her seminal book. See W. Johnson, "On Agency"; D. White, "Revisiting *Ar'n't I a Woman*," in *Ar'n't I a Woman*, 1–12. As Jim Downs notes, "Historians of slavery and capitalism—which has emerged as a leading theme in the field as of late—potentially risk reproducing the logic of slaveholders by emphasizing economics, even when their aim is to restore humanity to enslaved people and to demonstrate their contribution to the broader economy." Jim Downs, "When the Present Is Past," in Berry and Harris, *Sexuality and Slavery*, 190.

29. Berlin and Morgan, "Introduction," in *Cultivation and Culture*, 1–2.

30. Wood, "Slave Labor Camps." Edward Baptist also insists on calling plantations "labor camps." Baptist, *Half Has Never Been Told.* A plantation has been traditionally defined by the size of the estate and labor on it, including the use of "considerable" slave labor and a clear division of labor and management. See Hilliard, "Plantations and the Molding of the Southern Landscape."

31. T. Jones, *Experience and Personal Narrative of Uncle Tom Jones*, 23. Italics original.

32. hooks, "Homeplace," 47.

33. Douglass, *My Bondage and My Freedom*, 429. Over the past fifty years, historians have clearly demonstrated how fundamental family was to enslaved people's daily lives, to their survival, and to their understandings of freedom. For works within the North American/US context, see Gutman, *Black Family in Slavery and Freedom*; J. Jones, *Labor of Love, Labor of Sorrow*; Malone, *Sweet Chariot*; Stevenson, *Life in Black and White*; Berlin and Rowland, *Families and Freedom*; Schwartz, *Born in Bondage*; Dunaway, *African-American Family in Slavery and Emancipation*; and H. Williams, *Help Me to Find My People.* More recently, scholars have shown how enslaved people's conception of family was far more varied and expansive than the traditionally defined nuclear family. See Hunter, *Bound in Wedlock*; J. Johnson, *Wicked Flesh*; and J. Morgan, *Reckoning with Slavery.* This is particularly important when exploring the wide range of enslaving that took place on the continent, including Native slavery. See J. Brooks, *Captives and Cousins.*

34. T. Jones, *Experience and Personal Narrative of Uncle Tom Jones*, 23.

35. For one of the earliest and most influential iterations of this, see A. Davis, "Reflections on the Black Woman's Role." The ability to comprehend how people in the past, like the present, are able to experience and hold such conflicting sensations characterizes much of the path-breaking work of Black feminist scholars from multiple disciplines, including but certainly not limited to Angela Davis, bell hooks, Patricia Hill Collins, Kimberlé Crenshaw, Katherine McKittrick, Stephanie Camp, Daina Ramey Berry, Leslie M. Harris, Jessica Johnson, and Jennifer Morgan.

36. Scholars have discussed the important differences between labor performed for

enslavers and that performed for self and community, yet homemaking is rarely considered as a part of that labor. For Berlin and Morgan, for instance, "The work of slaves divides into that done for the master and that done for themselves. Slave societies thus involved two interrelated and overlapping economies." Homemaking labor, on the other hand, suggests that meaningful work could be performed without a direct connection to any form of "economy." Berlin and Morgan, "Introduction," in *Cultivation and Culture*, 2.

37. While the term homemaking has deeply gendered connotations, it was practiced by all people. There is a clear reason why it would be associated with women, for historians have demonstrated how the domestic became a gendered female idea and space in nineteenth-century America, and how home likewise determined women's identities and lived experiences, including the gendered expectation that men and women would exist in "separate spheres." Yet if we think about homemaking in a more expansive way—not only as the domestic practices commonly associated with women's work—it becomes clear that men, just like women, actively participated in making a home. See McGowan, "Materials of Home."

38. I am certainly not the first nor the only scholar who argues that plantations were more than worksites. More recently scholars from various disciplines have been rethinking how to categorize and narrate the plantation. In 2019 the McNeil Center for Early American Studies at the University of Pennsylvania convened a symposium, Investigating Mid-Atlantic Plantations: Slavery, Economies, and Space, that featured new ways of viewing the plantation, including highlighting the role and place of home. See also Holmes, "Within the House of Bondage."

39. As historians like Stephanie Jones-Rogers have shown, enslavers' mansions, slave cabins, and the broader plantation landscape were all integral sites of the slave trade and market. Jones-Rogers, *They Were Her Property*, esp. chap. 4.

40. Some of the seminal surveys of American homes and housing reiterated for scholars that only certain types of housing could equal a home. Gwendolyn Wright, *Building the Dream*; Foy and Schlereth, *American Home Life, 1880–1930*; Thompson, *American Home*.

41. Architectural historian Jobie Hill has cataloged a dozen common slave housing types found in the twentieth-century photographic collection of the Historic American Buildings Survey, which points to the wide range of building styles possible for slave dwellings. Hill, "Humanizing HABS," 58–60.

42. Memoirs and interviews of formerly enslaved people show this. When forced to work in the main house, Peter Bruner "had to sleep on the floor and have nothing but a few ragged quilts." Many enslaved women and men like Bruner who worked in the "Big House" were required to sleep near their owners, sometimes in a nearby room or, in the case of Louis Hughes, on the dining room floor. Edgar Bendy told a WPA interviewer, "I didn't have no house of my own, 'cause de marster, he give me de room in he house." Bruner, *A Slave's Adventures toward Freedom*, 13; Hughes, *Thirty Years a Slave*, 24; Edgar Bendy, in FWP-WPA, *Slave Narratives*, vol. 16, pt. 1, 66.

43. Based on excavations in South Carolina, archaeologist Leland Ferguson maintains that since slave dwellings were very small, most domestic activities took place outside these structures. Ferguson, *Uncommon Ground*, 68.

44. Home, in this case, may signify an enslaved person's connection to what Anthony Kaye refers to as the slave "neighborhood," a union of people, activities, and spaces that enslaved residents conceived. Kaye, *Joining Places*, esp. 4–12.

45. Battle-Baptiste, *Black Feminist Archaeology*, 94. Grey Gundaker likewise argues for the integration of more than physical dwellings to the study of the material and spatial elements of home for Black Americans. Grey Gundaker, "Home Ground," in *Keep Your Head to the Sky*, 14.

46. New work employing material culture sources and methodology in studies of Blackness, Indigeneity, enslavement, colonialism, and other oppressive contexts shows just how fruitful this can be. See, for example, contributions to the continuing series Enslavement and Its Legacies in *Winterthur Portfolio*.

47. Camp, *Closer to Freedom*, 94. Camp's path-breaking work, both in book and article form, has been essential to my evolution as a scholar and the development of this book. Within *Closer to Freedom*, Camp builds on work by architectural historians and archaeologists, though the questions animating her scholarship tended to apply less to the actual built environment and more to how the constraints of that built environment confined and opened up enslaved women's lives. Yet her interdisciplinary approach encouraged me to explore the material and spatial realities of the plantation as well as the ways that these spaces can tell us much about the constant struggle between enslaver and enslaved that made them.

48. Saidiya Hartman calls this imbalance and inadequacy "the slipperiness and elusiveness of slavery's archive." Hartman, *Lose Your Mother*, 17.

49. Michel-Rolph Trouillot describes the "cycle of silences," wherein silences emerge at four points in historical production: the creation of sources, archives, narratives, and history. Trouillot, *Silencing the Past*, 26. Others have questioned whether the use of the term "silence" is adequate to convey the destruction, intentional obfuscation, and concealment that has been so commonplace in archives across time and space. See Moss and Thomas, *Archival Silences*. For more on the violence of the archive, see the articles in the October 2016 special issue of *History of the Present* 6, no. 2.

50. As Maria R. Montalvo contends, enslavers intentionally crafted the archive of slavery—in particular the legal archive—for their own benefit, acting as historians and archivists in their own rights. Too often we simply replicate what they desired us to. Montalvo, *Enslaved Archives*.

51. Miles, *All That She Carried*, 300; Hartman, "Venus in Two Acts," 12; Fuentes, *Dispossessed Lives*, 7. Italics original.

52. Tiya Miles likewise argues for the inclusion of more and different kinds of sources in the study of slavery. Miles, *All That She Carried*, 291–304. Rather than focus on material sources as broadening and expanding the archive of the African Diaspora, Jenny Sharpe encourages us to also explore the immaterial, in particular "the intangible quality of affects, dreams, spirits, and visions that art and literature introduce into material archives." J. Sharpe, *Immaterial Archives*, 3.

53. Scholars including Dell Upton, Rhys Isaac, Bernard L. Herman, Edward A. Chappell, Larry McKee, and Clifton Ellis have shown how enslavers sought to reaffirm their status, wealth, control, and power by altering the built environment. However, as Upton, Terrance W. Epperson, and Rebecca Ginsburg have demonstrated, enslaved individuals read the landscape differently, which allowed them to imbue it with their own meaning. The work of Leland Ferguson, Theresa A. Singleton, Patricia Samford, and others reveals that enslaved people found moments and spaces of their own to assert authority over their lives. At the same time, architectural and material culture

scholars such as Louis Nelson and Paul Farnsworth document the very real oppression and violence that shaped enslaved people's lives and physical world. Upton, *Holy Things and Profane*; Isaac, *Transformation of Virginia*; Herman, "Embedded Landscapes"; Edward A. Chappell, "Housing Slavery," in Carson and Lounsbury, *Chesapeake House*, 156–78; McKee, "Ideals and Realities"; Clifton Ellis, "Building for 'Our Family, Black and White,'" in Ellis and Ginsburg, *Cabin, Quarter, Plantation*, 141–55; Upton, "White and Black Landscapes"; Epperson, "Constructing Difference"; Ginsburg, "Escaping through a Black Landscape," in Ellis and Ginsburg, *Cabin, Quarter, Plantation*, 51–66; Ferguson, *Uncommon Ground*; Singleton, "Archaeology of Slave Life"; Samford, "Archaeology of African-American Slavery"; Nelson, "Architectures of Black Identity"; and Farnsworth, "Brutality or Benevolence in Plantation Archaeology."

54. Historians have been debating the objective, or not, nature of our discipline for decades, yet professional training still relies almost exclusively on texts as evidence. This dissuades historians from either seeking new source material or approaching old ones in new, experimental ways. As Jim Downs declares, "The efforts to scienticize history have discouraged interpretation and a healthy discourse of disagreement by deferring to empiricism. This does not mean that they should abandon the time-honored tradition of evidence, but they ought to rethink the use of evidence—not as a tool that could be counted and quantified and then added to a footnote but rather as an artifact that requires a closer inspection, a deeper meditation, with the hope that the document can generate more questions, introduce new perspectives, and open new paths of inquiry." Downs, "When the Present Is Past," 200.

55. Some of these plantations are studied in tandem with the broader estates owned by enslaving Southerners. I chose these plantations based on certain criteria: they had to be currently open to the public, maintain extant slave-era buildings, retain records of archaeological work performed on site, and have archival material related to the site or families on it during slavery.

56. I understand and share the concern about micro-history and the tendency to extrapolate wildly with findings at, for example, a specific plantation site. The work of archaeologists like Douglas Armstrong makes clear the faultiness of arguing that one site can stand in for the full variability of life for enslaved people. Beyond the clear contribution to historical knowledge of these particular sites, though, this kind of approach can still reveal connections across time and space, drawn out through comparative examples and reinforced through the use of cultural sources like memoirs, interviews, and oral histories. Armstrong, *Old Village and Great House*, xiv.

57. Stephanie Camp has argued that these "rival geographies" of slavery demonstrate that enslaved people maintained an alternate way of perceiving and using space in contrast to enslavers' wants and needs. Camp, *Closer to Freedom*, 7. Camp's work, like my own, builds on the seminal work of architectural historians like John Michael Vlach and Dell Upton, who have demonstrated how Black and white plantation residents had distinct understandings of, and thus distinct practices of engaging with, the built environment and landscape. Theorist Katherine McKittrick has likewise argued that enslavers' geographies of domination were never complete. McKittrick, *Demonic Grounds*.

58. Hunter et al., "Black Placemaking," 31. See also Radney, "Place in the Sun."

59. I specify that these practices include both the everyday and the exceptional, as influenced by Stephanie Camp's focus on the "hidden and informal" parts of slavery.

For me, this means that a study of homemaking cannot just include the infrequent and massive project of building a slave cabin. It must also be about the small actions and the (literally) hidden objects in those houses once they were built. Often the minutia of life is not written about, yet it may have been left behind elsewhere, stuck between two walls or dropped under a floorboard. Camp, *Closer to Freedom*, 3.

60. For examples of other such contexts, see Mosterman, *Spaces of Enslavement*; Harris, *Little White Houses*; K. Brown, *Gone Home*; K. Mitchell, *From Slave Cabins to the White House*.

Chapter One

1. Sources for this vignette include Leanna Schafer, "The South Yard Dwellings: The Taylor and Stewart Families," Montpelier's Digital Doorway, February 4, 2021, https://digital doorway.montpelier.org/2021/02/04/the-south-yard-dwellings-the-taylor-and-stewart -families/; "Archaeology Sites at James Madison's Montpelier," MAD-MF, JMM; Ketcham, *The Madisons at Montpelier*; *Homes of American Statesmen*, 181–97. Ralph Philip Taylor was born to an enslaved domestic servant (whose name has yet to be identified) in 1812, around the same time that slave carpenters completed the South Yard. While no documents have been found to identify which enslaved domestic servants lived where, Ralph's mother's and later his own status as trusted laborers from families enslaved at Montpelier for at least four generations suggests their residence in the South Yard. Montpelier currently interprets one of the two furnished dwellings in the South Yard as the residence of Ralph and his wife, Catherine, who was likely born a slave at Montpelier in the 1820s. Ralph's biographical information comes from Montpelier's Digital Doorway.

2. James's grandfather, Ambrose, took up residence at his estate in 1732, though several enslaved laborers had been working the land (and had built various structures) for years before that. Chambers, *Murder at Montpelier*, 88.

3. Hyland, "Montpelier: The History of a House," chap. 2.

4. Montpelier's archaeology and education departments refer to the mansion curtilage (a term signifying the land enclosing a house) as the "performative space." I am grateful for their input on this terminology, which I have slightly altered. Of particular influence is the work of Terry Brock, who discusses the performative landscape of plantations in his dissertation and applied these ideas to the Montpelier landscape during his tenure in its archaeology department. See Brock, "'All of Us Would Walk Together,'" esp. chap. 7. Brock's formulation of the "curated" nature of the Madisons' performative space was especially helpful. Terry P. Brock, "Exploring the Montpelier South Yard: Archaeology, Slavery, and Public Engagement at James Madison's Montpelier" (paper presented at Wilton House Lecture Series, February 2020, paper provided by Brock).

5. This included the rest of the "Home Farm," the 1,250 acres original to the eighteenth-century land patent of Ambrose Madison. Montpelier encompassed several farms located over 5,000 acres, but the Home Farm was the central agricultural complex. I use the same quarter designations as Montpelier's archaeology department. The department frequently finds new objects, landscapes, and activities embedded in the ground. Their updates, which come through newsletters and blog posts, are essential, if unusual, primary sources for historical work on Montpelier, including my own.

6. Douglas Chambers compiled several appendixes, from various primary sources,

documenting the known enslaved residents of Montpelier from the 1720s through 1850s. Chambers, *Murder at Montpelier*, 193–246.

7. As William Goodell argued in 1853, if "the slave could possess property . . . he might become a man, and becoming such, cease to be a slave." By "man," Goodell is referring not to the humanity of an enslaved person but to autonomy. The idea that an enslaved individual could have property, Goodell noted, would be equivalent to "the idea that the slave has *rights*." To grant enslaved people formal property ownership, to grant them autonomy over their things and their homes, would be to acknowledge their capacity for citizenship and freedom. Of course, in reality, enslaved individuals did possess property, and historians such as Dylan Penningroth and Roderick McDonald have shown the "ownership" of property like clothing, livestock, and domestic goods. Goodell, *American Slave Code*, 96; Penningroth, *Claims of Kinfolk*; R. McDonald, *Economy and Material Culture of Slaves*.

8. As archaeologists and architectural historians have argued for decades, the spatial patterning of artifacts and buildings in the plantation landscape reflected the power and identity of enslavers, and it allowed plantation owners to communicate which structures were for the white, slave-owning family and which were outbuildings meant for Black laborers. See, for example, Upton, *Holy Things and Profane*; Isaac, *Transformation of Virginia*; Herman, "Embedded Landscapes"; Edward A. Chappell, "Housing Slavery," in Carson and Lounsbury, *Chesapeake House*, 156–78; Clifton Ellis, "Building for 'Our Family, Black and White,'" in Ellis and Ginsburg, *Cabin, Quarter, Plantation*; Kealhoffer, "Creating Social Identity."

9. As the formative work of Dell Upton and John Michael Vlach as well as the more recent work of Whitney Battle-Baptiste has shown, enslaving and enslaved residents had their own spaces in and conceptions of the broader landscape. Upton, "White and Black Landscapes"; Vlach, *Back of the Big House*; Battle-Baptiste, *Black Feminist Archaeology*.

10. As Katherine McKittrick notes, the "social production of space," including physically establishing concealment, marginalization, and boundaries in the landscape, were "important social processes" for Black people as well as white. McKittrick, *Demonic Grounds*, xi.

11. See Demos, *A Little Commonwealth*; Ulrich, *A Midwife's Tale*; Shammas, *A History of Household Government in America*.

12. Boydston, *Home and Work*.

13. Richter, *At Home in Nineteenth-Century America*, esp. chap. 1.

14. Marla Miller argues that architectural transformations to a single household in Massachusetts reflect the broader evolution of work's separation from home in early America. These transformations include the expansion of the owners' formal rooms and the establishment of physical barriers between those rooms and the servants' living/laboring spaces. Marla Miller, "Labor and Liberty in the Age of Refinement."

15. This can be seen in the first chapter of Amy Richter's primary source collection on the ideal of home in the nineteenth century, which focuses on northern sources to reveal the separation between home and labor. In the remaining chapters that go beyond the ideal home, Richter does an excellent job of diversifying the source base. Richter, *At Home in Nineteenth-Century America*.

16. Glymph, *Out of the House of Bondage*, 3.

17. Camp, *Closer to Freedom*, 94.

18. Ira Berlin and Philip Morgan's 1993 edited collection clearly shows how prevalent this division was for enslaved people. Berlin and Morgan, "Introduction," in *Cultivation and Culture*, 2. The concept of a "slave economy" as distinct from that of the enslavers is prevalent throughout the literature on slavery, both the labor-focused works of the early 1990s and more recently with the turn to slavery and capitalism studies. See Berlin and Morgan, *Slaves' Economy*; J. Edwards, *Unfree Markets*. Rather than focusing on the economy that developed from this kind of labor, I am focused on how different conceptions of work shaped enslaved people's physical world, and how it reflects ideas related not only to labor but to home.

19. Memoirs and interviews of formerly enslaved people demonstrate that much of this chosen labor related to domestic work, to chores and tasks performed within and around dwellings meant to support the people closest to them. It is true that enslaved individuals did perform labor for their enslavers within their own dwellings. Many former slaves recalled their mothers or other female family members having to complete tasks at night for their owners, such as spinning cotton once they arrived at their dwellings after a full day's work. Yet others remembered quilting, making clothes, and cooking late into the night for themselves as much as for their enslavers. Martha Colquitt recalled that her mother and grandmother stayed up late into the night to sew and knit for the children, and they "done it 'cause dey wanted to. Dey wuz workin' for deyselves den." Martha Colquitt, in FWP-WPA, *Slave Narratives*, vol. 4, pt. 1, 243. For evidence of working late into the night for enslavers, see Emmaline Heard, in FWP-WPA, *Slave Narratives*, vol. 4, pt. 2, 149; Charlie Pye, in FWP-WPA, *Slave Narratives*, vol. 4, pt. 3, 186.

20. The half-mile approximation comes from Reeves, "Scalar Analysis of Early Nineteenth-Century Household Assemblages," 39. One of the simultaneous pleasures and difficulties of working on sites with active, robust archaeology programs is the constant unearthing of new materials. For instance, recent excavations of the Field Quarter may suggest that it was not in fact associated with field laborers but with other workers. Still, the spatial arrangement of the quarter reflects the lived experience of enslaved people on the plantation, regardless of whether they labored in the fields or elsewhere. Terry Brock (former assistant director of archaeology at Montpelier), virtual meeting with author, April 26, 2022.

21. Sharp, "An Architectural Portrait," 71–83, quote from 74.

22. Although James Madison did not officially inherit Montpelier until his father's death in 1801, he functioned as his father's executor and began overseeing work on the plantation by 1790. Letters to and from James Madison during this time (including dozens in Stagg, *Papers of James Madison Digital Edition*) show his deep interest and involvement in the building and landscaping activity of the entire plantation. Additionally, records from owners and overseers of plantations across the Atlantic world show the ceaseless activity taking place on these sites not only related to the planting and harvesting of crops but also to the continual process of building and renovating. C. Wells, "Planter's Prospect."

23. Bromell, *By the Sweat of the Brow*, 178–86.

24. "Soldiers' Families," *The Countryman* (Putnam County, GA), March 24, 1863.

25. Broadwater, *James Madison*, chap. 7.

26. Breen, *Tobacco Culture*.

27. This "pastoralization of housework," as historian Jeanne Boydston termed it,

rewrote women's work as a part of one's inherent nature rather than one's labor, thereby furthering the separation between home and labor evolving at this time. Boydston, *Home and Work*.

28. Letter, Dolley Madison to Anna Cutts, July 23, 1818, in Mattern and Shulman, *Selected Letters of Dolley Payne Madison*, 231.

29. The belief that Black bodies were naturally meant for manual labor began as early as the first European encounters with Africans, and this association would only increase with the racialization of slavery in the Americas. Morgan, *Laboring Women*.

30. James Madison, "Instructions for the Montpelier Overseer and Laborers," November [ca. 8], 1790, in Stagg, *Papers of James Madison Digital Edition*.

31. Narratives often recounted lofts used for slave sleeping spaces. See, for example, H. Brown, *Homespun Heroines*, 119; T. Burton, *What Experience Has Taught Me*, 18; Douglass, *My Bondage and My Freedom*, 37; Jackson-Coppin, *Reminiscences of School Life*, 9; Northup, *Twelve Years a Slave*, 49.

32. Finch, *Travels in the United States of America and Canada*, 247; "Montpelier, the Seat of Mr. Madison," *Daily National Intelligencer* (Washington, DC), August 9, 1820.

33. See Mark A. Trickett, "By the Harvest Moon's Light: Excavations of the Field Slave Quarters at the Home of James Madison, 2012–2013" (March 2014), MAD-MF, JMM.

34. Finch, *Travels in the United States of America and Canada*, 236.

35. Peter Wood observes that earthen floors may, in fact, have been an intentional choice of enslaved people, as many "traditional cultures" had the skill to make such floors as hard as concrete. Additionally, this type of flooring was often better at insulating houses from cold than plank, which allowed cold air to seep in. Wood, "Whetting, Setting and Laying Timbers," 7. Evidence for the possibility of wooden floors in the Field Quarter cabins comes from the slope/cut near the subfloor pits. "Archaeology Sites at James Madison's Montpelier," 63, MAD-MF, JMM.

36. Freed slaves commonly referred to their state while enslaved as akin to livestock or chattel, and sometimes they described their dwellings in the same way. In a speech published in one of his autobiographies, Frederick Douglass argued that enslaved people are "impiously inserted in a master's ledger, with horses, sheep, and swine . . . he is sheltered only by the wretched hovel that a master may dwell in a magnificent mansion." Douglass, *My Bondage and My Freedom*, 429–30. Writing of slavery, Henry Bleby described enslaved laborers as "penned" into their dwellings, like a pig into a pen, and how they were "lodged in log huts, on the bare ground. . . . The wind whistled, and the rain and snow blew in through the cracks." Bleby, *Josiah*, 26.

37. Reeves, "Scalar Analysis of Early Nineteenth-Century Household Assemblages," 40–41.

38. Although Virginia passed slave codes in the 1790s meant to regulate enslaved people's access to purchasing goods, these laws discouraged few Virginians (white or Black), and people continued to spend money on things they wanted. See Galle, "Costly Signaling and Gendered Social Strategies," 23.

39. Hyland, "Montpelier: The History of a House," chap. 1. Brenda Stevenson has shown the ways that the internal slave trade shaped both types of household structures in Virginia. Stevenson, *Life in Black and White*.

40. Archaeologists and architectural historians have noted that the colonial era tended toward more "unsupervised" slave housing. The same might also be said of physical areas

away from the enslaver's mansion. See McKee, "Ideals and Realities," 198; Vlach, *Back of the Big House*, 154–55.

41. Davies, *Jeffersonian America*, 141–42.

42. Prunty, "Renaissance of the Southern Plantation."

43. Kelly, "Change and Continuity in Coastal Bénin," 96.

44. This was one of the many gendered divisions of labor on plantations. As Berlin and Morgan argue, "Almost universally, skilled labor was men's work," and since, as Catharine Bishir notes, "Construction . . . was still predominantly a traditional craft directly dependent on the skills of artisans," enslaved builders were typically men. Berlin and Morgan, "Introduction," in *Cultivation and Culture*, 19; Bishir, "Black Builders in Antebellum North Carolina," 425. Throughout the literature on slave architecture, terms like builder, artisan, carpenter, and skilled slave have an invisible modifier of male. It is important to note, though, that the scholarly gendering of "skilled" labor as male misrepresents the diversity and meaning of work, focusing only on the labor performed for the enslaver and not the skilled work that enslaved people performed for themselves and their loved ones.

45. Hilde, *Slavery, Fatherhood, and Paternal Duty*.

46. Accounts from West Africa reveal the use of a communal yard for socializing, burying one's dead, raising poultry, and gardening. This was labor meant to benefit families, and the same was likely true for the communal yard of the Field Quarter. See Heath and Bennett, "'The Little Spots Allow'd Them,'" 39.

47. Mark A. Trickett, "By the Harvest Moon's Light" (March 2014), MAD-MF, JMM, 14.

48. Lee, "Beads, Coins, and Charms."

49. Garrett Fesler, "Excavating the Spaces and Interpreting the Places of Enslaved Africans and Their Descendants," in Ellis and Ginsburg, *Cabin, Quarter, Plantation*, 27–49.

50. "Archaeology Sites at James Madison's Montpelier," 54, MAD-MF, JMM.

51. "Cutts Memoir II," transcribed by Lee Langston-Harrison, Catherine Allgor, and James T. Connolly, in Allgor, *Queen of America*, 156.

52. "Montpelier, the Seat of Mr. Madison."

53. "English Garden" and "Landscape Garden," in Curl, *Oxford Dictionary of Architecture and Landscape Architecture*, 428–30. As Julianne Berckman argues, the Madisons' performative core contains "characteristics of the English landscape style of the eighteenth century (actually a combination of the ideas of William Shenstone and Lancelot Brown) with its lawns, vistas, groves of trees, garden temple, ha-ha hedge and absence of fountain plantings." Berckman, "Development of the Mansion Grounds of 'Montpelier,'" 5.

54. Wulf, *Founding Gardeners*. This included the use of ha-has: shallow ditches used as a boundary but that do not interrupt the vista. Mary Cutts remembered the use of these in the Montpelier rear lawn: "Behind the house was another portico, not so large as the one in front; from this you stepped down on an extensive lawn, bounded by ha ha." "Cutts Memoir II," 158.

55. Reeves and Greer, "Within View of the Mansion," 75.

56. Another practical purpose may have been to deter wind and thus erosion. Terry P. Brock, "Two Fences: Archaeological Investigations of the South Yard Fence Line" (March 2020), 32, MAD-MF, JMM.

57. Brock, "Two Fences" (March 2020), 31, MAD-MF, JMM. Stephanie McCurry has

shown how nineteenth-century South Carolina property holders also used fences as a means of establishing not only boundaries of landownership but boundaries of power. McCurry, *Masters of Small Worlds*, 9–11.

58. Brock, "Two Fences" (March 2020), 31, MAD-MF, JMM.

59. For James's death and Dolley's relocation, see Ketcham, *The Madisons at Montpelier*, 177.

60. Brock, "Two Fences" (March 2020), 47, MAD-MF, JMM.

61. Reeves and Greer, "Within View," 71–72.

62. "Cutts Memoir II," 156. See also "Archaeology Sites at James Madison's Montpelier," 55, MAD-MF, JMM.

63. "Montpelier, the Seat of Mr. Madison."

64. "Cutts Memoir II," 156–57.

65. Evidence of the wallpaper has been found in the mansions of the Hermitage and Belmont Plantations near Nashville, Tennessee. For this and more on Americans' reading and reception of the book, see Ward, "Fénelon and Classical America," 186. For more on Jefferson's interest in the book, see Hayes, *Road to Monticello*, 27.

66. Lafayette apparently told Cutts of his meeting with Milly. "Cutts Memoir II," 156.

67. For more on Madison's views on slavery (and antislavery), see Broadwater, *James Madison*, chap. 7.

68. It is possible she could read, as textual and material evidence reveals that at least some South Yard residents were literate. Letters from various enslaved people can be found in the Papers of Dolley Madison, housed at the Library of Congress, as well as online in *The Dolley Madison Digital Edition* (https://rotunda.upress.virginia.edu/dmde/). Additionally, two slate pencils were found during archaeological excavation of the South Yard kitchen. Hope Smith, "The South Kitchen Objects: A Preliminary Analysis of Artifacts Recovered during the 1990–1996 Field Seasons at James Madison's Montpelier" (2015), 12, MAD-MF, JMM.

69. "Cutts Memoir II," 156.

70. Trickett, "By the Harvest Moon's Light" (March 2014), 2, MAD-MF, JMM.

71. Finch, *Travels in the United States of America and Canada*, 239.

72. Letters from carpenters and architects, including James Dinsmore, Hugh Chisholm, and Benjamin Henry Latrobe, written between 1809 and 1811 reveal James's clear involvement in the renovations at Montpelier, even while he was in Washington, DC. See Stagg, *Papers of James Madison Digital Edition*. The buildings constructed during this time were not the first in the South Yard, as several dwellings existed on the site beforehand. "Archaeology Sites at James Madison's Montpelier," 42–51, MAD-MF, JMM.

73. The kitchen building was the only brick structure within the South Yard. Built in the eighteenth century, decades before the other buildings in the Yard, it served first as a dwelling for enslavers while enslaved and possibly free carpenters built the mansion. There was more than one kitchen along the perimeter of the Madisons' home core; this particular one in the South Yard served the household of James's mother, Nelly, who lived separately from her son and daughter-in-law in the southern half of the mansion. However, similarities in foodways objects found around the South Yard kitchen and in middens associated with James and Dolley elsewhere suggest a possible crossover between the two households. Smith, "The South Kitchen Objects" (2015), 25, 40, MAD-MF, JMM.

74. *Homes of American Statesmen*, 194. Typical dinners lasted at least two hours and were described as sumptuous, abundant, and elegant. See Ketcham, *Madisons at Montpelier*, 25. The Madisons were also famous for their outdoor fêtes. Dolley wrote to her sister about a party on July 4, 1820, when they had "ninety persons to dine with us at one table—fixed on the lawn, under a thick arbour. The dinner was profuse and handsome." See "Cutts Memoir II," 155.

75. For more on the culinary labor and worksites of enslaved Southerners, see K. Deetz, *Bound to the Fire*.

76. Archaeologists have argued that the South Yard's proximity to the Madison mansion likely altered the activities present in the South Yard, gearing them more toward enslavers rather than toward themselves and their families. Reeves and Greer, "Within View," 75.

77. We do not know all the enslaved people who lived in the South Yard, though Elizabeth Downing Taylor discusses many who did in her book about Paul Jennings, James Madison's enslaved personal attendant. E. Taylor, *A Slave in the White House*. Additionally, James Madison's Montpelier continues to do incredible work recovering information on domestic and other enslaved residents. "The Naming Project," Montpelier's Digital Doorway, https://digitaldoorway.montpelier.org/project/say-their-names/.

78. Although the kitchen near the north dwelling, between which enslaved residents maintained a swept yard, was certainly an area of labor, it was also likely a dwelling. Many plantation kitchens functioned as living quarters for the cook. K. Deetz, *Bound to the Fire*, 28–32.

79. Sidney W. Mintz brought the study of yards into the purview of scholars in the 1970s with his work on Caribbean house yards. Mintz, *Caribbean Transformations*. Garrett Fesler and other landscape archaeologists have begun to find and explore examples in the Chesapeake and beyond. Fesler, "Excavating the Spaces."

80. It was the paucity of artifacts between the South Yard structures that indicated the potential of swept yards. "Archaeology Sites at James Madison's Montpelier," 49, MAD-MF, JMM. For more on the techniques to discern swept yards in the landscape, see Heath and Bennett, "'The Little Spots Allow'd Them,'" 48.

81. Leanna Schafer, "South Yard Dwellings: Household Items," Montpelier's Digital Doorway, February 4, 2021, https://digitaldoorway.montpelier.org/2021/02/04/south-yard-dwellings-household-items/.

82. Annie Young, in FWP-WPA, *Slave Narratives*, vol. 13, 359.

83. Antebellum Black yards were likely comparable to those of the postbellum era, which scholars have found to be gendered. These more recent yards typically have an inner area worked by women, whose labor was culturally associated with the domestic, while the outer rim contains structures like storage sheds and smokehouses or communal hunting lodges that were more typically used by men. Outside this active yard are other major dependencies, including barns, that are exclusively used for nondomestic tasks. Heath and Bennett, "'The Little Spots Allow'd Them,'" 44. Whitney Battle-Baptiste also argues that women and children usually maintained the swept yards. Battle-Baptiste, "Sweepin' Spirits," 87. See also A. Young, "Gender and Landscape."

84. Excavations of the South Yard dwellings also found sewing materials and cooking vessels. Schafer, "South Yard Dwellings: Household Items." The literature on enslaved women's work, especially their domestic labor, is extensive and shows how the ideal of

domesticity and women's role in the home was at once denied to and expected of them. See, for example, Fox-Genovese, *Within the Plantation Household*; J. Jones, *Labor of Love, Labor of Sorrow*; Glymph, *Out of the House of Bondage*; Finley, *An Intimate Economy*.

85. See Schafer, "South Yard Dwellings: Household Items."

86. For more on the multiple functions and meanings of brooms in enslaved people's lives, see Stacey L. Young, "Brooms," in Katy-Hyman and Rice, *World of a Slave*, 1:80–83.

87. See Parry, *Jumping the Broom*.

88. As Patrick O'Neil has shown, enslavers sometimes interfered in slave wedding ceremonies, and since many of our accounts of these practices come from white perspectives, the practice of jumping the broom may represent more of what slave owners desired of these unions than what the enslaved people did. Yet even O'Neil recognizes that if slave communities were able to "withdraw to their own spaces," they could more fully engage in rituals that expressed their desires of marriage and family. This affirms the importance of home, among other spaces, where enslaved people might feel a sense of ownership. O'Neil, "Bosses and Broomsticks," 31.

89. Though Tyler Parry asserts that enslaved domestic servants often did not adopt this ritual, likely because they were forced to lodge so close to enslavers, he does note that it happened at least occasionally, so it is possible that slave couples in the South Yard participated in the practice. Parry, *Jumping the Broom*, 37.

90. Archaeologists have interpreted later nineteenth-century yards with layers of trash as resistance against slave owners who insisted on clean, uncluttered areas around and in dwellings. See Samford, "Archaeology of African-American Slavery and Material Culture," 97. But it does not necessarily follow that it was the decision of an enslaver—Madison in this case—to sweep yards clean. It may, in fact, have been something enslaved people wanted and performed on their own, regardless of their owner's demands. Or, it is possible that both enslaved *and* free residents desired yard spaces be swept clean. For more on the practical function of sweeping yards, see Terry P. Brock, "Exploring the Montpelier South Yard: Archaeology, Slavery, and Public Engagement at James Madison's Montpelier" (paper presented at Wilton House Lecture Series, February 2020, paper provided by Brock).

91. Battle-Baptiste, "Sweepin' Spirits," 88–89.

92. Heath and Bennett, "'The Little Spots Allow'd Them,'" 45.

93. "Descendants' Project," *James Madison's Montpelier*, accessed March 20, 2023, www.montpelier.org/resources/descendants-project.

94. Battle-Baptiste, "Sweepin' Spirits," 88.

95. Montpelier Archaeology Department, "Summer Field Update," *2022 Summer Newsletter*, email message, July 3, 2022.

96. Terry P. Brock has also argued that a swept yard "suggests intentional activity by African Americans to create distinction between their workspace and homespace." Terry P. Brock, "Identifying the South Yard: Interrogating Landscapes of Home and Work Yards Enslaved African Americans at Montpelier" (paper presented at the Society for Historical Archaeology 2018 meeting, New Orleans, LA, January 3–7, 2018; paper provided by Brock).

97. "Archaeology Sites at James Madison's Montpelier," 49, MAD-MF, JMM.

98. Strasser, *Waste and Want*.

99. Poplar Forest, owned by Thomas Jefferson, is located some 100 miles southwest of Montpelier. Archaeologists have argued that artifact distributions in yards there reflect

residents' perspective on how to best dispose of trash. Heath and Bennett, "'The Little Spots Allow'd Them,'" 49–50.

100. Mark A. Trickett, "South Yard Excavation Report: Excavations at the South East Duplex and the Southern Portion of the Mansion Grounds Fence Line, 2008" (August 2009), 35, MAD-MF, JMM. This pattern of discarding trash outside the mansion's view has been noted for other Montpelier structures, including an eighteenth-century slave dwelling. See Trickett, "South Yard Excavation Report" (August 2009), 63, MAD-MF, JMM.

101. "Archaeology Sites at James Madison's Montpelier," 49, MAD-MF, JMM.

102. Montpelier Archaeology Department, "Summer Field Update."

103. See Gundaker, "Gardens and Yard Art"; Westmacott, *African American Gardens and Yards*; Brock, "'All of Us Would Walk Together,'" 319.

104. Mintz, *Caribbean Transformations*, 231–32; Fesler, "Excavating the Spaces," 31; Battle-Baptiste, *Black Feminist Archaeology*, 100. Heath and Bennett note that archaeologists should anticipate finding buildings and artifacts related to chores and workspaces within yards. Heath and Bennett, "'The Little Spots Allow'd Them,'" 42–44.

105. Men and women, free and enslaved, adults and children smoked tobacco during times of both work and relaxation, and these two highly decorated pipes were most likely used by enslaved residents of the South Yard as they moved through their day. Terry P. Brock, "A Masonic Pipe and Stories of Freedom," Montpelier's Digital Doorway, November 1, 2018, https://digitaldoorway.montpelier.org/2018/11/01/a-masonic-pipe-and-stories-of-freedom/. See also Agbe-Davies, "The Production and Consumption of Smoking Pipes," 275.

106. Brock, "Two Fences" (March 2020), 47, MAD-MF, JMM. Archaeologists found a set of postholes eight feet from each of the two South Yard duplexes, which they suggest may have been for porches or "shades." This post-in-ground construction is distinct from the timber-frame construction of dwellings, further suggesting it was added after the dwellings were built and thus potentially after the Madisons were no longer on site. Reeves and Greer, "Within View," 75.

107. "Cutts Memoir II," 158.

108. Interestingly, Mary Cutts also wrote of the "superannuated slaves" at Montpelier "who love their homes." She declared that "they stay with their indulgences, happy, because contented, until death leaves the log cabin free for other occupants!" In certain instances, then, Cutts was willing to recognize that enslaved people did, in fact, have homes. Yet this argument was not rooted in the feelings of enslaved people. Rather, it was meant as evidence of the Madisons' benevolence, who were (from Cutts's perspective) so good to their slaves that they were content to stay living in slavery until their deaths. Their ability to call this place home ultimately depended, for Cutts, on their enslavement there. "Cutts Memoir II," 157.

109. As Alan Taylor notes, by 1800, approximately half of the Tidewater's and Piedmont's white households held enslaved people, though most owned only a few individuals. By the time of the Revolution, the number of Piedmont families owning around 100 slaves (a number that the Madisons, if taking James, Nelly, and other inheritors of James Sr.'s property, approximated) began to decline, making the dozens of enslaved people living at Montpelier unusual compared to the broader region. Alan Taylor, *Internal Enemy*, 46.

110. Wulf, *Founding Gardeners*, 199–201.

111. It should be noted that while they may have looked "nicer," the South Yard duplexes had several disadvantages to those in the Stable Yard. The plank walls were particularly susceptible to weather. The raised, wooden floor did not provide the thermal exchange that dirt floors did. Plus, very little of the buildings' surface area faced south for southern exposure warmth during winters. Reeves and Greer, "Within View," 75.

112. Szczesiul, *Southern Hospitality Myth*.

113. *Homes of American Statesmen*, 194.

114. Terrence Epperson notes that the incorporation of enslaved domestic workers into the private spaces of enslavers reflects the constant tension between incorporation and exclusion. Epperson, "Constructing Difference," 168–69.

115. *Homes of American Statesmen*, 188.

116. Terry P. Brock, "The South West Yard: Uncovering Transitional Landscapes at James Madison's Montpelier" (2016), 105, MAD-MF, JMM. Similar walls have been seen at other plantations, such as at Drayton Hall and Mt. Vernon. See Brock, "The South West Yard" (2016), 107, MAD-MF, JMM.

117. Brock, "The South West Yard" (2016), 23–24, 85–88, MAD-MF, JMM.

118. Brock, "The South West Yard" (2016), 25, MAD-MF, JMM.

119. At Somerset Plantation in North Carolina, the owner separated a row of twenty-one slave cabins from his mansion using only a fence and walkway, similar to the walkway that separated Thomas Jefferson's Monticello mansion from Mulberry Row, the procession of buildings for enslaved living and laboring that Jefferson placed directly adjacent to the mansion. Harrison, "Reconstructing Somerset Place," 32.

120. Letter, John H. B. Latrobe to Charles Carroll Harper, August 4, 1832, in Semmes, *John H. B. Latrobe and His Times*, 239.

121. Clifton Ellis, "Building for 'Our Family, Black and White,'" in Ellis and Ginsburg, *Cabin, Quarter, Plantation*, 141–59.

122. Anishanslin, *Portrait of a Woman in Silk*, 101–2.

123. Finch, *Travels in the United States of America and Canada*, 243–44.

124. Hyland, "Montpelier: The History of a House," chap. 1.

125. Moffatt and Carrière, "A Frenchman Visits Norfolk," 204.

126. Vlach, *Planter's Prospect*.

127. This was not always the case. The Baroness Anne-Marguerite-Henriette Hyde de Neuville's drawing of Montpelier, made in 1818, did not hide the reality of enslaved labor, including two Black figures (a woman and small child) painting the mansion's fence posts. In this way, Neuville articulated the racialization of home and labor on Southern plantations. As an exile, perhaps Neuville felt some kind of connection to those whom society dismissed or ignored. The New-York Historical Society featured Neuville's watercolors in the exhibit *Artist in Exile: The Visual Diary of Baroness Hyde de Neuville*, which ran in 2019–20.

128. "Monticello and Montpelier," *Daily National Intelligencer*, August 15, 1820, in Stagg, *Papers of James Madison Digital Edition*. Translation provided by Stagg.

129. Letter, James Dinsmore to James Madison, October 29, 1809, in Stagg, *Papers of James Madison Digital Edition*.

130. Mark A. Trickett, "Pine Allée Report" (2010), 3, MAD-MF, JMM; Terry P. Brock, "The Pine Alley: Final Report" (April 2022), 7, Brock Research and Consulting, The Montepelier Foundation, JMM.

131. Quote from Gray, "A Tour of Virginia in 1827," 467. For more on the temple, or pavilion as Jefferson sometimes called it, see Beiswanger, *A Temple in the Garden*.

132. "Cutts Memoir II," 158.

133. For more on temples, see Cybele Gontar, "The Neoclassical Temple" (October 2003), in *Heilbrunn Timeline of Art History* (New York: Metropolitan Museum of Art, 2000), www.metmuseum.org/toah/hd/neoc_2/hd_neoc_2.htm.

134. See Burstein and Isenberg, *Madison and Jefferson*.

135. Davies, *Jeffersonian America*, 307.

136. "Archaeology Sites at James Madison's Montpelier," 36, MAD-MF, JMM.

137. Kim Tinkham and Matthew Reeves, "Mansion Cellars Report: Excavations of the Cellar Spaces for the Main Block of the Mansion (2003–2005 Seasons)" (2010), MAD-MF, JMM; Matthew Reeves, "Mundane or Spiritual?: The Interpretation of Glass Bottle Containers Found on Two Sites of the African Diaspora," in Ogundiran and Saunders, *Materialities of Ritual in the Black Atlantic*, 176–97.

138. Trickett, "Pine Allée Report" (2010), 3, MAD-MF, JMM; Brock, "The Pine Alley: Final Report" (April 2022), 12–14, Brock Research and Consulting, The Montpelier Foundation, JMM.

139. Trickett, "Pine Allée Report" (2010), 4, MAD-MF, JMM.

140. *Homes of American Statesmen*, 188.

141. Ketcham, *The Madisons at Montpelier*, 178; Letter, John Payne Todd to Dolley Madison, April 6, 1844, *Dolley Madison Digital Edition*, accessed July 26, 2022.

142. E. Taylor, *A Slave in the White House*, 152.

143. Reeves and Greer, "Within View of the Mansion," 69.

144. The post-Madison history of Montpelier, including the extensive changes made by the duPont family in the twentieth century, is discussed in Hyland, "Montpelier: The History of a House," chaps. 3, 4, and 5.

145. As of December 2022, James Madison's Montpelier includes many elements of the antebellum version of the plantation, including a reconstruction of the entire South Yard, the Stable Quarter log cabin, and several "ghosted" cabins in the Field Quarter.

146. Brock, "Exploring the Montpelier South Yard"; Leanna Schafer, "The South Yard Dwellings: Furniture," Montpelier's Digital Doorway, February 3, 2021, https://digitaldoorway.montpelier.org/2021/02/03/the-south-yard-dwellings-furniture/; Reeves and Greer, "Within View," 77–78.

Chapter Two

1. Sources for this vignette include Cy Hart, in FWP-WPA, *Slave Narratives*, vol. 11, pt. 1, 380–81; Willis Hart, interview by Alice Eley Jones, June 19, 1986, transcript, SSHS; SSHS Tour, Vera M. Cecelski (site director), June 20, 2018; Letter, Paul C. Cameron (Paul) to Duncan Cameron (Duncan), February 1, 1842, folder 871, CFP; Letter, Mary Anderson to Duncan, March 28, 1807, CFP. One of the four Horton Grove houses is known as the "Hart house," as members of the Hart family lived there until the mid- to late twentieth century. Ephram's son, Cy Hart, gave an interview to the WPA in 1937, recalling a story told to him that Paul Cameron purchased Ephram and sent him to the Stagville quarter known as Snow Hill. When the Hart family moved into the Horton Grove house is unclear. SSHS staff claim that the family was living in the house by at least the 1880s, so it is certainly possible that the move took place during the era of

slavery. Ephram is the spelling in the WPA narrative; Efraim and Ephraim are other spellings within the family. Efraim Hart, interview by Alice Eley Jones, July 2, 1986, transcript, SHSS; Jean B. Anderson, "A Preliminary Report on Stagville Plantation: The Land and the People" (June 1977), North Carolina Division of Archives and History, Wilson Library, University of North Carolina at Chapel Hill.

2. I use the name Stagville to refer to both Stagville Plantation specifically (which centered on the Bennehan house) and the larger Bennehan-Cameron complex in North Carolina (which included multiple farms and slave quarters with specific names) more generally. Unless otherwise noted, biographical information on the Bennehan-Camerons comes from Jean Anderson, *Piedmont Plantation*.

3. The exact number of enslaved people the Cameron siblings claimed as property is nearly impossible to pin down as the records are extremely inconsistent. Jean Bradley Anderson argues that 1860 US Census–Slave Schedule numbers add up to at least 900, plus some 100 additional enslaved people identified through archival sources. Yet a search of the 1860 census does not yield such high numbers, particularly for Orange County (Jean Anderson asserts that the census shows 592 for Orange, while my search found less). Paul Cameron claimed to have enslaved approximately 650 people on his Orange County estate before the Civil War, but this number is unreliable (and likely low) as it was given while Paul pled for a pardon after the war. In any case, the Orange County numbers would not have included the 199 laborers in Alabama and Mississippi (according to the 1860 US Census–Slave Schedule), so a conservative total still reaches almost 850 enslaved people. Jean Anderson, *Piedmont Plantation*, 95. 1860 US Census–Slave Schedules for Orange County, NC; Person County, NC; Greene County, AL; Tunica County, MS. Additionally, in September 1863, Paul wrote to his brother-in-law George Mordecai that he could not absorb any of George's laborers since he had "the care of at least 800 slaves." Letter, Paul to George W. Mordecai, September 18, 1863, folder 93, George W. Mordecai Papers #522, SHC.

4. The staff of SSHS, with John Sweet and University of North Carolina at Chapel Hill students, has mapped nearly a dozen slave quarters through GIS, as shown on a map provided by site director Vera Cecelski. Vera Cecelski, email message to author, March 20, 2018. See also figure 1, "Cameron Plantations," in Carl Lounsbury and George W. McDaniel, "Recording Plantation Communities: Report on the Architectural and Historical Resources at Stagville" (July 1980), Wilson Library, University of North Carolina at Chapel Hill.

5. Benson J. Lossing, a traveler, rode through Stagville in 1848 and commented upon the size, prosperity, and diversified operation of the plantation: "This plantation extends parallel with the rivers, a distance of fifteen miles, and covers an area of about sixty square miles It is well managed, and yields abundant crops of wheat, corn, oats, cotton, tobacco, potatoes, and other products of the Northern and Middle States. One thousand negroes were upon it, under the direction of several overseers. Its hills are crowned with fine timber, and I observed several large flocks of sheep and herds of cattle upon the slopes. It is probably the largest landed estate in the Carolinas, perhaps in the Union." Lossing, *Pictorial Field-Book of the Revolution*, 557. The crops grown remained virtually the same from Richard Bennehan's to Paul Cameron's management and included wheat, tobacco, corn, rye, and oats, among others. Enslaved laborers planted and harvested cotton for utilitarian purposes, rather than for the market; the land in North Carolina simply would not support the kind of cotton plantations that would develop in the Deep South.

6. Letter, Paul to Duncan, January 30, 1835, folder 743, CFP.

7. Coontz, *Social Origins of Private Life*.

8. Nineteenth-century conceptions of privacy built on the castle doctrine of English common law. This precept, going back at least to the sixteenth century, held that every man's home was his castle and every man king of his own home. Only he could decide who entered. Privacy was thus deeply connected to physical homeplace. White Americans believed the home to be the "moral nexus between liberty, privacy, and freedom of association," and as such the physical house should never be violated. Cuddihy and Hardy, "A Man's House Was Not His Castle"; quote from Radin, "Property and Personhood," 991; Sharfstein, "Atrocity, Entitlement, and Personhood in Property." See also Lane, *American Privacy*.

9. Architectural and social historians have shown that widespread physical alterations in late eighteenth-century elite Virginia houses—including the dwelling's orientation to the road and the closing of personal spaces to visitors through the introduction of central passageways—demonstrate the gentry's desire for greater privacy, causing a retreat from both public life and sociability. Glassie, *Folk Housing in Middle Virginia*, 120–22; Upton, "Vernacular Domestic Architecture in Eighteenth-Century Virginia"; Isaac, *Transformation of Virginia*, 302–5; Mark R. Wenger, "Town House and Country House: Eighteenth and Early Nineteenth Centuries," in Carson and Lounsbury, *Chesapeake House*, 144–45. See also Heck, "Palladian Architecture and Social Change," 315–37.

10. Marie Gordon (Pryor) Rice, "Reminiscences" (1920), 3, Virginia Historical Society, Richmond.

11. For more on state and local laws pertaining to slavery, particularly in the Carolinas, see L. Edwards, *People and Their Peace*. For more on slave patrols, see Hadden, *Slave Patrols*.

12. Glymph, *Out of the House of Bondage*, 169.

13. In the words of historian Martha Ackelsberg, "to be chattel . . . means to have no private life." Ackelsberg, *Resisting Citizenship*, 84.

14. Enslaved individuals, particularly women, had little authority over their own bodies, and the violence enacted on them through mechanisms like rape and forced reproduction make clear the stakes of exploring privacy within the institution of slavery. This work has particularly focused on the bodies of enslaved women, though "privacy" as a term is less used. See, for example, D. White, *Ar'n't I a Woman?*; Morgan, *Laboring Women*; D. Owens, *Medical Bondage*.

15. Hartman is describing postbellum Black domestic sites, but the description is apt for those in slavery, as well. Hartman, *Scenes of Subjection*, 160.

16. Northup, *Twelve Years a Slave*, 49.

17. Whitney Battle-Baptiste has likewise shown that privacy was indeed something desired and felt by enslaved people, for slave dwellings were considered "counter-public" spaces: public from white perspectives and private for Black. Battle-Baptiste, *Black Feminist Archaeology*, 97.

18. Albert Raboteau discussed the use of secluded spaces like forests, gorges, groves, and the "hush arbor" to perform spiritual practices. Raboteau, *Slave Religion*, 215. For more on enslaved people's appropriation of swamplands, see Nevius, *City of Refuge*.

19. Camp, *Closer to Freedom*, 6–7.

20. Katherine McKittrick discusses how enslaved people reimagined captive spaces as ones of defiance and even emancipation. This includes the garret that antislavery writer

Harriet Jacobs inhabited for seven years while formulating a plan to escape slavery with her children. Once in the North, Jacobs documented this and other harrowing, traumatic moments of her life under slavery in *Incidents in the Life of a Slave Girl.* McKittrick, *Demonic Grounds*, esp. chap. 2.

21. The academic quest to identify "Africanisms" in Black American culture can be traced back at least eighty years. See Herskovits, *Myth of the Negro Past.*

22. For the argument that context is essential when exploring Africanisms, see, for instance, Jamieson, "Material Culture and Social Death."

23. While we may not know the exact names of those who handled the objects, we do have a robust database of names associated with Stagville, in large part because of the work of Herbert Gutman. Gutman, *Black Family in Slavery and Freedom*, esp. chap. 4.

24. Mark P. Leone and Gladys-Marie Fry have argued that hidden spaces were "sacred" for enslaved people and could bring protection to those who used them. Leone and Fry, "Conjuring in the Big House Kitchen," 382.

25. *Surveillance* is a loaded term in contemporary scholarly discourse, but in reference to Southern slavery, it means the sustained observation of the movement and actions of enslaved bodies in space for the purpose of controlling those individuals and punishing misbehavior. This definition is derived from studies of the relationship between surveillance and architecture, including the writings of Michel Foucault, for whom surveillance is, by definition, disciplinary. Surveillance, in this definition, ultimately functions as a method of control, often compelled by sexual desire. See Foucault, *Discipline and Punish.* An important contribution to surveillance studies is the application of theories and historical analyses of race and slavery. In particular, the work of Simone Browne reveals a distinct form of "racializing surveillance" that aimed to police racial norms. Browne, *Dark Matters*, 16–18.

26. See Andrzejewski, *Building Power*, esp. introduction.

27. The "carceral landscape" of slavery, as Walter Johnson refers to it, makes clear that enslavement was a spatial and material condition, along with an economic and legal one. W. Johnson, *River of Dark Dreams*, 209–43. Scholars have revealed the roots of the US prison industrial complex in the racial structures that supported slavery. See M. Alexander, *New Jim Crow.* Some, like Dennis Childs, show a direct line from plantation to prison. Childs, *Slaves of the State.*

28. J. B. C. Axelrod and Rise B. Axelrod suggest these three broad criteria for determining whether an institution is panoptic. Axelrod and Axelrod, "Reading Frederick Douglass through Foucault's Panoptic Lens," 117.

29. Breeden, *Advice among Masters*, 118.

30. Cyrus Bellus, in FWP-WPA, *Slave Narratives*, vol. 2, pt. 1, 142. Containment, as Stephanie Camp has argued, was an essential method of control for owners. Camp, *Closer to Freedom*, esp. 28–34.

31. This design, put forth by cultural geographer Merle Prunty more than fifty years ago, has been substantiated as the predominant form of plantation design throughout the Americas. Prunty, "Renaissance of the Southern Plantation." Theresa Singleton shows how enslavers used this arrangement to increase surveillance capabilities. Singleton, "Nineteenth-Century Built Landscape of Plantation Slavery"; Singleton, "Slavery and Spatial Dialectics on Cuban Coffee Plantations." For discussion of the many different plantation layouts, see Vlach, *Back of the Big House.*

32. Paul Cameron noted "the line of buildings" in a letter to his father. Letter, Paul to Duncan, October 23, 1850, folder 1081, CFP.

33. Joseph, "Resistance and Compliance," 21.

34. In 1807 word spread of a foiled plot by two enslaved men to poison Duncan's father. The Bennehans and Camerons were two of the area's most important families, and their union catalyzed Stagville's massive growth in the following six decades. The attack on one branch, then, was like an attack on the other. Letter, Mary Anderson to Duncan, March 28, 1807, CFP.

35. Letter, Paul to Duncan, February 1, 1842.

36. Latta, *History of My Life and Work*, 114. Latta was born at Fishdam, one of the many farms/quarters that comprised the Bennehan-Cameron's North Carolina Stagville complex in the 1850s.

37. Latta, *History of My Life and Work*, 114.

38. Abner Jordan, in FWP-WPA, *Slave Narratives*, vol. 11, pt. 2, 35.

39. Nathans, *A Mind to Stay*, esp. chaps. 1 and 2.

40. Jean B. Anderson noted that Thomas D. Bennehan purchased a young enslaved girl named Betty at a Stagville store auction on August 10, 1824. Jean B. Anderson, "JBA Research Notes: Blacks I," SHSS.

41. Anderson recorded slave accounts for the Stagville store. Jean B. Anderson, "JBA Research Notes: Blacks I," SHSS.

42. The Camerons kept quarter-by-quarter lists of enslaved laborers. Based on names listed under different quarters between 1834 and 1845, it is likely that Paul (who oversaw plantation operations during this period) would have ordered these rearrangements. See folders 3654, 3657, 3662, CFP.

43. Paul often complained about the poor health of his slaves (including rampant sexually transmitted diseases) in letters to his father.

44. One Virginian planter succinctly described the "ends aimed at in building negro cabins" as "First, the health and comfort of the occupants; Secondly, the convenience of nursing, surveillance, discipline, and the supply of wood and water; and thirdly, economy of construction." Breeden, *Advice among Masters*, 129. Archaeologist Larry McKee found at least part of the planter's description true, arguing that a primary motive of plantation management publications in advocating improved housing was to enhance the control of enslaved people. McKee, "Ideals and Realities." Edward Chappell picked up on the planter's third point and argued that alterations in slave housing around the Atlantic world had more to do with economics and politics than a concern over the welfare of enslaved living conditions. Edward A. Chappell, "Accommodating Slavery in Bermuda," in Ellis and Ginsburg, *Cabin, Quarter, Plantation*, 67–98.

45. Letter, Paul to Rebecca Cameron, January 28, 1836, folder 762, CFP.

46. As archaeologist Charles Orser asserts, "descriptions provided by . . . former slaves imply that most slave housing was simple, inadequate, and far from ideal." Orser, *Material Basis of the Postbellum Tenant Plantation*, 15.

47. No written documentation has been found about who made the stick or who may have used it at Stagville. Artifact records and employees at SSHS specify that the object was found in the Bennehan house walls, but no report exists of exactly when the walking stick was found or by whom. Vera Cecelski, email message to author, July 17, 2019.

48. Among several common types of hickory in North Carolina are pignut hickory,

which is commonly found around Durham County, where Stagville is located. Will Cook, "Summer Key to the Common Trees of Durham County, North Carolina," 1999, http://people.duke.edu/~cwcook/trees/durhamtreekey.html; Will Cook, "Trees, Shrubs, and Woody Vines of North Carolina—Durham County," Carolina Nature, accessed July 19, 2020, www.carolinanature.com/trees/durhamtrees.html; "Pignut Hickory," Carolina Nature, accessed July 19, 2020, www.carolinanature.com/trees/cagl.html.

49. Alice Eley Jones suggests the maker may have debarked the stick using hot coals, rather than through whittling. Alice Eley Jones, "Sacred Places and Holy Ground: West African Spiritualism at Stagville Plantation," in Gundaker, *Keep Your Head to the Sky*, 106.

50. Austin, "Defining the African-American Cane," 222; Hinson, "Walking Sticks," 378; Vlach, *Afro-American Tradition in Decorative Arts*, 27–44.

51. Lucille Peaks Turner, interview by Alice Eley Jones, June 26, 1986, transcript, SSHS.

52. In the limited literature on African American walking sticks produced or used during slavery, all examples provided are by male makers.

53. Jean Anderson, *Piedmont Plantation*, 11. Exactly who was a part of the crew that worked on the 1799 addition is not specified in Bennehan's records.

54. While the original story-plus-loft structure measured 24 by 16 feet, the two-story supplement was itself 32 by 22 feet. Descriptive List of Property Owned by Richard and Thomas Bennehan, folder 2110, CFP. Although the document is undated, Jean Bradley Anderson estimates the date to be December 1816. Jean Anderson, *Piedmont Plantation*, 189n10. The document in the Wilson Library also contains a penciled "[1816]" at the top. See also National Register of Historic Places, Stagville, Durham County, North Carolina, 1973, NRHP.

55. Bishir, "Black Builders in Antebellum North Carolina."

56. Bishir, "Black Builders in Antebellum North Carolina."

57. Bennehan had employed a carpenter to oversee construction of the original house and home complex in the 1780s, and while there is no extant documentation of him doing so for the 1799 addition, the size and quality of the building make it likely that he would have hired one again. Memorandum of Mr. Bennehan's Houses, folder 3553, CFP. As Carl Lounsbury argues, there were four levels of complexity in regard to building in antebellum North Carolina. The Bennehan house can be ascribed to the second level, which required the use of an experienced craftsman overseeing the work of laborers but not yet to the level of employing a trained architect (as far as the documents reveal). Lounsbury, "Building Process in Antebellum North Carolina." James Johnston, an enslaver near Edenton, North Carolina, hired out sawyers, bricklayers, and masons for the construction of his mansion at Hayes Plantation. Bishir, "'Severe Survitude to House Building,'" 384–85, 390.

58. Slave Ledger, June 1810, folder 3617, CFP; letter, Duncan to Thomas D. Bennehan, November 26, 1819, folder 474, CFP.

59. Bishir, "'Severe Survitude to House Building,'" 388.

60. List of Taxable Property, August 1778, folder 2107, CFP; List of Taxable Property, August 1799, folder 2108, CFP.

61. For more on timber framing in the eighteenth century, see Willie Graham, "Timber Framing," in Carson and Lounsbury, *Chesapeake House*, 206–38.

62. Carl Lounsbury has noted that many slave-owning clients used their own enslaved

labor force (along with some hired artisans) to finish the exterior and interior of buildings. Lounsbury, "Building Process in Antebellum North Carolina," 442.

63. Samford, *Subfloor Pits and the Archaeology of Slavery*; Samford, "Archaeology of
African-American Slavery and Material Culture"; Neiman, "Lost World of Monticello";
A. Young, "Risk Management Strategies among African-American Slaves"; Leone and
Fry, "Conjuring in the Big House Kitchen"; Moses, "Enslaved African Conjure and
Ritual Deposits on the Hume Plantation."

64. Samford, "Archaeology of African-American Slavery and Material Culture," 107.
See also J. Young, *Rituals of Resistance*, esp. chap. 3.

65. Samford, "Archaeology of African-American Slavery and Material Culture," 107.

66. Sharon Moses has argued that enslaved Americans adapted African conjure practices and material culture based on their unique circumstances, creating new expressions
of these rituals. Moses, "Enslaved African Conjure and Ritual Deposits on the Hume
Plantation." For more on adaptations of African religion, cultural practices, and material
culture, see Orser, "Archaeology of African-American Slave Religion"; Wilkie, "Secret
and Sacred."

67. Chireau, *Black Magic*, 12. See also Jeffrey Anderson, *Conjure in African American
Society*.

68. Documenting the American South records eleven descriptions of conjuring by
six different formerly enslaved writers. See Marcella Grendler, Andrew Leiter, and Jill
Sexton, "Guide to Religious Content in Slave Narratives," Documenting the American South, University Library, University of North Carolina at Chapel Hill, https://
docsouth.unc.edu/neh/religiouscontent.html. Conjuring is still practiced in communities throughout the African Diaspora and is a deeply significant part of spiritual, creative, academic, and activist work. See, for instance, Otero, *Archives of Conjure*.

69. Wilkie, "Magic and Empowerment on the Plantation."

70. Raboteau, *Slave Religion*, 276.

71. Austin, "Defining the African-American Cane," 222.

72. Cardinall, *Tales Told in Togoland*, 98.

73. We do not know if the cane would have been used by a man or woman for conjuring, as magic was practiced by individuals of both genders. Jeffrey Anderson, *Conjure
in African American Society*, 42. As Alexis Wells-Oghoghomeh makes clear, though,
the specific gendered experiences of enslaved women shaped how they conceived of
evil, death, and other spiritual and religious elements. Wells-Oghoghomeh, *Souls of
Womenfolk*.

74. A. Jones, "Sacred Places and Holy Ground," in Gundaker, *Keep Your Head to the
Sky*, 106. I am indebted to Jones's work on Stagville and attempt to historicize and expand her interpretations.

75. Many WPA narratives include references to snakes; for example, Charlie Daven-
port, in FWP-WPA, *Slave Narratives*, vol. 9, 35; Bert Mayfield, in FWP-WPA, *Slave
Narratives*, vol. 7, 16; Mattie Logan, in FWP-WPA, *Slave Narratives*, vol. 13, 190.

76. Lawal, "African-American Expressions," 45.

77. Andrew Boone, in FWP-WPA, *Slave Narratives*, vol. 11, pt. 1, 132.

78. Annie B. Boyd, in FWP-WPA, *Slave Narratives*, vol. 7, 58.

79. Harre Quarls, in FWP-WPA, *Slave Narratives*, vol. 16, pt. 3, 223.

80. Bibb, *Narrative of the Life and Adventures of Henry Bibb*, 25–26.

81. Cardinall, *Tales Told in Togoland*, 98.

82. Moses, "Enslaved African Conjure and Ritual Deposits on the Hume Plantation," 30.

83. Jennifer G. Garlid, "Stagville Field School in Historical Archaeology: A Nineteenth Century Slave Cabin" (September 1979), 20–22, North Carolina Department of Cultural Resources, Division of Archives and History, Historic Sites Section, accessed at SHSS. Archaeologists also found evidence of floorboards in the slave cabin remains. Garlid, "Stagville Field School," 12.

84. Archaeologists recovered material suggesting a door in the slave cabin. Garlid, "Stagville Field School," 25.

85. M. G. Harasewych and Fabio Moretzsohn note that *Cyprae moneta* typically range in size from ⅔ to 1¾ inch and contain two flattened sides, the dorsal face with an oval outline and the ventral with narrow, long aperture and thick lips. The dorsal is typically faint yellow, and the shell usually contains white or yellowish teeth, base, and margins. Harasewych and Moretzsohn, *Book of Shells*, 327.

86. Hogendorn and Johnson, *Shell Money of the Slave Trade*; T. Green, *A Fistful of Shells*.

87. Ogundiran, "Of Small Things Remembered," 438; Pearce, "Cowrie Shell in Virginia," 39–54.

88. Depositional (which I tend to refer to as physical and spatial contexts) and other contexts are important to analyzing and interpreting the shell in part because it is faulty to simply assume that cowrie shells were held only by enslaved hands. The presence of an actual African artifact at a plantation site seems to suggest a firm resolution by enslaved people to maintain a connection to the place, material culture, and practices of their ancestors. However, scholars have cautioned against the automatic association of cowrie shells with enslaved people, for historical records also demonstrate European use of the cowrie shell. Pearce, "To Whom Do They Belong?"; Pearce, "Cowrie Shell in Virginia," 3–4; Hildburgh, "Cowrie Shells as Amulets in Europe."

89. For a general overview of the types and functions of shells (including cowrie) used by enslaved people, see "Shells," in Katy-Hyman and Rice, *World of a Slave*, 2:420–22.

90. Warren R. Perry, Jean Howson, and Barbara A. Bianco, eds., *New York African Burial Ground Archaeology Final Report*, vol. 1 (Washington, DC: Howard University for US General Services Administration, Northeastern and Caribbean Region, February 2006), 386.

91. Querying the Digital Archaeological Archive of Comparative Slavery in 2020 revealed three cowrie shell artifacts in North America, all of them from Virginia: one at Monticello and two at Mt. Vernon. See the Digital Archaeological Archive of Comparative Slavery (www.daacs.org/).

92. Pearce, "Cowrie Shell in Virginia," 56, 68.

93. L. Jones, "Crystals and Conjuring at the Charles Carroll House," 3.

94. These artifact assemblages were found in the area of the Carroll house where enslaved people lived and labored. Russell, "Material Culture and African-American Spirituality at the Hermitage," 63–64.

95. Garlid, "Stagville Field School," 20–22. Although spirit bundles can include materials such as these, the intentional association of these fragments with the cowrie shell cannot be determined.

96. In these cases, archaeologists suggest that, due to associations with a pit feature or

other artifacts used in conjuring, enslaved people intentionally placed or concealed these cowrie shells where they were later found.

97. Descriptive List of Property Owned by Richard and Thomas Bennehan, folder 2110, CFP; Will of Richard Bennehan, April 24, 1820, Orange County, North Carolina, folder 2177, CFP. The carpenter's notes about Richard Bennehan's original homeplace included "2 Cabins Log Bodys," which are believed to have been slave cabins. Memorandum of Mr. Bennehan's Houses, folder 3553, CFP.

98. Will of Thomas D. Bennehan, April 28, 1845, folder 2178a, CFP.

99. Architectural dating from Garlid, "Stagville Field School," 44.

100. Garlid, "Stagville Field School," 44.

101. The cabin was located approximately two hundred feet from the mansion. Distance calculated from map in Garlid, "Stagville Field School," 8.

102. Aleckson, *Before the War*, 58.

103. This was a common choice for plantation "big houses." Vlach, *Planter's Prospect*.

104. Vera Cecelski reported that preliminary archaeological work performed in 2017 revealed the presence of at least two eighteenth-century roadbeds around the Bennehan house, indicating the land had been cleared by that time. Vera Cecelski, email message to author, July 17, 2019.

105. During the winter, when the leaves have fallen, one can view the foundation of the slave cabin from the Bennehan house. This provides confirmation that the Bennehans would have been able to easily surveil the house when those trees were not there. Vera Cecelski, email message to author, August 7, 2019.

106. C. Alexander, *Battles and Victories of Allen Allensworth*, 28.

107. Craft, *Running a Thousand Miles for Freedom*, 31.

108. Additional evidence on enslaved people's use of locks comes from written sources. The carpenter at Orange Hall Plantation in South Carolina purchased padlocks to keep his possessions safe from prying hands. Historian Roderick A. McDonald found evidence of homemade wooden locks, keys, and bolts to secure dwellings in Jamaica, while some Louisiana enslaved laborers purchased locks. While traveling throughout the Southern states, Frederick Law Olmsted recounted slave homes at two plantations that included indoor closets with locks. Some cabins even contained external locks for enslaved laborers to secure their cabins while working during the day. McDonnell, "Money Knows No Master," 37; McDonald, *Economy and Material Culture of Slaves*, 75, 109, 145–46; Olmsted, *A Journey in the Seaboard States*, 111, 422.

109. Garlid's archaeology report notes: "One chunk of timber labeled 'Part of Lock' by Tom Funk." Garlid, "Stagville Field School," 16. Enslaved laborers in eighteenth-century Barbados had homemade wooden locks on their doors. Handler and Lange, *Plantation Slavery in Barbados*, 299. Edward Chappell notes that, in one case, enslaved people in the Chesapeake simply wedged a peg into holes in the inner doorjamb, showing the innovative use of materials for locks. Edward A. Chappell, "Hardware," in Carson and Lounsbury, *Chesapeake House*, 278.

110. Archaeologists have identified the use of locks in or near slave dwellings across the United States, including at Montpelier in Virginia, as well as in Georgia. Padlock on display in South Yard, James Madison's Montpelier, Orange County, VA; Otto and Burns, "Black Folks and Poor Buckras," 189.

111. Ogundiran, "Cowries and Rituals of Self-Realization in the Yoruba Region,

ca. 1600–1860," in Ogundiran and Saunders, *Materialities of Ritual in the Black Atlantic*, 68–86. Toby Green also notes the use of cowries in "protective shrines hidden from public view" within Yorùbá households. T. Green, *Fistful of Shells*, 19.

112. Lee, "Beads, Coins, and Charms."

113. McCord, *Africans at Home*, 7.

114. Lee, "Beads, Coins, and Charms"; Wilkie, "Magic and Empowerment on the Plantation."

115. Tom Hawkins, in FWP-WPA, *Slave Narratives* vol. 4, pt. 2, 132. In addition to reminiscences, archaeological assemblages recovered from slave cabin sites include horse-shoes. Patricia M. Samford, "Investigations of a Probable Slave Quarter at Rich Neck Plantation," Colonial Williamsburg Foundation Library Research Report Series 0395 (Williamsburg: Colonial Williamsburg Digital Library, 1991), https://research.colonial williamsburg.org/DigitalLibrary/view/index.cfm?doc=ResearchReports%5CRR0395 .xml&highlight=.

116. Pearce, "The Cowrie Shell in Virginia," 73.

117. Thomas acquired a whip from his friend, Mr. Browne, who left it to Thomas when he died. Letter, to Thomas D. Bennehan, August 5, 1834, folder 736, CFP.

118. Although these restoration projects did not keep records or produce reports, Vera Cecelski reports that the forked sticks were found during this work. Vera Cecelski, email message to author, July 17, 2019.

119. Letter, Paul to Duncan, October 17, 1850, folder 1081, CFP.

120. Betty Holman Hayes remembered the nogging in their house in Horton Grove. Betty Holman Hayes, interview by Alice Eley Jones, July 8, 1986, transcript, SSHS.

121. For more on the range of nineteenth-century slave dwellings, see Vlach, *Behind the Big House*, chap. 11.

122. Carl Lounsbury has argued that enslaved people provided the majority of labor for slave dwelling–construction in North Carolina, and thus the construction crew at Horton Grove would have consisted of enslaved laborers. Lounsbury, "Building Process in Antebellum North Carolina," 437. This was also true throughout the US South. As Peter Wood asserts, "Southern plantations were North America's first 'predominantly black institutions' and the vast majority of houses on plantation property were con-structed and occupied by Afro-Americans." Wood, "Whetting, Setting and Laying Timbers," 3. However, it should be noted that some enslavers did hire outside labor to construct slave cabins. See McDonald, *Economy and Material Culture of Slaves*, 133.

123. Jean B. Anderson, "JBA Research Notes: Enslaved II," SHSS. Paul, as owner of Stagville, bucked the ancestral tradition of living at the Bennehan house, instead living in the far grander Greek Revival mansion at Fairntosh, just over a mile from the old fam-ily house. But Paul still personally visited Stagville's many slave quarters and worksites. Fairntosh was Paul's father's plantation. Jean Anderson, *Piedmont Plantation*, chap. 5.

124. Completed in 1860, the Horton Grove barn and stable structure is truly a triumph of enslaved craftsmanship, considered by many architectural historians to be one of the most impressive agricultural buildings of the era. Even if Cameron hired free carpen-ters and artisans for the project, enslaved laborers performed much of the work on the structure. Vernacular Architecture Forum, *From Farm to Factory in Durham County*, 6–7.

125. Architectural historians have proposed construction dates of 1859 to 1860 for the

houses, though it is difficult to ascribe a firm date. Vernacular Architecture Forum, *From Farm to Factory in Durham County*, 5.

126. A. Jones, "Sacred Places and Holy Ground," 106.

127. Sydney Nathans meticulously re-searched and re-created the story of the forced migration of these enslaved people from Stagville to Cameron's Deep South plantations, and their eventual purchase of the Greensboro plantation land after emancipation. The total number of laborers (196) relocated from North Carolina to Alabama and Mississippi comes from Nathans, *A Mind to Stay*, 40, 65, 71, 75. By 1860, the number at both Deep South plantations would be 199, an increase of only three. 1860 US Census–Slave Schedules, Greene County, AL, and Tunica County, MS.

128. Nathans, *A Mind to Stay*, 254n6. Milton appears in the letters of the Camerons as a trusted courier in the 1830s, moving from Fairntosh to other areas of the estate and even beyond. Nathans, *A Mind to Stay*, 255n27. Jean B. Anderson relates how Pompey and Lewis were demoted from waggoners after being caught selling whiskey and coffee to their fellow enslaved laborers. Jean Anderson, *Piedmont Plantation*, 100.

129. Letter, Paul to Duncan, August 2, 1850, folder 1079, CFP.

130. These numbers come from estimates provided by SSHS staff. Sydney Nathans affirms this, noting two dozen people in each house. SHSS Tour, June 20, 2018; Nathans, *A Mind to Stay*, 94.

131. National Register of Historic Places, Horton Grove Complex, 1978, 2, NRHP.

132. Hart interview; Hayes interview; Turner interview.

133. Forked twigs have also been used by Native Americans and European Americans, and particularly by the latter for "water witching," thought to be helpful in divining veins of water for mining. Vogt and Golde, "Some Aspects of the Folklore of Water Witching." For more on dowsing, see J. Kaplan, "New Religious Movements and Globalizations," 95.

134. "Popular Errors, Prejudices, and Superstitions," 366.

135. A. Jones, "Sacred Places and Holy Ground," 93, appendix.

136. Chireau, *Black Magic*, 50; A. Jones, "Sacred Places and Holy Ground," 106.

137. Silvia Witherspoon, in FWP-WPA, *Slave Narratives*, vol. 1, 430. See also Singleton, "The Archaeology of Slave Life," 157.

138. Latta, *History of My Life and Work*, 115.

139. Nathans, *To Free a Family*.

140. Doc Edwards was living at Fairntosh, the Cameron family home near Stagville, during his 1937 Work Progress Administration interview. Doc Edwards, in FWP-WPA, *Slave Narratives*, vol. 11, pt. 1, 297.

141. Janie Cameron Riley, interview by Alice Eley Jones, July 7, 1986, transcript, SSHS. Descendants of those enslaved at Stagville recalled migration patterns both within North Carolina and beyond to Southern or Northern cities in the late nineteenth and early twentieth centuries.

Chapter Three

1. Sources for this vignette include Letter, Betsy Whitfield (Betsy) to Nathan Whitfield (Nathan), May 20, 1845, Book 8, Reel 2, WFP; "Slave Migration," Accession 92-076, WFP; Rainville, *Hidden History*; Gundaker, "Gardens and Yard Art," 897; Letter,

A. Comstock to Nathan, October 24, 1842, Book 2, Reel 1, WFP. In her May 20, 1845, letter to Nathan, Betsy wrote about the death of Cresy's child. Cresy may have lived at Gaineswood, but given the size of Chatham, far more enslaved people likely lived there. Searching through the dozens of documents related to the multiple forced migrations Whitfield imposed on his enslaved laborers shows several possible indications of "Cresy" or "Crisy," though the poor handwriting does not provide conclusive evidence. It is possible Cresy may have been purchased after the move to Alabama, but it seems more likely she participated in the forced move along with the enslaved Shallowell residents. Comstock's letter to Nathan in 1842 expressed condolences over the deaths of the Whitfield children.

2. The Whitfields most often referred to Chatham Plantation as the "lower plantation" in their letters. Virginia Van Der Veer Hamilton, among other historians, designate this plantation Chatham, and for consistency and clarity I do as well. Hamilton, *Alabama*, xvi–xvii.

3. These kinds of family trees and the recording of important familial information (vital dates and names) became increasingly popular and prevalent among white Americans in the nineteenth century. Winner, *A Cheerful and Comfortable Faith*, 168. Henry Goings, who found himself uprooted multiple times throughout his life in slavery, declared that "the slave has no Family Bible in which to record the births, marriages and deaths of his domestic circle." Goings, *Rambles of a Runaway*, 3.

4. See *IndiVisible: African-Native American Lives in the Americas*, traveling exhibit of the National Museum of the American Indian. To belong in a place is to be, as philosopher and sociologist Jan Willem Duyvendak articulates, "where one can collectively be, express and realize oneself . . . a material and/or symbolic place with one's own people and activities." Duyvendak, *Politics of Home*, 38.

5. "Statement from Meeting of New York Negroes."

6. Quoted in Gutman, *Black Family in Slavery and Freedom*, 471.

7. V. Brown, "Social Death and Political Life in the Study of Slavery," 1232–33. Death practices can be explored as part of what Brown calls the politics of survival. As Christina Sharpe explores, though, the metaphors and materiality of Black mourning provide a complicated connection between Black death, trauma, and survival. She examines the "wake" from several different perspectives: the watery rootlessness of the slave ship's wake; the wake held around the burial of a loved one; and waking to consciousness. As she argues, "while the wake produces Black death and trauma . . . we are, still produce in, into, and through the wake an insistence on existing." C. Sharpe, *In the Wake*, 11. This is not to say that death practices and sites did not differ across time and space. Erik Seeman has shown how, across the eighteenth-century Atlantic world, Black cemeteries and funerary practices depended on numerous local factors and changes in enslaving. Seeman, *Death in the New World*, chap. 6.

8. Wells-Oghoghomeh, *Souls of Womenfolk*, 152.

9. V. Brown, *Reaper's Garden*, 249.

10. Gundaker, "At Home on the Other Side," 53.

11. J. Warren, "To Claim One's Own," 112.

12. Almost all writing on Gaineswood describes the mansion in this way, from official historic site materials to coffee-table books to academic articles. The house was not referred to as Gaineswood until 1856. Jerry J. Nielsen, "Limited Archaeological

Investigations at Gaineswood, Demopolis, Alabama" (Department of Anthropology, University of Alabama, 1973), 4, Gaineswood Plantation, Demopolis, AL. The Alabama Historical Commission now owns the Gaineswood site, but the Friends of Gaineswood is in charge of operating it. This group includes descendants of the white Whitfield family, who have a strong tradition of family history, some of which does not align with the interpretations presented here. I am grateful for their perspective as well as for that of the Alabama Historical Commission's director of the Historic Sites Division, Eleanor Cunningham.

13. Eleanor Cunningham, phone call with author, July 20, 2021.

14. Lynn Rainville has documented more than 150 historic Black cemeteries in central Virginia through a painstaking process of documentary research and field work that included several paid research assistants. Even so, she notes that "many more unmarked or forgotten burials remain to be photographed and recorded." Rainville, *Hidden History*, 1.

15. One example of this monovision (and one that scholars often use uncritically) is Vlach, *Afro-American Tradition in Decorative Arts*, 27–44. For a much-needed correction of this monovision, see Jamieson, "Material Culture and Social Death."

16. Saidiya Hartman explores the idea of slave as continual "stranger." Hartman, *Lose Your Mother*.

17. The Alabama Historic Cemeteries Register includes seventy "primarily African-American" cemeteries. The vast majority of these are post-emancipation graveyards, and the list is not exhaustive; it functions more as a voluntary listing and includes information as the Alabama Historical Commission receives it. It does not, for instance, include the several Lauderdale County slave burial grounds referenced in this chapter, all of which have impressive levels of documentation thanks to the work of local historians and genealogists. Additionally, comparing the list with that of the crowd-sourced Black genealogy website AfriGeneas makes clear the need of comparing and balancing different resources on Black cemeteries in the state. Alabama Historical Commission, "The Alabama Historic Cemetery Register," May 3, 2019, https://ahc.alabama.gov/cemetery programPDFs/Alabama_Historic_Cemetery_Register%20May%202019.pdf. I am aware there is a serious gap in my source base with only limited descendant voices present. As Deanda Johnson wrote, "Under the assumption that the objects 'speak for themselves,' researchers often impose meaning on the objects, failing to utilize a valuable resource right under their noses—the descendant community." I have attempted to research and review descendants' important work on slave burial grounds and practices in Alabama and beyond; but I was not able to contact descendants of enslaved people at Chatham or Gaineswood for this chapter. D. Johnson, "Seeking the Living among the Dead," 3.

18. Very little has been written about Nathan Whitfield outside of his construction of Gaineswood. Few references to his North Carlina plantation have made it into public or academic sources. Based on letters in the Whitfield Family Papers, it appears he and his family referred (at least at times) to his Lenoir County, North Carolina, plantation as Shallowell. On one letter envelope, for instance, he scrawled the name of Shallowell over and over. See Envelope, Reel 1, Book 1, WFP. See also Letter, Nathan to Betsy, February 20, 1835, Book 4, Reel 1, WFP.

19. The liminality of slavery greatly limited the possibility of finding connection and establishing a sense of belonging anywhere or to anyone. See Hartman, *Lose Your Mother*; Smallwood, *Saltwater Slavery*.

20. In the past several decades, historians have foregrounded the antebellum era's massive, forced relocation of nearly one million enslaved people to the Deep South in the history of slavery, the US South, and the nation as a whole. Ira Berlin, Robert Gudmestad, Walter Johnson, Stephen Deyle, and others have shown how the interstate slave trade deeply affected enslaved people's lives as well as the region's and nation's economic and political future. Berlin, *Generations of Captivity*; Robert H. Gudmestad, "Slave Resistance, Coffles, and the Debates over Slavery," in W. Johnson, *Chattel Principle*, 79; Deyle, *Carry Me Back*. Life after forced migration, however, has played less a role in these investigations of the Second Middle Passage. Damian Alan Pargas is one exception to this, exploring the "assimilation and integration" of enslaved people after forced migration. However, his study focuses almost exclusively on those individuals who were sold, not those transported with an enslaving family. Pargas, *Slavery and Forced Migration*, 6–7, part 2. Asking if and how enslaved people attempted to reestablish roots through physical actions like mortuary practices allows us to further explore the impact of forced migration, including how relocation shaped homemaking on Southern plantations.

21. Rothman, *Slave Country*.

22. Barrett, "The Whitfields Move to Alabama," 113. Barrett's work provides important information on the migration but barely touches on the experience of enslaved people in it.

23. Letter, Betsy to Nathan, March 10, 1835, Book 8, Reel 2, WFP.

24. Goings, *Rambles of a Runaway*, 16.

25. Historians have demonstrated the centrality of the experience of migration to enslaved people. Damian Alan Pargas has described forced migration as "a central experience in the lives of Black slaves throughout the New World," while Ira Berlin described them as comprising the "migration generations," indicating just how transformative the experience was in their lives. Pargas, *Slavery and Forced Migration*, 2; Berlin, *Generations of Captivity*.

26. Deyle, *Carry Me Back*, 4. Deyle notes that the internal slave trade began earlier in the eighteenth century but took on a much larger scale after the American Revolution.

27. Pickard, *The Kidnapped and the Ransomed*, 57.

28. The Second Middle Passage was only one form of forced migration within the antebellum era, as roughly twice the number were moved intrastate (many, again, because of a sale), and more still were moved between rural to urban areas after being rented (or "hired"). Deyle, *Carry Me Back*, 4; Pargas, *Slavery and Forced Migration*, 2; J. Martin, *Divided Mastery*.

29. Letter, James Whitfield to Nathan, November 22, 1835, Book 4, Reel 1, WFP; Buckingham, *Slave States of America*, 248.

30. Walter Johnson, "Introduction," in W. Johnson, *Chattel Principle*, 1. Several slave narratives recounted this feeling, including Peter Still: "Then came a heavy sinking of the heart at the thought, that he must thenceforth be exposed to all the reputed hardships of the South. The constant toil in the great cotton fields, the oppressive heat, the danger of fearful sickness, and the deeper dread of cruel overseers—all these fell upon his hopes like snow upon the violets that have peeped out too soon." Pickard, *The Kidnapped and the Ransomed*, 71.

31. Gudmestad, "Slave Resistance, Coffles," 79.

32. Pargas, *Slavery and Forced Migration*, 57.

33. O'Donovan, *Becoming Free in the Cotton South*, 20.

34. Letter, J. R. Bryan to Nathan, September 15, 1829, Book 5, Reel 2, WFP. He asked his agent to hire out these men and women in Alabama; see also Book 4, Reel 1, and Book 5, Reel 2, WFP.

35. A List of Nathan B. Whitfield's negroes sent to Marengo County Alabama by and in care of John B. Whitfield the 17th day February 1834, Accession 92-076, WFP.

36. Letter, Nathan to Betsy, April 10, 1834, Accession 92-076, WFP.

37. Scholars have been particularly interested in the connections between forced migration and the slave trade, in part because they were two sides of the same coin. The slave trade necessarily meant the coerced relocation of enslaved individuals, and often forced migration was tied to the sale of enslaved people. Yet not all who experienced forced migration in the antebellum era had been sold. Some 40 percent or more of those moved within the Second Middle Passage did so as a part of, as Lacy Ford puts it, "a presumably more benign forced migration with slaveholding families." But, as the experience of enslaved people reveals, this process was in no way benign, nor was it separated from the market and the slave trade. Enslavers who found their labor supply lacking purchased slaves before embarking on the trek westward, as Nathan Whitfield did. Lacy Ford, "Reconsidering the Internal Slave Trade: Paternalism, Markets, and the Character of the Old South," in W. Johnson, *Chattel Principle*, 147.

38. Letter, Nathan to Betsy, April 13, 1835, Book 1, Reel 1, WFP. The state's limitations on importing enslaved laborers had put a damper on the Alabama trade, making enslaved individuals particularly valuable. As Whitfield's cousin and brother-in-law Gaius told him, "Try and buy all the slaves you can they are better than Carolina money at the time." Letter, Gaius Whitfield to Nathan, March 21, 1835, Box 1, Accession 96-040, WFP. For more on the Alabama ban, see Thornton, *Politics and Power in a Slave Society*, 319–20.

39. Bills of sale, Folder 6, Box 1, Accession 96-040, WFP.

40. Nathan's and Gaius's fathers were brothers, and Nathan married Gaius's half sister.

41. A List of Nathan Whitfield's negroes started for Marengo County, Alabama the 13th April 1835, Accession 92-076, WFP; Letter, Nathan to Betsy, April 24, 1835, Box 1, Accession 96-040, WFP.

42. Goings, *Rambles of a Runaway*, 15.

43. Pargas, *Slavery and Forced Migration*, 110–11.

44. Whitfield complained about how slow the enslaved caravan moved. Letter, Nathan to Betsy, April 18, 1835, Box 1, Accession 96-040, WFP. The estimated mileage is based on documents in the WFP. We know that the migrants stopped in Augusta, Georgia, making their route look quite like the one that cars take today.

45. Letter, Nathan to Betsy, April 24, 1835, Accession 92-076, WFP. Josiah Washington agreed "to deliver to the said Nathan B. Whitfield at his plantation in Marengo County Alabama." Agreement between Whitfield and Washington, April 29, 1835, Folder 4, Box 1, Accession 92-076, WFP.

46. A List of Nathan Whitfield's negroes started for Marengo County, Alabama the 13th April 1835, Accession 92-076, WFP.

47. Letter, Nathan to Betsy, April 18, 1835, Box 1, Accession 96-040, WFP.

48. Nathans, *A Mind to Stay*, 52.

49. Betsy wrote to Nathan in May 1829 that "the cotton is planted and the hands is preparing the new ground." Letter, Betsy to Nathan, May 8, 1829, Book 4, Reel 1, WFP.

50. Nathan Whitfield owned 67 enslaved people in Marengo County in 1850, and 249 enslaved people in Marengo County by 1860. See the 1850 and 1860 US Census–Slave Schedules, Marengo County, AL. A visitor to Nathan's plantation noted both cotton and corn in its fields. Letter, Joseph Borden to Nathan, May 20, 1840, Book 3, Reel 1, WFP.

51. Coelho and McGuire, "Biology, Diseases, and Economics." Sydney Nathans notes a strain of malaria unique to the Black Belt. Nathans, *A Mind to Stay*, 47.

52. Pickard, *The Kidnapped and the Ransomed*, 136.

53. Many African American proverbs, sermons, and songs indicate the Christian belief in heaven as a forever home. As Kerran Sanger argues, when African Americans sang of "going home" or "went home," they were talking about heaven, but even more than that, they were talking about freedom. Sanger, *When the Spirit Says Sing!*, 112–13; Gundaker, "At Home," 27.

54. Vlach, *Afro-American Tradition in Decorative Arts*, 141.

55. J. Young, *Rituals of Resistance*, 166.

56. Rainville, *Hidden History*, 52; King, "Separated by Death and Color," 126.

57. This belief of a pseudo-purgatory, anthropologist Robert Hertz and others argue, is an example of Black Americans combining an African cosmology with a Christian one. See Jamieson, "Material Culture and Social Death," 51.

58. Puckett, "Folk Beliefs of the Southern Negro," 103.

59. On maintaining connections with ancestors, see Sobel, *World They Made Together*. Archaeologists have documented the role of magic in Black Southern life, which is not the same as superstition. See Wilkie, "Secret and Sacred."

60. Rainville, *Hidden History*, 54; A. Jones, "Sacred Places and Holy Ground," in Gundaker, *Keep Your Head to the Sky*, 106.

61. As Ross Jamieson argues, "Mortuary remains are a form of ritual communication in which fundamental social values are expressed. . . . The control of symbolic instruments such as mortuary practices by slave owners and overseers was an attempt to alienate the slaves from claims of belonging to a legitimate social order, and instead to make the master-slave relationship the dominant cultural force." Jamieson, "Material Culture and Social Death," 54.

62. Gundaker, "Home Ground," 15.

63. Joseph Downer notes that few studies have been conducted of African practices in the same time period, making direct connections between American and African practices less certain. Downer, "Hallowed Ground, Sacred Place," 26–27.

64. Jamieson, "Material Culture and Social Death," 55

65. Downer, "Hallowed Ground, Sacred Place," 113.

66. Patterson, *Slavery and Social Death*.

67. My work does not negate Patterson's contention that the slave trade ruptured ties; as the exploration of forced migration shows, it continued to hurt families even after the Atlantic trade dwindled. But a rupture does not have to be complete or permanent, nor does it forever stop enslaved people's desire to find belonging and roots.

68. Faulkner, "Pantaloon in Black," 129.

69. Breeden, *Advice among Masters*, 124.

70. From more on how enslaved people's "trash" can tell us much about their lives and circumstances, see Ywone D. Edwards, "'Trash' Revisited: A Comparative Approach to Historical Descriptions and Archaeological Analysis of Slave Houses and Yards," in Gundaker, *Keep Your Head to the Sky*, 245–72.

71. Letter, William Blackledge to Nathan, March 16, 1826, Book 5, Reel 2, WFP.

72. Rainville, *Hidden History*, 54–55.

73. V. Brown, *Reaper's Garden*, 249.

74. Gundaker, "At Home," 25–53. Of course, it is erroneous to assume that all enslaved people related to all deaths the same way and that there was a single, monolithic understanding of what should come after.

75. Ann Tashjian and Dickran Tashjian, "The Afro-American Section of Newport, Rhode Island's Common Burying Ground," in Meyer, *Cemeteries and Gravemarkers*, 163–96.

76. Sometimes there were more than two burial grounds. In northern Alabama, the Wheeler Plantation contained three segregated cemeteries. Linda France Stine, "Archaeological Explorations at the Wheeler Plantation, Lawrence County, Alabama" (1997), 3, Office of Archaeological Research, University of Alabama Museums, accessed via Digital Archeological Record, https://core.tdar.org/document/210614/archaeological -explorations-at-the-wheeler-plantation-lawrence-county-alabama.

77. For how burial grounds reinforced hierarchy, see Laqueur, "Bodies, Death, and Pauper Funerals."

78. Vernacular Architecture Forum, *From Farm to Factory in Durham County*, 7; Jean B. Anderson, "A Preliminary Report on Stagville Plantation," 103–6.

79. "The John Coffee Servants Cemetery Kidsville," Local History-Genealogy Department, Florence-Lauderdale Library, Lauderdale County, AL.

80. At Hickory Hill Plantation near the Forks of Cypress, genealogists say that records and family tradition both attest to the burial of enslaved domestic servants immediately east of the walled enslaving Coffee family cemetery. The Florence City Historical Board probed the area and noted the presence of bodies. "John Coffee Servants Cemetery Kidsville." The work of genealogists, family historians, and descendants is featured on the website Find a Grave, which is a particularly useful resource for individual graves and burial grounds. See "Hickory Hill Slave Cemetery," Find a Grave, December 17, 2018, www.findagrave.com/cemetery/2677503/hickory-hill-plantation-slave-cemetery.

81. The small number of enslaved individuals buried (whether actually or reputedly) near an enslaving family were almost certainly those with direct working relationships to enslavers—butler, housemaid, coach, jockey.

82. James Jackson, the white Jackson family progenitor, died in 1840, leaving a will with the first and last names of eighty-five enslaved individuals. National Register of Historic Places, Forks of Cypress Cemetery, Lauderdale County, Alabama, 1999, NRHP. James Garman also suggests that the interment of enslaved individuals within white family burial plots may have been a means of "visually linking the bodies of slaves in the burying ground with the masters who survived them." Garman, "Viewing the Culture Line," 82.

83. Isaam Morgan, in FWP-WPA, *Slave Narratives*, vol. 1, 284.

84. Hugh B. Matternes, "Cemeteries," in Katy-Hyman and Rice, *World of a Slave*, 1:99–102.

85. Rainville, *Hidden History*, 13–14.

86. "Archaeology Sites at James Madison's Montpelier," 4, 14–17, MAD-MF, JMM; Kirchler, "Reinterpreting a 'Silent' History," 103, 166.

87. David S. Rotenstein, "The River Road Moses Cemetery: A Historic Preservation Evaluation" (2018), 13 (report prepared for the River Road African American community descendants, Silver Spring, MD), https://montgomeryplanning.org/wp-content /uploads/2020/07/Moses-Cemetery-Report-FINAL-LR-with-MIHP-form.pdf.

88. Downer, "Hallowed Ground, Sacred Place," 114.

89. For more on the concept of "margins," see hooks, "Marginality as Site of Resistance." For a challenge to hooks, see McKittrick, *Demonic Grounds*, 52–59.

90. Michael Trinkley, "Graves," in Katy-Hyman and Rice, *World of a Slave*, 1:255; Jean B. Anderson, "JBA Research Notes," SHSS. Other plantation sites in this study also maintained cemeteries near slave quarters. At Silver Bluff, James Henry Hammond's first plantation, the burial site was in the west-central section of the property, miles from his Silverton mansion. At Patton Place, oral histories testify to the proximity of the slave cemetery to the quarter, on the other side of the creek from the Patton mansion. See James D. Scurry, J. Walter Joseph, and Fritz Hamer, "Initial Archeological Investigations at Silver Bluff Plantation Aiken County, South Carolina" (October 1980), 38, Institute of Archaeology and Anthropology, University of South Carolina, https:// scholarcommons.sc.edu/archanth_books/161/; *Varner-Hogg Plantation*, 2:27, 109.

91. Archaeologist Rebecca Ginsburg has demonstrated how Black people physically experienced and comprehended the landscape—especially the "secret and disguised world" of woods, rivers, and paths rarely traversed—in more fluid and detailed ways than white. Rebecca Ginsburg, "Escaping through a Black Landscape," in Ellis and Ginsburg, *Cabin, Quarter, Plantation*, 54. Christine Simmons notes that slave burials most often took place at night, not only because of the cover of darkness but also because of the necessities of work during the day. Christine N. Simmons, "Grave Matters: African-American and Slave Cemeteries, Anne Arundel County, Maryland" (2004), 3–4, Anne Arundel Genealogical Society, https://aagensoc.org/.

92. As Grey Gundaker has demonstrated, "Diverse African peoples, as well as African Americans, associate certain bodies of water, trees, inverted or pierced vessels, and otherworldly colors such as white and silver with ancestors and/or spirits." Gundaker, "Gardens and Yard Art," 897.

93. Brooks, "Exploring the Material Culture of Death," 7. Brooks notes that enslaved burial grounds in the Chesapeake tended to be located close to water less than those in the Low Country, though that might have been the product of the landscape: there was more waterfront in the latter.

94. Kirchler, "Reinterpreting a 'Silent' History," 166; Alabama Historical Commission, "Alabama Historic Cemetery Register," 2019; "Rebecca Magby," Find a Grave, February 19, 2010, www.findagrave.com/memorial/48342892/rebecca-magby; "John W. Magbee," Find a Grave, March 10, 2011, www.findagrave.com/memorial/66730522. It is unclear how heavily wooded this area was in the nineteenth century, but it is very likely there was some tree cover.

95. Rainville, *Hidden History*, 14–15.

96. Alabama Historical Commission, "A Guide to Common Alabama Grave Markers," accessed February 10, 2011, https://ahc.alabama.gov/cemeteryprogramPDFs/Guideto CommonAlabamaGraveMarkers.pdf.

97. Rainville, *Hidden History*, 14.

98. Gundaker, "At Home," 32.

99. The vast majority of those enslaved by the Whitfields would have lived and labored at Chatham, not Gaineswood. In surmising the whereabouts of a particular slave cemetery in Hanover County, Virginia, Lynn Rainville states, "With a living population of two dozen people over at least one generation, one could expect that the enslaved community was provided with a separate burial ground to accommodate its dead." It does not seem a stretch to apply a similar logic to other plantations, including Chatham. Rainville, *Hidden History*, 15.

100. Enslaved residents of Gaineswood may have had their own burial site separate from those at Chatham.

101. Mortuary objects have been a key part of material culture studies since James Deetz's seminal work in the 1970s. J. Deetz, *In Small Things Forgotten*.

102. When no object remains, slave burial sites have been found by archaeologists through ground depressions that form after the decomposition of coffins and resultant soil resettlement.

103. Stokes, "Gone but Not Forgotten," 178. See also Jamieson, "Material Culture and Social Death," 54.

104. Additionally, it is important to note that Richard Meyer has demonstrated the influence of both ethnicity and regionalism on cemeteries and grave markers. Richard E. Meyer, "Ethnicity and Regionalism," in Meyer, *Cemeteries and Gravemarkers*, 161–62. In this way, antebellum slave cemeteries in Piedmont Virginia, Low Country South Carolina, and Black Belt Alabama may have looked and functioned differently, even if all those buried within them shared a common racial background and legal status. However, considering the uprooting of more than one million people from the Upper South to the Lower South, those distinctions plausibly blurred in the antebellum era; as people moved, so did their ideas and practices.

105. K. D. M. Snell investigates how gravestones served as markers of belonging and attachment, and how they functioned to help root people to a place. Snell, "Gravestones, Belonging and Local Attachment."

106. Robert Shepherd, born enslaved in Georgia, recalled all three elements of the post-death ritual. Robert Shepherd, in FWP-WPA, *Slave Narratives*, vol. 4, pt. 3, 251–52. Alexis Wells-Oghoghomeh provides a vivid description of enslaved people's death rituals, relying particularly on narratives like Shepherd's from Georgia. But these line up well with narratives from other states, including those from Alabama. See Wells-Oghoghomeh, *Souls of Womenfolk*, 151–59; FWP-WPA, *Slave Narratives*, vol. 1.

107. Material evidence of shrouds, with brass straight-pins to fasten them, have been found in slave burial grounds, including the extensively excavated African Burial Ground in New York City. Charles D. Cheek and Daniel G. Roberts, "The Archeology of 290 Broadway Volume II Archaeological and Historical Data Analyses" (report prepared for Jacobs Edwards and Kelcey and US General Services Administration, 2009), 77, www.gsa.gov/cdnstatic/largedocs/Volume_II_290Broadway.pdf. See also Frohne, *African Burial Ground in New York City*, 117–18. Women were central to the rituals of death, particularly in cleaning and dressing the body. See Brock, "Burial Customs."

108. Jamieson, "Material Culture and Social Death," 53; Hugh B. Matternes, "Coffins and Caskets," in Katy-Hyman and Rice, *World of a Slave*, 1:128–29; Trinkley, "Graves," in

Katy-Hyman and Rice, *World of a Slave*, 1:254–58. Archaeologists have identified commonly used woods for coffins as pine, poplar, elm, maple, cedar, and other softwoods. Coffins were ubiquitous in the New York African Burial Ground, though evidence suggests that some enslaved people were buried with just a shroud. Frohne, *African Burial Ground in New York City*, 116. National Register of Historic Places, Forks of Cypress Cemetery, 7. The use of coffins can be identified through the regularity of depressions in the cemetery ground.

109. Brock, "Burial Customs," 20; Vlach, *Afro-American Tradition in Decorative Arts*, 139.

110. The burial was sometimes distinct from the funeral, which might take place days, weeks, or even months after.

111. See Downer, "Hallowed Ground, Sacred Place," 34.

112. Unusually, some of the rocks have etchings that range from unadorned initials to full names and vital dates, though it appears that most of the marked graves denote individuals who died after abolition. The number of probable burials, however, far exceeds the number of marked graves. Whether those graves were never marked or were once marked with stones or materials that disintegrated or were stolen is unknown. John Welch Prewitt, who was a slave trader, once held some 6,000 acres of land and established a separate burial ground for his enslaved laborers sometime in the 1820s. Thankfully, a number of the burials have been identified. "Old Prewitt Slave Cemetery," Find a Grave, January 1, 2000, www.findagrave.com/cemetery/25175/old-prewitt-slave-cemetery.

113. Jamieson, "Material Culture and Social Death," 50.

114. Puckett, "Folk Beliefs of the Southern Negro," 104.

115. As genealogist Nadia Orton notes, just in the last sixty years, an untold number of slave cemeteries have been wiped from the landscape by "freeway construction, eminent domain, 'urban renewal' programs, and gentrification." Nadia Orton, "Recovering and Preserving African American Cemeteries," *National Trust for Historic Preservation Leadership Forum* (blog), June 2, 2016, https://forum.savingplaces.org/blogs/special-contributor/2016/06/02/recovering-and-preserving-african-american-cemeteries.

116. Jamieson, "Material Culture and Social Death," 50. It appears that the practice of placing vessels on graves was a long-standing one in the Caribbean. Textual evidence from islands like Barbados note the practice of enslaved people placing food and drink (and thus vessels) atop graves, a tradition that lasted on the island until at least the 1820s. This practice of placing ceramics atop graves may have a much longer and diasporic presence. See Handler and Lange, *Plantation Slavery in Barbados*, 205–6.

117. Broken plates were a key component of the funerary rituals performed at Freedman's Cemetery in Dallas, Texas, and these ceramics were acquired for this specific purpose. For more on Freedman's Cemetery, see Peter, *Freedman's Cemetery*.

118. Bolton, "Decoration of Graves of Negroes in South Carolina." Bolton is now remembered primarily as a historian and bibliographer of chemistry, but he was also a life member of the American Folklore Society, presumably because of his deep interest in alchemy and magic. Perhaps this was what drew him to the burial practices and artifacts of postbellum Black Southerners, who held a particular interest to many late nineteenth-century scholars as they were assumed to be continuing practices of conjuring and witchcraft associated with enslaved Americans. "In Memoriam: Henry Carrington Bolton."

119. "Southern Superstitions," *Washington Post*, February 25, 1908.

120. Georgia Writer's Project, *Drums and Shadows*, 147. Language in quotations from this source changed to standard English for ease of reading.

121. Georgia Writer's Project, *Drums and Shadows*, 130–31.

122. While Vlach can be criticized for his monovision about African retentions, his work in cataloging the objects is well-grounded. He describes the wide variety of grave markers found in African American cemeteries: "Most of these items are pottery or pressed-glass containers, but many different objects are encountered, including cups, saucers, bowls, clocks, salt and pepper shakers, medicine bottles, spoons, pitchers, oyster shells, conch shells, white pebbles, toys, dolls' heads, bric-a-brac statues, light bulbs, tureens, flashlights, soap dishes, false teeth, syrup jugs, spectacles, cigar boxes, piggy banks, gun locks, razors, knives, tomato cans, flower pots, marbles, bits of plaster, toilet tanks." Vlach, *Afro-American Tradition in Decorative Arts*, 139.

123. While investigating Black cemeteries in central Virginia, Lynn Rainville has documented three dozen antebellum cemeteries and found that only 5 percent of slave gravestones were inscribed. Rainville, *Hidden History*, 2.

124. Lee Freeman, genealogist at the Florence-Lauderdale Library, has composed nearly two dozen memorials to enslaved and free Black Americans who are assumed to be buried in the Hickory Hill slave graveyard, including three to unnamed Coffee-owned men who drowned in the Tennessee River in 1840. "Unnamed Coffee Slave," Find a Grave, December 18, 2018, www.findagrave.com/memorial/195423011/unnamed -coffee_slave; Lee Freeman, email message to author, June 8, 2020. For more on the men's deaths, see "Unfortunate Casualty," *Florence Enquirer*, 1840, Hickory Hill Plantation and Cemetery digital exhibit, accessed November 27, 2021, https://shoalsBlack history.omeka.net/items/show/747. Shoals Black History houses numerous digital exhibits displaying primary sources from state and regional archives, including an exhibit on Hickory Hill Plantation and Cemetery. The website is a community collaboration between Project Say Something, the Florence-Lauderdale Public Library, the University of North Alabama Public History Program, and the people of the Shoals.

125. Bills of sale, Hickory Hill Plantation and Cemetery digital exhibit, accessed November 27, 2021, https://shoalsBlackhistory.omeka.net/exhibits/show/enslaved-people -who-were-owned/enslaved-people-who-were-owned.

126. Historical Marker, photograph, "Hickory Hill Plantation Slave Cemetery," Historical Marker Database, accessed November 27, 2021, www.hmdb.org/m.asp?m=138778. The Florence Historical Board asserts that the markers were likely common fieldstones.

127. John Coffee was the patriarch of the Coffee family and a key participant in the Creek War of 1813–14 that violently appropriated Native lands. His Hickory Hill Plantation was about three miles north of Florence, Alabama. For more on John Coffee, see G. Chappell, "John Coffee." Joshua Coffee, John's son, administered the plantation after his father's death in 1833, though a significant portion of those owned by John went to his other son, Alexander, who owned the plantation with the Coffee Servant's Cemetery some 4 miles west of Florence. See Lewis, "John Coffee."

128. "John Coffee Servants Cemetery Kidsville."

129. "Annie M. Coffee," Find a Grave, accessed November 27, 2021, www.findagrave .com/memorial/195424480/annie-m_-coffee (no longer active).

130. The third inscribed tombstone in the Coffee "Servants Cemetery" is that of Katty, the "wife of David Smith," who died in 1842. Unlike the other two gravestones, Katty's

includes neither a reference to her loyalty or faithfulness nor a notation of who erected it. It is possible David himself erected the tombstone. The language on his tombstone is telling: "Hutchins" referred to David's first enslaver, a name he did not choose but that he may have chosen to expunge after slavery's end (considering it does not appear on Katty's stone). Its inclusion on his own tombstone is likely more reflective of white people's choices, specifically those of Mary Coffee Campbell, than his own. Coffee Servants Cemetery, surveyed by Orlan Irons, January 5, 1989, RootsWeb, accessed November 27, 2021, https://sites.rootsweb.com/~allauder/cem-coffeeservantblack.htm; "'Old Uncle Dave': The Oldest Man in Lauderdale Dead," *Florence Times*, July 18, 1890, accessed via "1890s Obituaries," RootsWeb, November 27, 2021, http://sites.rootsweb.com/~allauder/obits -florencetimes1890.htm.

131. Garman, "Viewing the Culture Line," 80–82.

132. Bolton, "Decoration of Graves of Negroes in South Carolina."

133. David Roediger argued that the placement of bodies in graves reflects a clear African retention. Vlach echoes this, as do several scholars, with little evidence to support them. Roediger, "And Die in Dixie," 170–71; Vlach, *Afro-American Tradition in Decorative Arts*, 147.

134. The same bodily orientation has been found at the slave cemetery at Montpelier. "Archaeology Sites at James Madison's Montpelier," 16–17, MAD-MF, JMM. Downer asserts it is "far-fetched" to assume that enslaved people's burial orientation was (or at least was *only*) an African retention. Downer, "Hallowed Ground, Sacred Place," 33–34. See also Jamieson, "Material Culture and Social Death," 52.

135. Emmaline Heard, in FWP-WPA, *Slave Narratives*, vol. 4, pt. 2, 159.

136. Rachleff, "An Abolitionist Letter to Governor Henry W. Collier of Alabama," 252.

137. Rachleff, "An Abolitionist Letter to Governor Henry W. Collier of Alabama."

138. These personal goods were also meant to help the spirit as they ascended into the next life. Vlach, *Afro-American Tradition in Decorative Arts*, 139–41.

139. In middle-class and elite white cemeteries, markers and their inscriptions were meant in part to emphasize the deceased's individuality, demarcating them as discrete entities even within a family plot or cemetery. As Jennifer Van Horn argues in the context of eighteenth-century Charleston, white residents' gravestones both displayed an individual's standing and worked to bind those individuals "into a highly visible community that transcended the boundary of death." Van Horn, *Power of Objects*, 156–58, quote from 156.

140. Rainville, *Hidden History*, 3.

141. National Register of Historic Places, Forks of Cypress Cemetery, 6.

142. As the National Register of Historic Places Nomination Form notes, the postbellum monuments appear to "physically defer to the antebellum, Civil War era ones," an interesting physical manifestation of the importance of enslaving to this family. National Register of Historic Places, Forks of Cypress Cemetery, 5.

143. National Register of Historic Places, Forks of Cypress Cemetery, 7.

144. In the early twentieth century, Elise Clews Parsons asserted that African Americans were tied more to the particular place of the cemetery than a particular plot within it. Simmons, "Grave Matters," 7. On the other hand, archaeologists contend that a

cemetery with seemingly haphazard arrangement might still reflect conscious groupings of individuals, sometimes in social status, perhaps even by age, but often in families. Downer, "Hallowed Ground, Sacred Place," 10–11.

145. Phebe did not die until 1848, and so lived more than a decade in Alabama. Letter, William Whitfield to Nathan, May 25, 1848, Book 7, Reel 2, WFP.

146. Hale, *Historic Plantations of Alabama's Black Belt*, chap. 6. Isaac is highlighted on the Gaineswood tour, though more research is needed to explore his many contributions to the mansion and the plantations. Gaineswood Tour, Paige Smith (Director), June 27, 2018.

147. Two men named Isaac are named in Whitfield's lists of enslaved laborers in Alabama by 1832. Box 1, Accession 96-040, WFP.

148. It is not clear exactly how the members of this community continued to lay one another to rest here. As is so often the case with slave cemeteries, this site contains markers with no text, making it unclear exactly who was buried in this cemetery or when.

149. An Eagle Scout and his troop in the early 1990s recovered this information and honored the deceased with plaques including their names and familial units.

150. See the 1870 US Census and 1880 US Census, Lauderdale County, AL.

151. National Register of Historic Places, Forks of Cypress Cemetery, 7.

152. Bill of sale, Hickory Hill Plantation and Cemetery digital exhibit, accessed November 27, 2021, https://shoalsBlackhistory.omeka.net/exhibits/show/enslaved-people-who-were-owned/item/774.

153. Southern Claims Commission, 1874, Freedmen and Southern Society Project. Found at "Webb Coffee," Find a Grave, December 28, 2018, www.findagrave.com/memorial/195614203/webb-coffee.

154. *Florence Gazette*, April 6, 1881, Hickory Hill Plantation and Cemetery digital exhibit, accessed November 27, 2021, https://shoalsBlackhistory.omeka.net/exhibits/show/enslaved-people-who-were-owned/item/637.

155. "Rebecca Coffee," Find a Grave, December 27, 2018, www.findagrave.com/memorial/195592171/rebecca-coffee. See also Dyas Collection—John Coffee Papers, Tennessee State Library and Archives, https://sos.tn.gov/products/tsla/dyas-collection-john-coffee-papers-1770-1917.

156. "Sally Coffee," Find a Grave, accessed November 27, 2021, www.findagrave.com/memorial/195467391/sally-coffee (no longer active); "Washington Coffee," Find a Grave, accessed November 27, 2021, www.findagrave.com/memorial/195463001/washington-coffee (no longer active).

157. "John Kemper," Find a Grave, December 31, 2018, www.findagrave.com/memorial/195693565/john-kemper.

158. Photograph and obituary of Simon Jackson, Hickory Hill Plantation and Cemetery digital exhibit, accessed November 27, 2021, https://shoalsBlackhistory.omeka.net/exhibits/show/enslaved-people-who-were-owned/item/789.

159. Ester Whitfield, 1870 Census, Marengo County, AL; Vinea Whitfield, 1880 US Census, Marengo County, AL. The 1827 bill of sale notes, "1 woman Chloe 30 years old & 2 children Venus & Rony aged 4 & 6 years $452, 1 girl Esther 10 years, $226." Bills of sale, Folder 6, Box 1, Accession 96-040, WFP. Then, in Whitfield's list of enslaved laborers sent to Marengo County, Chloe is listed first, followed by Esther, Rony, David

(name crossed off), and Venus. A List of Nathan B. Whitfield's negroes sent to Marengo County Alabama by and in care of John B. Whitfield the 17th day February 1834, Accession 92-076, WFP.

160. Smith, *To Serve the Living.*

161. Cornelia Winfield, in FWP-WPA, *Slave Narratives*, vol. 4, pt. 4, 178.

Chapter Four

1. Sources for this vignette include testimony from witnesses in Brazoria County Court (BCC), Case #453, Probate Records, Folder 2 (copies of BCC, Case #453 documents are available for viewing at V-HP); Amy C. Earls and Mary Beth S. Tomka, "Historic and Prehistoric Archaeological Excavations at Varner-Hogg Plantation State Historical Park Brazoria County, Texas," October 1994, 84–88, V-HP. Although the plantation is now known as Varner-Hogg Plantation State Historic Site, I use the term Patton Place throughout this chapter to refer to the plantation, as it was owned specifically by the Pattons between 1834 and the 1869. Nineteenth-century sources likewise refer to it as such. See receipts for work done at Patton Place, BCC, Case #690, Probate Records, Folder 6 (copies of BCC, Case #690 documents are available for viewing at V-HP). Interview with Francis H. Evans, V-HP; *Varner-Hogg Plantation*, 2:52.

2. I do not use a surname for Rachel until after emancipation, when records begin to show her using one of two last names. Charles Grimm, one of the white community members who described Rachel in this way, used the term "mistress" not so much as a reference to her position as Columbus's sexual companion but instead as a reference to her position in Columbus's household. Answers of Charles Grimm, BCC, Case #453, Probate Records, Folder 2. Scholars have understandably derided the terms "slave mistress" and "concubine," arguing that they erase sexual violence and distort the reality of life for enslaved women. See Emily Owens, "On the Use of 'Slave Mistress,'" *Black Perspectives*, August 21, 2015, www.aaihs.org/on-the-use-of-slave-mistress/; Martha S. Jones, "Julian Bond's Great-Grandmother a 'Slave Mistress?' How the *New York Times* Got it Wrong," History News Network, August 26, 2015, https://historynewsnetwork.org/article/160451. Still others emphasize the importance of using the language of the era and place, including Alexandra Finley, who argues that the term "concubine" has historically been used to describe relations between enslaver and enslaved wherein coercion is present, thereby negating concerns that such a term elides the force involved. Finley, *An Intimate Economy*, 11–12. I therefore use the terms that Rachel's contemporaries used to describe her, including "lady," "mistress," and "wife," but I do so with full recognition that these people practiced and supported the very system that perpetuated her enslavement. In using their words, though, I lean into their doubled function: first, that these words were used by white people who believed in their power yet sought to strip Rachel of the very status that attended them; and second, that they can nonetheless also signal Rachel's own aspirations.

3. An intimate relationship does not mean that it was kind or consensual. But, as Emily Owens and Alexandra Finley argue, consent was not even a choice or possibility for enslaved women. Through attention to Rachel's domestic strategies, we can move beyond the false binary of consent and violation and explore instead how Black women sought to define themselves within and outside of these relationships and the homes they

created in the process. E. Owens, *Consent in the Presence of Force*; Finley, *An Intimate Economy*.

4. Answers of Charles Grimm.

5. It is in the documents of the two BCC cases (#690, Probate Records, and #453, Probate Records) surrounding Columbus Patton's insanity and later his estate that we find the most information on Rachel's life.

6. Statement Accompanying Exhibit "B," 1860, BCC, Case #690, Probate Records, Folder 3.

7. Thavolia Glymph, for instance, asserts that proslavery, and even antislavery, descriptions of enslaved women as dirty and difficult to manage were meant to strip these women of their womanhood and thus their ability to be mothers, wives, and domestic ideals. Glymph, *Out of the House of Bondage*, 94–95.

8. D. White, *Ar'n't I a Woman?*

9. Scott, *Southern Lady*, xi.

10. For more on the ideal of Southern ladyhood, see Scott, *Southern Lady*, esp. chap. 1.

11. Heneghan, *Whitewashing America*. As Alexandra Finley contends, domestic labor included a woman's prudent shopping, signifying that public activities constituted a core part of a woman's domesticity. Finley, *An Intimate Economy*, 5.

12. As women's historians argued beginning in the 1970s, these two spheres—the private and public—were never separate but always shaping and influencing and interfering in the other. Cott, *Bonds of Womanhood*; Kerber, "Separate Spheres, Female World, Woman's Place."

13. In some ways, Rachel—who maintained great influence in the enslaver's home and possessed purchasing power through access to capital—was exceptional in relation to the millions of other people enslaved in the United States. At the same time, her position was not singular. Alexis Neumann's work on enslaved-enslaver relationships, particularly on incestual ones, has helped me think through the exceptional versus representational issue. Neumann approaches different case studies through the lens of "the exceptional normal," which allows us to see cases that on the surface may seem exceptional but that are, in fact, representative of widespread ideologies and actions. Neumann, "American Incest," 10. For my work, this includes the fact that Rachel lived in a world where relationships (sexual or not) between enslaved people and their enslavers were common, and the fear, manipulation, and violence that kept her position precarious was the same experienced by millions of other enslaved and free women. For more on enslaved-enslaver relationships, see Stevenson, "What's Love Got to Do with It?"

14. Not that these records *meant* to archive Rachel's existence. Much of the testimony and documents in the cases existed to prove or disprove the sanity of her enslaver, Columbus. His brother, sisters, and nephew used Rachel as a pawn to prove their case, yet in focusing part of their case on her, they unintentionally recorded her existence for us. Very few records outside the two Brazoria County Court cases tell us about Rachel, but these documents give us insight into her intimate patterns of domestic life with Columbus. We do, though, have her own words—through the intermediary of a lawyer—from a postbellum court case: *Bartlett v. Adriance*, BCC, Case #2997. I am indebted to John R. Lundberg for finding and sharing this case with me.

15. As with so much evidence of enslaved people's lives, these court documents do

not come from Rachel's own hand or mouth but from those who practiced or defended the institution of slavery. The court testimony, for instance, comes from white, male Texans, most of whom were enslavers, overseers, doctors, merchants, or otherwise part of the region's slaving system. As Alexandra Finley has shown, this kind of testimony often reveals more about the speaker's own worldview than about those they attempt to describe. The violence of the archive shrouds the voices, personalities, beliefs, and actions of enslaved women like Rachel. Reading these documents leaves one with few firm declarations and far more questions. Yet reasonable and responsible speculation—in concert with additional evidence—allows us to move beyond the history we know now, a history we assume is correct because it has been so long articulated, but which is itself part conjecture based on available sources. Finley, *An Intimate Economy*, 69.

16. Too often, Rachel has been portrayed only as a side character in Columbus's story, an extraordinary but tragic figure whose story does not exist apart from her enslavers. Ann Patton Malone, perhaps the first historian to write about the relationship, described Rachel, Columbus, and the Patton family ordeal as "straight out of William Faulkner," thereby reinforcing the white male perspective and diverting us from asking questions about Rachel. In fact, Malone concludes that the significance of this relationship lay in what it can tell us about enslavers by providing "us with evidence of the regard with which many female slaves were held by their owner-consorts." Malone, *Women on the Texas Frontier*, 44–46. This is not to say that scholars do not recognize the power imbalance, the role of coercion, or the role of violence. But most typically, in the context of antebellum Texas, historians have viewed these enslaver-enslaved intimate relationships as mere illustrations of the frontier experience or the state's unique legal system, a way of demonstrating something bigger and supposedly more important about the institution of slavery in the Lone Star State. See, for example, Carroll, *Homesteads Ungovernable*. Scholars of slavery—and more specifically of sexuality and intimacy—have made massive strides to correct this analytical and interpretive imbalance, though not in the context of antebellum Texas. See especially Berry and Harris, *Sexuality and Slavery*. For more on the history of slavery in Texas, see Campbell, *Empire for Slavery*; and Torget, *Seeds of Empire*.

17. The exact year of the Pattons' migration is not clear, but it was likely 1832 or 1833. It appears that at least two additional enslaved people—Jake and Solomon—made this journey with Rachel and the Pattons, as all three had been born in Kentucky. Rachel Patton, 1880 US Census, Brazoria County, TX; Jacob Steele, line number 1001, and Solomon Williams, line number 1003, 1867 Voter Registration List, Brazoria County, TX. It is possible many more than three made this journey; V-HP currently states that sixty enslaved people came with the Pattons, although staff could not confirm where that number came from. I do not refer to Rachel or any other enslaved laborers owned by the Pattons as part of the Patton family. As such, any references to the Pattons during the era of slavery describe the white Patton family members.

18. We do not know Rachel's exact age at the time of the move. The 1880 US Census lists her age as sixty, putting her birth year at 1820, though multiple estate inventories suggest her birth year to have been around 1814. 1880 US Census, Brazoria County, TX; Inventory of John D. Patton, 1840, Record of Wills, V-HP (original at BCC); Estimative Inventory of Property Owned by Columbus R. Patton, 1854, Record of Wills, V-HP; Inventory of C. R. Patton Estate, July 1857, Record of Wills, V-HP. It is unclear exactly who owned Rachel in her early years, but A. S. Tyler of Kentucky recalled that he "left

her" with Columbus in 1833, when she would have been a teenager. Whether this transfer took place in Kentucky or Texas is not explicitly stated, though a close consideration of Tyler's testimony suggests it took place in Kentucky. Answers of A. S. Tyler, BCC, Case #453, Probate Records, Folder 2.

19. The Pattons appear to have viewed their property as family-owned rather than as individually owned, sometimes even jointly claiming their property, both in land and in people. The estimate of enslaved individuals owned by the family in the late 1830s to the early 1840s ranges from fifty-six to sixty-six, depending on the exact year and the family members in question. See *Varner-Hogg Plantation*, 2:53; and Inventory of John D. Patton, 1840. Charles F. Patton claimed eighty-three enslaved laborers in 1860. 1860 US Census–Slave Schedule, Brazoria County, TX.

20. In an interview, Anthony Christopher, a man who had been enslaved on Patton Place, remembered "lots of cotton and corn and cane to make sugar and cattle and hawgs and hosses and plenty [of enslaved laborers] to work de place." Interview with Anthony Christopher, in Rawick, *American Slave*, 718. This region of Texas became known as the Sugar Bowl, with Patton Place consistently ranking in the first or second tier of sugar producers in Brazoria County. Watts, "A History of the Texas Sugar Industry"; *Varner-Hogg Plantation*, 2:55, 63.

21. Like the Madisons at Montpelier, the Pattons used a natural barrier and dividing line (in this case a creek) to visually separate their home from the dwellings of enslaved field laborers. On the other side of Varner Creek, enslaved residents used the same handmade bricks to build double-pen cabins for themselves alongside the plantation's many work buildings. Interview with Anthony Christopher, in Rawick, *American Slave*, 722. This separation between what enslavers coded as home (their own space) and labor (enslaved people's space) continued into the twentieth-century interpretation of the site. A 1983 institutional document recorded that "Varner Creek flows through the length of the site, separating the main residential area from the former industrial site," aka the enslaved living and laboring site. *Varner-Hogg Plantation*, 1:40.

22. Kelley, *Los Brazos de Dios*, 63–64.

23. The exact construction date of the mansion is not documented, though most sources point to its completion between 1835 and 1836. See, for instance, Historic American Buildings Survey, "Varner-Hogg Plantation House, Varner Hogg State Park Museum, West Columbia, Brazoria County, TX," HABS TX-251, Library of Congress; *Varner-Hogg Plantation*, 2:101; and "The Patton Family," 8, V-HP. Quote from Answers of Charles Grimm. It is unclear exactly when the relationship between Rachel and Columbus began, though as early as 1833, A. S. Tyler saw something "brewing" between them. Answers of A. S. Tyler. It should be noted that several witnesses to Rachel and Columbus's interactions did not explicitly use the terminology of "wife." For these men, there could be a distinction between cohabitating with a woman ("concubine or kept woman and not . . . a wife") and calling her his wife. In another case involving an enslaved-enslaver intimate relationship, witnesses and the judge distinguished between the woman Sobrina as a "kept" woman and as a wife, and the judge of the case provided the above quote distinguishing between the two. See Gillmer, *Slavery and Freedom in Texas*, 40–45.

24. Columbus Patton never acknowledged children with any woman, and the court records never mention any progeny. Family history and local lore suggest that Henry

Patton, who is listed as German-born in the 1850 and 1860 US Censuses and "my Dutch boy" in Columbus's will, might be Columbus and Rachel's child, but very little confirming evidence exists for that.

25. Common-law marriages were common enough during the nineteenth century to necessitate a growing debate about their legitimacy in the courts. See Dubler, "Governing through Contract."

26. Hunter, *Bound in Wedlock*, 8.

27. See Finley, *An Intimate Economy*, 81.

28. Rachel knew that Texas laws made manumission extremely difficult, and she seemed to believe that Columbus had done everything he could to give her as much freedom as possible, particularly within his will. In an 1870 court case, Rachel declared that "it was the intention of Columbus R. Patton to give your petitioner [Rachel] her freedom as far as he could do so under the then existing laws of the state of Texas." BCC, Case #2997.

29. Gillmer, *Slavery and Freedom in Texas*, 32.

30. Sarah Ford, in FWP-WPA, *Slave Narratives*, vol. 16, pt. 2, 42.

31. Domestic manuals, advice literature, and even novels presented a white middle-class moral order that separated home from the outside world, in the process negating the economic and productive value of women's domestic work by recasting it as altruistic, feminine love. See Boydston, *Home and Work*, esp. chap. 7.

32. See Clinton, *Plantation Mistress*; Fox-Genovese, *Within the Plantation Household*; Jones, *Labor of Love, Labor of Sorrow*; Glymph, *Out of the House of Bondage*.

33. As Anne Firor Scott argued more than fifty years ago, no woman of any class or race could ever live up to the fantasies of white Southern womanhood. Scott, *Southern Lady*. Yet the ideal was still racialized and classed in ways that excluded particular people—including enslaved Black women—from ever taking advantage of the small but real power that such fantasies offered to some women. See A. Kaplan, "Manifest Domesticity," 581–606; A. Burton, "Toward Unsettling Histories of Domesticity." The ideal of the Southern lady was inherently juxtaposed to the slave; ladyhood, therefore, was also racialized. See Farnham, *Education of the Southern Belle*, esp. intro.

34. This was part of the Pattons' goal with the court case: to establish that Rachel controlled Columbus and thus that the will should be voided. Yet it seems unlikely that so many different individuals would testify to the same point and would claim to have seen it firsthand if there were not some truth to it. Those who spoke of Rachel's stature held a range of relationships to the Pattons, from former Patton Place overseers to doctors who administered to enslaved residents to longtime friends. The differences in occupation and status meant that some witnesses felt her authority more directly; an overseer, for instance, interacted with Rachel in ways different from a family friend. All, however, were frequent visitors to the plantation and had ample opportunities to witness Rachel's behavior and attitude. To these observations and interactions they brought shared raced and gendered beliefs about the roles enslaved people should and should not hold on the plantation; it was this belief system that Rachel challenged in her determination to act and be treated as the lady of the house.

35. Answers of George O. Jarvis, BCC, Case #453, Probate Records, Folder 2.

36. Texas historians note that family and community members' positions toward bi-

racial relationships "hardened" beginning around the 1850s as slavery further ensconced itself in the state. Carroll, *Homesteads Ungovernable*, 73. But it seems that the Patton family was in conflict with Rachel from nearly the beginning.

37. St. Clair Patton worked as overseer sometime before his death in 1849. "The Patton Family," 5, V-HP. Mat worked as overseer for most of 1852 through 1854. BCC, Case #690, Probate Records, Folder 4.

38. These conflicts could be traced back to interactions with or opinions they had of Rachel. Answers of Charles Grimm. A. S. Tyler, who lived in Kentucky, wrote to Columbus expressing concern about the "great many difficulty with his relations and overseer on the account of the negro girl Rachel." Answers of A. S. Tyler.

39. See Berlin and Morgan, "Introduction," in *Cultivation and Culture*, 1–45.

40. Answers of John Adriance, BCC, Case #453, Probate Records, Folder 2.

41. Answers of Charles Grimm.

42. Sarah Ford, in FWP-WPA, *Slave Narratives*, vol. 16, pt. 2, 43.

43. Answers of E. S. Jackson, BCC, Case #453, Probate Records, Folder 2.

44. Answers of George O. Jarvis.

45. Clinton, *Plantation Mistress*; Fox-Genovese, *Within the Plantation Household*; Glymph, *Out of the House of Bondage*; D. White, *Ar'n't I a Woman?*; Finley, *An Intimate Economy*; Jones-Rogers, *They Were Her Property*. Jones-Rogers has urged us to reconsider what we mean by the term "mistress" in relation to white enslaving women, employing the term to signify "a woman who govern[ed]." Jones-Rogers, *They Were Her Property*, xiv–xv.

46. Answers of Charles Grimm.

47. Answers of E. S. Jackson.

48. Scott, *Southern Lady*, 31. The work of Southern women of various classes, races, and ethnicities often went unacknowledged and unpaid. See Delfino and Gillespie, *Neither Lady nor Slave*.

49. Malone, *Women on the Texas Frontier*, 15–20.

50. Gillmer, *Slavery and Freedom in Texas*, 37. As Catherine Clinton has argued, the "planter's wife was in charge not merely of the mansion but the entire spectrum of domestic operations." Clinton, *Plantation Mistress*, 18.

51. Answers of E. S. Jackson. WPA narratives from southeastern Texas, including Gus Johnson and Lucy Lewis, discuss enslaving women/plantation mistresses whipping slaves. Gus Johnson, in FWP-WPA, *Slave Narratives*, vol. 16, pt. 2, 208; Lucy Lewis, in FWP-WPA, *Slave Narratives*, vol. 16, pt. 3, 16.

52. Answers of George O. Jarvis.

53. Jones-Rogers, *They Were Her Property*, esp. chap. 3. Rachel was not unique in this. As Jessica Marie Johnson contends, Black women were not unwilling to use the violence and cruelty of enslavement for their own benefit, particularly if it gave them some level of control over their own safety and security. J. Johnson, *Wicked Flesh*, 3.

54. Answers of George O. Jarvis.

55. Answers of Charles Grimm.

56. Dr. Collins likewise remembered that Rachel made her management of overseers and workmen loud enough "where Mr. Patton could hear it." Answers of Dr. Collins, BCC, Case #453, Probate Records, Folder 2.

57. Answers of E. S. Jackson.

58. Answers of Charles Grimm.

59. Answers of George O. Jarvis. E. S. Jackson also asserted that, "I never knew Mr Patton to whip Rachel or have her whipped." Answers of E. S. Jackson.

60. Answers of Dr. Collins; Answers of Charles Grimm.

61. Answers of Dr. Collins.

62. Answers of Horace Cone, BCC, Case #453, Probate Records, Folder 2.

63. See *Varner-Hogg Plantation*. This observation is also based on tours taken of the mansion, though it should be noted that Varner-Hogg is currently reworking the mansion tour, including the reinterpretation of other sites on the plantation.

64. This estimated date (1840s) is based on when Annie and her two daughters were no longer living at Patton Place.

65. As Francis Evans remembered, "It was built for comfort in a hot climate." Interview with Francis H. Evans.

66. Daniel J. Crouch, "Varner-Hogg Plantation State Historical Park Archaeological Investigations" (February 1982), 60, V-HP.

67. Hart and Kemp, *Lucadia Pease and the Governor*, 27.

68. "Eliza M. Hill Estate Personal Property 1848," provided by Hal Simmons-Hassell of the Texas Historical Commission. Simmons-Hassell lists Hill as being at Osceola Plantation, but she may have died at Waverly Plantation, where it seems she and her third husband, William Green Hill, lived. William Green Hill moved with his children to Osceola around 1860. See appendix A, "Thomas Westall Family Genealogy," in Brazosport Archaeological Society, "Henson G. Westall-Andrew E. Westall-Thomas Henrie Westall, Bell Grove Plantation" (March 2016), 6, http://bmns.org/wp-content/uploads/2020/04/BellGrove.pdf.

69. For a useful overview of the history and historiography of matrimonial property laws in Texas, see Carroll, *Homesteads Ungovernable*, esp. 228–33.

70. Bushman, *Refinement of America*, 267–79.

71. Clark, *American Family Home*, 41–42; Grier, *Culture and Comfort*; K. Deetz, *Bound to the Fire*; S. Williams, *Savory Suppers and Fashionable Feasts*, esp. chap. 3; Perrot and Gurrand, "Scenes and Places," 367.

72. In the late eighteenth and early nineteenth centuries, more American households began to move their entertaining to specified and separate living areas (particularly parlors). Mark R. Wenger, "Town House and Country House: Eighteenth and Early Nineteenth Centuries," in Carson and Lounsbury, *Chesapeake House*, 145–46.

73. Furniture terms have been kept as they were written in the inventory. Inventory of John D. Patton, 1840.

74. The 1854 and 1857 inventories note $450, but no further description is provided. Estimative Inventory of Property Owned by Columbus R. Patton, 1854; Inventory of C. R. Patton Estate, July 1857.

75. For more on the importance of sideboards, see Ames, *Death in the Dining Room*. For more on sofas and the parlor, see Grier, *Culture and Comfort*.

76. Answers of George O. Jarvis.

77. Answers of E. S. Jackson.

78. Kent Anderson Leslie likewise notes of another enslaved-enslaver relationship that the couple's "behaving as intimates" included "sitting in the parlor or by the fire in David Dickson's bedroom, talking over business and other matters of concern to them both." Leslie, *Woman of Color, Daughter of Privilege*, 45–46.

79. The two "talk[ed] together as husband and wife." Gillmer, *Slavery and Freedom in Texas*, 37.

80. Gillmer, *Slavery and Freedom in Texas*, 33.

81. Answers of E. S. Jackson. It is open to question who, if anyone, from the community would have dined with Rachel and Columbus. Perhaps white women refused to socialize on the plantation. Peggy Pascoe argues as much about Leah and Alfred Foster in Fort Bend County, Texas. Pascoe, *What Comes Naturally*, 18.

82. Earls and Tomka, "Historic and Prehistoric Archaeological Excavations at Varner-Hogg," 84–88.

83. We do not have receipts or textual documentation of who purchased and used these objects, yet we cannot discount the possibility that Rachel did. Neither archaeologists nor historians have linked these artifacts to Rachel, in large part because scholars so often associate material abundance with white residents and material deprivation with Black residents of plantations. David Babson argues that archaeologists often assume a person's racial category when artifacts of certain value or aesthetics are found. Babson, "Archaeology of Racism and Ethnicity on Southern Plantations," 24.

84. Quote from Kelley, *Los Brazos de Dios*, 1–2. For more on Brazoria County plantations, see Lundberg, *Texas Lowcountry*.

85. There is an East and West Columbia, both of which were referred to at various times in the nineteenth century as Columbia. Kemp, "The Capitol (?) at Columbia."

86. The population of Columbia was just 300 in 1844. Brazoria, located down the Brazos River a few miles from Columbia, was larger, with a population of 800 in 1844. Creighton, *A Narrative History of Brazoria County, Texas*, 162.

87. Restrictions of mobility were one of enslavers' many mechanisms of control, something that enslaved individuals constantly resisted. Camp, *Closer to Freedom*; Pryor, *Colored Travelers*.

88. Answers of E. S. Jackson.

89. Account against C. R. Patton by Jordan Hill, January 1860[?], BCC, Case #690, Probate Records, Folder 4.

90. Answers of John Adriance.

91. Jones-Rogers, *They Were Her Property*, xiv–xv.

92. Answers of John Adriance.

93. "Fashion, Women's," in Kindell, *World of Antebellum America*, 320.

94. See, for instance, DuPlessis, *Material Atlantic*; Walker, *Exquisite Slaves*; Monica Miller, *Slaves to Fashion*.

95. Lucy Lewis, in FWP-WPA, *Slave Narratives*, vol. 16, pt. 3, 15.

96. Sarah Ford, in FWP-WPA, *Slave Narratives*, vol. 16, pt. 2, 45.

97. Hilde, *Slavery, Fatherhood, and Paternal Duty*.

98. Even after emancipation, when investments in land and dwellings increased, formerly enslaved people still spent much of their available earnings on clothing. See Barnes, "Land Rich and Cash Poor," 33; William Hampton Adams and Steven D. Smith, "Historical Perspectives on Black Tenant Farmer Material Culture: The Henry C. Long General Store Ledger at Waverly Plantation, Mississippi," in Singleton, *Archaeology of Slavery and Plantation Life*, 329–30.

99. Knowles, "Fashioning Slavery."

100. S. White and G. White, *Stylin'*; Foster, *New Raiments of Self*; Shaw, "Slave Cloth and Clothing Slaves"; Knowles, "Patches of Resistance on the Badges of Enslavement."

101. Camp, "The Pleasures of Resistance," 535.

102. Wilson, *Adorned in Dreams*, 247.

103. Answers of George O. Jarvis. It is interesting that Jarvis explicitly mentions young ladies, as historian Anya Jabour argues that it was young, white women who most exemplified the mythic ideal of the Southern belle. Even though Rachel was no longer "young" by contemporary standards, she likely also knew that they were the women most admired in Southern culture for their fashion, beauty, and ladyhood. Jabour, *Scarlett's Sisters*.

104. Answers of John Adriance.

105. Answers of Thomas Cayce, BCC, Case #453, Probate Records, Folder 2.

106. Fox-Genovese, *Within the Plantation Household*, 213–16.

107. Dalrymple, *American Victorian Costume*; Setnik, *Victorian Fashions for Women and Children*.

108. Answers of Isaac Tinsley, BCC, Case #453, Probate Records, Folder 2.

109. Knowles, "Patches of Resistance," 4.

110. J. Wells, *Women Writers and Journalists*, 50. For an exploration of the dangers of fashion in the nineteenth century, particularly its use in deceiving viewers of the wearer's true identity and intent, see Halttunen, *Confidence Men and Painted Women*.

111. That which was fashionable for a white woman would be seen as gauche for a Black woman. We can see this in visual culture of the antebellum era, including Edward Williams Clay's well-known cartoon series, which pictured Black women and men wearing fashionable clothing "incorrectly." See the digitized "Life in Philadelphia Collection," Library Company of Philadelphia, accessed August 28, 2022, https://digital.librarycompany.org/islandora/object/Islandora%3ALINP1.

112. Answers of Isaac Tinsley.

113. Answers of George O. Jarvis.

114. Baum, *Counterfeit Justice*, 28.

115. Information and Petition in the case of Columbus R. Patton, BCC, Case #453, Probate Records, Folder 1.

116. C. F. Patton Decree, BCC, Case #453, Probate Records, Folder 1; Brother, Sisters, and Nephew Contest C. R. Patton's Will, January 27, 1857, BCC, Case #453, Probate Records, Folder 1.

117. Brother, Sisters, and Nephew Contest C. R. Patton's Will. For more on asylums in South Carolina during antebellum era, see McCandless, *Moonlight, Magnolias, and Madness*, part 2.

118. Sarah Ford, in FWP-WPA, *Slave Narratives*, vol. 16, pt. 2, 42. When exactly this relocation took place is hazy. Sarah asserts it occurred after Columbus's death, which happened in September 1856, whereas Adriance noted that Charles only began to take an active role on the plantation in February 1858. At that time, Charles (with the consent of his siblings and nephew) took up residence and management of Patton Place. John Adriance Papers, V-HP (originals at the Dolph Briscoe Center for American History, University of Texas at Austin). It is possible, if not likely, that enslaved folks felt Charles's influence on the plantation for years before this, as he desired to play a larger role in the management of the place.

119. Sarah Ford, in FWP-WPA, *Slave Narratives*, vol. 16, pt. 2, 42.

120. The only indication we have of the material conditions of the slave quarters comes

from a WPA interview with Anthony Christopher, who recalled that he and other en-slaved residents of Patton Place had "good brick quarters and wood floors . . . [with a] fireplace where mama keep de cookin' pots." Interview with Anthony Christopher, in Rawick, *American Slave*, 719.

121. Notice of Last Will and Testament (of C. R. Patton), January 1857, BCC, Case #453, Probate Records, Folder 1. Charles Grimm, who worked as overseer on the site for several years, verified that the handwriting on the last will and testament document matched that of Columbus Patton. Answers of Charles Grimm. Grimm declared that both Adriance and Underwood were present when the will was found, but Adriance disputed that Underwood was there. Answers of John Adriance.

122. Columbus also left a significant sum, $5,000, to "my Dutch Boy Henry Patton." Will of C. R. Patton, dated June 1, 1853, BCC, V-HP.

123. It was assumed that Mat Patton, Columbus's nephew, would be chief inheritor of Columbus's estate. Horace Cone, among others, asserted that Columbus wanted Mat to become "the Patton of the family" after his death. Answers of Horace Cone. When Mat's father died, Columbus became his guardian and took great pains to raise him, even paying for his education in Kentucky. See Answers of A. S. Tyler. But Mat fell out of favor with Columbus, in part because, while acting as overseer, Mat whipped Rachel.

124. Amendment to the Petition of the Heirs, BCC, Case #453, Probate Records, Folder 2.

125. Will of C. R. Patton, dated June 1, 1853. Maria died in 1856, before the will was found, and thus never received any of the stipulated annual stipend. Document Filed about the State of the Patton Estate by J Adriance, May 1856, BCC, Case #453, Probate Records, Folder 1. Whether an intimate relationship between Maria and Columbus existed is unknown. No other sources have been found to support that idea.

126. Answers of Charles Grimm.

127. BCC, Case #2997.

128. Mat eventually took himself out of the lawsuit and had his portion cashed out. He was apparently fed up with the lawsuit; he was also perhaps tired of dealing with Rachel again, with whom he had sparred many times before. BCC, Case #453, Probate Records, Folder 2.

129. BCC, Case #453, Probate Records, Folder 1.

130. BCC, Case #2997.

131. John Adriance, January 3, 1859, BCC, Case #690, Probate Records, Folder 3. A December 1858 petition from John Adriance to the Brazoria County court notes the successful distribution of several enslaved laborers based on Columbus's will, including Rachel's choice of living arrangements; but that document does not indicate where or with whom she chose to reside. Petition from John Adriance on C. R. Patton estate, Petition #21585807, December 30, 1858, Race and Slavery Petitions, Digital Library on American Slavery, University of North Carolina at Greensboro, https://library.uncg .edu/slavery/petitions/details.aspx?pid=12749.

132. After noting that "in accordance with said agreement further your Petitioner has suffered the negro woman Rachel to choose for herself the place where or family in which she should live," Adriance then mentions that Jake and Solomon, who had the same ability to live where they desired, "too thus far remained on said plantation." The

use of "too" here suggests the possibility that Rachel also was on the plantation during the year (1858) that Adriance summarized for the court. Statement Accompanying Annual Account 1858, January 3, 1859, BCC, Case #690, Probate Records, Folder 3.

133. Sarah Ford, in FWP-WPA, *Slave Narratives*, vol. 16, pt. 2, 42.

134. John Adriance Papers, V-HP. Anthony Christopher, Deenie's brother, spoke of her as "Marse Patton's gal. He wasn't married and he keeps Deenie up to de big house." Interview with Anthony Christopher, in Rawick, *American Slave*, 722. This is very likely Ardenia Bates, to whom Charles left a gray horse and $50 worth of gold in his will. Will of Charles F. Patton, February 4, 1870, BCC, Case #904.

135. It is unclear why Rachel may have chosen to live in Hayr's house, or what exactly she did for him in it. As a white, single man with some property but no enslaved laborers, Rachel may have provided the kinds of domestic services that were expected of women, the same kind she had managed at Patton Place for a decade. The 1860 census lists Hayr as sixty years old, born in North Carolina, and having $20,000 in real estate. He is the only person listed in his household. 1860 US Census, Brazoria County, TX. The census lists no personal estate, nor is Hayr found in the 1860 slave schedule.

136. Mrs. Rachel of C. R. Patton Estate to A. Underwood & Co, March 5, 1859, BCC #690, Probate Records, Folder 5.

137. Statement Accompanying Exhibit "B," 1860, BCC, Case #690, Probate Records, Folder 3.

138. Receipt from A. Underwood & Co. for Rachel of C. R. Patton Estate, BCC, Case #690, Probate Records, Folder 4. John Adriance's statements to the court suggest that he used her annual allowance to pay for her shopping. Adriance stated in 1858 that he "has engaged to pay her [Rachel] the sum of one hundred dollars a year, the [?] of which yearly allowance to said woman Rachel which the present time has been paid & a part of the same appears in the account of Nash & Barrow." Statement Accompanying Annual Account 1858, January 3, 1859.

139. It is possible that Rachel learned to sew while she lived as a domestic laborer at Patton Place or later as lady of the place. Sewing was a necessary part of any lady's domesticity, including those who ran the household of Southern plantations. Fox-Genovese, *Within the Plantation Household*, 120–28.

140. Early Victorian (ca. 1840s) dresses tended to take between six and nine yards of fabric for both bodice and skirt. A mid-Victorian (1850–60s) bodice and skirt required anywhere from approximately six to eighteen yards, though the latter might have been out of place in Texas. Jennifer Rosbrugh, "How Much Yardage Do I Need?," Historical Sewing, September 12, 2018, https://historicalsewing.com/how-much-yardage-do-i-need.

141. For an example of such embellishments on a finished dress, see Promenade Dress of Silk Plush with Fringing, designer unknown, Great Britain, ca. 1855–57, Victoria and Albert Museum (T.324&A&B-1977), accessed June 25, 2021, http://www.vam.ac.uk/content/articles/h/history-of-fashion-1840-1900/.

142. For an example, see Bonnet, designer unknown, Great Britain, ca. 1845, Victoria and Albert Museum (T.1039-1913), accessed June 25, 2021, http://www.vam.ac.uk/content/articles/h/history-of-fashion-1840-1900/.

143. It is of course possible that Rachel fashioned this outfit for another woman as a way of making money. Knowing Rachel's penchant for chic clothing, though, it is just as likely she made this ensemble for herself.

144. Statement Accompanying Exhibit "B," 1860, BCC, Case #690, Probate Records, Folder 3.

145. Petition to Court to Sell Land for Debts, 1855, BCC, Case #453, Probate Records, Folder 1.

146. What exactly is meant by the statement that Rachel caused trouble is uncertain, and it may not have been anything good, positive, or useful for other enslaved folks. Sarah Ford never recalled that the enslaved residents of Patton Place held a grudge against Rachel, though her demands to be called Miss Rachel likely were not met with excitement. But the way in which Sarah remembered Rachel versus other enslaved individuals with some measure of authority on Patton Place is striking. After emancipation, Sarah's family left Patton Place to build their own home near Columbia, and sometime afterward, Big Jake—the Black foreman remembered for his particularly cruel punishments of enslaved laborers—asked to stay with them. As Sarah put it, "De black folks all hated him so dey wouldn't have no truck with him and he ask my papa could he stay." Perhaps there was not this kind of long-term hostility toward Rachel. Sarah Ford, in FWP-WPA, *Slave Narratives*, vol. 16, pt. 2, 46.

147. Statement Accompanying Exhibit "B," 1860, BCC, Case #690, Probate Records, Folder 3. Adriance noted that "your Petitioner rather permitted it to be done than procured it to be done, but it was done with Petitioners approbation, and recognition of the necessity of the case." Cincinnati was the site of relocation for many formerly enslaved concubines and their children. See S. Green, *Remember Me to Miss Louisa*.

148. A later court case noted that she was "transported to the distant city of Cincinnati . . . contrary to the wishes of your petitioner," that is, Rachel. BCC, Case #2997.

149. BCC, Case #2997.

150. Estate of C. R. Patton for Rachel Bartlett to W. F. Swain, BCC, Case #690, Probate Records, Folder 5; John Jackson to Court about C. R. Patton Estate, BCC, Case #690, Probate Records, Folder 3.

151. Many enslaved women who maintained intimate relationships with their enslavers practiced domestic and skilled trades. As Brenda Stevenson notes, seamstresses were a particularly "popular" choice of enslavers. Stevenson, "What's Love Got to Do with It?," 107.

152. Her bill from W. F. Swain in June 1870 also listed her as Rachel Bartlett, as did her Freedmen's Bureau complaint. Estate of C. R. Patton for Rachel Bartlett to W. F. Swain.

153. 1880 US Census, Brazoria County, TX.

154. By 1883, Columbus Patton's estate was run dry, with all its assets exhausted. Rachel no longer received the allowance that Columbus's will promised her for life and that she had sued John Adriance to ensure. We do not know how Rachel handled this further change in circumstances, but it must have come as a blow after having fought for what she argued was due to her by the Patton Estate. Petition for Discharge and Final Exhibit, BCC, Case #690, Probate Records, Folder 3; BCC, Case #2997.

155. This may be David C. Roberts, a white man living in Brazoria County who would have been twenty-eight years old at the time of the assault. 1860 US Census, Brazoria County, TX; Line 768, 1867 Voter Registration List, Brazoria County, TX.

156. Complaint filed April 16, 1867, Texas, Freedmen's Bureau Field Office Records, 1865–1870, Columbia, Roll 15, Register of complaints, vol. 80, Apr. 1867–Nov. 1868.

157. John Adriance was required to pay the court costs and the case was settled out of

court. It is not clear exactly what the settlement amount paid to Rachel was, though it was likely less than she requested.

158. Answers of A. S. Tyler, E. S. Jackson, George O. Jarvis, Charles Grimm, John Adriance, and Horace Cone.

Chapter Five

1. Sources for this vignette include Hammond's Plantation Journal in JHHP, SCL; Letters, JHHP, LC; James Henry Hammond, "Speech of Hon. James H. Hammond, of South Carolina, On the Admission of Kansas, Under the Lecompton Constitution: Delivered in the Senate of the United States, March 4, 1858," Washington, D.C., 1858, American Antiquarian Society, Worcester, MA.

2. For more on the simultaneous confidence and anxieties of enslavers, see Karp, *This Vast Southern Empire*; Paulus, *Slaveholding Crisis*.

3. Most scholars have argued that Redcliffe was a "show" plantation distinct from Hammond's other plantations (Silver Bluff, Cowden, and Cathwood). While it is true that Redcliffe was different, it was still understood as part of the profit-driven, capitalist pursuit of slavery. Some point to his use of land for vineyards as an indication of how Hammond saw this property as different from his other plantations, yet those vineyards would produce, from Hammond's perspective, the next major plantation crop. For more on the distinction between show and working plantations in South Carolina, see Cabak and Groover, "Bush Hill."

4. Stephanie McCurry asserts that of the four million people enslaved in the United States in 1860, some three million remained on plantations during the Civil War, held there by their enslavement but in many cases actively fighting against slavery nonetheless. McCurry, *Confederate Reckoning*, 5, 8.

5. As Thomas Barrie contends, "Home is the center of most people's lives, the place they may depart from, but to which they always return. As a bulwark against the uncertainty of their lives, it serves as the hub of their personal world, and its safety and stability are essential to their sense of wellbeing." Barrie, *House and Home*, 16.

6. Philips, *Looming Civil War*. Religious conviction was a primary influencer in nineteenth-century expectations of the future, but status in Southern society also shaped one's hopes. See also Wright and Dresser, *Apocalypse and the Millennium*.

7. Historians have tended to emphasize the intentions of enslavers when exploring sites like Redcliffe. Drew Gilpin Faust, whose biography of Hammond remains the best work on the enslaver, maintained that he built Redcliffe to flaunt "the wealth, taste, and refinement he acquired in his years as plantation master." Faust, *James Henry Hammond and the Old South*, 335. Others have followed suit, including Carol Bleser, whose valuable work on the Hammond family emphasized James's focus on Redcliffe as a reflection of his problematic self-assurance and egotism, though she also recognizes how the enslaver desired it to be something handed down for generations. Bleser, *The Hammonds of Redcliffe*.

8. The term "monumental architecture" most often refers to man-made structures meant for public or communal use rather than for private residences. But the term also suggests any building that is substantially larger than it practically needs to be. Such a description could be applied to the rather monumental size of Redcliffe as well as to its nature as a kind of monument to Hammond and to slavery. For more on monumental

architecture and its relationship to power and behavior, see Trigger, "Monumental Architecture."

9. John Michal Vlach has noted, "Because it is often the case that only the mansion house remains, the impression conveyed by plantation sites today is exclusively one of wealth and comfort," and thus of the lives and vision of enslavers. Vlach, *Back of the Big House*, 183.

10. For more on Hammond's early life and marriage to Catherine Fitzsimons, see Faust, *James Henry Hammond*, esp. chaps. 1 and 4. The Silver Bluff site served as an Indian trading post before and after the Revolution. It passed through multiple hands before coming into the ownership of the Fitzsimons, who apparently did a rather poor job of realizing its potential. See James D. Scurry, J. Walter Joseph, and Fritz Hamer, "Initial Archeological Investigations at Silver Bluff Plantation Aiken County, South Carolina" (October 1980), 38, Institute of Archaeology and Anthropology, University of South Carolina, https://scholarcommons.sc.edu/archanth_books/161/.

11. Inventory of Silver Bluff Plantation, December 8, 1831, Reel 1, JHHP, SCL.

12. More than thirty familial groups had been at Silver Bluff for years when Hammond took his initial inventory. Genealogists and RPSHS staff believe these families can be traced back to the site as early as 1775. "Silver Bluff Plantation," RPSHS.

13. Inventory of Silver Bluff Plantation, December 8, 1831, Reel 1, JHHP, SCL.

14. For more on Hammond's relationship to paternalism, see Faust, *James Henry Hammond*.

15. Plantation Journal, December 13, 1831, Reel 1, JHHP, SCL.

16. Plantation Journal, January 12, 1840, Reel 1, JHHP, SCL.

17. Plantation Manual, Reel 2, JHHP, SCL.

18. Records of enslaved deaths, Reel 1, JHHP, SCL.

19. Plantation Journal, September 4, 1841, Reel 1, JHHP, SCL.

20. Elizabeth and Mary are listed with Hannah Shubrick in Hammond's Inventory of Silver Bluff Plantation, December 8, 1831, Reel 1, JHHP, SCL.

21. Plantation Journal, November 5, 1841, Reel 1, JHHP, SCL. Runaway attempts (sometimes multiple indicated in each notation) in the first decade of ownership include those documented in Plantation Journal, December 10, 1831; January 5, 1832; January 24, 1832; May 11, 1835; June 18, 1835; May 16, 1838; February 17, 1839; July 3, 1839; October 17, 1839; February 12, 1840; July 4, 1841, Reel 1, JHHP, SCL.

22. Scurry, Joseph, and Hamer, "Initial Archeological Investigations at Silver Bluff," 28.

23. Plantation Journal, Reel 1, JHHP, SCL.

24. These were part of remarks added to a copy of Hammond's Plantation Manual, in Plantation Book, 1857–58, Reel 14, JHHP, SCL.

25. Caitlyn Rosenthal explores how these kinds of experiments were central to the development of sophisticated, capitalistic management techniques on Southern and Caribbean plantations. Rosenthal, *Accounting for Slavery*.

26. In South Carolina, these techniques can be traced back even further to the late eighteenth century. See Joseph, "Resistance and Compliance," 21; Joseph, "White Columns and Black Hands," 67; Babson, "Plantation Ideology and the Archaeology of Racism." For more on changes to the antislavery movement, see Sinha, *Slave's Cause*.

27. McKee, "Ideals and Realities," 195–213; Edward A. Chappell, "Accommodating Slavery in Bermuda," in Ellis and Ginsburg, *Cabin, Quarter, Plantation*, 67–98.

28. Renee Ballard et al., "Slave Quarters Historic Structure Report: Redcliffe Plantation, Beech Island, SC" (July 2002), 1, RPSHS.

29. Hammond did not explicitly note whether these were double-pen cabins, but the width of the houses and the use of double-pen cabins elsewhere on his estate (including at Redcliffe) suggest it.

30. Clay-Clopton, *A Belle of the Fifties*, 216. Elizabeth Laney, former park interpreter at RPSHS, maintains this section of Clay-Clopton's reminiscences describes Silver Bluff, not Redcliffe. Clay-Clopton used the term "Redcliffe" to refer to all four of the Hammond plantations within her writings. Tour of RPSHS with Elizabeth Laney, June 11, 2018.

31. The settlement plan called for nine new houses, which if double-pen, likely had from six to ten residents in each. Therefore, nearly one hundred enslaved people may have been relocated to this new settlement. Plantation Journal, July 27, 1842, Reel 1, JHHP, SCL.

32. Scurry, Joseph, and Hamer, "Initial Archeological Investigations at Silver Bluff," 38.

33. Property purchase, Reel 2, JHHP, SCL. List of Negroes sent to Green Valley, Fairfield District, in Plantation Journal, Reel 1, JHHP, SCL.

34. They may have been able to see one another still, although Hammond's strict regulations required that anyone moving between his plantations have a pass card, and even that only applied to husbands and wives. Plantation Book, 1857–58, Reel 14, JHHP, SCL.

35. Plantation Journal, January 2, 1839, Reel 2, JHHP, SCL.

36. Hammond was not always at the Silverton house. In January 1841, he moved his family to Columbia, South Carolina. However, he often returned to Silverton to monitor proceedings at Silver Bluff and would return full-time by December 1843. Hammond had moved to Columbia to pursue his political career, but he was socially and politically ousted due to a personal scandal involving inappropriate sexual relations with his nieces. Journal, February 24, 1852, Reel 4, JHHP, SCL.

37. October 30, 1845, Records of enslaved births, Reel 1, JHHP, SCL.

38. Letter, James Henry Hammond (James) to Harry Hammond (Harry), February 19, 1856, Reel 9, JHHP, SCL.

39. It is not clear that James Henry Hammond always chose enslaved babies' names, though it appears he often did. Neumann, "American Incest," 61.

40. As Libra R. Hilde notes, "White men fathered enslaved children who then grew up to realize they were somehow different and who struggled to find a sense of belonging and a place in the world." Hilde, *Slavery, Fatherhood, and Paternal Duty*, 192.

41. The 1870 US Census listed all the Johnsons as mulatto. 1870 US Census, Barnwell County, SC.

42. Faust, *James Henry Hammond*, 315.

43. Letter, James to Marcus Claudius Marcellus Hammond (Marcus), September 25, 1852, Reel 9, JHHP, SCL.

44. Bibb, *Narrative of the Life and Adventures of Henry Bibb*, 38.

45. Letter, C. Fitzsimons to James, November 17, 1852, Reel 9, JHHP, SCL.

46. Letter, James to Marcus, September 25, 1852, Reel 9, JHHP, SCL.

47. Inventories of the various plantations in 1852 and 1853 do not list Louisa, but the 1854 record does. Reel 10, JHHP, LC. Still, the fact that she almost certainly gave birth

at Silver Bluff in 1853 indicates she was back there by at least the time of the birth, if not by the time of impregnation. Records of enslaved births, Reel 1, JHHP, SCL. Additionally, Faust notes that Louisa was back at Silver Bluff by March 1853. Faust, *James Henry Hammond*, 317.

48. Catherine and their two daughters were back by 1855. See Letter, James to William Gilmore Simms (William), May 10, 1855, Reel 10, JHHP, LC.

49. Letter, James to Harry, December 20, 1852, in Faust, *James Henry Hammond*, 313.

50. Like so many enslaved women, Sally and Louisa provided multiple types of labor for their enslaver: productive, reproductive, and sexual. For more on the many types of labor required of enslaved women, see Finley, *An Intimate Economy*.

51. Journal, February 24, 1852, Reel 4, JHHP, SCL.

52. November 28, 1853, Records of enslaved births, Reel 1, JHHP, SCL; Letter, James to Harry, February 19, 1856, Reel 9, JHHP, SCL.

53. October 25, 1855, Records of enslaved births, Reel 1, JHHP, SCL. Hammond wrote that Edmund was almost surely his: "Her second I believe is mine." Letter, James to Harry, February 19, 1856, Reel 9, JHHP, SCL.

54. Cathwood is sometimes spelled Kathwood, particularly if referring to the more contemporary community there. Carol Bleser argues, though, that James Henry Hammond renamed what was part of Catherine's dowry "Cathwood," after his wife. Bleser, *The Hammonds of Redcliffe*, 14.

55. Letter, James to Marcus, September 13, 1858, Reel 10, JHHP, SCL.

56. Hammond numbered his enslaved laborers at 290 in 1857. List of Negroes, Reel 14, JHHP, SCL.

57. Plantation Book, 1849–58, Reel 14, JHHP, SCL.

58. Contract, James and Charles Axt, October 13, 1859, Reel 14, JHHP, LC. See also Faust, *James Henry Hammond*, 317–18. Several different enslaved laborers were frequently sent on business to Augusta, but Henderson's more permanent removal, for years at a time, would have been quite different. Plantation Journal, Reel 1, JHHP, SCL.

59. Faust, *James Henry Hammond*, 319. It appears that one reason Hammond sent Henderson away was because of Henderson's rebellious "wild & daring spirit," which made him a poor domestic servant.

60. Faust, *James Henry Hammond*, 317–18. Henderson ran away from his apprenticeship at least once, after which the viticulturist bound his hands and legs, suspended him from the ceiling, and whipped him enough to cause other German immigrants in the area to alert Hammond to the violence. Hammond, in Washington, DC, for his Senate post, asked his colleague Alexander Stephens to investigate. Stephens judged that the viticulturist was not in the wrong and reported that Henderson was "very cheerful" and thus happy with his situation. Neither Stephens nor Hammond considered the treatment brutal and thus not bad enough to cause Henderson to be sent home.

61. Plantation Book, 1849–58, Reel 14, JHHP, SCL; Plantation Journal, January 25, 1862, Reel 2, JHHP, SCL.

62. Plantation Journal, April 23, 1862, Reel 2, JHHP, SCL.

63. Letter, James to Harry, February 19, 1856, Reel 9, JHHP, SCL.

64. Historians have pushed back against Eugene Genovese and others who argued that paternalism was the driving force shaping relations within slavery. These scholars insist that the slave trade, plus enslavers' own conceptions of property and capitalist

convictions, limited the force that paternalism actually held in real life. It could be a strong proslavery argument but did not hold the same sway over individual actions. See Gutman, *Power and Culture*; W. Johnson, *Soul by Soul*; Tadman, *Speculators and Slaves*; Baptist, *Half Has Never Been Told*; Ford, *Origins of Southern Radicalism*. Those who have intensely studied James Henry Hammond, however, see him as a powerful case study about how mastery so deeply warped his mind that he could believe in the fallacy of paternalism while simultaneously raping his "children." See Faust, *James Henry Hammond*; Neumann, "American Incest."

65. Like other enslavers, James sometimes referred to his enslaved laborers as "my black family." The first time Hammond uses the term in writing is a few years after acquiring Silver Bluff. Plantation Journal, December 16, 1834, Reel 1, JHHP, SCL. Obviously, though, this term takes on a different meaning when used in the context of the Johnson family.

66. James would go on to lament that this was "folly" because his children were undependable and could not run the estate well. Letter, James to Marcus, September 13, 1858, Reel 10, JHHP, SCL. He was increasingly worried that his children would be massive failures, unable to take over management of his large estate, and that Redcliffe would fall out of Hammond hands. See Bleser, *The Hammonds of Redcliffe*, 64–65.

67. Scholars have discussed several reasons why Hammond wanted to build Redcliffe: a need for a more healthful location than Silverton, a desire to be recognized by his peers, as recompense for having to give up his earlier home in Columbia, and as a status symbol for himself and his family. Bleser, *The Hammonds of Redcliffe*, 14–15; Weber, "Power, Prestige, and Influence," 281–82.

68. James bragged that on a cloudless day he could see every building in nearby Augusta, Georgia. Faust, *James Henry Hammond*, 335.

69. Almost immediately after coming into possession of the house and property, Hammond noted, "I may have to build an entire new establishment before I can be comfortable there." Letter, James to William, April 25, 1855, Reel 10, JHHP, LC. He was aware, though, that his finances were not unlimited, and thus did not want to "speculate too grandly." Letter, James to William, June 30, 1855, Reel 10, JHHP, LC.

70. Letter, Marcus to James, February 19, 1858, Reel 10, JHHP. Not all found Redcliffe so pleasing. Architectural historians have sneered at and mocked its mansion. Roger G. Kennedy, for instance, called it "a graceless barn of a place . . . a representative of the harsh, unapologetic, egocentric and querulous man who built it." Of course, that only reiterates the point that Hammond's home was a monument to himself, which included the harshness and ego that enslaving generated in him. Kennedy, *Architecture, Men, Women and Money in America*, 361.

71. For more on James Madison's perspective on slavery, see Broadwater, *James Madison*, esp. chap. 7.

72. Speech, December 1861, Reel 10, JHHP, SCL.

73. Speech, December 1861, Reel 10, JHHP, SCL.

74. Faust, *Ideology of Slavery*.

75. For more on the simultaneous fears and confidence of enslavers in late antebellum South Carolina, see Bruckho, "'Slave Traffick.'"

76. See, for instance, Diary 1841–46, Reel 13, JHHP, SCL.

77. Fehrenbacher, *Slaveholding Republic*.

78. Letter to James, 1838, Reel 4, JHHP, LC.

79. Journal, February 24, 1852, Reel 4, JHHP, SCL.

80. Hammond, "Speech of Hon. James H. Hammond."

81. Letter, James to William, May 10, 1855, Reel 10, JHHP, LC.

82. Four months after purchasing the property, Hammond wrote to William Simms with his plans for the mansion's design. Letter, James to William, June 30, 1855, Reel 10, JHHP, LC. He continued to write to Simms about the design and construction, and how he had "constant thoughts [about] my new residence." Letter, James to William, January 20, 1857, Reel 10, JHHP, LC. For a list of Hammond's books, see the catalog of the Redcliffe Library, Reel 4, JHHP, SCL.

83. He vociferously declared he did not want to get back into politics, but how truthful that statement was (in light of the still-powerful belief in republicanism's disinterested leader ideal) is unclear. See Plantation Journal, November 29 and 30, 1857, Reel 1, JHHP, SCL.

84. See letters in part 1 of Bleser, *The Hammonds of Redcliffe*.

85. Hammond, "Speech of Hon. James H. Hammond." James hired a contractor but used his own enslaved labor: "no carpenters but my own & one or two hirelings." Letter, James to Harry, May 29, 1857, Reel 10, JHHP, SCL. James noted the use of Sullivan and Ben for building Redcliffe in Plantation Journal, December 30, 1856, Reel 1, JHHP, SCL. James regarded his enslaved workforce as central to his wealth, noting "[I] Shall build [Redcliffe] and make myself comfortable out of Capital." Plantation Journal, October 12, 1855, Reel 1, JHHP, SCL.

86. Hammond, "Slavery in the Light of Political Science," 661.

87. Savage, *Standing Soldiers, Kneeling Slaves*, 4.

88. Letter, James to Harry, September 21, 1855, Reel 10, JHHP, SCL.

89. Roger Kennedy argues that Greek Revival was at its height from the 1820s through the 1840s, though it did not fully die until the Civil War. But it had so fully taken hold in the United States that it became part of the national architecture and was thus used and legible by a wide range of Americans in the nineteenth century. Kennedy, *Greek Revival America*, 1–6.

90. Letter, James to William, June 30, 1855, Reel 10, JHHP, LC. The piazzas had to be reconstructed in the 1880s, including the removal of the second-floor balconies, due to wet rot. The house as it stands now therefore does not reflect its original classical symmetry. National Register of Historic Places, Redcliffe, Aiken County, South Carolina, 1973, NRHP.

91. These are three of the six characteristics Roger Kennedy argues were displayed in all three forms of American Greek Revival. Kennedy, *Greek Revival America*, 4–5. The Redcliffe mansion's entry is not symmetrical, as the outdoor staircase ascends to the far right of the front, but the remainder of the home is very much so, set on a central hall plan with an equal number of windows on either side of the front door. Other classical notes included pedimented windows.

92. Talbot Hamlin called Greek Revival the first "American Architecture." Hamlin, *Greek Revival Architecture in America*, 22.

93. Kennedy, *Greek Revival America*, 1. Kennedy argues that the slave-owning South's Greek Revival was distinct from that elsewhere, especially in the North, where it reflected the reform-minded aspirations of citizens. Perhaps the greatest proponent of the

political nature of Greek Revival is Talbot Hamlin, who produced the most influential work on the style. Hamlin, *Greek Revival Architecture in America*. Architectural historian W. Barksdale Maynard, however, argues that the popularity of Greek Revival had more to do with aesthetic preferences and cultural aspirations of Americans than with their political prescriptions. Maynard, *Architecture in the United States*, esp. chap. 5. Scholars have also emphasized that the popularity of Greek Revival did not mean that antebellum Americans were in fact more ordered or reasoned that those before or after. As historian David Brion Davis has noted, "In spite of a façade of ordered symmetry in the houses and public buildings of the Greek Revival, ante-bellum America was not ruled by a mild and tolerant spirit of reason." D. Davis, "Some Ideological Functions of Prejudice in Ante-bellum America," 115.

94. Throughout his papers, including in his school-age journals, Hammond evinced a fascination with classical history, literature, poetry, and other subjects. Clearly a product of his education, this fixation shaped his ideology for his entire life, as evidenced by his late 1850s speeches. Faust, *James Henry Hammond*, esp. chap. 1; Sugrue, "South Carolina College."

95. As Heidi Amelia-Anne Weber puts it, "The intrinsic union of this architectural style and slave ownership was ever present." Weber, "Power, Prestige, and Influence," 284. See also Gowans, *Images of American Living*; Gamble, "The White-Column Tradition."

96. Severns, *Southern Architecture*, 45.

97. Letter, James to William, January 10, 1861, Reel 14, JHHP, LC.

98. Contract, James and Charles Axt, October 13, 1859, Reel 14, JHHP, LC.

99. Henderson is denoted as living in the "Yard," and though it is not clear which plantation's Yard, this term most often applied to Redcliffe. Plantation Book, 1849–58, Reel 14, JHHP, SCL.

100. Letter, F. G. Kron to James, April 2, 1860, Reel 10, JHHP, SCL.

101. For an early discussion of the ways that architectural tenets (specifically Georgian values of organization and hierarchy) paralleled the social structure of slavery, and thus were useful in plantation design in South Carolina, see Joseph, "Early American Period and Nineteenth Century," 64.

102. Diary, May 12, 1855, in Bleser, *Secret and Sacred*, 266.

103. Bluestone, "A. J. Davis's Belmead Picturesque Aesthetics."

104. The Redcliffe Yard, designed in accordance with the best management principles of the day, was therefore also to be a material argument against abolitionists who wanted to display the brutal treatment of enslaved people. As James O. Breeden, editor of a collection of plantation management sources, makes clear, those who thought and wrote about slave management on this level never constituted a majority of enslavers. Still, their general goal of implementing more systematic methods of enslaving permeated the culture, supporting and enhancing the ideology of paternalism that many in the South argued lay at the core of why slavery should continue. To better justify slavery in the face of increasing national criticism, slave owners needed to demonstrate why enslaved people were better off in slavery. For a general overview of the antebellum trend of slave management studies, see Breeden, *Advice among Masters*, xvii–xxii.

105. Ballard et al., "Slave Quarters Historic Structure Report"; Andrew Agha and David Jones, "Preliminary Archaeology Report, Spring 2003, Redcliffe Plantation," South Carolina Department of Parks, Recreation and Tourism, RPSHS. For more on

Hammond's emphasis on clean quarters, see "Cleaning Up," Plantation Manual, in Plantation Book, 1857–58, Reel 14, JHHP, SCL.

106. By 1857, at least two enslaved families were living at Redcliffe, with several more added in the coming years. Records of enslaved births, Reel 1, JHHP, SCL.

107. Monica Beck found a similar use of cabin orientation for enslavers' surveillance of slave living spaces at Brattonsville in backcountry South Carolina. Beck, "'A Few Ways Off from the Big House,'" 126.

108. "Cleaning Up," Plantation Manual, in Plantation Book, 1857–58, Reel 14, JHHP, SCL.

109. Breeden, *Advice among Masters*, 123.

110. Plantation Book, 1857–58, Reel 14, JHHP, SCL.

111. Agha and Jones, "Preliminary Archaeology Report," 18.

112. If this yard was indeed swept, there was likely a sense of ownership over it by enslaved people in the cabins. As Monica Beck argues, enslaved people's yard sweeping at another Piedmont South Carolina plantation suggests a feeling of mutual ownership— enslaver and enslaved—over this shared space. Beck, "'A Few Ways Off from the Big House,'" 128.

113. Speech, December 1861, Reel 10, JHHP, SCL.

114. Plantation Journal, April 6, 1862; July 28, 1864, Reel 2; Confederate Bonds, Reel 2, JHHP, SCL.

115. November 10, 1861, Reel 2, JHHP, SCL.

116. June 28, 1863, Reel 2, JHHP, SCL.

117. August 30, 1863, Reel 2, JHHP, SCL. It is certainly possible more enslaved people owned by Hammond escaped to Union lines, particularly once James became incapacitated and could not easily travel to oversee his other nearby plantations.

118. Amy Taylor, *Embattled Freedom*, 60.

119. Plantation Journal, November 10, 1861; January 30, 1862; February 10, 1862; April 6, 1862; June 29, 1863; August 8, 1863, Reel 2, JHHP, SCL.

120. Clay-Clopton, *A Belle of the Fifties*, 232.

121. In December 1860, Harry and his wife moved to Silverton. Another one of James's sons, Edward Spann Hammond, had a plantation in Mississippi. Plantation Journal, December 4, 1860, Reel 1; November 29, 1862, Reel 2, JHHP, SCL.

122. Letter, Harry to brother, September 3, 1865, Reel 11, JHHP, SCL.

123. *Acts of the General Assembly of the State of South Carolina*, 291–304.

124. Betty Farrow, in FWP-WPA, *Slave Narratives*, vol. 16, pt. 2, 34.

125. Orser, *Material Basis of the Postbellum Tenant Plantation*, esp. chap. 4.

126. Browder, Brooks, and Crass, *Memories of Home*.

127. Mark Reinberger, in his examination of sharecropping dwellings in the Georgia Piedmont, notes that "shared dwellings were one of the aspects of slavery most emphatically avoided by free blacks." Reinberger, "Architecture of Sharecropping," 126.

128. 1870 US Census, Barnwell County, SC. The census lists "Sarah Johnson," but her age and other personal info, including names of children, match. Plus, the fact that Louisa is next door suggests this is Sally.

129. "The African-American Experience," 2018, RPSHS.

130. As Louisa is listed as a "farm laborer," it is likely she worked her mother's land, alongside her brother, sister, and children. 1870 US Census, Barnwell County, SC.

131. The next house over, at what may have been the Silverton house, was a white family who employed several Johnson children. 1870 US Census, Barnwell County, SC. Henderson, Sally and John Henry Hammond's son, was not living with his mother in 1870; perhaps his vintner skills gave him a choice to pursue a life beyond farming.

132. John Shaw Billings Scrapbook Collection, no. 67, 1955, South Caroliniana Library, University of South Carolina.

133. This does not mean they did not feel a sense of ownership over their homes. Although enslaved people had been legally unable to own property, they did possess it, providing many with a sense of ownership, even if it was not recognized by the courts or individual enslavers. In fact, historian Dylan Penningroth has shown that in areas of the South where plantation workforces had been relatively stable in the 1850s, freed people claimed ownership of parcels of land that they defined as "home." Penningroth, *Claims of Kinfolk*, 158.

134. J. Smith, "More Than Slaves, Less Than Freedmen," 264.

135. Breeden, *Advice among Masters*, 129.

136. Plantation Manual, List of Negroes, October 5, 1845, Reel 1, JHHP, SCL.

137. By 1880, they had moved to the Hammond Township, closer to Redcliffe. 1880 US Census, Aiken County, SC.

138. In the years after emancipation, some formerly enslaved people continued to live in the same cabins they had been enslaved in. Orser, *Material Basis of the Postbellum Tenant Plantation*, 90–93.

139. Du Bois, "Problem of Housing the Negro."

140. G. McDaniel, *Hearth and Home*, 137. McDaniel notes that this was not a uniquely African American characteristic, nor were housing types and evolutions in them directly related to one's race. Still, improvisation was a necessary coping mechanism that continued from slavery into freedom.

141. John Shaw Billings, the last Hammond descendant to own Redcliffe from 1935 to 1975, left a trove of scrapbooks that included old photographs marked with his own captions. This one reads "A Happy Family, Redcliffe, SC," a comment perhaps on Billings's perception of Black laborers on his property. It is not clear exactly where on the Redcliffe property this photograph was taken, whether closer to the Redcliffe mansion or farther out as the Hammond estate transitioned from slavery to tenancy. Regardless, the lean-to addition is suggested by the three piers beneath one side of the cabin; typically, only two piers hold up the short side of a cabin (as with the Redcliffe Yard houses). The middle pier suggests a prior design, while the planks may have been replaced to cover the full length of the newly extended sides. See "A Happy Family, Redcliffe, SC," Scrapbook from the John Shaw Billings Papers, Accession no. 7108, Photo Album 3, held at South Caroliniana, University of South Carolina, Columbia.

142. Byrd, "Loot, Occupy, and Re-envision," 78.

143. Emmaline Heard, in FWP-WPA, *Slave Narratives*, vol. 4, pt. 2, 152.

144. Andrea Roberts has done extensive recovery work with descendants to identify postbellum Black settlements and towns in Texas, and she argues that the naming practices of these "freedom colonies" was a part of the broader practice of Black placemaking. The Texas Freedom Colonies Project, www.thetexasfreedomcoloniesproject.com/.

145. Anson Harp, in FWP-WPA, *Slave Narratives*, vol. 14, pt. 2, 239.

146. For a general overview of postbellum migration patterns, see Phillips, *Daily Life during African American Migrations*, 1–32.

147. Archaeologists and anthropologists use the term "shifting" rather than "migrating" to describe much of the movement of Black Southerners in the immediate postbellum era. Shifting includes movement between individual farms within or across different regions as well as between farms on the same property. Shifting was likely easier for tenant or sharecropping families, as it allowed individuals to remain within established kin and social networks. In distinction to shifting, migration refers to movement from one area to another or from a rural to urban environment. See Orser, *Material Basis of the Postbellum Tenant Plantation*, 112.

148. Why and when Sallie and her husband changed their last name to Wigfall is not clear. James refers to her as Sally/Sallie Smith until he dies, and her first husband's last name appears to have been Mason. Records of enslaved births, Reel 1, JHHP, SCL. There was a nearby enslaving family named Wigfall, and several formerly enslaved people who lived in the area took that last name after emancipation. Along with the Johnsons and Smiths/Wigfalls, surnames like Shubrick, Fuller, Ball, Clark, Goodwin—surnames that had appeared in plantation records throughout the many decades of Hammond's enslaving—appeared on the voter registration list for Silverton Township in 1868 and in the 1870 and 1880 US Censuses. See the 1868 Voter Registration List, Barnwell County, SC; 1870 US Census, Barnwell and Edgefield Counties, SC; 1880 US Census, Barnwell and Aiken Counties, SC.

149. Hammond recorded that Sallie lived at Redcliffe in 1857 when she gave birth to her daughter, Eliza. Records of enslaved births, Reel 1, JHHP, SCL.

150. No husband is listed in the 1880 US Census, but Ella had two children by that time. 1880 US Census, Aiken County, SC.

151. In 1880, Sallie (going by the nickname Sarah) had the last name of Bruce and was married to a man named John Bruce. They together had ten children in the home, one of which (Josephine, born at Redcliffe during slavery) is listed as John's stepdaughter. 1880 US Census, Aiken County, SC.

152. These households would not have the newfound privacy that more dispersed settlements experienced, but they too relied on family that lived nearby or even in the same building.

153. A friend of Harry Hammond's mentioned "Aunt Sallie" being at church with all the Redcliffe folks in an 1889 letter. "The African-American Experience," 2018, RPSHS.

154. The US Census is not clear about whether a dwelling means a separate building.

155. This included Dennis, Sallie's son and Ella's brother, who went on to run a successful grocery store in Augusta that he passed down to his son. When Clarence, Dennis's son, died in 1959, the *Charleston News and Courier* remembered him as a "wealthy son of . . . Dennis Wigfall, reportedly a slave of Gov. James Henry Hammond." *Charleston News and Courier*, February 25, 1959. The Henleys were the last Black family to leave Redcliffe when it was sold to the state of South Carolina in 1975. "The African-American Experience," 2018, RPSHS.

156. It is important to note that emancipation did not easily lead to improvements in standards of living or access to necessities or desired goods. Archaeologists have shown how difficult it is to differentiate or separate antebellum and postbellum material culture

on plantation sites that were occupied before and after the war. Digging into the physical remains of postbellum Black Southern life reveals that living conditions were, for many, similar to that in slavery. Theresa A. Singleton, "Archaeological Implications for Changing Labor Conditions," in Singelton, *Archaeology of Slavery and Plantation Life*, 303; Wilkie, *Creating Freedom*, 245.

157. Agha and Jones, "Preliminary Archaeology Report." For more on African American consumerism in the late nineteenth and early twentieth centuries, see Mullins, *Race and Affluence*; Ownby, *American Dreams in Mississippi*.

158. Harry devised a scheme to keep much of the 14,000-acre estate in Hammond hands after the war, but by the early twentieth century, portions of the land were sold off until only a few hundred acres around Redcliffe remained in Hammond/Billings control. Bleser, *The Hammonds of Redcliffe*, 136–37, 307.

159. There has been a concerted effort to establish public monuments and memorials to slavery around the Atlantic world. See Phulgence, "Monument Building, Memory Making, and Remembering Slavery." However, the American monument landscape is still overwhelmingly white. See Monument Lab, *National Monument Audit*, accessed October 7, 2022, https://monumentlab.com/audit.

160. C. Smith, *How the Word Is Passed*, 51. Whitney Plantation is one of the few historic plantation sites that functions exclusively as a site of commemoration for enslaved Americans. At Whitney, site administrators use not only extant and relocated plantation architecture but also text- and sculpture-based memorials to commemorate those who lived, labored, loved, and died while enslaved on the plantations.

161. Architectural historians, including Tara Dudley and Catherine W. Bishir, push us to view buildings constructed by enslaved and free Black Americans as examples of their skill and genius in architecture, design, construction, and more. Dudley, *Building Antebellum New Orleans*; Bishir, *Crafting Lives*.

162. Alan Rice has discussed how plantations can be understood as *lieux de memoire*, an idea put forward by theorist Pierre Nora, wherein sites have multiple layers of memories, some of them in conflict. In this way a plantation can represent white Southern memory *and* Black Southern memory. Yet it takes more than a simple recognition of that to actually shift our perspective from the dominant white Southern memory so clearly represented in the landscape and interpretation of historic plantation sites. Alan Rice, "Museums, Memorials and Plantation Houses in the Black Atlantic," 230. Some writers have begun to describe plantations as Confederate monuments, which in some ways is true, as both the Confederacy and plantation landscapes were at their core about supporting the same social, economic, and political ideologies and realities. Yet in adding this other framework—one where plantations are also monuments to Black lives—we may find another way of countering the Lost Cause mythology that still persists at so many historic sites. For the former, see Chase Quinn, "Why the 'Romance' of Plantation Estates Is More Dangerous Than Confederate Statues," *Guardian*, June 24, 2020, www .theguardian.com/commentisfree/2020/jun/24/romance-plantation-estates-dangerous -confederate-statues; for the latter, see the writings and work of artist and activist John Sims, including his op-ed series in the *Tampa Bay Times* and the Monuments, Markers, and Memory 2021 Symposium Series convened with the University of South Florida.

163. The Henleys lived at Redcliffe since at least 1857, when Hammond recorded the birth of their son John there. Records of enslaved births, Reel 1, JHHP, SCL. They lived

in the double-pen cabin at a right-angle to and just feet from the house Sallie Smith/ Wigfall/Bruce and her family occupied for years, until the mid-1970s.

164. Chelsea Stutz, "Strength to Go Forward—Dr. Breanne Henley," South Carolina State Parks, accessed August 10, 2021, https://southcarolinaparks.com/stories/strength -to-go-forward-dr-breanna-henely.

165. Instagram post, Breanna Henley, May 11, 2021. Post and photograph included with consent of Breanna Henley, email message to author, August 31, 2022.

Conclusion

1. Sources for this vignette include Matthew Reeves, ed., "Historical, Archaeological and Architectural Research at the Gilmore Cabin" (no date), MAD-MF, JMM.

2. JMM dates the cabin to 1873. "Historical, Archaeological and Architectural Research at the Gilmore Cabin," 5.

3. Descendants have been working more than two decades with JMM to ensure that a more honest and equitable history of the site is told. In 2021, the Montpelier Foundation made the enormously important step of committing to structural parity, thereby creating a shared governance structure with descendants. But in March 2022, the Foundation's board of directors reversed their decision and soon after fired several staff members who spoke out against this unacceptable reversal. Thanks to the persistent work of the Montpelier Descendants Committee, who launched a campaign that drew thousands of signatures and widespread media attention, the board recommitted to structural parity in May 2022 and re-hired the unjustifiably fired staff members soon thereafter. For more on the controversy and the renewed promise of Montpelier, see James French, "Montpelier: A Model for Reconciliation in Peak Polarization," *Washington Post*, May 16, 2022, www.washingtonpost.com/opinions/2022/05/16 /montpelier-model-reconciliation-peak-polarization/.

4. Quote from Oubre, *Forty Acres and a Mule*, 134.

5. "Get a Home," *Free Man's Press* (Austin, TX), August 1, 1869.

6. General Ormsby M. Mitchel, private letter to the editor of the *New York Evening Post*, in Finding Freedom's Home: Archaeology at Mitchelville digital exhibit, accessed May 7, 2023, https://beaufortcountysc.gov/mitchelville/.

7. Letter, Selina Gray to Mary Custis Lee, November 1872, Mary Custis Lee Papers, Virginia Historical Society, Richmond, VA.

8. Margrett Nillin, in FWP-WPA, *Slave Narratives*, vol. 16, pt. 3, 153.

9. Bragg, *Men of Maryland*, 75.

10. Schweninger, *Black Property Owners in the South*.

11. Du Bois, *Black Reconstruction*, 601.

12. Black activists focused on the home as one of the centers for racial uplift during the Jim Crow era. See, for example, Gaines, *Uplifting the Race*; M. Mitchell, *Righteous Propagation*.

13. B. K. Bruce, "Possibilities of Christmas," *Christian Recorder*, December 23, 1880.

14. Du Bois, "Problem of Housing the Negro."

15. Royce, *Origins of Southern Sharecropping*; Mancini, *One Dies, Get Another*. For more on broad changes to the Southern labor market and economy after emancipation, see Gavin Wright, *Old South, New South*.

16. See, for example, Orser, "Artifacts, Documents and Memories of the Black Tenant

Farmer," 51. A number of formerly enslaved people in Georgia recalled the re-use of slave cabins as sharecropper cabins. See Georgia Writers' Project, *Drums and Shadows*, 32.

17. Robert Perkinson lays out the evolution of convict leasing in Texas, including its relationship to the institution of slavery, which he argues is the origin of the state's contemporary penal system. Perkinson, *Texas Tough*.

18. At least forty-eight convicts worked at Patton Place in 1874 and 1875, making bricks and working a sugar crop. See J. K. P. Campbell, "Inspection Report," October 1, 1874, State Archives Records relating to the Penitentiary, Texas State Archives, Austin, Texas, in *Varner-Hogg Plantation*, 2:71. The convict leasing system operated in Texas from the late 1860s through the 1910s, providing labor on plantations and railroads, among other industries. Private companies initially ran the system, and the state took control in the 1880s.

19. 1880 US Census, Orange County, VA; 1880 US Census, Aiken County, SC; 1880 US Census, Brazoria County, TX.

20. Hunter, *To 'Joy My Freedom*; Sharpless, *Cooking in Other Women's Kitchens*.

21. 1880 US Census, Orange County, VA. All these pieces are now in the Smithsonian's National Museum of African American History and Culture (NMAAHC) collection. The objects were donated by Clara Ellis Payne, granddaughter of Frank and Polly May Ellis. Through her notes, we know the pieces were owned by members of the Ellis family, including some items that belonged to her grandparents, Frank and Polly May. A few may also date to the generation prior, to Squire May and his second wife, Roseanna, the great-grandfather and step-great-grandmother of the donor. Squire and Roseanna also lived in Orange County, Virginia. Thank you to the NMAAHC for providing the known provenance of these objects. Records of marriage from "Virginia, U.S., Select Marriages, 1785–1940," Ancestry.com, accessed February 15, 2022, https://www.ancestry.com/search/collections/60214/.

22. This was one verse sung at meetings of the Exodusters, a group of Black Southerners who touted the benefits of migration and who moved to Kansas seeking greater freedom in the late 1870s. Quote from Fleming, "'Pap' Singleton," 67. For more on the Exodusters, see Painter, *Exodusters*.

23. Nieman, *To Set the Law in Motion*.

24. Isaac Croom held thirteen individuals in bondage at Magnolia Grove in 1860, while his Marengo County plantation contained 219 enslaved persons. 1860 US Census–Slave Schedule, Greene County, AL; 1860 US Census–Slave Schedule, Marengo County, AL; Cunningham, "Magnolia Grove."

25. Eleanor Cunningham (director of the Alabama Historical Commission's Historic Sites Division) related that the dating for Magnolia Grove's construction is based on building techniques as well as on deeds for land purchases. Isaac Croom began buying land on the western edge of town in 1836 and purchased the last lot that made up Magnolia Grove in 1839. Eleanor Cunningham, email message to author, July 17, 2019.

26. A team from the Alabama Department of Corrections found the cowrie shell and other objects during restoration/stabilization of the slave cabin in 2009. Drilled through the center of the cowrie shell is a hole where a brass pendant (secured by brass washer and pin) contains fiber remnants, which the Alabama Historical Commission suggests came from a tassel. Perhaps previously used as a personal adornment or charm, the cowrie shell may have been in the family for much longer than the 1870s dating

suggests. Eleanor Cunningham, "Artifacts or Ratifacts?: Objects Recovered from within the Walls of the Slave House, Magnolia Grove Historic Site, Greensboro, AL" (May 18, 2009), unpublished report, Alabama Historical Commission, provided by Cunningham.

27. George W. Mordecai, who was married to Paul's sister and who thus legally owned some enslaved Stagville residents, experienced financial ruin in the late 1850s and sold many people, including Elijah, Lucy, and their seven children. The nine of them are marked as "sold" (penned in George's handwriting) in his 1859 slave list of Jones Quarter. Inventory of Jones Quarter, folder 289, George W. Mordecai Papers #522, SHC.

28. Letter, Paul to George W. Mordecai, May 29, 1865, folder 95, George W. Mordecai Papers #522, SHC.

29. Albertus Hope, a white man, testified before the South Carolina Klan trial that he went to a local Klan meeting because he feared for his property and family, having to walk his yard several nights to ensure no Black men committed "outrages," specifically arson. Simply put, Hope declared, "I was in the Klan, which we organized for protection— to protect my house and family." United States Circuit Court, *Proceedings in the Ku Klux Trials at Columbia, S.C.*, 446, 461.

30. Excerpt from order of General Meade, in McPherson, *A Political Manual for 1868*, 320.

31. Works Progress Administration interviews contain hundreds of recollections of Black Southerners' fear of the KKK, including the targeting of their homes.

32. Smallwood and Crouch, "Texas Freedwomen during Reconstruction," 46.

33. Letter, H. C. Thompson to Mary Ellen Hedrick, November 22, 1869, Box 8, Hedrick Papers, David M. Rubenstein Rare Book and Manuscript Library, Duke University, Durham, NC.

34. Du Bois, "The Problem of Housing the Negro," 535.

35. Rothstein, *Color of Law*; K. Taylor, *Race for Profit*; Browne, *Dark Matters*.

36. Holt, *The Movement*.

37. High-profile police murders of Black individuals in their own homes—including Breonna Taylor, Atatiana Jefferson, and Botham Jean—only reinforce that this racialized history of home is not past.

38. Adams, *Wounds of Returning*, 5.

39. This includes Montpelier, Stagville, Gaineswood, Varner-Hogg, and Redcliffe, all of which have worked (to varying degrees) to alter their tours, site interpretation, and public programming over the past few decades. But the number of sites similarly pursuing a more robust inclusion or a centering of Black history is far greater, and is increasing. Whitney Plantation in Louisiana is one of the few (and was one of the earliest) historic plantations re-dedicated to telling the stories of enslaved people, while some like McLeod Plantation in South Carolina have been working to make the plantation a site of shared memory. Along with Montpelier, other presidential plantation sites have further included slavery and enslaved residents their interpretation, though with pushback from visitors and the public. See C. Smith, *How the Word Is Passed*, 8–84; Graves, "'Return and Get It'"; Hannah Knowles, "As Plantations Talk More Honestly about Slavery, Some Visitors Are Pushing Back," *Washington Post*, September 8, 2019, www .washingtonpost.com/history/2019/09/08/plantations-are-talking-more-about-slavery -grappling-with-visitors-who-talk-back/. For recent studies of the successes and

continued failures of narrating slavery at historic museums and sites, see Skipper, *Behind the Big House*; Alderman et al., *Remembering Enslavement*.

40. Randall Kenan, "The Descendants," *Garden and Gun*, February–March 2018, https://gardenandgun.com/feature/the-descendants/.

Appendix

1. Founded originally as the Classical Institute of the South, the project changed its name to the Decorative Arts of the Gulf South soon after the Historic New Orleans Collection acquired it. For more on the research project and the database it has helped create, see "Decorative Arts of the Gulf South," Historic New Orleans Collection, accessed June 13, 2022, www.hnoc.org/research/decorative-arts-gulf-south.

2. Much of what I encountered corresponded to the early 2000s findings of Jennifer Eichstedt and Stephen Small, who in an analysis of 122 historic plantation sites in Virginia, Georgia, and Louisiana, discovered that the vast majority ignored, marginalized, or trivialized the role, experiences, and spaces of enslaved individuals. In fact, they reported that there were "thirty-one times as many mentions of furniture at these sites than of slavery or those enslaved." Eichstedt and Small, *Representations of Slavery*, 109. See also Mooney, "Looking for History's Huts." This has begun to change in the past decade, due in large part to the efforts of descendants, public historians, and activists, including groups like the Slave Dwelling Project. But this work has not necessarily trickled down to smaller, less-well-funded, or private sites.

3. As Tiya Miles recently described it, "Every scholar of . . . the history of slavery, must confront the conundrum of the archives." Miles, *All That She Carried*, 300. To be fair, some scholars assert that the traditional archive is not silent when it comes to enslaved people; *historians* have silenced enslaved people in the archive. Additionally, the recent turn toward making the archive itself a subject of historical analysis has shown not only the violence of it but also the opportunities in it, if read in new ways.

4. Many different disciplines utilize material culture sources and methodology, including history, literature, archaeology, art history, and sociology. See, for example, Woodward, *Understanding Material Culture*. As a historian, I approach material culture as a means of better understanding the past, which shapes how I articulate and practice material culture, including in ways different from those contemplating the present.

5. This has been a core tenet of material culture studies for more than half a century, including in the work of Henry Glassie, a pioneer of American material culture and vernacular architecture. Glassie argues that most of mankind has been nonliterate, and thus unable to participate in the creation of documentary evidence. Because those who recorded their thoughts, experiences, and lives represent such a small (generally elite) class of actors, written sources tell far less than is typically assumed. Glassie, *Folk Housing in Middle Virginia*, 8–12. Glassie and other Americanists built on the work of those studying a different place and era, such as medieval historian Lynn White, who advocated for more than a decade that "if historians are to attempt to write the history of mankind, and not simply the history of mankind as it was viewed by the elite and specialized segments of the race who had the habit of scribbling, they must take a fresh view of the records," including the artifacts they left behind. L. White, *Medieval Technology and Social Change*, vii.

6. Pitt-Rivers, "On the Evolution of Culture," 23; Kenneth L. Ames, "Meaning in

Artifacts: Hall Furnishings in Victorian America," in Schlereth, *Material Culture Studies in America*, 208.

7. The built environment, or built landscape, refers to any human-made alteration to the natural world. As Rebecca Ginsburg and Clifton Ellis describe it, it is the "buildings, yards, streets, fields, alleys, obscure trails, dusty lanes, fences, and tree lines and all other elements of our surroundings that are the product of human intervention, however slight." Clifton Ellis and Rebecca Ginsburg, "Introduction," in *Cabin, Quarter, Plantation*, 2.

8. Upton, "Material Culture Studies, a Symposium," 85.

9. Additionally, the preservation movement has too long ignored or underappreciated Black historic sites, and the resulting lack of recognition (and funding) has further racialized the American landscape. See Leggs, "Growth of Historic Sites"; Lynn-Tinen, "Reclaiming the Past as a Matter of Social Justice."

10. This constant unearthing of new evidence may be concerning for historians, particularly those whose interpretations are presented in static print form. It is possible that new sources might emerge to corroborate or contradict the arguments in a book or article. Rather than view this potential as anxiety-inducing, we can recognize it as exciting and encouraging, prompting a reassessment of the past. Historians are constantly fighting against the notion that the past is past; we want to make clear to the public that history is always changing and evolving. The use of archaeology and other alternative archives allows historians to practice what we preach.

11. Instead of categorizing and dissociating different material forms, assemblages (a term traditionally used by archaeologists but more recently brought into historical scholarship) bring multiple object types into conversation with one another and with other cultural products (pamphlets, poetry, prints, etc.). See Van Horn, *Power of Objects*; Anishanslin, *Portrait of a Woman in Silk*.

12. Descendants may be the most important group to whom historians should listen. Public historians and archaeologists have long recognized this and have written about the opportunities and struggles of working with descendant communities. See, for example, McDavid, "Descendants, Decisions, and Power"; McDavid, "Archaeologies That Hurt"; Colwell, "Collaborative Archaeologies and Descendant Communities"; National Council on Public History, "The Making of James Madison's Montpelier's 'The Mere Distinction of Colour' Q&A," parts 3 and 4, History@Work, February 2019, https://ncph.org/history-at-work/.

13. The sheer number of explanatory paragraphs in monographs and articles about material culture suggest that scholars feel the need to continue justifying their approaches in the face of skepticism. My work, like that of others who make historical arguments based on nontextual sources, has been met with some spirited resistance and suspicion, including by stellar social historians. Such misgivings helped me refine my own method and made me more careful with speculative thinking and writing.

14. This is particularly important, once again, when investigating those whom the archive has erased, obfuscated, or distorted in the historical record. As Saidiya Hartman suggests, speculative arguments are one way to "negotiate the constitutive limits of the archive." Hartman, "Venus in Two Acts," 11.

15. Jules David Prown's method, perhaps the most influential in material culture studies, substantially shaped my approach, but so did several important "state of the field"

anthologies. Prown, "Mind in Matter"; Schlereth, *Material Culture Studies in America*; Martin and Garrison, *American Material Culture*; Ulrich et al., *Tangible Things*. Additionally, scholars have worked to translate material culture methodology into more accessible guides for students, including Harvey, *History and Material Culture*; Daniel Waugh, "Analyzing Material Objects," *World History Commons*, accessed June 22, 2022, https://worldhistorycommons.org/analyzing-material-objects; Debby Andrews, Sarah Carter, Estella Chung, Ellen Garvey, Shirley Wajda, and Catherine Whalen, "Twenty Years, Twenty Questions to Ask an Object," workshop at the American Studies Association meeting, Los Angeles, California, November 6–9, 2014, https://networks.h-net.org/twenty-questions-ask-object-handout.

16. At the same time, the process is not perfectly linear and often requires moving back and forth as needed. Even though Prown argued for a strict adherence to his particular step sequence, his point was intended to ensure that the researcher not move forward too quickly. Additionally, one will not need to take each step for every single object or source examined. As one builds these skills, the more natural the process becomes and the more one is able to discern when to jump forward or when to return to a previous step. Prown, "Mind in Matter," 7.

17. Rosemary Troy Krill explains that an object has "multiple layers of meaning, including the viewpoints of the maker, owner, and everyone who subsequently has interacted with the objects." Krill, *Early American Decorative Arts*, ix. Archaeologist Ian Hodder defines context as any and all environments that are relevant to an object, with "relevant" conveying the "relationships[s] necessary for discerning the object's meaning." Hodder, *Reading the Past*, 139. Historians who utilize material culture evidence can learn much from historical archaeologists about sensitivity to context. See particularly J. Deetz, *In Small Things Forgotten*.

18. This may lead to a cacophony of contexts, yet as historical archaeology demonstrates, "To be meaningful, contexts must incorporate the many, sometimes discordant voices of the people actively contributing to the unique cultures of their historical times and places." De Cunzo and Hermann, "Preface," x.

19. Prown, "Mind in Matter," 10.

20. This includes employing best practices of the public history field, such as shared authority with descendant communities, collaboration with stakeholders and academics, and active research, including archaeology programs. For more on best practices at sites of slavery, see Gallas and DeWolf Perry, *Interpreting Slavery at Museums and Historic Sites*; Rose, *Interpreting Difficult History at Museums and Historic Sites*.

BIBLIOGRAPHY

Primary Sources

MANUSCRIPTS AND ARCHIVES

Angleton, TX
    Brazoria County Clerk's Office, Cases #453, #690, #904, #2997
Auburn, AL
    Auburn University Special Collections and Archives
        Whitfield Family Papers
Beech Island, SC
    Redcliffe Plantation State Historic Site
Chapel Hill, NC
    University of North Carolina, Wilson Library, Southern Historical Collection
        Cameron Family Papers #133
        George W. Mordecai Papers #522
Columbia, SC
    University of South Carolina, South Caroliniana Library
Dallas, TX
    Southern Methodist University, Fondren Library
        James Henry Hammond Papers, microfilm (originals at South Caroliniana
            Library, University of South Carolina)
            Records of the Ante-Bellum Southern Plantations from the Revolution
                through the Civil War Series A, Part I
Demopolis, AL
    Gaineswood Plantation
Durham, NC
    Duke University, David M. Rubenstein Rare Book and Manuscript Library
    Stagville State Historic Site
Florence, AL
    Florence-Lauderdale Library
Orange County, VA
    James Madison's Montpelier
Richmond, VA
    Virginia Historical Society
West Columbia, TX
    Varner-Hogg Plantation State Historic Site
Worcester, MA
    American Antiquarian Society

PERIODICALS

Charleston (SC) News and Courier
Christian Recorder (Philadelphia, PA)

The Countryman (Putnam County, GA)
Daily National Intelligencer (Washington, DC)
Florence (AL) Enquirer
The Free Man's Press (Austin, TX)
Southern Workman (Hampton, VA)
Washington Post

ONLINE PRIMARY SOURCES

Federal Writers' Project, Work Projects Administration. *Slave Narratives: A Folk History of Slavery in the United States from Interviews with Former Slaves.* 17 vols. Washington, DC: Library of Congress, 1941. www.loc.gov/collections/slave-narratives-from-the-federal-writers-project-1936-to-1938/about-this-collection/.
Historic American Buildings Survey/Historic American Engineering Record/Historic American Landscapes Survey, Library of Congress, Prints and Photographs. www.loc.gov/pictures/collection/hh.
National Archives and Records Administration, Record Group 79: Records of the National Park Service; National Register of Historic Places and National Historic Landmarks Program Records. https://catalog.archives.gov/id/20812721.
Stagg, J. C. A., ed. *The Papers of James Madison Digital Edition.* Charlottesville: University of Virginia Press, 2010. https://rotunda.upress.virginia.edu/founders/JSMN.html.

PUBLISHED PRIMARY SOURCES

Acts of the General Assembly of the State of South Carolina Passed at the Sessions of 1864–65. Columbia: Julian A. Selby, Printer to the State, 1865.
Aleckson, Sam. *Before the War, and After the Union: An Autobiography.* Boston: Gold Mind, 1929.
Alexander, Charles. *Battles and Victories of Allen Allensworth.* Boston: Sherman, French, 1914.
Allgor, Catherine, ed. *The Queen of America: Mary Cutts's Life of Dolley Madison.* Charlottesville: University of Virginia Press, 2012.
Ball, Charles. *Fifty Years in Chains; or, the Life of an American Slave.* New York: H. Dayton, 1859.
Bibb, Henry. *Narrative of the Life and Adventures of Henry Bibb.* New York: Published by the Author, 1849.
Bleby, Henry. *Josiah: The Maimed Fugitive.* London: Wesleyan Conference Office, 1873.
Bleser, Carol, ed. *The Hammonds of Redcliffe.* Columbia: University of South Carolina Press, 1997.
———, ed. *Secret and Sacred: The Diaries of James Henry Hammond, a Southern Slaveholder.* Columbia: University of South Carolina Press, 1997.
Bolton, Henry Carrington. "Decoration of Graves of Negroes in South Carolina." *Journal of American Folklore* 4, no. 14 (July–September 1891): 214.
Bragg, George F. *Men of Maryland.* Baltimore, MD: Church Advocate Press, 1914.
Breeden, James O., ed. *Advice among Masters: The Ideal in Slave Management in the Old South.* Westport, CT: Greenwood Press, 1980.

Brown, Hallie Q. *Homespun Heroines and Other Women of Distinction*. Xenia, OH: Aldine Publishing Company, 1926.

Brown, William Wells. *Narrative of William W. Brown, a Fugitive Slave*. Boston: Anti-slavery Office, 1847.

Bruner, Peter. *A Slave's Adventures toward Freedom, Not Fiction, but the True Story of a Struggle*. Oxford, OH: n.p., 1918.

Buckingham, James Silk. *The Slave States of America*. Vol. 1. London: Fisher, Son, 1842.

Burton, Thomas Williams. *What Experience Has Taught Me: An Autobiography of Thomas William Burton*. Cincinnati, OH: Press of Jennings and Graham, 1910.

Cardinall, Allan W. *Tales Told in Togoland*. London: Oxford University Press, 1970.

Clay-Clopton, Virginia. *A Belle of the Fifties: Memoirs of Mrs. Clay of Alabama*. New York: Doubleday, 1905.

Craft, William. *Running a Thousand Miles for Freedom; or, the Escape of William and Ellen Craft from Slavery*. London: William Tweedie, 1860.

Davies, Richard Beale. *Jeffersonian America: Notes on the United States of America Collected in the Years 1805–6–7 and 11–12 by Sir Augustus John Foster*. San Marino, CA: Huntington Library, 1954.

Douglass, Frederick. *My Bondage and My Freedom*. New York: Miller, Orton and Mulligan, 1855.

Du Bois, W. E. B. "The Problem of Housing the Negro; III. The Home of the Country Freedmen." *Southern Workman* 30, no. 10 (October 1901): 535.

Faulkner, William. "Pantaloon in Black." In *Go Down, Moses*. Reprint. New York: Vintage Books, 2011.

Finch, John. *Travels in the United States of America and Canada*. London: Longman, Rees, Orme, Brown, Green, and Longman, 1833.

Fleming, Walter L. "'Pap' Singleton: The Moses of the Colored Exodus." *American Journal of Sociology* 15 (July 1909): 61–82.

Georgia Writers' Project. *Drums and Shadows: Survival Studies among the Georgia Coastal Negroes*. Athens: University of Georgia Press, 1989.

Goings, Henry. *Rambles of a Runaway from Southern Slavery*. Edited by Calvin Schermerhorn, Michael Plunkett, and Edward Gaynor. Charlottesville: University of Virginia Press, 2012.

Goodell, William. *The American Slave Code in Theory and Practice; Its Distinctive Features Shewn by Its Statutes, Judicial Decisions, and Illustrative Facts*. New York: American and Foreign Anti-Slavery Society, 1853.

Hahn, Steven, Steven F. Miller, Susan E. O'Donovan, John C. Rodrigue, and Leslie S. Rowland, eds. *Freedom: A Documentary History of Emancipation, 1861–1867*. Ser. 3, vol. 1, *Land and Labor, 1865*. Chapel Hill: University of North Carolina Press, 2017.

Hart, Katherine, and Elizabeth Kemp, eds. *Lucadia Pease and the Governor: Letters, 1850–1857*. Austin, TX: Encino Press, 1974.

Henson, Josiah. *Uncle Tom's Story of His Life: An Autobiography of the Rev. Josiah*. London: Christian Age Office, 1876.

Homes of American Statesmen; with Anecdotical, Personal, and Descriptive Sketches. Hartford, CT: O. D. Case, 1855.

Hughes, Louis. *Thirty Years a Slave: From Bondage to Freedom; The Institution of Slavery as Seen on the Plantation and in the Home of the Planter.* Milwaukee: South Side Printing, 1897.

"In Memoriam: Henry Carrington Bolton." *Journal of American Folklore* 16, no. 63 (October–December 1903): 275.

Jackson-Coppin, Fanny. *Reminiscences of School Life, and Hints on Teaching.* Philadelphia: A. M. E. Book Concern, 1913.

Jones, Thomas H. *Experience and Personal Narrative of Uncle Tom Jones.* Boston: H. B. Skinner, 1854.

Latta, M. L. *The History of My Life and Work.* Raleigh: Self-published, 1903.

Lossing, Benson J. *Pictorial Field-Book of the Revolution.* Vol. 2. New York: Harper and Brothers, 1852.

Mattern, David B., and Holly C. Shulman, eds. *The Selected Letters of Dolley Payne Madison.* Charlottesville: University of Virginia Press, 2003.

McCord, David James. *Africans at Home, from the Forthcoming Number of the "Southern Quarterly Review."* July 1854. https://archive.org/details/africansathomefroomcco _0/page/n1/mode/2up.

McPherson, Edward. *A Political Manual for 1868, Including a Classified Summary of the Important, Executive, Legislative, Politico-Military, and General Facts of the Period, from April 1, 1867, to July 5, 1868.* Washington, DC: Philp and Solomons, 1868.

Northup, Solomon. *Twelve Years a Slave: Narrative of Solomon Northup.* Auburn, NY: Derby and Miller, 1853.

Olmsted, Frederick Law. *A Journey in the Seaboard States: With Remarks on Their Economy.* New York: Dix and Edwards, 1856.

Pickard, Kate E. R. *The Kidnapped and the Ransomed: Being the Personal Recollections of Peter Still and His Wife 'Vina' after Forty Years of Slavery.* Syracuse, NY: William T. Hamilton, 1856.

"Popular Errors, Prejudices, and Superstitions." *Illustrated Magazine of Art* 1, no. 6 (1853): 366–67.

Puckett, Newbell Niles. "Folk Beliefs of the Southern Negro." PhD diss., Yale University, 1925.

Rawick, George P., ed. *The American Slave: A Composite Autobiography.* Vol. 3, pt 2. Westport, CT: Greenwood Press, 1979.

Semmes, John Edward. *John H. B. Latrobe and His Times, 1803–1891.* Baltimore, MD: Norman, Remington, 1917.

"Statement from Meeting of New York Negroes, January 25, 1831, New York." In *Becoming American: The African-American Journey*, edited by Howard Dodson, Christopher Paul Moore, and Roberta Young, 95. New York: Sterling Publishing, 2009.

United States Circuit Court (4th Circuit) South Carolina. *Proceedings in the Ku Klux Trials at Columbia, S.C.: In the United States Circuit Court, November Term, 1871.* Columbia, SC: Republican Printing, 1872. Huntington Library, San Marino, CA.

Varner-Hogg Plantation State Historical Park, Brazoria County, Texas. 2 vols. Columbia: Texas Parks and Wildlife Department, 1983.

Weld, Theodore Dwight. *Slavery as It Is: Testimony of a Thousand Witnesses.* New York: American Anti-Slavery Society, 1839.

Secondary Sources

BOOKS

Ackelsberg, Martha A. *Resisting Citizenship: Feminist Essays on Politics, Community, and Democracy*. New York: Routledge, 2010.

Adams, Jessica. *Wounds of Returning: Race, Memory, and Property on the Postslavery Plantation*. Chapel Hill: University of North Carolina Press, 2007.

Agbe-Davies, Anna S. "The Production and Consumption of Smoking Pipes along the Tobacco Coast." In *Smoking and Culture: The Archaeology of Tobacco Pipes in Eastern North America*, edited by Sean Rafferty and Rob Mann, 273–304. Knoxville: University of Tennessee Press, 2004.

Alderman, Derek H., Candace Forbes Bright, David L. Butler, Perry L. Carter, Stephen P. Hanna, and Amy E. Potter. *Remembering Enslavement: Reassembling the Southern Plantation Museum*. Athens: University of Georgia Press, 2022.

Alexander, Michelle. *The New Jim Crow: Mass Incarceration in the Age of Colorblindness*. New York: New Press, 2010.

Ames, Kenneth L. *Death in the Dining Room and Other Tales of Victorian Culture*. Philadelphia: Temple University Press, 1992.

Anderson, Jean Bradley. *Piedmont Plantation: The Bennehan-Cameron Family and Lands in North Carolina*. Durham, NC: Historic Preservation Society of Durham, 1995.

Anderson, Jeffrey E. *Conjure in African American Society*. Baton Rouge: Louisiana State University Press, 2005.

Andrzejewski, Anna Vemer. *Building Power: Architecture and Surveillance in Victorian America*. Knoxville: University of Tennessee Press, 2008.

Anishanslin, Zara. *Portrait of a Woman in Silk: Hidden Histories of the British Atlantic World*. New Haven, CT: Yale University Press, 2016.

Armstrong, Douglas V. *The Old Village and Great House: An Archaeological and Historical Examination of Drax Hall Plantation, St. Ann's Bay, Jamaica*. Urbana: University of Illinois Press, 1990.

Austin, Ramona M. "Defining the African-American Cane." In *American Folk Art Canes: Personal Sculpture*, edited by George H. Meyer, 222–27. Seattle, WA: Marquand Books, 1992.

Ball, Erica. *To Live an Antislavery Life: Personal Politics and the Antebellum Black Middle Class*. Athens: University of Georgia Press, 2012.

Baptist, Edward. *The Half Has Never Been Told: Slavery and the Making of American Capitalism*. New York: Basic Books, 2014.

Barrie, Thomas. *House and Home: Cultural Contexts, Ontological Roles*. New York: Routledge, 2017.

Battle-Baptiste, Whitney. *Black Feminist Archaeology*. New York: Routledge, 2016.

———. "Sweepin' Spirits: Power and Transformation on the Plantation Landscape." In *Archaeology and Preservation of Gendered Landscapes*, edited by Sherene Baugher and Suzanna M. Spencer-Wood, 81–94. New York: Springer, 2010.

Baum, Dale. *Counterfeit Justice: The Judicial Odyssey of Texas Freedwoman Azeline Hearne*. Baton Rouge: Louisiana State University Press, 2009.

Beck, Monica L. "'A Few Ways Off from the Big House': The Changing Nature of

Slavery in the South Carolina Backcountry." In *The Southern Colonial Backcountry: Interdisciplinary Perspectives on Frontier Communities*, edited by David Colin Crass, Martha A. Zierden, Richard D. Brooks, and Steven D. Smith, 108–36. Knoxville: University of Tennessee Press, 1998.

Beckert, Sven. *Empire of Cotton: A Global History*. New York: Alfred A. Knopf, 2014.

Beiswanger, William L. *A Temple in the Garden: A Short History*. Charlottesville, VA: Thomas Jefferson Memorial Foundation, 1984.

Berlin, Ira. *Generations of Captivity: A History of African-American Slaves*. Cambridge, MA: Harvard University Press, 2003.

Berlin, Ira, and Philip D. Morgan, eds. *Cultivation and Culture: Labor and the Shaping of Slave Life in the Americas*. Charlottesville: University Press of Virginia, 1993.

————, eds. *The Slaves' Economy: Independent Production by Slaves in the Americas*. New York: Routledge, 1991.

Berlin, Ira, and Leslie S. Rowland, eds. *Families and Freedom: A Documentary History of African-American Kinship in the Civil War Era*. New York: New Press, 1997.

Berry, Daina Ramey, and Leslie M. Harris, eds. *Sexuality and Slavery: Reclaiming Intimate Histories in the Americas*. Athens: University of Georgia Press, 2018.

Bishir, Catherine W. *Crafting Lives: African American Artisans in New Bern, North Carolina, 1770–1900*. Chapel Hill: University of North Carolina Press, 2013.

Boles, John B. *Black Southerners, 1619–1869*. Lexington: University Press of Kentucky, 1983.

Boydston, Jeanne. *Home and Work: Housework, Wages, and the Ideology of Labor in the Early Republic*. New York: Oxford University Press, 1990.

Breen, T. H. *Tobacco Culture: The Mentality of the Great Tidewater Planters on the Eve of the Revolution*. Princeton, NJ: Princeton University Press, 1988.

Broadwater, Jeff. *James Madison: A Son of Virginia and a Founder of the Nation*. Chapel Hill: University of North Carolina Press, 2012.

Brock, Terry P. "Burial Customs." In *Enslaved Women in America: An Encyclopedia*, edited by Daina Ramey Berry and Deleso A. Alford, 20–21. Santa Barbara, CA: Greenwood, 2012.

Bromell, Nicholas Knowles. *By the Sweat of the Brow: Literature and Labor in Antebellum America*. Chicago: University of Chicago Press, 1993.

Brooks, James. *Captives and Cousins: Slavery, Kinship, and Community in the Southwest Borderlands*. Chapel Hill: University of North Carolina Press, 2003. Published for the Omohundro Institute of Early American History and Culture, Williamsburg, Virginia.

Browder, Tonya Algerine, Richard David Brooks, and David Colin Crass. *Memories of Home: Dunbarton and Meyers Mill Remembered*. Savannah River Archaeological Research Heritage Series, no. 1. Columbia: South Carolina Institute of Archaeology and Anthropology, University of South Carolina, 1993.

Brown, Karida L. *Gone Home: Race and Roots through Appalachia*. Chapel Hill: University of North Carolina Press, 2018.

Brown, Vincent. *The Reaper's Garden: Death and Power in the World of Atlantic Slavery*. Cambridge, MA: Harvard University Press, 2008.

Browne, Simone. *Dark Matters: On the Surveillance of Blackness*. Durham, NC: Duke University Press, 2015.

Burstein, Andrew, and Nancy Isenberg. *Madison and Jefferson*. New York: Random House, 2010.

Bushman, Richard. *The Refinement of America: Persons, Houses, Cities*. New York: Vintage Books, 1992.

Byrd, Dana E. "Loot, Occupy, and Re-envision: Material Culture of the South Carolina Plantation, 1861–1867." In *The Civil War and the Material Culture of Texas, the Lower South, and the Southwest*. David B. Warren Symposium, no. 3. Houston: Museum of Fine Arts, Houston, 2012.

Camp, Stephanie M. H. *Closer to Freedom: Enslaved Women and Everyday Resistance in the Plantation South*. Chapel Hill: University of North Carolina Press, 2004.

Campbell, Randolph B. *An Empire for Slavery: The Peculiar Institution in Texas, 1821–1865*. Baton Rouge: Louisiana State University Press, 1991.

Carroll, Mark. *Homesteads Ungovernable: Families, Sex, Race, and the Law in Frontier Texas, 1823–1860*. Austin: University of Texas Press, 2001.

Carson, Cary, and Carl R. Lounsbury, eds. *The Chesapeake House: Architectural Investigation by Colonial Williamsburg*. Chapel Hill: University of North Carolina Press with Colonial Williamsburg Foundation, 2013.

Chambers, Douglas B. *Murder at Montpelier: Igbo Africans in Virginia*. Jackson: University Press of Mississippi, 2005.

Childs, Dennis R. *Slaves of the State: Black Incarceration from the Chain Gang to the Penitentiary*. Minneapolis: University of Minnesota Press, 2015.

Chireau, Yvonne P. *Black Magic: Religion and the African American Conjuring Tradition*. Berkeley: University of California Press, 2003.

Clark, Clifford Edward, Jr. *The American Family Home, 1800–1960*. Chapel Hill: University of North Carolina Press, 1986.

Clinton, Catherine. *The Plantation Mistress: Woman's World in the Old South*. New York: Pantheon, 1984.

Collins, Patricia Hill. *Black Feminist Thought: Knowledge, Consciousness, and the Politics of Empowerment*. 2nd ed. London: Routledge, 2000.

Coontz, Stephanie. *The Social Origins of Private Life: A History of American Families, 1600–1900*. New York: Verso, 1988.

Cott, Nancy. *The Bonds of Womanhood: 'Woman's Sphere' in New England, 1780–1835*. New Haven, CT: Yale University Press, 1977.

Creighton, James A. *A Narrative History of Brazoria County, Texas*. Angleton, TX: Brazoria County Historical Commission, 1975.

Crenshaw, Kimberlé. *On Intersectionality: Essential Writings*. New York: New Press, 2023.

Curl, James Stevens. *Oxford Dictionary of Architecture and Landscape Architecture*. 2nd ed. New York: Oxford University Press, 2006.

Dalrymple, Priscilla Harris. *American Victorian Costume in Early Photographs*. New York: Dover Publications, 2013.

De Cunzo, Lu Ann, and Bernard L. Hermann. "Preface." In *Historical Archaeology and the Study of American Culture*, edited by Lu Ann Cunzo and Bernard L. Hermann, ix–xi. Winterthur, DE: Henry Francis du Pont Winterthur Museum, 1996.

Deetz, James. *In Small Things Forgotten: An Archaeology of Early American Life*. New York: Anchor Books/Doubleday, 1977.

Deetz, Kelley Fanto. *Bound to the Fire: How Virginia's Enslaved Cooks Helped Invent American Cuisine*. Lexington: University Press of Kentucky, 2017.

Delfino, Susanna, and Michele Gillespie, eds. *Neither Lady nor Slave: Working Women of the Old South*. Chapel Hill: University of North Carolina Press, 2002.

Demos, John. *A Little Commonwealth: Family Life in Plymouth Colony*. New York: Oxford University Press, 1970.

Deyle, Steven. *Carry Me Back: The Domestic Slave Trade in American Life*. New York: Oxford University Press, 2005.

Du Bois, W. E. B. *Black Reconstruction*. New York: Harcourt, Brace, 1935.

Dudley, Tara. *Building Antebellum New Orleans: Free People of Color and Their Influence*. Austin: University of Texas Press, 2021.

Dunaway, Wilma A. *The African-American Family in Slavery and Emancipation*. New York: Cambridge University Press, 2003.

DuPlessis, Robert S. *The Material Atlantic: Clothing, Commerce, and Colonization in the Atlantic World, 1650–1800*. New York: Cambridge University Press, 2016.

Duyvendak, Jan Willem. *The Politics of Home: Belonging and Nostalgia in Europe and the United States*. New York: Palgrave Macmillan, 2011.

Edwards, Justene Hill. *Unfree Markets: The Slaves' Economy and the Rise of Capitalism in South Carolina*. New York: Columbia University Press, 2021.

Edwards, Laura F. *The People and Their Peace: Legal Culture and the Transformation of Inequality in the Post-Revolutionary South*. Chapel Hill: University of North Carolina Press, 2009.

Eichstedt, Jennifer L., and Stephen Small. *Representations of Slavery: Race and Ideology in Southern Plantation Museums*. Washington, DC: Smithsonian Institution Press, 2002.

Elliott, Mary. "Legacies of Placc." In *Make Good the Promises: Reclaiming Reconstruction and Its Legacies*, edited by Kinshasha Holman Conwill and Paul Gardullo, 154–71. Washington, DC: Smithsonian Institution, 2021.

Ellis, Clifton, and Rebecca Ginsburg, eds. *Cabin, Quarter, Plantation: Architecture and Landscapes of North American Slavery*. New Haven, CT: Yale University Press, 2010.

Epperson, Terrence. "Constructing Difference: The Social and Spatial Order of the Chesapeake Plantation." In *I, Too, Am America: Archaeological Studies of African-American Life*, edited by Theresa A. Singleton, 159–72. Charlottesville: University of Virginia Press, 1999.

Farnham, Christie Anne. *The Education of the Southern Belle: Higher Education and Student Socialization in the Antebellum South*. New York: New York University Press, 1994.

Faust, Drew Gilpin. *The Ideology of Slavery: Proslavery Thought in the Antebellum South, 1830–1860*. Baton Rouge: Louisiana State University Press, 1981.

———. *James Henry Hammond and the Old South: A Design for Mastery*. Baton Rouge: Louisiana State University Press, 1982.

Fehrenbacher, Don E. *The Slaveholding Republic: An Account of the United States Government's Relations to Slavery*, completed and edited by Ward M. McAfee. New York: Oxford University Press, 2001.

Ferguson, Leland. *Uncommon Ground: Archaeology and Early African America, 1650–1800*. Washington, DC: Smithsonian Institution Press, 1992.

Finley, Alexandra J. *An Intimate Economy: Enslaved Women, Work, and America's Domestic Slave Trade*. Chapel Hill: University of North Carolina Press, 2020.

Ford, Lacy. *Origins of Southern Radicalism: The South Carolina Upcountry, 1800–1860*. New York: Oxford University Press, 1988.

Foster, Helen Bradley. *New Raiments of Self: African American Clothing in the Antebellum South*. New York: Berg, 1997.

Foucault, Michel. *Discipline and Punish: The Birth of the Prison*. Translated by Alan Sheridan. New York: Pantheon, 1977.

Fox-Genovese, Elizabeth. *Within the Plantation Household: Black and White Women of the Old South*. Chapel Hill: University of North Carolina Press, 1988.

Foy, Jessica H., and Thomas J. Schlereth, eds. *American Home Life, 1880–1930: A Social History of Spaces and Services*. Knoxville: University of Tennessee Press, 1992.

Frohne, Andrea E. *The African Burial Ground in New York City: Memory, Spirituality, and Space*. Syracuse, NY: Syracuse University Press, 2015.

Fuentes, Marisa. *Dispossessed Lives: Enslaved Women, Violence, and the Archive*. Philadelphia: University of Pennsylvania Press, 2016.

Gaines, Kevin K. *Uplifting the Race: Black Leadership, Politics, and Culture in the Twentieth Century*. Chapel Hill: University of North Carolina Press, 1996.

Gallagher, Gary W., and Alan T. Nolan, eds. *The Myth of the Lost Cause and Civil War History*. Bloomington: Indiana University Press, 2000.

Gallas, Kristin L., and James DeWolf Perry, eds. *Interpreting Slavery at Museums and Historic Sites*. New York: Rowman and Littlefield, 2015.

Gillmer, Jason A. *Slavery and Freedom in Texas: Stories from the Courtroom, 1821–1871*. Athens: University of Georgia Press, 2017.

Glassie, Henry. *Folk Housing in Middle Virginia: A Structural Analysis of Historic Artifacts*. Knoxville: University of Tennessee Press, 1975.

Glymph, Thavolia. *Out of the House of Bondage: The Transformation of the Plantation Household*. New York: Cambridge University Press, 2008.

———. *The Women's Fight: The Civil War's Battles for Home, Freedom, and Nation*. Chapel Hill: University of North Carolina Press, 2020.

Gowans, Alan. *Images of American Living*. New York: Lippincott, 1964.

Green, Sharony. *Remember Me to Miss Louisa: Hidden Black-White Intimacies in Antebellum America*. Dekalb: Northern Illinois University Press, 2015.

Green, Toby. *A Fistful of Shells: West Africa from the Rise of the Slave Trade to the Age of Revolution*. Chicago: University of Chicago Press, 2019.

Grier, Katherine C. *Culture and Comfort: Parlor Making and Middle-Class Identity, 1850–1930*. Rev. ed. Washington, DC: Smithsonian Books, 2010.

Gundaker, Grey. "At Home on the Other Side: African American Burials as Commemorative Landscapes." In *Places of Commemoration: Search for Identity and Landscape Design*. Vol. 19, edited by Joachim Wolschke-Bulmahn, 25–54. Washington, DC: Dumbarton Oaks Research Library and Collection, 2001.

———. "Gardens and Yard Art." In *Encyclopedia of African-American Culture and History*. Vol. 3, 2nd ed., 896–99. Detroit: Macmillan Reference USA, 2006.

———, ed. *Keep Your Head to the Sky: Interpreting African American Home Ground*. Charlottesville: University of Virginia Press, 1998.

Gutman, Herbert. *The Black Family in Slavery and Freedom, 1750–1925*. New York: Pantheon Books, 1976.

———. *Power and Culture: Essays on the American Working Class*. New York: Pantheon, 1987.

Hadden, Sally E. *Slave Patrols: Law and Violence in Virginia and the Carolinas*. Cambridge, MA: Harvard University Press, 2001.

Hale, Jennifer. *Historic Plantations of Alabama's Black Belt*. Charleston, SC: History Press, 2009.

Halttunen, Karen. *Confidence Men and Painted Women: A Study of Middle-Class Culture in America, 1830–1870*. New Haven, CT: Yale University Press, 1982.

Hamilton, Virginia Van Der Veer. *Alabama: A History*. New York: W. W. Norton, 1984.

Hamlin, Talbot. *Greek Revival Architecture in America: Being an Account of Important Trends in American Architecture and American Life Prior to the War between the States*. New York: Oxford University Press, 1944.

Handler, Jerome S., and Frederick W. Lange. *Plantation Slavery in Barbados*. Cambridge, MA: Harvard University Press, 1978.

Harasewych, M. G., and Fabio Moretzsohn. *The Book of Shells: A Life-Size Guide to Identifying and Classifying Six Hundred Seashells*. Chicago: University of Chicago Press, 2010.

Harris, Dianne. *Little White Houses: How the Postwar Home Constructed Race in America*. Minneapolis: University of Minnesota Press, 2013.

Hartman, Saidiya V. *Lose Your Mother: A Journey along the Atlantic Slave Route*. New York: Farrar, Straus and Giroux, 2007.

———. *Scenes of Subjection: Terror, Slavery, and Self-Making in Nineteenth-Century America*. New York: Oxford University Press, 1997.

Harvey, Karen, ed. *History and Material Culture: A Student's Guide to Approaching Alternative Sources*. London: Routledge, 2009.

Hayes, Kevin J. *The Road to Monticello: The Life and Mind of Thomas Jefferson*. New York: Oxford University Press, 2008.

Heneghan, Bridget T. *Whitewashing America: Material Culture and Race in the Antebellum Imagination*. Jackson: University Press of Mississippi, 2003.

Herskovits, Melville J. *The Myth of the Negro Past*. Reprint. Boston: Beacon Press, 1958.

Hilde, Libra R. *Slavery, Fatherhood, and Paternal Duty in African American Communities over the Long Nineteenth Century*. Chapel Hill: University of North Carolina Press, 2020.

Hilliard, Sam B. "Plantations and the Molding of the Southern Landscape." In *The Making of the American Landscape*, edited by Michael P. Conzen, 104–26. New York: Routledge, 1990.

Hinson, Glenn. "Walking Sticks." In *The New Encyclopedia of Southern Culture*. Vol. 14, *Folk Life*, edited by William Ferris, 376–69. Chapel Hill: University of North Carolina Press, 2010.

Hodder, Ian. *Reading the Past: Current Approaches to Interpretation in Archaeology*. New York: Cambridge University Press, 1986.

Hogendorn, Jan, and Marion Johnson. *The Shell Money of the Slave Trade*. New York: Cambridge University Press, 1986.

Holt, Thomas C. *The Movement: The African American Struggle for Civil Rights*. New York: Oxford University Press, 2021.

hooks, bell. "Homeplace: A Site of Resistance." In *Yearning: Race, Gender, and Cultural Politics*, 41–49. Boston: South End Press, 1990.

———. "Marginality as Site of Resistance." In *Out There: Marginalization and Contemporary Cultures*, edited by Russell Ferguson, Martha Gever, Trinh T. Minh-Ha, and Cornel West, 341–43. Cambridge, MA: MIT Press, 1990.

Hunter, Tera W. *Bound in Wedlock: Slave and Free Black Marriage in the Nineteenth Century*. Cambridge, MA: Belknap Press of Harvard University Press, 2017.

———. *To 'Joy My Freedom: Southern Black Women's Lives and Labor after the Civil War*. Cambridge, MA: Harvard University Press, 1998.

Isaac, Rhys. *The Transformation of Virginia, 1740–1790*. Chapel Hill: University of North Carolina Press, 1982.

Jabour, Anya. *Scarlett's Sisters: Young Women in the Old South*. Chapel Hill: University of North Carolina Press, 2007.

Johnson, Jessica Marie. *Wicked Flesh: Black Women, Intimacy, and Freedom in the Atlantic World*. Philadelphia: University of Pennsylvania Press, 2020.

Johnson, Walter, ed. *The Chattel Principle: Internal Slave Trades in the Americas*. New Haven, CT: Yale University Press, 2004.

———. *River of Dark Dreams: Slavery and Empire in the Cotton Kingdom*. Cambridge, MA: Harvard University Press, 2013.

———. *Soul by Soul: Life inside the Antebellum Slave Market*. Cambridge, MA: Harvard University Press, 2009.

Jones, Jacqueline. *Labor of Love, Labor of Sorrow: Black Women, Work, and the Family, from Slavery to the Present*. New York: Vintage Books, 1986.

Jones-Rogers, Stephanie. *They Were Her Property: White Women as Slave Owners in the American South*. New Haven, CT: Yale University Press, 2019.

Kaplan, Jeffrey. "New Religious Movements and Globalizations." In *Introduction to New and Alternative Religions in America*. Vol. 1, edited by Eugene V. Gallagher and W. Michael Ashcraft, 84–125. Westport, CT: Greenwood Press, 2006.

Karp, Matthew. *This Vast Southern Empire: Slaveholders at the Helm of American Foreign Policy*. Cambridge, MA: Harvard University Press, 2016.

Katy-Hyman, Martha B., and Kym S. Rice, eds. *World of a Slave: Encyclopedia of the Material Life of Slaves in the United States*. Vol. 1. Santa Barbara, CA: Greenwood, 2010.

———, eds. *World of a Slave: Encyclopedia of the Material Life of Slaves in the United States*. Vol. 2. Santa Barbara, CA: Greenwood, 2011.

Kaye, Anthony E. *Joining Places: Slave Neighborhoods in the Old South*. Chapel Hill: University of North Carolina Press, 2009.

Kealhoffer, Lisa. "Creating Social Identity in the Landscape: Tidewater, Virginia, 1600–1750." In *Archaeologies of Landscape, Contemporary Perspectives*, edited by Wendy Ashmore and A. Bernard Knapp, 58–82. Hoboken, NJ: Blackwell Publishers, 1999.

Kelley, Sean M. *Los Brazos de Dios: A Plantation Society in the Texas Borderlands, 1821–1865*. Baton Rouge: Louisiana State University Press, 2010.

Kelly, Kenneth G. "Change and Continuity in Coastal Bénin." In *West Africa during the Atlantic Slave Trade: Archaeological Perspectives*, edited by Christopher R. DeCorse, 81–100. London: Leicester University Press, 2001.

Kennedy, Roger G. *Architecture, Men, Women and Money in America, 1600–1860*. New York: Random House, 1985.

———. *Greek Revival America*. New York: Rizzoli, 2010.

Ketcham, Ralph. *The Madisons at Montpelier: Reflections on the Founding Couple*. Charlottesville: University of Virginia Press, 2009.

Kindell, Alexandra, ed. *The World of Antebellum America: A Daily Life Encyclopedia*. Vol. 2. Santa Barbara, CA: Greenwood, 2018.

Knowles, Katie. "Patches of Resistance on the Badges of Enslavement: Enslaved Southerners, Negro Cloth, and Fashionability in the Cotton South." In *Clothing and Fashion in Southern History*, edited by Ted Ownby and Becca Walton, 3–31. Jackson: University Press of Mississippi, 2020.

Krill, Rosemary Troy. *Early American Decorative Arts, 1620–1860: A Handbook for Interpreters*. New York: Rowman and Littlefield, 2010.

Lane, Frederick S. *American Privacy: The 400-Year History of Our Most Contested Right*. Boston: Beacon Press, 2009.

Lasch, Christopher. *Haven in a Heartless World: The Family Besieged*. New York: Basic Books, 1977.

Lawal, Babtunde. "African-American Expressions." In *The New Encyclopedia of Southern Culture*. Vol. 23, *Folk Art*, edited by Carol Crown and Cheryl Rivers, 43–49. Chapel Hill: University of North Carolina Press, 2013.

Leslie, Kent Anderson. *Woman of Color, Daughter of Privilege: Amanda America Dickson, 1849–1893*. Athens: University of Georgia Press, 1996.

Lundberg, John R. *The Texas Lowcountry: Slavery and Freedom on the Gulf Coast, 1822–1895*. College Station: Texas A&M University Press, 2024.

Lynn-Tinen, Erin. "Reclaiming the Past as a Matter of Social Justice: African American Heritage, Representation and Identity in the United States." In *Critical Perspectives on Cultural Memory and Heritage: Construction, Transformation and Destruction*, edited by Veysel Apaydin, 255–68. London: University College London Press, 2020.

Malone, Ann Patton. *Sweet Chariot: Slave Family and Household Structure in Nineteenth-Century Louisiana*. Chapel Hill: University of North Carolina Press, 1992.

———. *Women on the Texas Frontier: A Cross-Cultural Perspective*. El Paso: Texas Western Press, 1983.

Mancini, Matthew J. *One Dies, Get Another: Convict Leasing in the American South, 1866–1928*. Columbia: University of South Carolina Press, 1996.

Martin, Ann Smart, and J. Ritchie Garrison, eds. *American Material Culture: The Shape of the Field*. Winterthur, DE: Henry Francis du Pont Winterthur Museum, 1997.

Martin, Jonathan D. *Divided Mastery: Slave Hiring in the American South*. New York: Cambridge University Press, 2004.

Maynard, W. Barksdale. *Architecture in the United States, 1800–1850*. New Haven, CT: Yale University Press, 2002.

McCandless, Peter. *Moonlight, Magnolias, and Madness: Insanity in South Carolina from the Colonial Period to the Progressive Era*. Chapel Hill: University of North Carolina Press, 1996.

McCurry, Stephanie. *Confederate Reckoning: Power and Politics in the Civil War*. Cambridge, MA: Harvard University Press, 2010.

———. *Masters of Small Worlds: Yeoman Households, Gender Relations, and the Political Culture of the Antebellum South Carolina Low Country*. New York: Oxford University Press, 1995.

McDaniel, George W. *Hearth and Home: Preserving a People's Culture*. Philadelphia: Temple University Press, 1982.

McDonald, Roderick. *The Economy and Material Culture of Slaves: Goods and Chattels on the Sugar Plantations of Jamaica and Louisiana*. Baton Rouge: Louisiana State University Press, 1993.

McDonnell, Lawrence T. "Money Knows No Master: Market Relations and the American Slave Community." In *Developing Dixie: Modernization in a Traditional Society*, edited by Winfred B. Moore Jr., Joseph F. Tripp, and Lyon G. Tyler Jr., 31–44. New York: Greenwood Press, 1988.

McKee, Larry. "The Ideals and Realities behind the Design and Use of 19th Century Virginia Slave Cabins." In *The Art and Mystery of Historical Archaeology: Essays in Honor of James Deetz*, edited by Mary C. Beaudry and Anne Yentsch, 195–213. Boca Raton, FL: CRC Press, 1992.

McKittrick, Katherine. *Demonic Grounds: Black Women and the Cartographies of Struggle*. Minneapolis: University of Minnesota Press, 2006.

Meyer, Richard E., ed. *Cemeteries and Gravemarkers: Voices of American Culture*. Logan: Utah State University Press, 1989.

Miles, Tiya. *All That She Carried: The Journey of Ashley's Sack, a Black Family Keepsake*. New York: Random House, 2021.

Miller, Monica L. *Slaves to Fashion: Black Dandyism and the Styling of Black Diasporic Identity*. Durham, NC: Duke University Press, 2009.

Mills, Cynthia, and Pamela H. Simpson, eds. *The Lost Cause: Women, Art, and the Landscapes of Southern Memory*. Knoxville: University of Tennessee Press, 2003.

Mintz, Sidney W. *Caribbean Transformations*. Chicago: Aldine Publishing Company, 1974.

Mitchell, Koritha. *From Slave Cabins to the White House: Homemade Citizenship in African American Culture*. Urbana: University of Illinois Press, 2020.

Mitchell, Michele. *Righteous Propagation: African Americans and the Politics of Racial Destiny after Reconstruction*. Chapel Hill: University of North Carolina Press, 2004.

Montalvo, Maria R. *Enslaved Archives: Slavery, Law, and the Production of the Past*. Baltimore, MD: Johns Hopkins University Press, forthcoming.

Morgan, Jennifer L. *Laboring Women: Reproduction and Gender in New World Slavery*. Philadelphia: University of Pennsylvania Press, 2004.

———. *Reckoning with Slavery: Gender, Kinship, and Capitalism in the Early Black Atlantic*. Durham, NC: Duke University Press, 2021.

Morris, Christopher. "Within the Slave Cabin: Violence in Mississippi Slave Families." In *Over the Threshold: Intimate Violence in Early America*, edited by Christine Daniels and Michael V. Kennedy, 268–85. New York: Routledge, 1999.

Moss, Michael, and David Thomas, eds. *Archival Silences: Missing, Lost and, Uncreated Archives*. New York: Routledge, 2021.

Mosterman, Andrea C. *Spaces of Enslavement: A History of Slavery and Resistance in New York*. Ithaca, NY: Cornell University Press, 2021.

Mullins, Paul R. *Race and Affluence: An Archaeology of African America and Consumer Culture*. Boston: Springer, 2002.

Nathans, Sydney. *A Mind to Stay: White Plantation, Black Homeland*. Cambridge, MA: Harvard University Press, 2017.

———. *To Free a Family: The Journey of Mary Walker*. Cambridge, MA: Harvard University Press, 2012.

Nevius, Marcus P. *City of Refuge: Slavery and Petit Marronage in the Great Dismal Swamp, 1763–1856*. Athens: University of Georgia Press, 2020.

Nieman, Donald G. *To Set the Law in Motion: The Freedmen's Bureau and the Legal Rights of Blacks, 1865–1868*. Millwood, NY: KTO Press, 1979.

O'Donovan, Susan Eva. *Becoming Free in the Cotton South*. Cambridge, MA: Harvard University Press, 2007.

Ogundiran, Akinwumi, and Paula Saunders, eds. *Materialities of Ritual in the Black Atlantic*. Indianapolis: Indiana University Press, 2014.

Orser, Charles E., Jr. *The Material Basis of the Postbellum Tenant Plantation: Historical Archaeology in the South Carolina Piedmont*. Athens: University of Georgia Press, 1988.

Ortega, Mariana. *In-Between: Latina Feminist Phenomenology, Identity, and the Self*. Albany: State University of New York Press, 2016.

Otero, Solimar. *Archives of Conjure: Stories of the Dead in Afrolatinx Cultures*. New York: Columbia University Press, 2020.

Oubre, Charles F. *Forty Acres and a Mule: The Freedman's Bureau and Black Land Ownership*. Baton Rouge: Louisiana State University Press, 1978.

Owens, Deirdre Cooper. *Medical Bondage: Race, Gender, and the Origins of American Gynecology*. Athens: University of Georgia Press, 2017.

Owens, Emily A. *Consent in the Presence of Force: Sexual Violence and Black Women's Survival in Antebellum New Orleans*. Chapel Hill: University of North Carolina Press, 2023.

Ownby, Ted. *American Dreams in Mississippi: Consumers, Poverty, and Culture, 1830–1998*. Chapel Hill: University of North Carolina Press, 1999.

Painter, Nell Irvin. *Exodusters: Black Migration to Kansas after Reconstruction*. New York: W. W. Norton, 1976.

Pargas, Damian Alan. *Slavery and Forced Migration in the Antebellum South*. New York: Cambridge University Press, 2015.

Parry, Tyler D. *Jumping the Broom: The Surprising Multicultural Origins of a Black Wedding Ritual*. Chapel Hill: University of North Carolina Press, 2020.

Pascoe, Peggy. *What Comes Naturally: Miscegenation Law and the Making of Race in America*. New York: Oxford University Press, 2009.

Patterson, Orlando. "Slavery, Alienation, and the Female Discovery of Personal Freedom." In *Home: A Place in the World*, edited by Arien Mack, 159–87. New York: New York University Press, 1993.

———. *Slavery and Social Death: A Comparative Study*. Cambridge, MA: Harvard University Press, 1982.

Paulus, Carl Lawrence. *The Slaveholding Crisis: Fear of Insurrection and the Coming of the Civil War*. Baton Rouge: Louisiana State University Press, 2017.

Penningroth, Dylan C. *The Claims of Kinfolk: African American Property and*

Community in the Nineteenth-Century South. Chapel Hill: University of North Carolina Press, 2003.

Perkinson, Robert. *Texas Tough: The Rise of America's Prison Empire*. New York: Metropolitan Books, 2010.

Perrot, Michelle, and Roger-Henri Gurrand. "Scenes and Places." In *A History of Private Life*. Vol. 4, *From the Fires of Revolution to the Great War*, edited by Michelle Perrot, 339–449. Cambridge, MA: Belknap Press of Harvard University Press, 1990.

Peter, Duane E., ed. *Freedman's Cemetery: A Legacy of a Pioneer Black Community in Dallas, Texas*. Plano, TX: Geo-Marine, 2000.

Philips, Jason. *Looming Civil War: How Nineteenth-Century Americans Imagined the Future*. New York: Oxford University Press, 2018.

Phillips, Kimberley L. *Daily Life during African American Migrations*. Santa Barbara, CA: Greenwood Press, 2012.

Pitt-Rivers, A. Lane-Fox. "On the Evolution of Culture." In *The Evolution of Culture and Other Essays*, edited by J. L. Myers, 20–44. Oxford: Clarendon Press, 1906.

Prince, Valerie Sweeney. *Burnin' Down the House: Home in African American Literature*. New York: Columbia University Press, 2005.

Pryor, Elizabeth Stordeur. *Colored Travelers: Mobility and the Fight for Citizenship before the Civil War*. Chapel Hill: University of North Carolina Press, 2016.

Raboteau, Albert. *Slave Religion: The "Invisible Institution" in the Antebellum South*. New York: Oxford University Press, 1978.

Rainville, Lynn. *Hidden History: African American Cemeteries in Central Virginia*. Charlottesville: University of Virginia Press, 2014.

Reeves, Matthew. "Scalar Analysis of Early Nineteenth-Century Household Assemblages: Focus on Communities of the African Atlantic." In *Beyond the Walls: New Perspectives on the Archaeology of Historical Households*, edited by Kevin R. Fogle, James A. Nyman, and Mary C. Beaudry, 23–46. Gainesville: University Press of Florida, 2015.

Rice, Alan. "Museums, Memorials and Plantation Houses in the Black Atlantic: Slavery and the Development of Dark Tourism." In *The Darker Side of Travel: The Theory and Practice of Dark Tourism*, edited by Richard Sharpley and Philip R. Stone, 224–46. Bristol: Channel View Publications, 2009.

Richter, Amy G. *At Home in Nineteenth-Century America: A Documentary History*. New York: New York University Press, 2015.

Roberts, Alaina E. *I've Been Here All the While: Black Freedom on Native Land*. Philadelphia: University of Pennsylvania Press, 2021.

Rose, Julia. *Interpreting Difficult History at Museums and Historic Sites*. Lanham, MD: Rowman and Littlefield, 2016.

Rosenthal, Caitlyn. *Accounting for Slavery: Masters and Management*. Cambridge, MA: Harvard University Press, 2018.

Rothman, Adam. *Slave Country: American Expansion and the Origins of the Deep South*. Cambridge, MA: Harvard University Press, 2007.

Rothstein, Richard. *The Color of Law: A Forgotten History of How Our Government Segregated America*. New York: Liveright Publishing Corporation, 2017.

Royce, Edward. *The Origins of Southern Sharecropping*. Philadelphia: Temple University Press, 1993.

Samford, Patricia M. *Subfloor Pits and the Archaeology of Slavery in Colonial Virginia*. Tuscaloosa: University of Alabama Press, 2007.

Sanger, Kerran L. *When the Spirit Says Sing!: The Role of Freedom Songs in the Civil Rights Movement*. New York: Routledge, 1995.

Saunt, Claudio. *Unworthy Republic: The Dispossession of Native Americans and the Road to Indian Territory*. New York: W. W. Norton, 2020.

Savage, Kirk. *Standing Soldiers, Kneeling Slaves: Race, War, and Monument in Nineteenth-Century America*. New ed. Princeton, NJ: Princeton University Press, 2018.

Schlereth, Thomas J., ed. *Material Culture Studies in America*. Nashville: American Association for State and Local History, 1982.

Schwartz, Marie Jenkins. *Born in Bondage: Growing Up Enslaved in the Antebellum South*. Cambridge, MA: Harvard University Press, 2001.

Schweninger, Loren. *Black Property Owners in the South, 1790–1915*. Urbana: University of Illinois Press, 1990.

Scott, Anne Firor. *The Southern Lady: From Pedestal to Politics, 1830–1930*. Chicago: University of Chicago Press, 1970.

Seeman, Erik R. *Death in the New World: Cross-Cultural Encounters, 1492–1800*. Philadelphia: University of Pennsylvania Press, 2010.

Setnik, Linda. *Victorian Fashions for Women and Children: Society's Impact on Dress*. Atglen, PA: Schiffer Publishing, 2012.

Severns, Kenneth. *Southern Architecture: 350 Years of Distinctive American Building*. New York: Dutton, 1981.

Shammas, Carole. *A History of Household Government in America*. Charlottesville: University of Virginia Press, 2002.

Sharpe, Christina. *In the Wake: On Blackness and Being*. Durham, NC: Duke University Press, 2016.

Sharpe, Jenny. *Immaterial Archives: An African Diaspora Poetics of Loss*. Chicago: Northwestern University Press, 2020.

Sharpless, Rebecca. *Cooking in Other Women's Kitchens: Domestic Workers in the South, 1865–1960*. Chapel Hill: University of North Carolina Press, 2010.

Singleton, Theresa A. "The Archaeology of Slave Life." In *Before Freedom Came: African-American Life in the Antebellum South*, edited by Edward D. C. Campbell Jr. and Kym S. Rice, 155–75. Charlottesville: University Press of Virginia, 1991. Published in conjunction with an exhibition of the same title, organized by the Museum of the Confederacy, July 1991–June 1992.

——, ed. *The Archaeology of Slavery and Plantation Life*. Orlando, FL: Academic Press, 1985.

——. "Nineteenth-Century Built Landscape of Plantation Slavery in Comparative Perspective." In *The Archaeology of Slavery: A Comparative Approach to Captivity and Coercion*, edited by Lydia Wilson Marshall, 96–110. Carbondale: Southern Illinois University Press, 2014.

Sinha, Manisha. *The Slave's Cause: A History of Abolition*. New Haven, CT: Yale University Press, 2016.

Skipper, Jodi. *Behind the Big House: Reconciling Slavery, Race, and Heritage in the U.S. South*. Iowa City: University of Iowa Press, 2022.

Smallwood, James M., and Barry A. Crouch. "Texas Freedwomen during

Reconstruction." In *Black Women in Texas History*, edited by Bruce A. Glasrud and Merline Pitre, 38–72. College Station: Texas A&M University Press, 2008.

Smallwood, Stephanie. *Saltwater Slavery: A Middle Passage from Africa to American Diaspora*. Cambridge, MA: Harvard University Press, 2007.

Smith, Clint. *How the Word Is Passed: A Reckoning with the History of Slavery across America*. Boston: Little, Brown, 2021.

Smith, Suzanne. *To Serve the Living: Funeral Directors and the African American Way of Death*. Cambridge, MA: Belknap Press of Harvard University Press, 2010.

Sobel, Mechal. *The World They Made Together: Black and White Values in Eighteenth-Century Virginia*. Princeton, NJ: Princeton University Press, 1989.

Stevenson, Brenda E. *Life in Black and White: Family and Community in the Slave South*. New York: Oxford University Press, 1996.

Stewart, Catherine A. *Long Past Slavery: Representing Race in the Federal Writers' Project*. Chapel Hill: University of North Carolina Press, 2016.

Strasser, Susan. *Waste and Want: A Social History of Trash*. New York: Henry Holt, 1999.

Szczesiul, Anthony. *The Southern Hospitality Myth: Ethics, Politics, Race, and American Memory*. Athens: University of Georgia Press, 2017.

Tadman, Michael. *Speculators and Slaves: Masters, Traders, and Slaves in the Old South*. Madison: University of Wisconsin Press, 1989.

Taylor, Alan. *The Internal Enemy: Slavery and War in Virginia, 1772–1832*. New York: W. W. Norton, 2013.

Taylor, Amy Murrell. *Embattled Freedom: Journeys through the Civil War's Slave Refugee Camps*. Chapel Hill: University of North Carolina Press, 2018.

Taylor, Elizabeth Downing. *A Slave in the White House: Paul Jennings and the Madisons*. New York: Palgrave Macmillan, 2012.

Taylor, Keeanga-Yamahtta. *Race for Profit: How Banks and the Real Estate Industry Undermined Black Homeownership*. Chapel Hill: University of North Carolina Press, 2019.

Thompson, Eleanor McD., ed. *The American Home: Material Culture, Domestic Space, and Family Life*. Winterthur, DE: Henry Francis du Pont Winterthur Museum, 1998.

Thornton, J. Mills, III. *Politics and Power in a Slave Society: Alabama, 1800–1860*. Baton Rouge: Louisiana State University Press, 1978.

Torget, Andrew J. *Seeds of Empire: Cotton, Slavery, and the Transformation of the Texas Borderlands, 1800–1850*. Chapel Hill: University of North Carolina Press, 2015.

Trouillot, Michel-Rolph. *Silencing the Past: Power and the Production of History*. Boston: Beacon Press, 1995.

Tuan, Yi-Fu. *Space and Place: The Perspective of Experience*. Minneapolis: University of Minnesota Press, 1977.

Twombly, Robert, ed. *Andrew Jackson Downing: Essential Texts*. New York: W. W. Norton, 2012.

Ulrich, Laurel Thatcher. *A Midwife's Tale: The Life of Martha Ballard Based on Her Diary, 1785–1812*. New York: Alfred A. Knopf, 1990.

Ulrich, Laurel Thatcher, Ivan Gaskell, Sara J. Schechner, and Sarah Ann Carter. *Tangible Things: Making History through Objects*. New York: Oxford University Press, 2015.

Upton, Dell. *Holy Things and Profane: Anglican Parish Churches in Colonial Virginia*. Reprint. New Haven, CT: Yale University Press, 1997.

Van Horn, Jennifer. *The Power of Objects in Eighteenth-Century British America*. Chapel Hill: University of North Carolina Press, 2017. Published for the Omohundro Institute of Early American History and Culture, Williamsburg, Virginia.

Vernacular Architecture Forum. *From Farm to Factory in Durham County and the City of Durham*. 2016.

Vlach, John Michael. *The Afro-American Tradition in Decorative Arts*. Cleveland, OH: Cleveland Museum of Art, 1978. Published in conjunction with an exhibition of the same title, organized by the Cleveland Museum of Art, February 1, 1978–December 30, 1979.

———. *Back of the Big House: The Architecture of Plantation Slavery*. Chapel Hill: University of North Carolina Press, 1993.

———. *The Planter's Prospect: Privilege and Slavery in Plantation Paintings*. Chapel Hill: University of North Carolina Press, 2005.

Walker, Tamara J. *Exquisite Slaves: Race, Clothing, and Status in Colonial Lima*. New York: Cambridge University Press, 2017.

Ward, Patricia A. "Fénelon and Classical America." In *Fénelon in the Enlightenment: Traditions, Adaptations, and Variations*, edited by Stefanie Stockhorst, Christoph Schmitt-Maass, and Doohwan Ahn, 171–92. New York: Rodopi, 2014.

Warren, Jamie. "To Claim One's Own: Death and the Body in the Daily Politics of Antebellum Slavery." In *Death and the American South*, edited by Craig Thompson Friend and Lorri Glover, 110–30. New York: Cambridge University Press, 2014.

Warren, Wendy. *New England Bound: Slavery and Colonization in Early America*. New York: Liveright Publishing Corporation, 2017.

Wells, Jonathan Daniel. *Women Writers and Journalists in the Nineteenth-Century South*. New York: Cambridge University Press, 2011.

Wells-Oghoghomeh, Alexis. *The Souls of Womenfolk: The Religious Cultures of Enslaved Women in the Lower South*. Chapel Hill: University of North Carolina Press, 2021.

Westmacott, Richard. *African American Gardens and Yards in the Rural South*. Knoxville: University of Tennessee Press, 1992.

White, Deborah Gray. *Ar'n't I a Woman: Female Slaves in the Plantation South*. Rev. ed. New York: W. W. Norton, 1999.

White, Lynn, Jr. *Medieval Technology and Social Change*. Oxford: Oxford University Press, 1962.

White, Shane, and Graham J. White. *Stylin': African American Expressive Culture from Its Beginnings to the Zoot Suit*. Ithaca, NY: Cornell University Press, 1998.

Wilkie, Laurie A. *Creating Freedom: Material Culture and African-American Identity at Oakley Plantation, Louisiana, 1840–1950*. Baton Rouge: Louisiana University Press, 2000.

Williams, Heather Andrea. *Help Me to Find My People: The African American Search for Family Lost in Slavery*. Chapel Hill: University of North Carolina Press, 2012.

Williams, Susan. *Savory Suppers and Fashionable Feasts: Dining in Victorian America*. Knoxville: University of Tennessee Press, 1996.

Wilson, Elizabeth. *Adorned in Dreams: Fashion and Modernity*. Berkeley: University of California Press, 1985.

Winner, Lauren F. *A Cheerful and Comfortable Faith: Anglican Religious Practice in the*

Elite Households of Eighteenth-Century Virginia. New Haven, CT: Yale University Press, 2010.

Wood, Peter H. "Slave Labor Camps in Early America: Overcoming Denial and Discovering the American Gulag." In *Inequality in Early America*, edited by Carla Gardina Pestana and Sharon V. Salinger, 222–38. Hanover, NH: University Press of New England, 1999.

Woodward, Ian. *Understanding Material Culture*. London: Sage Publications, 2007.

Wright, Ben, and Zachary W. Dresser, eds. *Apocalypse and the Millennium in the American Civil War Era*. Baton Rouge: Louisiana State University Press, 2013.

Wright, Gavin. *Old South, New South: Revolutions in the Southern Economy since the Civil War*. New York: Basic Books, 1986.

Wright, Gwendolyn. *Building the Dream: A Social History of Housing in America*. Cambridge, MA: MIT Press, 1983.

Wulf, Andrea. *Founding Gardeners: The Revolutionary Generation, Nature, and the Shaping of the American Nation*. New York: Alfred A. Knopf, 2011.

Young, Amy. "Gender and Landscape: A View from the Plantation Slave Community." In *Shared Spaces and Divided Places: Material Dimensions of Gender Relations and the American Historical Landscape*, edited by Deborah L. Rotman and Ellen-Rose Savulis, 104–34. Knoxville: University of Tennessee Press, 2003.

Young, Jason R. *Rituals of Resistance: African Atlantic Religion in Kongo and the Lowcountry South in the Era of Slavery*. Baton Rouge: Louisiana State University Press, 2007.

JOURNAL ARTICLES, THESES, AND DISSERTATIONS

Axelrod, J. B. C., and Rise B. Axelrod. "Reading Frederick Douglass through Foucault's Panoptic Lens: A Proposal for Teaching Close Reading." *Pacific Coast Philology* 39 (2004): 112–27.

Babson, David W. "The Archaeology of Racism and Ethnicity on Southern Plantations." *Historical Archaeology* 24, no. 4 (1990): 20–28.

——. "Plantation Ideology and the Archaeology of Racism: Evidence from the Tanner Road Site (38BK416), Berkeley County, South Carolina." *South Carolina Antiquities* 19, nos. 1–2 (1987): 35–47.

Barnes, Jodi A. "Land Rich and Cash Poor: The Materiality of Poverty in Appalachia." *Historical Archaeology* 45, no. 3 (2011): 26–40.

Barrett, Kayla. "The Whitfields Move to Alabama: A Case Study in Westward Migration, 1825–1835." *Alabama Review* 48, no. 2 (April 1995): 96–113.

Bauer, Brook, and Elizabeth Ellis. "Indigenous, Native American, or American Indian?: The Limitations of Broad Terms." *Journal of the Early Republic* 43, no. 1 (Spring 2023): 61–74.

Berckman, Julianne. "Development of the Mansion Grounds of 'Montpelier,' Home of James Madison." MA thesis, University of Connecticut, 1986.

Bishir, Catherine W. "Black Builders in Antebellum North Carolina." *North Carolina Historical Review* 61, no. 4 (October 1984): 423–61.

——. "'Severe Survitude to House Building': The Construction of Hayes Plantation House, 1814–1817." *North Carolina Historical Review* 68, no. 4 (October 1991): 373–403.

Bluestone, Daniel. "A. J. Davis's Belmead Picturesque Aesthetics in the Land of Slavery." *Journal of the Society of Architectural Historians* 71, no. 2 (June 2012): 145–67.

Brock, Terry Peterkin. "'All of Us Would Walk Together': The Transition from Slavery to Freedom at St. Mary's City, Maryland." PhD dissertation, Michigan State University, 2014.

Brooks, Christina. "Exploring the Material Culture of Death in Enslaved African Cemeteries in Colonial Virginia and South Carolina." *African Diaspora Archaeology Newsletter* 14, no. 3 (2011): article 1.

Brown, Vincent. "Social Death and Political Life in the Study of Slavery." *American Historical Review* 114, no. 5 (December 2009): 1231–49.

Bruckho, Erica A. "'Slave Traffick': The Informal Economy, the Law, and the Social Order of South Carolina Cotton Country, 1793–1860." PhD diss., Emory University, 2016.

Burton, Antoinette. "Toward Unsettling Histories of Domesticity." *American Historical Review* 124, no. 4 (October 2019): 1332–36.

Cabak, Melanie A., and Mark D. Groover. "Bush Hill: Material Life at a Working Plantation." *Historical Archaeology* 40, no. 4 (2006): 51–83.

Camp, Stephanie M. H. "The Pleasures of Resistance: Enslaved Women and Body Politics in the Plantation South, 1830–1861." *Journal of Southern History* 68, no. 3 (August 2002): 533–72.

Chappell, Gordon T. "John Coffee: Land Speculator and Planter." *Alabama Review* 23 (January 1969): 25–33.

Coelho, Philip R. P., and Robert A. McGuire. "Biology, Diseases, and Economics: An Epidemiological History of Slavery in the American South." *Journal of Bioeconomics* 1 (1999): 151–90.

Colwell, Chip. "Collaborative Archaeologies and Descendant Communities." *Annual Review of Anthropology* 45 (2016): 113–27.

Cuddihy, William, and B. Carmon Hardy. "A Man's House Was Not His Castle: Origins of the Fourth Amendment to the United States Constitution." *William and Mary Quarterly* 37, no. 3 (July 1980): 371–400.

Cunningham, Eleanor. "Magnolia Grove." In *Encyclopedia of Alabama*, May 12, 2011, last updated December 3, 2018. www.encyclopediaofalabama.org/article/h-3075.

Davis, Angela. "Reflections on the Black Woman's Role in the Community of Slaves." *Black Scholar* 3, no. 4 (December 1971): 2–14.

Davis, David Brion. "Some Ideological Functions of Prejudice in Ante-bellum America." *American Quarterly* 15, no. 2 (Summer 1963): 115–25.

Downer, Joseph A. "Hallowed Ground, Sacred Place: The Slave Cemetery at George Washington's Mount Vernon and the Cultural Landscapes of the Enslaved." MA thesis, George Washington University, 2015.

Dubler, Ariela R. "Governing through Contract: Common Law Marriage in the Nineteenth Century." *Yale Law Journal* 107, no. 6 (April 1998): 1885–1920.

Farnsworth, Paul. "Brutality or Benevolence in Plantation Archaeology." *International Journal of Historical Archaeology* 4, no. 2 (June 2000): 145–58.

Galle, Jillian E. "Costly Signaling and Gendered Social Strategies among Slaves in the Eighteenth-Century Chesapeake: An Archaeological Perspective." *American Antiquity* 75, no. 1 (January 2010): 19–43.

Gamble, Robert. "The White-Column Tradition." *Southern Humanities Review* (1977): 41–59.

Garman, James. "Viewing the Culture Line through the Material Culture of Death." *Historical Archaeology* 28, no. 3 (1994): 74–93.

Graves, Brian. "'Return and Get It': Developing McLeod Plantation as a Shared Space of Historical Memory." *Southern Cultures* 23, no. 2 (Summer 2017): 75–96.

Gray, Ralph D., ed. "A Tour of Virginia in 1827: Letters of Henry D. Gilpin to His Father," *Virginia Magazine of History and Biography* 76, no. 4 (1968): 444–71.

Guyatt, Nicholas. "'The Outskirts of Our Happiness': Race and the Lure of Colonization in the Early Republic." *Journal of American History* 95, no. 4 (March 2009): 986–1011.

Harris, Leslie M. "Names, Terms, and Politics." *Journal of the Early Republic* 43, no. 1 (Spring 2023): 149–54.

Harrison, Alisa Y. "Reconstructing Somerset Place: Slavery, Memory and Historical Consciousness." PhD diss., Duke University, 2008.

Hartman, Saidiya. "Venus in Two Acts." *Small Axe* 12, no. 2 (June 2008): 1–14.

Heath, Barbara J., and Amber Bennett. "'The Little Spots Allow'd Them': The Archaeological Study of African-American Yards." *Historical Archaeology* 34, no. 2 (2000): 38–55.

Heck, Marlene. "Palladian Architecture and Social Change in Post-revolutionary Virginia." PhD diss., University of Pennsylvania, 1988.

Herman, Bernard L. "The Embedded Landscapes of the Charleston Single House, 1780–1820." *Perspectives in Vernacular Architecture* 7 (1997): 41–57.

Hildburgh, W. L. "Cowrie Shells as Amulets in Europe." *Folklore* 53, no. 4 (December 1942): 178–95.

Hill, Jobie. "Humanizing HABS: Rethinking the Historic American Buildings Survey's Role in Interpreting Antebellum Slave Houses." MA thesis, University of Oregon, 2013.

Holden, Vanessa M. "'I Was Born a Slave': Language, Sources, and Considering Descendant Communities." *Journal of the Early Republic* 43, no. 1 (Spring 2023): 75–83.

Holmes, Erin M. "Within the House of Bondage: Constructing and Negotiating the Plantation Landscape in the British Atlantic World, 1670–1820." PhD diss., University of South Carolina, 2017.

Hunter, Marcus Anthony, Mary Patillo, Zandria F. Robinson, and Keeanga-Yamahtta Taylor. "Black Placemaking: Celebration, Play, and Poetry." *Theory, Culture and Society* 33, nos. 7–8 (December 2016): 31–56.

Hyland, Matthew G. "Montpelier: The History of a House, 1723–1998." PhD diss., College of William and Mary, 2004.

Jamieson, Ross W. "Material Culture and Social Death: African-American Burial Practices." *Historical Archaeology* 29, no. 4 (1995): 39–58.

Johnson, Deanda Marie. "Seeking the Living among the Dead: African American Burial Practices in Surry County, Virginia." MA thesis, College of William and Mary, 2004.

Johnson, Walter. "On Agency." *Journal of Social History* 37, no. 1 (Autumn 2003): 113–24.

Jones, Lynn. "Crystals and Conjuring at the Charles Carroll House, Annapolis,

Maryland." *African Diaspora Archaeology Newsletter* 7, no. 1 (January 2000): article 2. https://scholarworks.umass.edu/adan/vol7/iss1/2.

Joseph, J. W. "The Early American Period and Nineteenth Century in South Carolina Archaeology." *South Carolina Antiquities* 25 (1993): 63–75.

———. "Resistance and Compliance: CRM and the Archaeology of the African Diaspora." *Historical Archaeology* 38, no. 1 (2004): 18–31.

———. "White Columns and Black Hands: Class and Classification in the Plantation Ideology of the Lowcountry of Georgia and South Carolina." *Historical Archaeology* 27, no. 3 (1993): 57–73.

Kaplan, Amy. "Manifest Domesticity." *American Literature* 70, no. 3 (September 1998): 581–606.

Kemp, L. W. "The Capitol (?) at Columbia." *Southwestern Historical Quarterly* 48, no. 1 (July 1944): 3–9.

Kerber, Linda. "Separate Spheres, Female World, Woman's Place: The Rhetoric of Women's History." *Journal of American History* 75, no. 1 (June 1988): 9–39.

King, Charlotte. "Separated by Death and Color: The African American Cemetery of New Philadelphia, Illinois." *Historical Archaeology* 44, no.1 (2010): 125–37.

Kirchler, Leslie Brett. "Reinterpreting a 'Silent' History: Slave Sites at Four Virginia Plantations." PhD diss., University of Michigan, 2005.

Knowles, Katie. "Fashioning Slavery: Slaves and Clothing in the U.S. South, 1830–1865." PhD diss., Rice University, 2014.

Laqueur, Thomas. "Bodies, Death, and Pauper Funerals." *Representations*, no. 1 (February 1983): 109–31.

Lee, Lori. "Beads, Coins, and Charms at a Poplar Forest Slave Cabin." *Northeastern Historical Archaeology* 40 (2011): 104–22.

Leggs, Brent. "Growth of Historic Sites: Teaching Public Historians to Advance Preservation Practice." *Public Historian* 40, no. 3 (August 2018): 90–106.

Leone Mark P., and Gladys-Marie Fry. "Conjuring in the Big House Kitchen: An Interpretation of African American Belief Systems Based on the Uses of Archaeology and Folklore Sources." *Journal of American Folklore* 112, no. 445 (Summer 1999): 372–403.

Lewis, Herbert J. "John Coffee." In *Encyclopedia of Alabama*, March 28, 2011, last updated July 20, 2020. www.encyclopediaofalabama.org/article/h-3041.

Lounsbury, Carl. "The Building Process in Antebellum North Carolina." *North Carolina Historical Review* 60, no. 4 (October 1983): 431–56.

McDavid, Carol. "Archaeologies That Hurt; Descendants That Matter: A Pragmatic Approach to Collaboration in the Public Interpretation of African-American Archaeology." *World Archaeology* 34, no. 2 (October 2002): 303–14.

———. "Descendants, Decisions, and Power: The Public Interpretation of the Archaeology of the Levi Jordan Plantation." *Historical Archaeology* 31, no. 3 (1997): 114–31.

McGowan, Abigail. "The Materials of Home: Studying Domesticity in Late Colonial India." *American Historical Review* 124, no. 4 (October 2019): 1302–15.

Miller, Marla L. "Labor and Liberty in the Age of Refinement: Gender, Class, and the Built Environment." *Perspectives in Vernacular Architecture* 10 (January 2005): 15–31.

Mitchell, Elise A. "Black and African American." *Journal of the Early Republic* 43, no. 1 (Spring 2023): 85–100.

Moffatt, L. G., and J. M. Carrière. "A Frenchman Visits Norfolk, Fredericksburg and Orange County, 1816." *Virginia Magazine of History and Biography* 53, no. 3 (July 1945): 197–214.

Mooney, Barbara Burlison. "Looking for History's Huts." *Winterthur Portfolio* 39, no. 1 (Spring 2004): 43–70.

Moses, Sharon K. "Enslaved African Conjure and Ritual Deposits on the Hume Plantation, South Carolina." *North American Archeologist* 39, no. 2 (2018): 131–64.

Neiman, Fraser D. "The Lost World of Monticello: An Evolutionary Perspective." *Journal of Anthropological Research* 64, no. 2 (Summer 2008): 161–93.

Nelson, Louis P. "The Architectures of Black Identity: Buildings, Slavery, and Freedom in the Caribbean and the American South." *Winterthur Portfolio* 45, nos. 2–3 (Summer–Autumn 2011): 177–94.

Neumann, Alexis Broderick. "American Incest: Kinship, Sex, and Commerce in Slavery and Reconstruction." PhD diss., University of Pennsylvania, 2018.

Ogundiran, Akinwumi. "Of Small Things Remembered: Beads, Cowries, and Cultural Translations of the Atlantic Experience in Yorubaland." *International Journal of African Historical Studies* 35, nos. 2–3 (2002): 427–57.

O'Neil, Patrick W. "Bosses and Broomsticks: Ritual and Authority in Antebellum Slave Weddings." *Journal of Southern History* 75, no. 1 (February 2009): 29–48.

Orser, Charles E., Jr. "The Archaeology of African-American Slave Religion in the Antebellum South." *Cambridge Archaeological Journal* 4, no. 1 (1994): 33–45.

———. "Artifacts, Documents and Memories of the Black Tenant Farmer." *Archaeology* 38, no. 4 (July–August 1985): 48–53.

Otto, John Solomon, and Augustus Marion Burns III. "Black Folks and Poor Buckras: Archeological Evidence of Slave and Overseer Living Conditions on an Antebellum Plantation." *Journal of Black Studies* 14, no. 2 (December 1983): 185–200.

Pearce, Laurie E. "The Cowrie Shell in Virginia: A Critical Evaluation of Potential Archaeological Significance." MA thesis, College of William and Mary, 1992.

———. "To Whom Do They Belong?: Cowrie Shells in Historical Archaeology." *African American Archaeology* 9 (1993): 1–3.

Phulgence, Winston Francis. "Monument Building, Memory Making, and Remembering Slavery in the Contemporary Atlantic World." PhD diss., University of York, 2016.

Prown, Jules David. "Mind in Matter: An Introduction to Material Culture Theory and Method." *Winterthur Portfolio* 17, no. 1 (Spring 1982): 1–19.

Prunty, Merle C. "The Renaissance of the Southern Plantation." *Geographical Review* 45, no. 4 (October 1955): 459–91.

Rachleff, Marshall. "An Abolitionist Letter to Governor Henry W. Collier of Alabama: The Emergence of 'The Crisis of Fear' in Alabama." *Journal of Negro History* 66, no. 3 (1981): 246–53.

Radin, Margaret Jane. "Property and Personhood." *Stanford Law Review* 34 (1982): 957–1015.

Radney, El-Ra Adair. "A Place in the Sun: Black Placemaking in Pan African Detroit." *Journal of Black Studies* 50, no. 3 (April 2019): 316–40.

Reeves, Matthew, and Matthew Greer. "Within View of the Mansion: Comparing and Contrasting Two Early Nineteenth-Century Slave Households at James Madison's Montpelier." *Journal of Middle Atlantic Archaeology* 28 (2012): 69–80.

Reinberger, Mark. "The Architecture of Sharecropping: Extended Farms of the Georgia Piedmont." *Perspectives in Vernacular Architecture* 9 (2003): 116–34.

Roediger, David R. "And Die in Dixie: Funerals, Death, and Heaven in the Slave Community, 1700–1865." *Massachusetts Review* 22, no. 1 (Spring 1981): 163–83.

Russell, Aaron E. "Material Culture and African-American Spirituality at the Hermitage." *Historical Archaeology* 31, no. 2 (1997): 63–80.

Samford, Patricia. "The Archaeology of African-American Slavery and Material Culture." *William and Mary Quarterly* 53, no. 1 (January 1996): 87–114.

Sharfstein, Daniel J. "Atrocity, Entitlement, and Personhood in Property." *Virginia Law Review* 98, no. 3 (May 2012): 635–90.

Sharp, Henry Kerr. "An Architectural Portrait: Prospect Hill, Spotsylvania County, Virginia." MA thesis, University of Virginia, 1996.

Shaw, Madelyn. "Slave Cloth and Clothing Slaves: Craftsmanship, Commerce, and Industry." *Journal of Early Southern Decorative Arts* 33 (2012). www.mesdajournal .org/2012/slave-cloth-clothing-slaves-craftsmanship-commerce-industry/.

Singleton, Theresa. "Slavery and Spatial Dialectics on Cuban Coffee Plantations." *World Archaeology* 33, no. 1 (June 2001): 98–114.

Sklar, Kathryn Kish. "Reconsidering Domesticity through the Lens of Empire and Settler Society in North America." *American Historical Review* 124, no. 4 (October 2019): 1249–66.

Smith, John David. "More Than Slaves, Less Than Freedmen: The 'Share Wages' Labor System during Reconstruction," *Civil War History* 26, no. 3 (September 1980): 256–66.

Snell, K. D. M. "Gravestones, Belonging and Local Attachment in England, 1700–2000." *Past and Present*, no. 179 (May 2003): 97–134.

Stevenson, Brenda E. "What's Love Got to Do with It?: Concubinage and Enslaved Women and Girls in the Antebellum South." *Journal of African American History* 98, no. 1 (Winter 2013): 99–125.

Stewart, Whitney Nell. "The Racialized Politics of Home in Slavery and Freedom." PhD diss., Rice University, 2017.

———. "White/white and/or the Absence of the Modifier." *Journal of the Early Republic* 43, no. 1 (Spring 2023): 101–8.

Stokes, Sherrie. "Gone but Not Forgotten: Wakulla County's Folk Graveyards." *Florida Historical Quarterly* 70, no. 2 (October 1991): 177–91.

Sugrue, Michael. "South Carolina College: The Education of an Antebellum Elite." PhD diss., Columbia University, 1992.

Tilton, Lauren. "Race and Place: Dialect and the Construction of Southern Identity in the Ex-Slave Narratives." *Current Research in Digital History* 2 (2019). https://doi .org/10.31835/crdh.2019.14.

Trigger, Bruce G. "Monumental Architecture: A Thermodynamic Explanation of Symbolic Behaviour." *World Archaeology* 22, no. 2 (October 1990): 119–32.

Upton, Dell. "Material Culture Studies, a Symposium." *Material Culture* 17, nos. 2–3 (Summer–Fall 1985): 85–88.

———. "Vernacular Domestic Architecture in Eighteenth-Century Virginia." *Winterthur Portfolio* 17, nos. 2–3 (Summer–Autumn, 1982): 95–119.

———. "White and Black Landscapes in Eighteenth-Century Virginia." *Places* 2, no. 2 (1984): 59–72.

Vogt, Evon Z., and Peggy Golde. "Some Aspects of the Folklore of Water Witching in the United States." *Journal of American Folklore* 71, no. 282 (October–December 1958): 519–31.

Watts, Sandra Lee. "A History of the Texas Sugar Industry with Special Reference to Brazoria County." MA thesis, Rice University, 1969.

Weber, Heidi Amelia-Anne. "Power, Prestige, and Influence of the Nineteenth Century Upcountry Georgia, South Carolina and North Carolina Cotton Planters and Their Appropriation of the Greek Revival House." PhD diss., Kent State University, 2015.

Wells, Camille. "The Planter's Prospect: Houses, Outbuildings, and Rural Landscapes in Eighteenth-Century Virginia." *Winterthur Portfolio* 28, no. 1 (Spring 1993): 1–31.

Welter, Barbara. "The Cult of True Womanhood, 1820–1860." *American Quarterly* 18, no. 2 (Summer 1966): 151–75.

Wilkie, Laurie A. "Magic and Empowerment on the Plantation: An Archaeological Consideration of African-American World View." *Southeastern Archaeology* 14, no. 2 (Winter 1995): 136–48.

———. "Secret and Sacred: Contextualizing the Artifacts of African-American Magic and Religion." *Historical Archaeology* 31, no. 4 (1997): 81–106.

Wood, Peter. "Whetting, Setting and Laying Timbers: Black Builders in the Early South." *Southern Exposure* 8, no. 1 (Spring 1980): 3–8.

Young, Amy L. "Risk Management Strategies among African-American Slaves at Locust Grove." *International Journal of Historical Archaeology* 1, no. 1 (March 1997): 5–37.

INDEX

Page numbers in italics refer to illustrations.

abolition movement, 34, 90, 129, 134–35
Adams, Jessica, 160, 170n2
Adriance, John, 105, 112, 114, 116–23, 219nn131–32, 220n138, 221n147
African cosmologies, 82, 84
Alabama: Black Belt, 72; cotton cultivation, 79; Slave Code, 90
Aldridge, Mary Hester, 117
Alfred (enslaved by John Coffee), 89
Allensworth, Allen, 61
amulets and charms, 61–62, 67
ancestors, rituals and connection to, 80–82
Antrobus, John, 84–85, *85*
archaeological artifacts. *See* artifacts; material culture theory
architecture, 134–35; Black builders, 22, 53–54, 66, 103, 125, *126*, 135–36, 181n44, 232n161; Greek Revival, 136–37, 227n89, 227n91, 227–28n93; monumental, 150, 222–23n8; of plantation mansions, 127, 169n1; slavery's structure reflected in, 137–40
artifacts: as archival material, 7–9; assemblages from "restricted" spaces, 59; recovered from gravesites, 88–89, 96–97. *See also* material culture theory
author's sources and methodology, 163–68

barriers between slave and nonslave spaces, 23–25, 35–36
Bartlett, Rachel (Patton). *See* Patton, Rachel (Bartlett)
Battle-Baptiste, Whitney, 7, 32, 178n9, 183n83, 189n17
Baum, Dale, 116
beads, as artifact of African diaspora, 23

Bellus, Cyrus, 47
Ben (enslaved person at Redcliffe Plantation), 125
Bennehan, Rebecca (Cameron), 48
Bennehan, Richard, 47–48, 53–54, 60
Bennehan, Thomas, 60, 61, 62
Berlin, Ira, 5, 174n36, 179n18, 181n44
Betty (enslaved by John Coffee), 89
Bibb, Henry, 56, 131–32
Bishir, Catherine, 53–54, 181n44, 232n61
Black Belt cotton plantations, 72, 158
Blue, James, 94
Body, Annie B., 55
Bolton, Henry Carrington, 88, 89–90
Boone, Andrew, 55
borrow (trash) pits. *See* trash pits/middens
Brock, Terry, xii, 25, 33, 177n4, 184n96
brooms, 29, *31*. *See also* swept yards
Brown, Vincent, 2, 72, 81–82
Bruce, Blanche K., 156
Bruce, John, 148
burial grounds: on Chatham Plantation, 78–82; grave markers at slave burial grounds, 88–89, 91; location within landscape at Chatham Plantation, 82–86; material culture of slave burial grounds, 86–93; orientation of bodies, 90
burial practices, 72–73, 74, 198n7

Cameron, Anne, 64
Cameron, Duncan, 48, 53
Cameron, Paul, 43–44, 47–49, 64, 66, 78, 129, 157, 159, 187n1, 188n3, 196n124
Cameron, Rebecca Bennehan, 48
Cameron Grove Baptist Church, 69
Camp, Stephanie M. H., 7, 18, 45, 113, 175n47, 176n57, 176n59, 190n30

Campbell, Mary Coffee, 89
capitalism and hierarchies of labor, 19,
    173n28
Cardinall, Allan, 55
Cathwood Plantation, 133, 148, 225n54
Cayce, Thomas, 114
ceramic objects as grave artifacts, 88
Charles Carroll house, 59
charms and amulets, 61–62, 67
Chatham Plantation, *10*, 11, 71–75, 95–97;
    enslaved persons, rootedness of, 93–95;
    forced relocation of enslaved persons
    from, 74, 75–78, 91; material culture of
    slave burial grounds, 86–93; plantation
    landscape and location of slave burial
    grounds, 82–86; slave burial grounds,
    78–82
Chloe (enslaved person forced to mi-
    grate), 78, 95, 209n159
Clark, John, 104, 106
clothing: decorative embellishments, 119,
    120; of enslaved persons, 113; as expres-
    sions of class and power, 112–16, *115*
Cocke, Philip St. George, 139
Coffee, Alexander Donelson, 89
Coffee, John, 88–89, 94
Coffee, Joshua, 88, 94
Coffee, Judy, 94–95
Coffee, Rebecca, 94
Coffee, Sally, 95
Coffee, Washington, 95
Coffee, Webb, 94
coffins, 87. *See also* burial practices
Coleman, Rebecca Gilmore, 161
Collins, Lewis, 20
Confederacy, 142–43
conjuration, 40, 50, 55–56, 59–60, 67, 90,
    167
convict leasing, 156–57, 234nn17–18
cotton cultivation, 79, 103
Cotton Kingdom in Deep South, 75
Cowden Plantation, 133
cowrie shells, 57–59, *58, 59*, 61; in Mag-
    nolia Grove wall, 158, *159*
Craft, Ellen, 61
Craft, William, 61

Cresy (enslaved person at Chatham Plan-
    tation), 71–72, 73, 86, 198n1
Croom, Isaac, 157, 158, 234nn24–25
Cutts, Mary, 23, 25, 27, 34, 38

Dandridge (enslaved person at Stagville
    Plantation), 64
David (enslaved child forced to migrate),
    78, 95, 209n159
Davis, A. J., 139
death rituals, 72–73; and burial practices,
    74, 198n7. *See also* burial grounds
Decorative Arts of the Gulf South, xi,
    163, 236n1
Deep South, enslaved persons wish to
    avoid, 76–77
Dennis (enslaved by John Coffee), 89
divining rods/dowsing sticks, 62–68
domesticity: constraints upon enslaved
    women, 100–101; indoor/outdoor
    differences, 31–33; nineteenth-century
    ideals of, 4, 7, 105–6; racialized ideolo-
    gies of, 160; Southern women's roles
    in, 108–11. *See also* homemaking
Douglass, Frederick, 6
dowsing sticks/divining rods, 62–68
Du Bois, W. E. B., 146, 156, 160

Edwards, Doc, 68
Edwards, Ywone, 81
Elijah (enslaved person at Stagville Plan-
    tation), 158–59
Ellis, Frank, 157, *158*
Ellis, Polly May, 157, *158*
emancipation, 155–60; at Chatham Plan-
    tation, 94–95; Emancipation Procla-
    mation, 51; at Montpelier Plantation,
    153; at Patton Place, 121, 123; at Red-
    cliffe Plantation, 126–28, 143–48
enslavement. *See* slavery
Esther (Ester Whitfield, enslaved by
    Nathan Whitfield), 95, 209n159

Farrow, Betty, 143
Faulkner, William, 81
Fern, Mariah, 94

Fesler, Garrett, 23, 183n79
Finch, John, 20, 27, 36
Fitzsimons, Catherine (Hammond), 128, 131
Ford, Mike, 113
Ford, Sarah, 104, 105, 113, 116–17, 118, 221n146
Forks of Cypress Plantation (Alabama), 83, 91, *92*, 93–94
Foster, Augustus John, 22, 23, 39
Fox-Genovese, Elizabeth, 114, 172n27
Frank (enslaved person at Redcliffe Plantation), 142
Frank (enslaved person forced to relocate), 76
free Black Southerners: after emancipation, 126–27, 143–49, 155–56; surveillance of homes of, 159–60; and landownership, 156–57; rootedness of, in land, 72, 150–51
Freedmen's Bureau, 123
Fuentes, Marisa, 8

Gaineswood Plantation, 71, 72, 73, *73*, 86, 157, 235n39; as modern historic site, xii, 235n39
Garman, James, 89, 203n82
Gilmore, George, 153–54, 161
Gilmore Cabin, 153–54, *154*, 157
Glymph, Thavolia, xiii, 5, 18, 45, 171n12, 172n25, 172–73n27, 211n7
Goings, Henry, 76, 77
Granny Milly (enslaved woman at Montpelier), 25–27, 61
Great Migration, 69
Greek Revival architecture, 136–37, *137*, 227–28n95, 227n91
Green Valley Plantation, 130
Grey, Selina, 156
Grimm, Charles, 103, 105, 106, 107, 118, 210n2, 219n121
Gudgell, Henry, 51
Gundaker, Grey, 72–73, 80, 85–86, 175n45, 204n92

Haitian Revolution, 48
Haley, Alex, 94

Hammond, Catherine Fitzsimons, 128, 131
Hammond, Harry, 131, 132, 133, 144–45, 146, 149, 229n121, 232n158
Hammond, James Henry, 11, 125, 126, 127, 149–51; during Civil War, 142–43; and Redcliffe Plantation, 134–43; and Redcliffe Plantation after emancipation, 143–49; and Silver Bluff Plantation, 128–34; slavery, thoughts on, 125, 134–35
Harp, Anson, 147
Harper, Francis Ellen Watkins, 156
Harris, Leslie, xvii
Hart, Ephram, 11, 43
Hartman, Saidiya, 8, 45, 172n25, 175n48, 189n15, 199n16, 237n14
Hawkins, Thomas, 94
Hawkins, Tom, 62
Hayes, Rutherford B., 111
Hayr, James, 118–19
Heard, Emmaline, 90, 147
Henley, Anthony, 150
Henley, Breanna, 150–51, *151*
Henley, Lucy, 150
Hickory Hill Plantation (Alabama), 82, 83, 84, 88–89, 94–95, 203n80, 207n124, 207n127
Hill, Eliza, 108–9
historical methodology, 163–68, 176n54; and material culture theory, 163–68
Hogendorn, Jan, 57
Holden, Vanessa, xvii
homemaking: and Black placemaking, 12, 171n14; burial ground maintenance as, 75, 96–97; class, race, and social value influences on, 5; enslavers' denigration of enslaved peoples' homes, 49; and meaning-making, 1–2, 3–7, 12–13, 41–42; as site of labor, 16–18; as sphere of feminine duty, 4. *See also* domesticity
Homes of American Statesmen, 40–41, *41*
hooks, bell, 6
horseshoes, as good luck charms, 62
household goods, value of, 108–9
Hume Plantation, 56
Hunter, Tera, 103

industrialization, 17
Isaac (enslaved person at Chatham Plantation), 91

Jackson, Charles, 94
Jackson, E. S., 105–6, 107, 110, 207n59
Jackson, James, 83, 89, 93, 94, 203n82
Jackson, Joshua, 94
Jackson, Mariah, 94
Jackson, Nannie, 94
Jackson, Simon, 95
Jacob (enslaved by John Coffee), 89
Jacobs, Harriet, 45, 190n20
Jake (enslaved person at Patton Place Plantation), 117, 212n17, 219n132, 221n146
Jamieson, Ross, 80, 202n61
Jarvis, George O., 105, 106, 107, 110, 114, 115
Jefferson, Thomas, 24, 26, 38, 39, 150, 184n99, 186n119
Jerry (enslaved by John Coffee), 89
Jim (enslaved person at Stagville Plantation), 48, 53
Jinny (enslaved person forced to migrate), 78
Joanna (enslaved by John Coffee), 89
Joe (enslaved person at Stagville Plantation), 48
Johnson, Henderson, 131, 133, 137–38, 225nn58–60, 228n99, 230n131
Johnson, Louisa, 131–32, 133, 144, 157, 224–25n47, 225n50, 229n128, 229n130
Johnson, Marion, 57
Johnson, Sally, 131, 132, 133, 138, 144, 145, 157, 225n50, 229n128, 230n131
Jones, Alice Eley, 55, 67, 192n49, 193n74
Jones, Thomas, 5, 6
Jones-Rogers, Stephanie, 107, 112, 174n39, 215n45
Jordan, Abner, 48
Journal of the Early Republic Critical Engagements Forum, xviii

Kelley, Sean R., 103
Kemper, John, 95

Kemper, Sarah, 95
Ku Klux Klan, 160, 235n29

Lafayette, Marquis de, 26, 182n66
land: ownership for free Blacks, 156–57; rootedness in, 72, 93–95, 150–51
landscape design: barriers, human and natural, 23–27; of burial grounds, 84–86, 90; landscaping styles, 24; and private/public spaces at Montpelier Plantation, 18–23, 33–42; and private/public spaces at Stagville Plantation, 46–49
language and terminology used in book, xvii–xviii
Latrobe, John H. B., 36
Latta, Morgan, 48, 68
Lawal, Babtunde, 55
Lee, Robert E., 156
Lewis (enslaved person at Stagville Plantation), 53, 66, 197n128
Lewis, Lucy, 113
The Liberator (abolitionist newspaper), 90
Lomax, John, xviii
Lost Cause mythology, 2–3, 126, 170n7
Lucy (enslaved person at Stagville Plantation), 158–59

Madison, Ambrose, 177n2
Madison, Dolley, 10, 13, 15, 16, 19, 25, 33, 34, 42, 182n59, 183n74
Madison, James, Jr., 10, 13, 15, 16, 19, 179n22, 182n59, 182nn72–73; death of, 25, 33; design of South Yard, 27; dichotomy between democratic ideals and enslavement, 39–40; instructions to overseers, 20; labor reform movement, 34; landscaping style and practice, 24; separation of Black and white spaces, 16, 19–20, 23–25, 35–36, 41; slavery, thoughts on, 26
Madison, Nelly, 182n73
Magby Slave Cemetery, 84
Magnolia Grove, 157–58, *159*, 234nn24–25
Maria (enslaved by John Coffee), 89

Maria (enslaved person at Patton Place Plantation), 117, 219n125
Martin (enslaved by John Coffee), 89
Mason, George, 35
material culture theory, 163–68; and material evidence methodology, 7–9, 163–68
McCord, David James, 61
McDaniel, George, 146, 172–73n27, 230n140
Miles, Tiya, 8, 175n52, 236n3
Milly (enslaved by John Coffee), 89
Milton (enslaved person at Stagville Plantation), 66
Minda (enslaved by John Coffee), 89
Monticello, 59, 150, 186n119, 194n91
Montlezun-Labarthette, Baron de, 37, 40–41
Montpelier Foundation, 161, 223n3
Montpelier Plantation, 10, 10, 15–18, 17, 83–84; Anna Maria Thornton's watercolor of, 38, 39; Field Quarter, 19–23, 25, 32, 33, 41, 51, 179n20, 180n35, 181n46, 187n145; Homes of American Statesmen, 40–41, 41; as modern historic site, xii, 235n39; neoclassical temple/icehouse, 38–40; Pine Allée, 17, 38, 40; South Yard, 15, 16, 17, 20, 22, 24, 24–25, 27–33, 28, 30, 37, 47, 60, 67, 129, 154, 177n1, 182n68, 182nn72–73, 183n84, 185n106, 186n111, 187n145; South Yard and concealment of labor, 33–42; Stable Yard, 16, 23–27, 24, 186n111
Montpelier Slave Cemetery, 84
monuments: cemetery, 89, 93; to enslaved people, 149, 150, 232n159; monumental architecture, 222–23n8; plantation buildings as, 150, 232n162; public, function of, 136; to white supremacy on behalf of James Henry Hammond's legacy, 123, 126, 127, 134, 136, 139, 149
Mordecai, George W., 159, 188n3, 235n27
Morgan, Isaam, 83
Morgan, Philip D., 5, 174n38, 179n18, 181n44

Moses (enslaved by John Coffee), 89
Moses, Sharon, 56, 193n66
Mott, J. Rhett, 145

Nathans, Sydney, 48, 78, 197n127, 197n130, 202n51
Ned (enslaved person at Stagville Plantation), 48, 53
Nillin, Margrett, 156
Northup, Solomon, 45

objects, meaning of, 166–67. See also material culture theory
O'Donovan, Susan Eva, 77
Ogundiran, Akinwumi, 61
Old Prewitt Slave Cemetery (Alabama), 87–88, 206n112

Parry, Tyler, 29, 184n89
paternalism, 2, 49, 89, 113, 133–34, 139, 225–26n64, 228n104
patriarchy, 100, 113, 123, 132
Patterson, Orlando, 72, 80–81, 172n25
Patton, America, 117
Patton, Annie, 106
Patton, Charles F., 105, 116, 117, 118, 213n19, 218n118, 220n134
Patton, Columbus R., asylum residence and death, 116–17; domestic arrangements/relationship with Rachel, 99, 100, 103–5, 107–8, 110, 116, 122, 213–14nn23–24; family background, 102, 106; will and estate of, 117–18, 121, 214n34, 219nn121–23, 219n125, 219n31, 221n154
Patton, Margaretta, 117
Patton, Mat, 105, 108, 117–18, 219n123
Patton, Rachel (Bartlett): as mistress of Patton Place plantation, 102–8; plantation mansion and material goods of, 108–11; public roles of Southern women and, 111–16; removal from Patton place mansion and subsequent life, 116–22; social status and domestic duties of, 99–102, 122–23, 210n2, 211n13, 212n16
Patton, St. Clair, 105

Patton Place, *10*, 11, 99–102, *103*, 122–23;:
    archaeological excavations and ceram-
    ics, 110–11, *111*; household goods, 109–
    10; as modern historic site (Varner-
    Hogg), xii, 235n39; Patton family
    challenges to Rachel's power, 116–22;
    public performances of plantation mis-
    tresses and, 111–16; Rachel's authority
    as mistress, 102–8; and role of mistress
    and domestic authority, 108–11
Pearce, Laurie, 59, 62
Pease, Lucadia, 108
Peggy (enslaved person forced to re-
    locate), 76
Phebe (enslaved person at Shallowell
    Plantation), 81, 91
pipe fragments, 33, 185n105
plantation life: barriers between slave
    and nonslave spaces, 23–25, 35–36, 82,
    213n21; brutality and dehumanization,
    6; construction and renovation proj-
    ects, 53–54; domestic spatial arrange-
    ments, 22–23; as emblem of slavery,
    170n2; enslaved persons and surveilled
    spaces, 45–46, 60–61; hospitality to
    visitors, 34–35; housing for domestic
    servants, 27; material culture and con-
    cealed items, 7–9, 45–46, 49; narratives
    of, 2–3; nucleated village design, 22,
    47; outdoor spaces, importance of,
    23; performative core of plantation,
    6, *17*, 19, 20, 23–25, 27, 34; plantations
    as repositories of memory, 232n162;
    planters' privacy contrasted with
    surveillance of enslaved, 47, 60–61;
    scientific plantation management,
    49; separation of work/domestic life,
    18, 22–23; yards, swept clay, 28–29, *31*,
    31–33. *See also* slavery
Pompey (enslaved person at Stagville
    Plantation), 66
prisons and surveillance, 47, 190n27
privacy: domestic, in plantation man-
    sions, 109; of enslaved persons
    contrasted with slaveholders', 44–45;
    private/public spheres, 17–18, 101, 104

Proust, Marcel, 163, 168
Prown, Jules David, 168, 237–38n15, 238n16

Quarls, Harre, 56
Queen Ester (enslaved great-grand-
    mother of Alex Haley), 94

Raboteau, Albert, 55, 189n18
Rachleff, Marshall, 90
Rainville, Lynn, 91, 199n14, 205n99,
    207n123
Redcliffe Plantation, *10*, 11, 125–28, 222n3,
    222nn7–8, 224nn29–30, 226nn66–67,
    226n70, 227n91, 228n104, 232n158,
    235n39; after emancipation, 143–49;
    establishment and function, 134–43;
    mansion architecture, 135–37, *137*;
    as modern historic site, xii, 149–51,
    235n39; Redcliffe Yard after emanci-
    pation, 148–51; Redcliffe Yard slave
    quarters, *138*, 138–41, *140*, *141*, 146, *147*,
    228n104
Reeves, Matthew, xii, 21
Rice, Marie Gordon, 44
Roberts, D. C., 123
rootedness in land, 72, 79, 85–86, 93–95,
    150–51

Sallins, Rosa, 88
Samford, Patricia, 54
Sampson (enslaved by John Coffee), 89
Savage, Kirk, 136
Scott, Anne Firor, 101, 214n33
Second Middle Passage, 11, 75, 76–78,
    201n37
segregation of burial grounds, 82–86,
    89–90
Shallowell Plantation (North Carolina),
    75, 199n18
sharecropping: systems, 143–44, 156–57;
    cabins, 146, 229n127
Sharp, Henry, 19
shrouds, 81, 87, 91, 95, 205n107, 206n108.
    See also burial practices
Shubrick, Elizabeth, 129
Shubrick, Hannah, 129

Shubrick, Mary, 129
Silver Bluff Plantation, 127, 128–31, 139, 140, 204n90
Simon (enslaved by John Coffee), 89
Slave Narratives. See Works Progress Administration (WPA)
slave quarters: construction, 62–66; efforts to protect by enslaved residents, 61, 67; free houses contrasted with slave cabins, 146; hidden spaces, 141–42; lean-to structures, 146, *147*; surveillance and lack of privacy, 68, 129–30, 190n25; swept yards, 28–29, *31*, 31–33, 141, 183n83, 229n112
slavery: abolition movement, 134–35; antiliteracy mandates, 90–91; brutality, 128–29, 172n23; burial grounds, 74; enslaved-enslaver relationships, 103–4, 123, 211n13; enslaved people's clothing, 113; enslaved peoples' homemaking, 6; enslaved persons as wealth, 34, 135–36; family separation and forced resettlement, 66, 68, 75–78, 91, 201n37; impact on family structure, 22; and paternalistic attitudes, 2, 49, 113, 133–34, 139, 225–26n64; politics of survival, 2; reflected in architecture, 138–40; scientific methods of enslavement, 129–30; and sexual violence, 131–32; slave auctions, 48–49; slave cabins, 20–21, *21*, 57; slave codes, 90; slave narratives, 5–6, 55, 76; slave rebellions, fear of, 90; slave wedding ceremonies, 29, 31, 184n88; struggles between enslavers/enslaved, 12–13; surveillance and containment, 46–49, 66, 139–41, 145. *See also* plantation life
slave trade: 48, 56, 174n39, 180n39, 200n20, 200n26, 201n37, 202n67, 225n64; cowrie shells as currency, 57–58; and village structure in Africa, 22
Smith, Clint, 150
Smith, Jack, 129, 130, 148
Smith, Rose, 129, 130, 148
Smith, Sallie (Wigfall), 130, 148, 149, 151, 153, 155, 231nn148–49, 233n163

snakes, symbolism of, 51, 55
Sobrina (enslaved "spouse" of John Clark), 104, 106, 110, 213n23
Solomon (enslaved person at Patton Place Plantation), 117, 212n17, 219n132
spiritual beliefs and practices, 82
Stagville Plantation, *10*, 11, 43–46, 68–69, 188n5; archaeological artifacts, significance of, 54–55, 68–69; cowrie shell concealed in slave cabin, 56–62, *58*, *59*; Eno Quarter burial grounds, 84; forked sticks concealed in slave quarter wall, 62–68, *64*, *65*; Horton Grove slave dwellings, 62–66, *65*; house renovations, 51, 53; as modern historic site, xii, 235n39; security and surveillance, 46–49; walking stick concealed in wall, 49–56, *50*
Stevens, Kenneth, 137
Stewart, Catherine, xviii
Stills, Peter, 79
sugarcane, 103, 213n20, 234n18
Sukey (Dolley Madison's enslaved housemaid), 19
Sullivan (enslaved person at Redcliffe Plantation), 125, 126, 135, 227n39
surveillance and containment of enslaved persons, 46–49, 66, 139–141, 45. *See also* privacy
swept yards, 28–29, *31*, 31–33, 141, 149, 154, 183n78, 183n80, 183n83, 184n96, 229n112

Taylor, Amy Murrell, 142–43
Taylor, Ralph Philip, 10, 15, 28, 42, 177n1
Telemachus, 26, 61
terminology used in book, xvii–xviii
terrorism, white supremacist, during Reconstruction, 159–60
Thornton, Anna Maria, 38, *39*
tobacco, 33, 19, 185n105, 188n5
Todd, John Payne, 42
tombstones, 86–87, 208n139. *See also* burial practices
trash pits/middens, 23, *30*, 32–33, 149, 182n73
Turner, Joseph A., 19

Turner, Lucille Peaks, 51
Turner, Nat, 90

Upton, Dell, 164–65, 175n53, 176n57, 178n9

Venus (Vinea Whitfield, enslaved by
   Nathan Whitfield), 95, 209n159
Vodou religion, 55

Walker, Frank, 68
walking sticks, 49–51, 50, 52, 54, 55, 57, 62,
   166, 191n47, 192n52. *See also* Stagville
   Plantation
Warren, Jamie, 73
Washington, George, 24
Washington, Josiah, 78
Washington, Uncle Smart, 72
water, symbolism of, 71, 84, 86, 88, 204n92
Webb (enslaved by John Coffee), 89
wedding ceremonies, of enslaved people,
   29, 31, 183n88
Wells-Oghoghomeh, Alexis, 72, 193n73,
   205n106
white supremacy, 100, 123, 126, 127, 134–35,
   142, 149, 150, 159 60
Whitfield, Betsy, 71, 76, 78, 198n1

Whitfield, Ester (Esther, enslaved by
   Nathan Whitfield), 95
Whitfield, Gaius, 77, 201n38, 201n40
Whitfield, James, 76
Whitfield, Nathan, 11, 71–72, 75–78, 86,
   93, 95, 157, 199n18, 201n40, 202n50
Whitfield, Rony, 95
Whitfield, Vinea (Venus, enslaved by
   Nathan Whitfield), 95
Wigfall, Ella, 148, 149, 231n150
Wigfall, John, 148, 231n148
Wigfall, Sallie Smith, 148, 149, 231nn148–
   49, 231n151, 231n153, 231n155, 233n163
Willis (enslaved by John Coffee), 89
Wilson, Elizabeth, 113
Winfield, Cornelia, 96
witches, protection against, 62, 67
Witherspoon, Silvia, 67
work, mental contrasted with manual, 19
Works Progress Administration (WPA),
   xviii, 68, 143

yards, swept clay, 28–29, 31, 31–33, 149,
   154, 183n78, 183n80, 183n83, 184n96
Young, Jason, 79